Antiquity and Man

EDITED BY
JOHN D. EVANS, BARRY CUNLIFFE
AND COLIN RENFREW

Antiquity and Man

ESSAYS IN HONOUR OF GLYN DANIEL

MA, Ph.D., Litt.D., FSA
Disney Professor of Archaeology in
the University of Cambridge

THAMES AND HUDSON

Frontispiece: drawing of Glyn Daniel by Robert Tollast,
by kind permission of the Master and Fellows of
St John's College, Cambridge.

Jacket and title-page calligraphy by Will Carter
Maps by H. A. Shelley

Printed and bound in Great Britain

Foreword by His Royal Highness, The Prince of Wales

DELIGHTED as I am to have been asked to write a foreword to the Festschrift for Glyn Daniel, the very act of picking up my pen has reminded me that I left Cambridge ten years ago – a frightening indication of rapidly advancing decrepitude! Rather like David Wilson I find that my memory of daily life at Cambridge has become distinctly hazy, but I could not possibly forget the many expeditions I made in my first year to St John's College where I was supervised, entertained, amused and encouraged by Glyn Daniel. There is no doubt that having him as a supervisor made archaeology – and the process of learning – fun. I always remember greatly enjoying his rather irreverent approach to teaching, liberally spiced with anecdotes and numerous stories of encounters with archaeological forgers and confidence tricksters. Even now, ten years after the Archaeology and Anthropology Tripos, I find myself in fairly frequent correspondence with Glyn Daniel over various intriguing and complex people who write to me about archaeological matters of widely differing importance . . . !

Well I remember, too, those visits to The Flying Stag in Cambridge; lunches with a definite French influence; some hilarious stories of the joys and tribulations of editing *Antiquity* – and the delight of being entertained by Ruth. The significance of those gallic meals became only too clear when my supervisor arranged what I fondly imagined was to be an archaeological tour of the Dordogne region of France and of the megalithic monuments of Brittany during the Easter vacation. In a very short time my liver discovered that the tour was to consist principally of some of the best eating places in both those areas, a fact for which I have been eternally grateful to Glyn Daniel ever since. Owing to his inspired foreign supervision I succeeded a few months later in passing the tripos exam and then moved to the slightly more leisurely world of history!

As an old boy of the Archaeology and Anthropology faculty I was delighted when I heard that Glyn Daniel had been appointed professor some years ago – and, as Patron of the Royal Anthropological Institute, I twice attended his annual presidential lecture given at the University of London. I can hardly believe that now, finally, he is retiring. I count myself fortunate, and indeed privileged, that I am able to say I was taught at Cambridge by Glyn Daniel and I wish him and Ruth all possible happiness and contentment in the years to come.

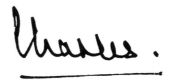

GLYN EDMUND DANIEL was born on 23 April 1914. He was educated at Barry County School and at University College, Cardiff, from which he went to St John's College, Cambridge, to read Geography and later Archaeology and Anthropology. He graduated with First Class Honours with Distinction and in 1938 obtained his PhD with a thesis on the spread of megalithic monuments in Western Europe, in the same year being elected to a Research Fellowship at his own college.

After the outbreak of the Second World War he joined the Royal Air Force in which, like a number of other distinguished archaeologists, he served as an Intelligence Officer from 1940 to 1945. From 1942 onwards he was in charge of photo-interpretation in India and South-East Asia, and in 1943 he was promoted to the rank of Wing Commander.

On his return to civilian life he became a Lecturer in Archaeology at the University of Cambridge and Fellow of St John's College, which has remained his base of operations during the rest of his career. In 1974 he succeeded Grahame Clark as Professor on the latter's retirement from the Disney Chair. He has been a Visiting Professor or special lecturer at many universities both in Britain and abroad, and is a Fellow of a number of foreign archaeological institutes and societies, including the German Archaeological Institute and the Istituto Italiano di Preistoria e Protostoria. From 1977 to 1980 he was President of the Royal Anthropological Institute of Great Britain and Ireland. In addition to his academic distinctions, he is a Knight (First Class) of the Danebrog. With the assistance of his wife, Ruth, he has edited *Antiquity*, in succession to Dr O. G. S. Crawford, the founder, for almost a quarter of a century.

In the 1950s he brought archaeology to a wider public as Chairman for six years of the BBC television programme 'Animal, Vegetable, Mineral?', and in 1955 he was elected 'Television Personality of the Year'. He is now a Director of Anglia Television and a Trustee of the Cambridge Arts Theatre.

Among his many contributions to publishing, perhaps the most outstanding is the 'Ancient Peoples and Places' series, which he created and of which he continues to be the General Editor and guiding spirit. He has himself written the hundredth volume, *A Short History of Archaeology* (1981).

Glyn Daniel's other publications include *A Hundred Years of Archaeology* (1950) (an enlarged edition was re-issued in 1975 as *A Hundred-and-fifty Years of Archaeology*), *The Prehistoric Chamber Tombs of England and Wales* (1950), *The Megalith Builders of Western Europe* (1958), *The Prehistoric Chamber Tombs of France* (1960), *The Idea of Prehistory* (1962), *The Origins and Growth of Archaeology* (1967) and *The First Civilizations* (1968), as well as *The Hungry Archaeologist in France* (1963) and two detective novels, *The Cambridge Murders* (1945) and *Welcome Death* (1954).

CONTENTS

PART III: ARCHAEOLOGY AND THE PUBLIC

PART IV: THE EDITOR OF 'ANTIQUITY'

NOTE Following current convention, dates corrected according to the tree-ring calibration of radiocarbon are indicated by 'BC' in capital letters; uncorrected dates are shown by lower-case letters ('bc').

PART I : THE HISTORY OF ARCHAEOLOGY

1 Introduction: On the Prehistory of Archaeology

John D. Evans

IT IS, I think, in all respects particularly appropriate that a volume in honour of Glyn Daniel should begin with a section consisting of essays on aspects of the history of archaeology. In the first place, the subject is one which he has made very much his own, enjoying equally its lighter anecdotal and its more serious scholarly and explanatory aspects. Secondly, and more importantly, by his constant and enthusiastic interest, and by his writings and lectures on every aspect of it over a period of several decades, beginning with that still very illuminating essay on the history of the Three Age concept published in 1943, he has probably done more than anyone else to win general recognition that it is not simply a fascinating byway of study, but a field of scholarship which is well worthy of the serious attention both of professional archaeologists and historians of science. The recent creation, by the International Congress of Prehistoric and Protohistoric Sciences, of a Commission on the History of Archaeology, of which he is most appropriately the Chairman, has now endorsed this judgment at the highest academic level, and should ensure that for the future research in this field will continue to receive due recognition and encouragement.

The need for historical perspective, the conviction that, as he himself has put it 'the present state of archaeology cannot be divorced from its past' (quoted in Willey and Sabloff 1974, 7), has always been a consideration which has been integral to his own approach to teaching and research. Having been a pupil of his in the days before even the *Hundred Years of Archaeology* was published, I can offer a personal testimony to the illumination produced not only by his formal lectures on the history of archaeology, but many times also by the introduction in course of a discussion during supervision of some apposite historical fact or anecdote which served to put a theory or a controversy into instant perspective for us. Understanding was enhanced and critical evaluation became possible once you understood the historical *raison d'être* of points of view which previously seemed obscure, obtuse or merely perverse.

All branches of human knowledge are the product of historical processes, of course, but the immediate relevance of this for those working on current problems varies from field to field. For archaeologists the relevance of understanding the historical background of their subject is undoubtedly high for a number of reasons. First of all, those reports of discovery which are the very foundation of our study are themselves historical documents. However consciously 'objective', they often need interpretation in the light of the state of knowledge and the preoccupations of scholars at the time when they were written. The availability of more modern, more accurately observed and recorded data does not make older observations obsolete, but their effective incorporation into the current body of information often demands an understanding of the conditions in which they were collected as well as of the field of archaeology to which they belong.

A second consideration relates to the discussion of theoretical problems. Much confusion could often be avoided by a real understanding of the ways in which ideas and theories have come into being and the course followed by subsequent discussion and argument about them. A notable example is offered by some of the recent writing on the 'evolution v. diffusion' theme. Naive and simplistic views on this subject have at times been attributed to earlier scholars which do not accurately represent their real position (notably to Gordon Childe, though he has been by no means the only sufferer). This not only does injustice to the individuals concerned, but it tends also to obscure the real issues and so to trivialize the current debate in some degree.

But perhaps the most important reason that can be given for studying the history of archaeology is that it enables us to understand better the processes which gave rise to its emergence as a separate and distinctive intellectual discipline. In order to attain full comprehension of these, however, we must also grasp their relationship to the major currents of thought and research which helped to produce our present scientific conception of the world and man's place in it. In itself this is a valuable educational exercise, and it is also one which is essential for the correct assessment both of the achievements of archaeology to date and its likely importance in the future.

Archaeology as we now understand it, namely the systematic study of the material remains of past human activity, and of the past environments in which that activity took place, is a product of the scientific revolution in Western Europe which began in the seventeenth century. Yet it is surely remarkable that there are so few anticipations of its possibilities among earlier civilizations, since the principles on which it is based are not particularly abstruse nor does the practice of excavation require any great technological resources. Historical studies were certainly much cultivated in many of these civilizations, and indeed an interest in the past seems to be a universal human characteristic and one which is attested by some of the oldest extant records from various parts of the world. Moreover, durable monuments of past human activity were at least as much in evidence in past times as they are today. Several thousand years ago the inhabitants of some parts of the world, notably Western Asia, Egypt, India and China, were already living in the midst of very impressive monumental remains of the past, and we know from their records that they were aware of this. Ancient artifacts and buried monuments must frequently have been brought to light by accident, and clearly sometimes aroused curiosity.

The Chinese seem to have been the people who displayed the most sustained interest in artifactual remains before modern times. The earliest evidence of this takes us back well over two thousand years. In the first century BC one writer, Yüan K'ang, outlined a periodization of tools and weapons on the basis of the material used to make them which not only resembles the Three Age system, but seems actually to have been based on the evidence of ancient artifacts (Cheng 1959, xvii; Chang 1968, 2). For instance, his intercalation of a jade period between those of stone and copper or bronze seems to some extent to be substantiated by the findings of modern archaeology in China; also the system is very specific about the relative date (in terms of the emperor reigning at the time) of the various innovations, and stresses the fact that the implements were buried with the dead. In the second century BC the historian Ssu-ma Ch'ien made systematic use of his observations of ancient sites in writing his History of China (Cheng 1959, xvi). He travelled widely to obtain first-hand impressions of many of these, and was the first to note the ruins of the Shang capital near Anyang.

But this early tradition of interest in antiquities became fossilized and did not in the end develop the promise which seems to be detectable in its first stages. Known as *chin shih hsüeh* (literally 'studies of bronzes and stones', but in fact embracing ancient artifacts, including architecture, made in many different materials), it became a kind of systematic antiquarianism with a relatively limited outlook and aims (Cheng 1959, xvi; Chang 1968, 3). Interest was focussed on the objects themselves, and particularly on

any inscriptions they bore, and both the objects themselves and the inscriptions were interpreted in terms of the by then standard Confucian model of Chinese history. Provenance and context were little regarded, even when any information about these was available, which was not very often, and there was for the most part no conception of the independent historical information which might be provided by these material remains.

There are a few very interesting exceptions to this generalization. One such is the study of over two hundred bronzes, together with some objects of jade, from various collections which was made by Lü Ta-lin, probably during the Northern Sung Dynasty, in which he gives the dimensions and weight of each, along with the place of origin, if known (Chang 1972, 3). Most remarkable, however, was the work of the eleventh century polymath Shen Kua, described by Needham as 'the most interesting character in all Chinese scientific history' (1954, 135). In a recent study of Shen Kua's observations on antiquities in his great work, the *Mêng Hsi Pi T'an* ('Brush Talks from the Dream Brook') Professor Xia Nai has demonstrated that his approach was in many respects remarkably modern. He recognized, for instance, that the study of antiquities must be based on the material evidence itself, without recourse to fanciful reconstructions or attempts to identify objects by linking them to references in ancient literature. He employed 'experimental archaeology' to discover the construction of bronze mirrors and the use of the scaled sight on an ancient crossbow, and he was intensely interested in the technological achievements of earlier periods (particularly with an eye to the reintroduction of lost skills). In his geological and palaeoclimatological studies, moreover, he seems to have anticipated some of the concepts of modern environmental archaeology (Xia Nai 1979, 139–41).

However, the penetrating intellect of Shen Kua had no permanent effect on the course of Chinese antiquarian studies, which continued down to the end of the nineteenth century in the mould in which they had already set by his time (Chang 1968, 3). Anticipations of the approach of modern archaeology in other parts of the world are even more sporadic than in China, and in no case do we find any attempt to follow them up in a systematic way. Apart from a few isolated instances, such as the remarkable excavations of Nabonidus of Babylon in the temple of Shamash at Sippar (Lloyd 1947, 176) and of his predecessor, Nebuchadrezzar II (Oates 1979, 161), and the inference drawn by Thucydides (I, 8) from the contents of the graves in Delos which had been excavated for religious reasons, there is little or no trace in the ancient Near East or

Europe of any efforts to utilize information from material remains for historical purposes. Inscriptions, of course, as in China, did arouse interest for a variety of reasons, not necessarily historical. In Egypt, for instance, as we know from ancient stories like that of Satni Khamois, son of Ramesses II, inscriptions on ancient tombs were often studied for their supposed magical powers rather than for information about those buried within (Maspero 1915, 115–82).

The reasons for this prolonged failure to make any effective use of material evidence for the reconstruction of the human past were conceptual rather than practical. M. I. Finley (1975, 22) has pointed out that the ancient Greeks were quite capable of carrying out systematic excavations of ancient sites if they had wished to. 'Technically', as he says, 'Schliemann and Sir Arthur Evans had little at their disposal that was not available to fifth century Athenians', who were also quite as able to link what was unearthed with their legendary past. What was lacking, according to Finley, was the motivation. They simply felt no need of a systematic account of the past in terms of its material remains. We can extend this explanation to the other early civilizations as well. The kind of history, economic, technological and social, to which archaeology can make such an effective contribution is the creation of modern Western society and it has developed as part of the scientific approach to man and the universe which began to emerge from the seventeenth century on. It is an integral part of this movement and can only be understood in that context.

Though the study of antiquity in Renaissance Europe began with the remains of historical periods, first ancient Greek and Roman, later also medieval, it was the gradual realization of the existence, and eventually also of the length, of the prehistoric period which was mainly responsible for the emergence of archaeology as an autonomous science of material remains. Until this happened archaeology remained an ancillary discipline, the handmaid of documentary history and the fine arts. Only the stimulus of grappling with a quite novel series of problems which could be solved by archaeological methods alone could have provided the impetus for its transformation. Progress in this field was itself dependent on the emergence of a new world-picture, replacing both the medieval and the newer mathematical and mechanical one, in which the concept of development in time was fundamental. This began to occur in the course of the eighteenth century, and at the same time also began the development of the new sciences of geology and palaeontology, both of which were destined to be closely linked with, and profoundly influence, that of prehistoric archaeology.

Paradoxically, early modern Western Europe, dominated as it was by a religion which was firmly tied to an account of the history of the world which allowed only a few thousand years for the whole process (however the numbers were calculated), was a more hostile environment for the birth of an outlook based on gradual developmental change than many earlier civilizations. Not only was the length of time which had elapsed since the creation of the world worked out with only small margins of error from the Biblical writings, but the main framework of the whole course of world history from then down to fully historical times was related there in narratives which were generally regarded as divinely sanctioned. Yet in the upshot the very rigidity of this account of the past and the religious significance with which it was invested seem to have acted in some degree as a stimulus to research. A religion which apparently rested so much of its claim to credibility on records of historical events must be capable of being proved or disproved by independent historical evidence. As the fashion for systematic observation of natural phenomena of all kinds grew in the seventeenth and eighteenth centuries the Biblical account was both attacked and defended more and more frequently through arguments derived from discoveries of the remains of the remoter past, whether geological, palaeontological or human.

In ancient Greece and China no such stimulus had existed. Chinese scholars had observed the evidence for the occurrence of major geological changes in the past, and some of them, like Shen Kua, had explained them as resulting from continuous sedimentary deposition (Needham 1959, 604), implying the lapse of a very long period of time. Such views aroused no controversy, because they did not run counter to any accepted dogma, but, as Needham remarks (1959, 604, note e) 'neither was any Geological Society founded to search for facts which should test them'. To a great extent the same might be said about similar speculation in ancient Greece concerning the explanation of geological phenomena and even the origins of man, despite evidence of occasional hostility to, and persecution of, the philosophers concerned. Perhaps if there had been a sharper clash in either country with well-defined and generally held beliefs a more widespread interest might have been generated in these problems.

At all events, the situation was very different in this respect in Western Europe as it emerged from the constraints of medieval thought. Observations of natural phenomena of all kinds led immediately to the question of how they could be fitted in with religious beliefs. Intelligent people were often extremely worried by the fact that such observations frequently seemed to be at variance with notions derived directly or indirectly from the Bible, but nevertheless were impelled by this very circumstance to continue their researches, wherever these might lead. Many, of course, were able sooner or later to find a, for them, satisfactory method of reconciling the two, but others were unable to do so. It is important to remember that thinkers of both kinds made important contributions, and major advances were sometimes made by those who ultimately were unsuccessful in breaking out of the limits imposed by the traditional views of their time. It is also very relevant to remember that these religious pre-occupations cut right across the divisions of what we are accustomed to think of as separate disciplines. In dealing with the emergence of new concepts concerning the shape of the past, therefore, it is even less possible than it would otherwise be to separate the development of the various embryonic sciences involved entirely from each other. The boundaries between them were in any case only gradually defined, and most scholars ranged freely across a number of fields.

In trying to understand how the intellectual climate arose in which archaeology could at last begin to develop it is therefore best to consider those general movements in thought which tended to produce it and which had made appreciable progress by the end of the eighteenth century. Among the many factors which played their part, two of the most significant were 1) the first assault on what Toulmin and Goodfield (1967, 182, 195) have aptly called the 'time-barrier', and 2) the emergence of the first ideas of evolution, particularly in the social and cultural development of man.

Although the full effect of such ideas was felt only in the course of the nineteenth century it was the culmination of a long process which spans the whole of the eighteenth century and many aspects of which can be traced back still further. At the same time it is true that during much of the eighteenth century there is observable a certain lack of co-ordination between detailed observation and theory (as noted by Stuart Piggott, below, in relation to studies of megalithic monuments), which no doubt often made the latter much less convincing. Added to the general reluctance to accept conclusions obviously at variance with generally accepted religious dogmas, this weakness goes far to explain the retardation of the effects of the new ideas and evidence which were coming to light.

The chronological problem was not really raised until the mid-eighteenth century, though it was implicit in Descartes' hypothetical account of the development of the earth and the planets in his *Principles of Philosophy*, and even more directly in the conclusions of Hooke and Steno later in the seventeenth century about the extent of the geological changes which had affected the surface of the earth. Descartes excuses himself for his historical speculations rather lamely by saying that his account of origins is useful to prove how the physical universe could have come into being, even though we know (through revelation) that it did not happen this way. (You cannot help feeling that he would have been very happy if he could have thought of the argument that Philip Henry Gosse called the 'Law of Prochronism', and used to explain away the fossil record two centuries later.) Hooke and Steno, though their methods anticipated the uniformitarianism of Lyell in so far as they were prepared to infer past geological processes from those still operating in their own time, were nevertheless not prepared to follow the argument through to its logical conclusion. While admitting that the evidence pointed to sweeping changes having taken place in the landscape and its living population, they were prepared to assume, in order not to conflict with the Biblical account, that in earlier times the earth's crust must have been more malleable and the forces operating on it more violent than now. Hooke, in his writings about the fossil record, saw the process as one of the progressive destruction of the originally perfect earth, while the organic creation 'originally of a much greater and gigantic standard; suppose ten times as big as at present', had 'dwindled and degenerated into a dwarfish progeny'.

During the first half of the eighteenth century the popularity of Newton's explanation of the universe as operating, following its initial creation by God, like a great machine tended to exclude all idea of a historical development far more completely than even Descartes' system. Interest in a historical approach to cosmology came back in the middle of the century, however, with the publication of Buffon's *Theory of the Earth* in 1749, and Kant's *General History of Nature and Theory of the Heavens* in 1755; and was kept up by Buffon's later *Epochs of Nature* (1778). All of these assumed a long time-scale. Kant's remarkable conception of a continuous and endless process of creation needed 'a series of millions of years and centuries before the sphere of ordered nature, in which we find ourselves, attained to the perfection which is now embodied in it'. Buffon in his *Epochs* put forward, on the basis of experiments with the cooling of spheres of different sizes, very precise figures for the ages of the various planets, and the time when life could have first appeared on them. Those for the earth were 74,832 and 35,983 respectively. Buffon's figures, in addition to being precise to the point of absurdity, were also far too low, and it was soon shown that his calculations were based on false assumptions. Nevertheless, the great popularity of his writings (particularly compared to the very limited and local influence of Kant's work) was important in getting the reading public accustomed to the idea of long spans of time in relation to cosmic processes.

Buffon's figures, however, were obtained only by extrapolation from indirect evidence. More direct and immediate were the arguments that could be drawn from geological observations, though, rather surprisingly, overt conflict with the Mosaic chronology was quite slow in appearing. Voltaire even complained that geology was nothing more than the handmaid of the Book of Genesis (Berry 1968, 19). Germany, with its long tradition of mining and mineralogical studies, and France took the lead in geological investigations at first, and during the eighteenth century a considerable mass of data was accumulated in those countries by the sustained work of relatively few people. Surprisingly again, it was at first the discovery in France in the 1750s, and later elsewhere, of extinct volcanoes that gave more trouble chronologically than the growing understanding of the formation of sedimentary deposits. On A. G. Werner's Neptunist hypothesis, as it came to be called, the formation of the latter could be fitted into the Mosaic span, even if only on the supposition of numerous deluges rather than one. It was more difficult to explain so much unrecorded volcanic activity in the short time available, and moreover this did not fit well into the Wernerian theory.

The repeated eruptions of volcanoes, whether extinct or not, also offered an opportunity of utilizing the deposits of successive eruptions to calculate how long a particular volcano had been active. Naturally, those who attempted to do so came up with most un-Mosaic figures. An amusing and also instructive instance of this is to be found in a once-popular travel book, Patrick Brydone's *Tour of Sicily and Malta*, first published in 1770. Arriving in Sicily, Brydone visited Mount Etna and there met with a local priest, Father Recupero, who had been making a study of Etna with the idea of writing a history of it, but was most embarrassed by the conclusions he had arrived at. Brydone wrote:

Signor Recupero who obligingly engages to be our Cicerone, has shown us some curious remains of antiquity; but they have all been so shaken and shattered by the mountain that hardly anything is to be found entire.

Near to a vault, which is now thirty feet below ground, and has probably been a burial place, there is a draw-well, where there are several strata of lavas, with earth (to a considerable thickness) over the surface of each stratum. Recupero has made great use of this as an argument to prove the great

antiquity of his mountain. For if it requires two thousand years or upwards to form but a scanty soil on the surface of a lava, there must have been more than that space of time betwixt each of the eruptions which have formed these strata.

But what shall we say of a pit sunk near Iaci, of a great depth? They pierced through seven distinct lavas one under the other, the surfaces of which were parallel, and most of them covered with a thick bed of rich earth. Now, says he, the eruption which formed the lowest of these lavas, if we may be allowed to reason by analogy, must have flowed from the mountain at least 14,000 years ago.

Recupero tells me that he is exceedingly embarrassed by these discoveries in writing the history of the mountain; that Moses hangs like a dead weight upon him, and blunts his zeal for inquiry; for that he really has not the conscience to make his mountain so young as that prophet makes the world. What do you think of these sentiments from a Roman Catholic divine? The bishop, who is strenuously orthodox – for it is an excellent see – has already warned him to be upon his guard, and not to pretend to be a better natural historian than Moses; nor to presume to urge anything that may in the smallest degree be deemed contradictory to his sacred authority.

Recupero's embarrassment was, in view of his cloth, specially acute, but reluctance to accept anything which conflicted with the Biblical account was generally extremely strong among professional scientists in the later eighteenth and early nineteenth centuries. The most awkward evidence was often produced by amateurs, as in Recupero's case, and in the two well-known instances in which evidence for the antiquity of man was offered. J. F. Esper, who found human remains associated with bones of extinct animals in caves near Gailenreuth in Franconia, and published an account of his discoveries, was a Catholic priest like Recupero, while John Frere of the Hoxne palaeoliths was a country gentleman. Neither discovery attracted much attention, and the antiquity of man did not become an issue before the nineteenth century. But the antiquity of the world had, as became very evident with the outbreak of the bitter Neptunist/Vulcanist controversy between the followers of Werner and Hutton in the 1790s.

While the idea of change and flux is widespread and ancient in human thought, that of ordered, evolutionary development through time is scarcely perceptible before modern times. Some faint glimmerings may perhaps be seen in ancient Ionian philosophy and the Epicurean Lucretius certainly gave a developmental account of human technology. Much of the essentially static world-picture of medieval times was not merely carried over into the European thought of the seventeenth and eighteenth centuries, but was actually reinforced in certain respects by the new concepts which emerged from the mathematical philosophy of Descartes and the mathematical physics of Newton. For a time most religious and infidel thinkers started from common assumptions, which included the ancient idea of the Chain of Being, transformed progressively from the hierarchical system of medieval thought into something which was more like the counterpart in the organic realm of the perfect order which, in the new philosophy, characterized that great machine, the universe.

The growth of this new vision of the world led to the gradual elimination of the pessimistic elements which seventeenth-century thought had inherited from earlier times. Earlier attitudes to the past, drawing on the traditional Christian view of the corruption of the world through man's sin, combined, especially from the Renaissance onwards, with notions of progressive degradation derived from classical antiquity, had tended to a pessimism which was only reinforced by the humanist worship of the achievements of classical civilization. As already noted above, such ideas even conditioned early theories about the tendency of geological change. In the course of the seventeenth century, however, confidence in the achievements of the 'moderns' began to grow, but this did not lead immediately to the appearance of ideas of 'progress' or 'evolution'. Instead, in the early eighteenth century the past came to be conceived in a way which corresponded in great measure with the mechanical conception of the workings of nature then current. Rather than a process, either of degeneration or evolution, the human past was conceived as 'a sequence of variations on a theme' (Toulmin and Goodfield 1967, 138). The theme was human nature, which was regarded as a constant, the same everywhere and at all times, with reason as its guiding principle. The variations were provided by the effects of the passions or of custom. Social and cultural patterns were linked to human nature and its vagaries according to laws which were fixed.

Such an outlook, the dominant one in the earlier eighteenth century, was certainly highly inimical to the development of any genuine historical approach in any field. Yet this viewpoint, entrenched as it seems, was only a brief halting place in a journey of thought which was to lead much further. Even in the early eighteenth century the idea of the Chain of Being was being reinterpreted once more. Not only was it becoming obvious that all the links did not exist

simultaneously, but at the same time a strong moral feeling gained ground in favour of admitting the possibility of progress in the scale of being. The Chain therefore came to be viewed as a Ladder to be climbed. Optimism led to dissatisfaction with the present, to the idea of progress towards a better future, and this had its effect on views of the past.

The idea of historical development as a process was first worked out by Giambattista Vico quite early in the century. Vico argued that human history exhibited a succession of stages, each developing out of, and conditioned by, its predecessor. Each period had its special characteristics which differentiated it from all others. They reflected the changing needs of men at different times, so that Vico also implied that human nature was not fixed or constant. Vico's ideas were out of tune with contemporary thinking, and he had little influence at the time. Indirectly, however, he did have some effect on J. G. Herder, who was also a pupil of Kant and affected by his cosmological views. In the 1780s Herder began to publish a very influential work in which he presented a somewhat rhapsodical view of the entire universe as the product of a historical process. He also seems to have been the first to argue systematically for the idea that human nature is not always the same everywhere, even if, as Collingwood recognized (1961, 91), it was not a really historical conception, since Herder regarded the psychological characteristics of each race as fixed and uniform. Since Herder did not accept transformism in the biological sphere either, his approach is not truly evolutionary, but it nevertheless had a great effect in encouraging developmental approaches to both the natural and human world.

However, for the general diffusion of the idea of a progressive development of human society perhaps the most influential writings of the later eighteenth century were those of the French *philosophes*, such as Voltaire, Turgot and Condorcet. Their motivation was to a great extent political, and their approach rather old-fashioned to the extent that they all subscribed to the idea of a constant and unchanging human nature. Nevertheless, Turgot was able to present a powerful picture of the links which bind each period to those which precede and follow it, and of the process by which knowledge is accumulated from one generation to another. 'All the ages of mankind are enchained, one with another, by a sequence of causes and effects that binds the present to the whole preceding past.' Men have 'formed from individual stores of knowledge a common treasure, that one generation transmits to another, like unto a heritage continually augmented by the discoveries of each century' (*Tableau philosophique*, quoted in Slotkin 1965, 358). Turgot's disciple, Condorcet, believed that 'the unlimited perfectibility of mankind . . . is a universal law' (*Sur l'instruction publique*, in Slotkin 1965, 364), and produced a hypothetical series of nine Epochs to demonstrate our progress so far.

Such heady speculations, not based on evidence any more than Lucretius' account of the technological progress of mankind, might seem to have little relation to the laborious, miscellaneous and generally uninspired activities of the typical eighteenth-century antiquaries. But they helped to set, and they exemplify, the tone of much writing later in that century. Ideas of progress, and of the development of human society and human

knowledge, were novel and exciting ones, particularly since they seemed to point to a glorious future for mankind. They were 'in the air', along with many other more or less vague evolutionary speculations, especially before the course of the French Revolution tarnished the glitter somewhat. Such continual speculation about the early development of man at least provided a strong stimulus to try to interpret the surviving evidence for these remote periods. Success in this task was indeed reserved for the nineteenth century, but the climate which inspired and encouraged those who achieved it was largely the creation of the later eighteenth century.

Bibliography

BERRY, W. B. N. 1968 *Growth of a Prehistoric Time Scale*, San Francisco.

CHANG, KWANG-CHIH, 1968 *The Archaeology of Ancient China*, New Haven and London.

CHENG, TE-KUN, 1939 *Archaeology in China*, vol.1, Cambridge.

COLLINGWOOD, R. G. 1961 *The Idea of History*, Oxford.

FINLEY, M. I. 1975 *The Use and Abuse of History*, London.

LLOYD, S. 1947 *Foundations in the Dust*, Oxford (revised edn, London and New York 1980).

MASPERO, SIR G. 1915 *Popular Stories of Ancient Egypt*, London and New York.

NEEDHAM, J. 1954 *Science and Civilisation in China*, vol.I, Cambridge.

1959 *Science and Civilisation in China*, vol.III, Cambridge.

OATES, J. 1979 *Babylon*, London and New York.

SLOTKIN, J. S. (ed.) 1965 *Readings in Early Anthropology*, New York.

TOULMIN, S. AND GOODFIELD, J. 1967 *The Discovery of Time*, London.

WILLEY, G. R. AND SABLOFF, J. A. 1974 *A History of American Archaeology*, London and San Francisco.

XIA NAI 1979 *Essays on Archaeology of Science and Technology in China*, Peking.

2 'Vast Perennial Memorials': The First Antiquaries look at Megaliths

Stuart Piggott

IN OFFERING this essay to Glyn Daniel it seemed appropriate to choose a subject, a fragment of the history of archaeology, which represents a field of study in which he has made notable contributions, and to embody in it a quotation from that greatest of early Welsh antiquaries, Edward Lhwyd. But when we turn to examine the history of our own discipline, we immediately face difficulties shared by all historians, and especially those concerned with science and allied intellectual activities, as to what approach we make to the past. Historians of science have of recent years concerned themselves with just this problem, and though they have not specifically included archaeology, it takes its place naturally within the general debate. It is therefore worth while briefly to review this from the archaeologist's standpoint.

One view, now generally held to be unsatisfactory, involves the fallacy of looking at the past in modern terms and with hindsight, and so selecting from early writers ideas or expressions of opinion which fit a preconceived concept of continuous 'progress' in any one field, always advancing towards its present state, and with each successive generation or individual building consciously or unconsciously on the ideas of its predecessors. This is, of course, a selected aspect of what Herbert Butterfield long ago devastatingly criticized as the 'Whig interpretation' of history (Butterfield 1931) and can lead to misleading simplifications or downright distortions. In one extreme form this can become historical determinism, where the development of the discipline is seen as explicable solely in terms of social needs, pressures or circumstances: 'in this as in other sociological interpretations of the history of science, there is little or any scope for the unique, the fortuitous and the visionary' (Kearney 1974, 221). On the other hand, while full biographical studies of the major figures of archaeology, as in other disciplines, are essential to our understanding of its early development, they must, as I tried to do with William Stukeley (Piggott 1950) and Michael Hunter has with John Aubrey (Hunter 1975), set their characters firmly within the intellectual climate of their times. Too often in archaeology there has been a tendency to take refuge in the anecdotal, and at worst to lapse into well-meaning but ineffectual antiquarian gossip with patronizing overtones of the 'dear old

Aubrey' type, though one admits the deckle-edged period charm of H.B. Walters' *The English Antiquaries* of 1934. What we are left with, and surely should be our aim, is an attempt to see the early development of archaeology as far as possible in terms of its own past, with its individual exponents thinking and acting as children of their age (as we are of our own), and assessing what now seem for us their praiseworthy or unfortunate contributions to the subject in relation to their contemporary social and intellectual context, and their individual world-picture.

Into what sort of picture of the past then would the first British antiquaries set the field monuments or other antiquities, prehistoric or later, which they were beginning to find intellectually challenging? One of the most difficult tasks for the historian of any science is to visualize an approach to his subject which he knows must have been wholly unlike his own, and framed in a totally different intellectual climate, and yet by reason of its very subject-matter having elements which he should be able to share. The first recognition of difference here must be that for the early antiquaries from the sixteenth, and well into the nineteenth century the human past was entirely historical and could not well be otherwise, since one of the cardinal historical sources available began its narrative with the Creation. Historical, but not in terms of history as most historians see and practise it today; it was providential and meaningful, with a pre-ordained man-centred pattern, and its documentary sources had a status unlike that which they have to us. These comprised, briefly, ancient history as contained in the Greek and Roman writers, and the Old Testament, and some miscellaneous material at best legendary and at worst forgeries which, though largely discredited by the seventeenth century, still exercised an unfortunate influence long after.

Consideration of what appear the most obviously straightforward of these sources, the classical writers, shows immediately that we are in an unfamiliar world. Writing of the sixteenth and seventeenth centuries, Momigliano has commented that 'when ancient history was studied for its own sake . . . it was meant either to provide materials for moral and political reflections or to help the understanding of texts read primarily for stylistic reasons. The truth and completeness of the traditional accounts was hardly questioned' (Momigliano 1966, 6). This attitude was long to endure, and the 'Ancient Authours' treated with uncritical reverence, particularly in the course of the intermittent quarrel of the Ancients and the Moderns, which involved the early scientists of the new Royal Society who dared to think they might have made intellectual advances since classical antiquity, and culminated in Swift's *Battle of the Books* of 1697. Old-fashioned men continued to side with the Ancients for decades to come, and not all antiquaries were necessarily abreast with the latest intellectual advances (Jones 1951).

When we turn from the secular to the sacred, the Old Testament, as the first fundamental authority for the Christian religion, would seem at first sight to have such supernatural prestige as to render discussion as irrelevant as irreverent, but what strikes one when reading the contemporary writers who were desperately trying to construct an overall historical chronology in the seventeenth and eighteenth centuries, is the way in which the Mosaic narrative seems to have been regarded more as an historical document far earlier than, but comparable to, Herodotus or Livy, than as divine revelation. The question of high antiquity was, from the Renaissance, unfortunately confounded by other minor and misleading sources which temporarily were held in high repute. The myth of Trojan Brutus died hard in English minds and the forgeries of Annius of Viterbo maintained adherents for centuries (Kendrick 1950; Piggott 1976, 58), and to add to these there came what Frances Yates has called a 'huge historical error', the acceptance of the mystical writings associated with the name of Hermes Trismegistus (in fact works of the second and third centuries AD) as of extreme antiquity and Egyptian origin, contemporary with or even earlier than Moses. These 'Christian, or rather semi-Christian compositions, fathered on the Egyptian god Thoth to lend them importance' were taken as 'the fount of primitive wisdom whence Plato and the Greeks derived the best that they knew', and that 'the author of the Hermetica was a man who lived about the time of Moses' was generally accepted. Their real date was in fact demonstrated as early as 1614 by Isaac Casaubon, but the Hermetic tradition in European thought remained a pervasive influence for long to come, and confused the understanding of ancient Egypt and its writing system to an unfortunate degree (Yates 1964; Pope 1975, 22–34).

With this puzzling series of historical documents – the Bible for the ancient Near East, Greek and Roman legend enshrined as fact in the classical texts, and dubious sources from Dictys the Cretan and Dares of Phrygia through the *Hermetica* to Geoffrey of Mon-

mouth and Annius – the seventeenth-century scholars made a brave attempt to construct a chronology. Mention of Ussher and 4004 BC has gained many a lecturer an easy undergraduate giggle, but James Ussher, Archbishop of Armagh, was no crackpot old clergyman. He was an historian of outstanding distinction, recognized as such in his own time and today: 'This great scholar', David Douglas has written, 'was immeasurably superior to most of his colleagues' in textual criticism, showing 'an exact scholarship which in its range and accuracy has been the wonder of subsequent critics' (Douglas 1939, 251–2). In his *Annals of the World* of 1658 (an English translation of an earlier Latin *Annales*) he used every means at his disposal to construct a viable system, consulting the leading mathematicians of the day when he came to use solar eclipses in the Biblical record to form a basis for an absolute chronology, including Napier's new discovery of logarithms. Science and theology were indistinguishably entwined: 'Napier himself regarded logarithms as a short cut to calculating the Number of the Beast' in Revelations (Kearney 1974, 226). And Sir Isaac Newton, whose concern for the Hermetist tradition and passion for Biblical scholarship tends to be forgotten, went further in astro-archaeology when he put up an adventurous 'short chronology' in his *Chronology of the Ancient Kingdoms Amended*, by using the precession of the equinox to date, by references to star positions in the *Argonautica*, the period of that famous voyage (Pope 1975, 194). Within the intellectual framework of the time, these chronological exercises were inter-disciplinary research at the highest level then attainable.

I have made this excursus into the historical picture presented to the early antiquaries because it seems not to have been considered before. Antiquarianism, however, as is well known, did not emerge from English historical scholarship, but from the Scientific Revolution of the seventeenth century, a topic widely discussed and with an intimidatingly large and often polemical bibliography which shows no signs of lessening. Since I and others have considered the scientific background to antiquarianism in Britain during the seventeenth century on more than one occasion, I need to no more than sketch a brief summary here. In what was to characterize the early days of the Royal Society but beginning before its formal foundation in 1662, the new mood, that of the Moderns as against the Ancients, was 'associated with pragmatic observation and experiment, objective record and ordered classification' of phenomena both natural and artificial: that great early scientist Robert Hooke saw the antiquary, concerned with man-made antiquities, as following a parallel line of intellectual investigation to

20

the 'Natural Antiquary' studying fossils, minerals and the earth's surface. Within this favourable climate of thought, it was inevitable that 'antiquities, as a part of the earth and landscape, followed fossils as subjects for investigation within the same scheme'. Museums and Cabinets of Curiosities, not devoted to sculpture, paintings and other works of art, were formed, containing on the other hand specimens of plants, animals, birds, fossils, minerals and so on – natural history museums in fact – and these often included not only ethnographical but archaeological material. The theme of these collections was taxonomy and classification, and so far as stone, bronze or iron antiquities, or prehistoric pots, were concerned, the early antiquaries of the sixteenth and seventeenth centuries were grappling with a problem which in its final form was faced by Thomsen in Copenhagen in the early decades of the nineteenth century (Piggott 1976, 101–8).

In the field, the same set of scientific problems was encountered. Chronology was not the primary question here, it was the recognition of unfamiliar artifacts as such, and then their classification into some sort of a taxonomic scheme. Once stone implements were recognized for what they were by comparison with ethnological examples in the new collection of curiosities being formed, and not classed among 'naturally formed stones', an important step had been taken in recognizing the tangible remains of a barbarian, if not literally a prehistoric, British and European past. Paradoxically, this recognition inhibited the rightful interpretation of prehistoric bronze tools and weapons, for in the context of a primitive past comparable in status to that of the recently encountered American Indians (Aubrey thought the ancient Britons 'were 2 or 3 degrees, I suppose, less savage than the Americans') bronze technology was often thought to be beyond the capabilities of such woad-painted savages, and must, in a telescoped chronology, be a Roman introduction. We shall see that it was a parallel fallacious argument, in this case architectural sophistication, that led Inigo Jones to assign Stonehenge to the Romans.

It was then within the context of a barbarian, pre-Roman, past, having a stone-using technology, possibly also that of bronze, and by Caesar's time iron, that the first antiquaries saw field monuments including megaliths. The technological and chronological sequence which Thomsen was to perceive does not seem to have been apprehended, even if Camden in 1637 realized that 'the Britans used brazen weapons' and Ole Worm in 1643 thought the same of the ancient Danes, who were after all well beyond the imperial frontier, and Pegge in 1787 used the same argument for Ireland (Evans 1881, 30–3). How widely

dispersed this general knowledge of antiquity was in the seventeenth and eighteenth centuries is difficult to assess. I have stressed elsewhere the obstacles that inadequate transport and roads presented to early antiquarian fieldwork (Piggott 1976, 115), and to this we must add the dissemination of new ideas among scholars dependent, outside Oxford and Cambridge, on their private libraries, technical correspondence (which took the place of the interchange of offprints today) and above all in circles of personal friendships. Mention of Ole Worm, and his highly influential works, the *Danica Monumentorum Libri Sex* of 1643 and the Catalogue of his museum of 1655, reminds us of a final general point: the way in which, with a very abbreviated chronology, the seventeenth century could unwittingly transfer the concept of its modern nation states into the remote prehistoric past, so that antiquities found in Denmark could be thought of as products of historical Danes, or if in North Germany, of Saxons.

Turning now to the way in which these intellectual circumstances determined the first antiquaries' approach to megalithic monuments, it may be instructive to follow, so to say, an individual case history, that of the three (originally four) huge standing stones known as The Devil's Arrows, near Boroughbridge in Yorkshire. They are conspicuous from the main road north, Watling Street and today A1, and were recorded by John Leland, in Kendrick's words 'one of our greatest English antiquaries, illustrious alike in splendour of vision and purpose' (Kendrick 1950, 49) around 1540 after leaving Boroughbridge: 'A little without this Towne on the West Parte of *Wateling-Streate* standith 4 great maine stones wrought above *in conum* by Mannes hand.' The tapering stones (in fact naturally shaped) are then further described at some length, and Leland concludes: 'I take them to be *trophaea a Romanis posita* in the side of Watheling-Streat, as yn a place moste occupied in Yorneying, and so most yn sighte.' We next come to William Camden, whose own explanation ('agreeable with some others in this point') as rendered in the 1695 *Britannia*, 'a Roman trophy raised by the high-way', points immediately to one of his numerous unacknowledged borrowings from Leland's MSS. For his 1695 Camden revision, Edmund Gibson as editor had secured the services of the Leeds antiquary, Ralph Thoresby, for this Yorkshire section, and Thoresby questions the Roman attribution, adding that 'a later Antiquary seems inclin'd to conclude them to be a British work', with a marginal reference to Plot's *History of Staffordshire* of 1686.

This introduces us to a significant figure, Dr Robert Plot (1640–96), first Keeper of the Ashmolean

Museum. Though disliked by Edward Lhwyd, who served under him and succeeded to the Keepership, and involved in an unfortunate little contretemps with Aubrey and Anthony Wood, 'the egregious Dr Plot' as Anthony Powell perhaps rightly called him (Powell 1948, 202) is interesting as reflecting the prevailing antiquarian mood of his times. He published two 'Natural Histories' or county surveys in the new manner encouraged by the Royal Society, for Oxfordshire in 1677 and Staffordshire in 1686, and Aubrey at one time intended handing over to him his own notes for North Wiltshire. Thoresby's note takes us to a reference to a standing stone at Kinver which Plot thinks 'may be accounted' British, and goes on to say of such antiquities 'which perhaps they may, and not without reason; whether we esteem them as *British Dieties* [*sic*], as the *Devil's Bolts* in Yorkshire and *Devil's coits* in *Oxford-shire*, have been proved to be at large; or some memorials of battles fought thereabout'. He then adds '*Kits-Coty-House* in *Kent*; *Roll-wright* in *Oxfordshire*; and *Stonehenge* in *Wiltshire*' as presumptively ancient British, though noting of the last that it was thought Roman by Inigo Jones and Danish by Walter Charleton. Here Plot is indebted to the ideas of Edward Stillingfleet (1635–99), who thought standing stones might be the gods of the ancient Britons, but he has changed his mind since he published his Oxfordshire volume nine years earlier, for here he champions Charleton and the Danes when describing the Rollright stone circle, which he thinks (as indeed had Camden) 'to have been the *Monument* of some *Victory*, and happily errected by *Rollo* the *Dane*'.

The antiquarian reader of the day seeking enlightenment on the Devil's Arrows might well by now be in a state of some confusion, but in 1709 another authority was available. Dr Thomas Gale, Dean of York from 1697 to his death in 1702, was a noted historian and numismatist, and a friend of Aubrey, who had prepared an edition of the Roman Antonine Itinerary still in manuscript on his death. This was revised and published by his son Roger in 1709, in Latin, with an engraving of the Devil's Arrows (which as we saw stand by the Roman road), and a comment which is a direct quotation from Leland, *trophaea a Romanis posita*, taking us back to the 1540s. Incidentally we have another link in those circles of friendship I mentioned earlier. Roger Gale was to become a friend of William Stukeley, and it was his father's transcript of part of Aubrey's *Monumenta Britannica* MS that Stukeley saw around 1718, and which fired him to devote his attention to Avebury and Stonehenge.

I have traced the story of the interpretation of a minor megalithic antiquity in detail from 1540 to 1709 because it so well illustrates the background of the more famous controversies that centred on Stonehenge. Here, as is well known, the familiar trio of claimants were once again in competition. Inigo Jones thought it an extraordinary sort of Roman temple in his posthumously published *Stone-Heng* of 1655; John Aubrey had long thought it British, and so, as a temple, attributable to the Druids, and this view, taken from the unpublished *Monumenta Britannica*, got into print in Gibson's 1695 edition of Camden's *Britannia*; Walter Charleton in his *Chorea Gigantum* of 1663 presented the monument 'restored to the Danes'. A Roman origin had been claimed for other prehistoric circles, such as those at Stanton Drew in Somerset, which William Musgrave, in his *Antiquitates Britanno-Belgicae* of 1719 described and planned among his Roman sepulchral monuments; Thomas Hearne thought Avebury Roman, as did others in the early eighteenth century. But Charleton's Danes deserve further comment, as they introduce what is to my mind a very significant aspect in seventeenth-century megalithic studies, even if Michael Hunter found the controversy 'disappointing' when he was searching for anticipations of modern archaeology among the seventeenth-century membership of the Royal Society, perhaps with a slight leaning towards the 'Whig interpretation' attitude (Hunter 1971, 117).

It all begins with the use made by British antiquaries of the works of the Danish scholar Ole Worm, in his two books of 1643 and 1655 already mentioned. John Aubrey knew the *Danicorum Monumentorum Libri Sex*, and from this 'altered my title of *Monumenta Druydum* to *Monumenta Britannica*' (Powell 1948, 182; Hunter 1975, 201), but seems uninfluenced by Worm's descriptions and rather crude illustrations of Danish megalithic monuments (largely denuded chambered tombs). Far otherwise with Charleton: 'The Doctor, dissatisfied with Mr *Jone's* Discourse, caus'd a Copy of it to be transmitted to Olaus Wormius, the celebrated Antiquary of *Denmark*, and *Wormius* return'd his Opinion of *Stone-Heng* in several Letters to Dr Charleton', recorded the anonymous editor of the 1725 reprint of Jones, Charleton, and Webb's rejoinder on behalf of the Romans. Charleton himself wrote: 'having diligently compared STONE-HENG with other Antiquities of the same kind, at this Day standing in *Denmark*, and finding a perfect *Resemblance* in most, if not all Particulars, observable on both Sides . . . I now at length conceive it to be Erected by the DANES, when they had this Nation in Subjection'. Worm's illustrations comprise, of course, nothing in the least like Stonehenge, but then, nor does that monument bear the faintest resemblance to a Roman temple. One of Jones's arguments was that it was too sophisticated, with its dressed stones, to belong to the technologically primitive ancient Britons, exactly as was said by others, as we saw, of bronze implements, and perhaps uncomfortably near in its mode of thought to those of us who championed Mycenaean influences. The rough barrow peristaliths shown by Worm could with more justice, in this sense, be compared with British circles such as Rollright, as was done by Plot, and within a past which had no prehistory, the fallacy of confusing modern nations with the antiquities of the area they covered was concealed.

But the question of British megalithic monuments having European counterparts quickly enlarged its scope. 'If you speake with my sonne who is at Dr Ternes in Lymestreet', wrote Sir Thomas Browne to Aubrey in 1672, 'hee will give you some account of stones like Rollrich stones, the which hee observed as he went from Magdeburg to Hamburg' (Keynes 1964, 374). Johan Picardt published his descriptions and illustrations of chambered tombs in the Netherlands in 1660, and others, such as Georg Keysler in 1720, those in North Germany (Bakker 1978). Keysler, who had lived in England, was an FRS and knew the antiquarian circle of the day, was fully conversant with the Stonehenge controversy, but in his *Antiquitates selectae septentrionales et celticae* (Hanover 1720) he pointed out that megalithic monuments existed in north Europe – *ut in Westphalia et Frisia orientali* – and so Stonehenge was Saxon: *monumentum vetus Anglo-Saxonicum*, the tomb of a Saxon king.

This was really going too far, and no English antiquary seems to have supported him; besides, by 1720 interest in the problem had waned. Earlier, other areas of Europe had also been considered, and when Professor James Garden of Aberdeen was in correspondence with Aubrey about a possible Druidic (and so Celtic) origin for stone circles, he wrote: 'In case anie of these monuments shall upon enquiry be found in France (where you know the Druids were in no less credit and reputation then in Brittaine) it would greatly contribute to the confirming of your opinion about them' (Gordon 1960). Garden, and others too, knew that there were stone circles in Britain outside the Danelaw, such as Callanish (of which a plan of sorts was published by Martin Martin in 1703), the Aberdeenshire circles themselves and the Orkney monuments recorded by Garden's friend James Wallace in his *Description of the Isles of Orkney* in 1693. There was also Wales, where Henry Rowlands was to publish the Anglesey antiquities in his *Mona Antiqua Restaurata* (1723), and it is here we turn with some sense of relief to Edward Lhwyd, who had the most penetrating intellect of them all. Lhwyd wrote to Rowlands (who published the letter in his book) in

1701: 'Cornwall affords store of these barbarous Monuments we have in Wales: some whereof are also, I presume, in all our neighbouring Countries of Europe'.

There was also Ireland, and when Lhwyd wrote to Rowlands, he had just made his famous visit to the great chambered tomb of Newgrange, after his tour in the Scottish Highlands (Ó Ríordáin and Daniel 1964; Herity 1967). He wrote about it not only to Rowlands, but to Dr Tancred Robinson and to Dr Thomas Molyneux, founder of the short-lived Dublin Philosophical Society, an offshoot of the Royal Society like that of Oxford, founded and run by Plot from 1683 to 1690 (Hoppen 1970). He sent Molyneux a plan made by his assistant William Jones, and in his letter said that although a Roman coin had been found on top of the Newgrange mound 'I cannot think this mount a work of the Romans, in regard the carving of the stones is plainly barbarous and the whole contrivance too rude for so polite a people'. He would have been 'very apt to regard it Danish' (alas, the Norse peoples had indeed got to Ireland too), but the coin shows it must be earlier and so, 'being neither Roman nor Danish, it remains it should be a place of sacrifice used by the old Irish' (Herity 1967, 129). But this cogent archaeological argument was to be wasted on Molyneux. He wrote his own account of Newgrange about 1710, and it was published in 1726 with a reprint of Boate's *Natural History of Ireland*. In it he decided that Newgrange and its adjacent tombs 'were designed by a way of a family monument for some great Danish prince, that chose to be interred near his country-dwelling, that might be hereabouts'. The Roman coins were 'by accident dropt, or deposited by design' by the Danes. And, so far as I am aware, this is their last appearance as putative builders of megalithic monuments in the British Isles.

Lhwyd had in fact made his main published pronouncement on this subject in 1695, when at Edmund Gibson's invitation he had joined the team of antiquarian advisers in the production of the new edition of Camden's *Britannia*. In his 'Additions' to the Pembrokeshire section, Lhwyd describes the chambered tomb of Pentre Ifan, not from first-hand observation but from the description and drawing of it in George Owen's MS *History of Pembrokeshire* of 1603 (Piggott 1978, 11). He suports Aubrey's ideas that such monuments were indigenous British tombs and temples, quoting in support James Garden and the Scottish evidence, place-names such as Tre'r Driw in Anglesey (on shaky ground here) and the story of St Patrick and the ring of idols called Cromm Cruaich. He opposes the views in favour of the Danes (despite his toying with the idea later at Newgrange) in a grand

23

phrase – 'Such vast perennial memorials, seem rather to be the work of a people settled in the country, than of such roving Pirats', who had 'but small leisure or reason for erecting such lasting Monuments'. The Danish monuments others had cited from Worm or Rudbeck were not strictly similar to those in Britain, least of all to Stonehenge, and 'I think it probable, should we make diligent enquiry, that there may be monuments of this kind still extant in the less frequented places of Germany, France and Spain; if not also in Italy'. This in fact was what later archaeologists were to find, and to interpret in many ways, as the vagaries of intellectual fashion became dignified as the application of alternative scientific paradigms. And Lhwyd went on: 'For as one Nation since the planting of Christianity hath imitated another in their Churches, Chapels, Sepulchral Monuments so also in the time of Paganism, the Rites and Customs in Religion must have been deriv'd from one Country to another', a statement disturbing or amusing, according to temperament, to those of us who remember Gordon Childe's megalithic missionaries and the climate of thought in which they were engendered.

This then was the picture of megalithic monuments formed by British antiquaries by the end of the seventeenth century. They were indigenous products, erected as tombs, memorials, ceremonial centres or temples by ancient Britons in a past which, while it could not yet be conceived of as prehistoric, was being pushed so far back beyond Caesar or Tacitus that it was being seen as anonymous and almost anhistoric. Their builders were barbarians with a stone technology (only very dubiously using bronze, and iron by Caesar's time), but yet capable of remarkable engineering and indeed, at Stonehenge, architectural feats. A parenthetical note of interest is that while admiration and respect were accorded to the megalith builders, the technology of the construction, involving large stone masses, was never considered as incredible, as it is sometimes today. The reason is not far to seek: the pre-industrial technology of the seventeenth century was, with few exceptions such as the use of gears, cranks and the block-and-tackle, very much that of remote antiquity. Huge stones were still being moved by simple means – half a dozen Egyptian obelisks were set up in Rome in the 1580s; St Peter's and other great churches were being erected, and nearer home St Paul's was being built between 1668 and 1716. One of the few antiquaries to mention the problem was Charleton, who did not see it as insuperable. He (and Inigo Jones) saw that the Stonehenge sarsens were likely to have been brought from the Avebury region, but it was surely not impossible for 'a whole Army of Men and Multitudes of Oxen, to transport the Stones thereof in

a plain and champain Country', in view of what had been done with Egyptian, Greek and Roman monuments. It is only today that an urban mind, divorced from the realities of simple technology, can be bewildered enough to take refuge in the world of marvel and mystery.

It is fitting to end this essay with William Stukeley, for what we have been considering were his immediate archaeological antecedents. What Aubrey and Lhwyd both saw, in their very different ways, was the need for a megalithic corpus with good illustrations: the *Monumenta Britannica* was to be this, and had Lhwyd lived, it looks as though the second volume of his *Archaeologia Britannica* would have contained such a survey. When Stukeley saw Gale's transcript of Aubrey (and evidently some of Lhwyd's or William Jones's drawings) he seems to have taken up the idea himself, with the detailed surveys of Avebury and Stonehenge as its core. Many of us have deplored the fact that though he had finished fieldwork at these sites by 1725, he did not publish his results until the 1740s, and then as part of an extraordinary exercise in religious polemic. Can we now perhaps see at least part of the answer? In the 1670s and 1680s some of the leading scholars and scientists of the day were deeply and actively concerned with getting Aubrey's *Monumenta*, and particularly the *Templa Druidum* section, into print, even if in the end they failed through no fault of their own. It is sometimes forgotten how briefly the English Intellectual Revolution flowered, beginning around 1640, interrupted by civil discord, and fading by the 1690s. By the 1720s the well-known decline in scientific and historical studies had set in, and neither the realm of learning nor the reading public was interested in a book on megalithic monuments, full of detailed surveys and drawings. To end with a paradox, perhaps we should see William Stukeley's greatness as a field archaeologist not in his being an innovator, but in his being provincial, old-fashioned and out-of-date, continuing the high tradition of Restoration antiquarianism unaware of the changed intellectual mood of the metropolis.

Bibliography

BAKKER, J.A. 1978 'Nordwestdeutsche Megalithgräber', in 'Niederländischen Berichten des 17 bis 19 Jahrhunderts.' *Die Kunde* NF XXVIII/XXIX, 21–31.

BUTTERFIELD, H. 1931 *The Whig Interpretation of History*, London.

Douglas, D. 1939 *English Scholars*, London.

Evans, J. 1881 *The Ancient Bronze Implements . . . of Great Britain and Ireland*, London.

Gordon, C. A. 1960 'Professor James Garden's letters to John Aubrey', *Misc. Third Spalding Club* III, 1–56.

Herity, M. 1967 'From Lhuyd to Coffey: new information from unpublished descriptions of the Boyne Valley tombs', *Studia Hibernica* VII, 127–45.

Hoppen, K.T. 1970 *The Common Scientist in the XVII century: a study of the Dublin Philosophical Society 1683–1708*, London.

Hunter, M. 1971 'The Royal Society and the origins of British archaeology', *Antiquity* XLV, 113–21; 187–92.

1975 *John Aubrey and the Realm of Learning*, London.

Jones, R.F. 1951 'The background of *The Battle of the Books*', in R.F. Jones *et al. The Seventeenth Century,* Stanford, 10–40; 'Science and criticism in the Neo-Classical age of English literature', *ibid*; 41—74.

Kearney, H.F. 1974 'Puritanism and the Scientific Revolution', in C. Webster (ed.) *The Intellectual Revolution of the Seventeenth Century*, 218–42.

Kendrick, T.D. 1950 *British Antiquity*, London.

Keynes, G. 1964 *The Works of Sir Thomas Browne*, IV, 374.

Momigliano, A. 1966 *Studies in Historiography*, London.

O'Riordain, S. P. and Daniel, G. 1964 *New Grange and the Bend of the Boyne*, London and New York.

Piggott, S. 1950 *William Stukeley: an Eighteenth Century Antiquary*, Oxford.

1976 *Ruins in a Landscape: Essays in Antiquarianism*, Edinburgh.

1978 *Antiquity Depicted: Aspects of Archaeological Illustration*, London and New York.

Pope, M. 1975 *The Story of Decipherment*, London and New York.

Powell, A. 1948 *John Aubrey and his Friends*, London.

Yates, F. A. 1964 *Giordano Bruno and the Hermetic Tradition*, London.

3   Dating the Earliest Iron Age in Scandinavia

Ole Klindt-Jensen

Ever since Otto Tischler proposed his tripartite division of the La Tène period in 1885, there has been lively discussion about Early Iron Age chronology, though not so much about the division into three phases as about details and the applicability of the system outside the sphere of Celtic culture. The three-period division did in fact become a model for research in neighbouring areas, but Tischler excluded Scandinavia, and his colleague and travelling companion, Ingvald Undset, was cautious in his pioneer work on the beginning of the Iron Age in northern Europe (Undset 1881, 440).

However, an important discovery had already been made by Emil Vedel, a distinguished amateur archaeologist who had defined a pre-Roman Iron Age on the basis of excavations and comparative studies. It is worth recollecting this early research in Scandinavia.

When Vedel's successful early career as lawyer and administrator in Schleswig was cut short after the war of 1864, he turned to archaeology. Appointed county prefect of the island of Bornholm two years later, he became aware of the numerous cremation pits which were threatened by agriculture and gravel digging, and decided to study these burial places. Upon excavating, he found resemblances to cremation graves under cairns. In a relatively short time he had exposed several cemeteries and compared their yields of antiquities with finds from other regions. During the course of this work he observed that a cemetery at Kannikegaard could be divided into several zones, each one reflecting a period, running from north to south.

In 1872 Vedel published the results of his investigations (Vedel 1872, 82–9; Gräslund 1974, 143). He distinguished between two periods of the pre-Roman Iron Age. The earlier was known from cairns of which some had Bronze Age graves. The later ones consisted of cremation pits containing brooches and belt hooks corresponding to those in the south from the La Tène period. He was not able to distinguish more periods, as this material bore no evident relationship to the

25

well-known continental finds of that time. However, he could trace a direct tradition from the Bronze Age and noticed that several groups of cremation pits appeared to be associated with Iron Age cairns in the cemeteries. Moreover, there were in these cemeteries no graves containing Roman imported glass and bronze objects, such as were known from other cemeteries. At Kannikegaard the pre-Roman cremation graves lay in the north, the graves with Roman imports in the centre, and still later graves in the south.

Vedel tried to date the pre-Roman Iron Age. Between 1868 and 1872 he had excavated about 1,550 cremation pits and realized that still more had been destroyed. The original number of graves was estimated to have been about 8,000. To this number should be added about three times as many graves at other cemeteries, unknown or destroyed – Vedel had acquired a pretty good knowledge of the density of cemeteries over the entire island. This would mean that between 40,000 and 50,000 people were buried in cremation pits. A statistical survey which had just been published made it possible to set the estimated number of inhabitants on the island in the seventh century AD at about 8,400. This meant a population of about 4,200 in AD 400, when the cremation period ended, a date which was quite precise. Two or three hundred years earlier the population would have been about 3,000, including infants, servants and thralls. Having in mind the large number of cremation pits it certainly meant that the cremation-pit period would have begun at least a hundred years BC. Adding to this date the period of the earliest Iron Age cairns, Vedel estimated the beginning of the Iron Age to be at least 200 BC, perhaps 300 or even 400 BC.

This bold supposition – which we now know to have been correct – was certainly astonishing, and obviously of importance to European research. Vedel decided to submit his hypothesis, in a cautious form, to the International Congress of Anthropology and Prehistoric Archaeology in Stockholm of 1874. At this distinguished gathering Vedel read his paper, which was printed next year in the copious report of the proceedings (Vedel 1875, 587). It is a striking fact that he was opposed by the secretary of the congress, Hans Hildebrand, the coming man in Swedish archaeology together with Montelius. He would neither accept a pre-Roman Iron Age in Scandinavia, nor allow that the Iron Age evolved from the Bronze Age civilization. He still maintained that iron was introduced by invasion (Hildebrand 1875, 592).

Vedel left the congress rather discouraged and did not repeat his arguments in support of an early beginning of the Iron Age; yet he was convinced that there had been a pre-Roman Iron Age leading directly to the Iron Age proper, since there was no evidence of the latter having been introduced by migration. These ideas were set forth in his monumental *Bornholm's Monuments and Antiquities* (1886).

Before the publication of this book he had received decisive support from Undset, who gave a positive and fair account of Vedel's work in *The Beginning of the Iron Age in Northern Europe* (1881). This original investigation (of which the first part earned its author a doctoral degree) was built up on a thorough knowledge of the literature and of about sixty collections, which he visited on his extensive travels. Undset came to the conclusion that there was a tradition that ran from the Bronze to the Iron Age and he argued against Hildebrand's view that a motif on a Bronze Age hanging bowl was inspired by a Celtic coin. This would have meant attaching a very late date indeed to the Bronze Age (Undset 1881, 342). Undset, then, acknowledged Vedel's arguments and accepted a pre-Roman Iron Age, best known on Bornholm but distinguishable in other areas of Scandinavia.

More finds and careful excavations soon supported these arguments. In Jutland an early cemetery at Aarre was found and published in 1894, and other graves provided further confirmation (Müller 1897, 431-74).

Then, in 1896, Montelius carried out his planned general survey of the Iron Age periods, which was a late acknowledgment of Vedel's work (Montelius 1896, 155). He was inspired by Tischler's three-period system regarding pre-Roman times. Even if he did not have parallels for the earlier periods of early and middle La Tène, he at any rate knew the late La Tène types in Scandinavia. It was evident that a direct application of the Celtic periods was not possible where the earlier phases were concerned. He therefore had to find representative native types to cover the two first periods, and he placed in Period I finds like Eskelhem and Røgerup, Bronze Age hoards with some few iron objects (today they are placed in the late Bronze Age). The idea of three periods had a certain appeal and was not without justification.

In more than one way this discussion was valuable. It stimulated more investigations aimed at bridging the gap between the Bronze Age and the third period of the Iron Age. Even if these remote years seemed to produce relatively few remains, this did not detract from the importance of the problem. South of the Danish border excavations led G. Schwantes to postulate a three-period system divided into Jastorf (a–c), Ripdorf and Seedorf periods, the last one equivalent to Period III (Schwantes 1911 (cf. Manhus IV 1912, 149)).

Subsequently the work proceeded along two lines, based respectively on a detailed chronological and a chorological division of the types. Here, thanks to the work of Erik Nylen, the investigations on Gotland have proved important. Part of this work has been published, but still more information has come from later excavations. The pre-Roman Iron Age has been divided into two periods, each subdivided into several phases, the more recent period being arranged in four chronological groups, A–D, while the gap between these and the earlier period is bridged (Nylen 1955 and later works).

Material has likewise come from other parts of Scandinavia, for instance from Jutland and Fyn, where extensive cemeteries, house sites and pits have provided impressive evidence. The three-period system has been used by C.J. Becker and E. Albrectsen in their detailed volumes on excavations there. More evidence has come from western Sweden and Dornholm (Becker 1961; Albrectsen 1954; Cullberg 1973; Klindt-Jensen 1981). The links with neighbouring areas have been studied, even connections with more remote cultures. In this context the stimulating work of C.A. Moberg, who influenced later publications, should be mentioned (Moberg 1941 and later works, e.g. *Acta Archaeologica* XXI (1950), 83; XXIII (1952), 1; XXV (1954), 1).

The second line in Scandinavian studies of the pre-Roman Iron Age is a continuation of the comparative method which was the basis of the original chronological work. It deals with the import of Celtic and Roman objects. At the same time discussions on the impact of Celtic culture on the Scandinavian phases have taken place. A series of remarkable objects have been published and consideration given to their relationship to the native surroundings. But here a time factor is involved in several instances. Thus the late Celtic Period I type of shield certainly left its mark on the Jutland shields, but these seem to belong to the next chronological period. Also the plastic style may have lasted a little longer in the north than in its original home. Mediterranean finds are certainly later than when they first appeared in their homeland. It is not easily explained, but some caution should be exercised when using imports for dating purposes (Albrectsen 1954, 70–82).

The work is proceeding. Excavations and finds are still adding to the material on which a sound chronology can be based. That this in the first instance should be supported by stratigraphy and cemetery topography is obvious, but no less important is careful classification according to types and common details. Associated finds are taken into consideration, even if this involves a certain statistical uncertainty (Gräslund 1974, 64; Malmer 1963, 11). On the basis of chronology cultural history is being built up.

Bibliography

ALBRECTSEN, E. 1954 'Fynske jernaldergrave I', *Førromersk jernalder*, Copenhagen.

BECKER, C.J. 1961 *Førromersk jernalder i Midt- og Sydjylland*, Copenhagen.

CULLBERG, K. 1973 *Ekehöken und Valtersberg*, Göteborg.

GRÄSLUND, B. 1974 'Relativ datering. Om Kronologisk metod i nordisk arkeologi', *Tor*, Uppsala.

HACHMANN, R. 1960 'Die Chronologie der jüngeren vorrömischen Eisenzeit', *Bericht der Römisch-Germanischen Kommission* XLI.

HILDEBRAND, H. 1975 'Sur le commencement de l'age du fer en Europe', in *Compte rendu du Congrès international d'Anthropologie et d'Archéologie préhistorique 2*, Stockholm, 587.

KLINDT-JENSEN, O. 1950 *Foreign Influences in Denmark's Early Iron Age*, Copenhagen.
1953 *Bronzekedelen fra Braa*, Aarhus.
1981 *Slusegaardgravpladsen*, III.

MALMER, M.P. 1963 *Metodproblem inom järnålderns konsthistoria*, Lund-Bonn.

MOBERG, C.–A. 1941 *Zonengliederungen der vorrömischen Eisenzeit in Nordeuropa*, Lund.

MONTELIUS, O. 1896 'Den nordiska jernalderns kronologi', *Svenska fornminnesföreningenstidskrift* IX, 155.

MULLER, S. 1897 *Vor Oldtid*, Copenhagen.

NYLEN, E. 1955 *Die jüngere vorrömische Eisenzeit Gotlands*, Stockholm.

SCHWANTES, G. 1911 *Die ältesten Urnenfriedhöfe bei Uelzen und Lüneburg*, Hanover.

TISCHLER, O. 1885 'Über die Gliederung der La-Tène-Periode', *Correspondenz-Blatt der deutschen Gesellschaft für Anthropologie, Ethnologie und Urgeschichte* XVI, 157.

UNDSET, I. 1881 *Jernalderens begyndelse i Nord-Europa*, Kristiania.

VEDEL, E. 1872 'Den aeldste Jernalders Begravelser paa Bornholm', *Aarbøger for nordisk Oldkyndighed og Historie*.
1875 'Sur l'origine de l'âge du fer en Scandinavie', *Compte rendu du Congrès international d'Anthropologie et d'Archéologie préhistorique 2*, Stockholm, 587.

4 The Near East: a Personal View

David and Joan Oates

IN THIS brief tribute to Professor Glyn Daniel we are concerned principally with new developments in the archaeology of the Near East in the years since the end of the Second World War. But what has happened in the last generation derived in part from the ideas and prejudices of our predecessors and especially from conditions of work that were largely imposed on them – as indeed they are on us – by financial, political and social factors far different from those that attended the development of archaeology in Western Europe or the United States. This is not to discount the influence of ideas and techniques of analysis that have been introduced from other disciplines in recent years. Some of these have been profitable, others less so – 'cross-fertilization' is often assumed to be by definition good, but no botanist would accept that all hybrids are improvements on the original stock. In the Near East the original stock of archaeological and historical techniques evolved in response to changing conditions over the course of a century. The history of archaeology during that time has been well documented, notably by Professor Daniel himself, but it is relevant here to consider briefly how and why major changes came about.

Money, or the lack of it, has always been a vital consideration, governing both the objectives of archaeological investigation and the methods employed. This was conspicuously so in the nineteenth century, when the principal and often the only reason for a Near Eastern expedition was to cast light on the historical and material background of the Old Testament. Since funds were largely provided through the agency of major museums in the wealthier countries of the West – for instance the British Museum and the Louvre – a return in the form of spectacular antiquities was expected. This has often been interpreted as greed, although a more respectable and undoubtedly genuine motive was the need to arouse public enthusiasm at home, a consideration that remains important to this day (see *Antiquity, passim*, espec. editorials since March 1958). The insistence on finds, however, meant that the excavator had to spend the bulk of a limited budget on employing vast numbers of low-paid local workmen, and could not afford the skilled staff to control or record their work. Again, this situation persisted well into the present century – indeed it was not until the last ten years that all Near Eastern countries abolished the system whereby a share of objects discovered was legally assigned to the excavator, thus finally relieving him and his sponsors of any lingering desire for material reward.

In such circumstances it is astonishing that some of the earliest pioneers – A. H. Layard at Nimrud and Nineveh, P. E. Botta at Khorsabad – left such accurate records of their Assyrian palaces, and it is notable that Layard also delighted his public at home with popular accounts of his work and journeys that remain among the best travel books ever written. But it is not surprising that their successors, even when in nominal charge of sponsored expeditions operating with official sanction, were less competent, and it is not often realized that much of the damage done on major Mesopotamian sites in the latter half of the nineteenth century was the work of looters serving a growing commercial market. Another factor at this time, resulting from the decipherment of the cuneiform script in the 1860s, was the emergence of a second category of scholar in ancient Near Eastern studies, interested primarily if not exclusively in textual evidence and anxious for the recovery of more and more documents, often with scant regard for their provenance. Public interest was assured by discoveries such as parts of the Mesopotamian Flood Legend, and the prestige of this new band of scholars was certainly enhanced by the fact that their discipline was in the traditional literary mode, far removed from the rude mechanics of excavation. This dichotomy led on occasion to absurd conflict. During the whole period of the German excavations at Ashur from 1902 to 1914, no epigraphist was ever present as a member of the expedition, whose staff was composed almost entirely of architects, and all textual information was thus denied to the excavator in the field.

But the Ashur expedition represents a great advance in archaeological technique which may be attributed very largely to the fact that, like the contemporary German expedition to Babylon, it was organized by the Deutsche Orient-Gesellschaft (D.O.–G.), a learned foundation principally concerned with the recovery of information rather than the enrichment of museum collections. As a result, not only was a large number of important buildings ranging over a long period meticulously excavated and recorded, but occupation elsewhere in the city was systematically sampled on a grid system. Furthermore, a deep sounding beneath the site of the temple of Ishtar carried the history of the site back for two thousand years, and is justly described by Seton Lloyd as the 'prototype of all stratigraphical investigations in later times'. The precedent was followed with notable success a generation later at Warka and Nineveh, giving our first stratified records of south and north Mesopotamian prehistory. Not all expeditions planned and financed with high academic motives achieved the same success. E. A. Wallis Budge of the British Museum – whose methods of acquiring material on his Near Eastern journeys were to say the least unscrupulous – was stung to reply to criticism of British work at Nineveh, 'More travellers than one who have seen the site of the American excavations at Nippur have failed to see there any exhibition of scientific digging.'

We have to this point been concerned with the effect of money and its sources on the development of Near Eastern archaeology. Our examples have been drawn from Mesopotamia but, *mutatis mutandis*, the same influences can be observed in the surrounding countries. Intertwined, however, were considerations of local and sometimes international politics. No Near Eastern excavator who has not some sense of diplomacy at least in relation to the customs and sensibilities of his host country has, or ever has had, much hope of success. It is no accident that Layard later became a distinguished ambassador, first in Turkey and then in Spain. At the local level it was abysmal failure to come to terms with the admittedly troublesome tribes of southern Mesopotamia that caused the precipitate withdrawal of the first American expedition to Nippur. Conditions in these neglected Arab provinces in the last decades of the Ottoman Empire were lawless, such government as existed was often corrupt, and perhaps men like Budge could reasonably question the need for honour among thieves. Thinking in international terms, it is no coincidence that the three European countries primarily concerned with archaeological exploration were established rivals in Near Eastern trade and its outlets to the Indian Ocean, and it is no criticism of the academic morality of the D.O.–G. to note that Ashur lay on the line of the Istanbul-Baghdad railway to be built – though never completed – by German engineers. One only wonders whether, but for this fact, the excavations would have been so well supported, although it is only fair to observe that D. G. Hogarth, C. L. Woolley and T. E. Lawrence were excavating on the line of the same railway where it crossed the Euphrates at Carchemish.

At all events the First World War and the dis-

memberment of the Arab provinces into separate states, with growing national feeling that eventually culminated in their complete independence, radically changed the position of foreign archaeological expeditions. Iraq and Palestine came at first under British, and Syria under French, mandate. One result was the promulgation of antiquities laws, the creation of national departments of antiquities, initially under foreign directors, and the setting up of national museums. This gave a measure of protection to ancient sites and regulated the conduct of excavations, stipulating for instance the minimum composition of an expedition staff and reserving all unique objects and a half share of other finds to the national collections, although the allocation of a share of duplicates to the expedition assured its museum sponsors for another generation some tangible return for their money.

Despite these developments, attitudes to excavation and the motives of excavators changed only slowly, although there was a gradual improvement in technique. Attention was still concentrated on the great city sites, partly because they held the promise of spectacular discoveries but partly – and reasonably – because of their obvious historical importance. In Mesopotamia, now Iraq, work began in the south, where the first vague image of Sumerian civilization was beginning to emerge from the mists of history. The French returned to Telloh and the Germans to Warka, while the British Museum sponsored a new excavation under the direction of Leonard Woolley at Ur. The comparison between Warka and Ur is of some interest, for both contributed enormously to our knowledge of Sumer by methods which were fundamentally different. The excavation of Warka, continuing to this day, has been – by most standards – free from financial worries, and has continously refined the meticulous techniques of excavation developed by the D.O.–G.'s earlier expeditions at Ashur and Babylon. The site presents special problems, since the most spectacular series of monumental public buildings of any early city in the world has been patiently unravelled from a mass of unbaked brick in which any wall might be no more than a few centimetres in height. If the excavators can be criticized it is for the arid technicality of their publications. Unlike Andrae at Ashur or Koldewey at Babylon, no director at Warka has yet produced a readable account for the general public of the history and monuments of this great city. Woolley at Ur was always short of money and consequently of staff, although the worst problems of supervision were mitigated by the importation of a few specialist workmen from his pre-war dig at Carchemish. Yet his personal combination of flair, industry and attention to detail resulted both in spectacular discoveries and in a series of final reports that are both exhaustive and readable, and – perhaps because money was short – he produced popular books of very high quality.

The second quarter of this century saw a number of significant developments. M.E.L. Mallowan's excavation of Arpachiyah in 1933 was the direct consequence of the deep sounding at Nineveh which he had conducted, and is one of the first examples in Mesopotamia of 'problem-oriented' archaeology in the current sense. It is no coincidence that this was the first enterprise of the new British School of Archaeology in Iraq whose interests, like those of the D.O.–G. long before, were essentially historical and academic. Founded as a memorial to Gertrude Bell who had fought long and hard for the establishment of the Iraq Antiquities Department, it was supported by private contributions and could not afford any permanent base in Iraq until 1948; it received no substantial grant from the British government until 1965. The creation of the B.S.A.I. was, however, only a minor symptom of a widespread change in attitudes to the purpose and thereby to the sponsorship of archaeological investigation in the 1930s, when national schools or institutes came to replace museums as the prime sponsors of research. Most important of all was the foundation of the Oriental Institute in Chicago, reflecting both the growing prestige of American scholars in Oriental studies and the emergence of the United States – after a period of gestation – as one of the world's richest centres of culture. The Institute conducted operations on the grand scale. Some were conventional, such as the re-excavation of Khorsabad, though even that project was associated with a field survey of Late Assyrian canal systems – a foretaste of things to come. More significant was the systematic excavation of sites in the Diyala plain east of Baghdad which produced the first and by far the longest archaeological sequence for the late fourth and early third millennia BC in Mesopotamia. The idea was well conceived and executed, with the result that this sequence, covering a vital six hundred years of Mesopotamian history, has passed into the textbooks as a universally applicable gospel when it is in fact an excellent source for an outlying province of Sumer, and no more.

A change in the Iraqi attitude to foreign expeditions in the mid-1930s brought a diffusion of effort from what had hitherto been regarded as the classic centres of ancient culture in Babylonia and Assyria. Syria in particular benefited from this switch of interest, notably with the discoveries at Mari by the French expedition under André Parrot, a rewarding combination of survey and excavation by the Oriental Institute in the 'Amuq plain, and Mallowan's excavations at Chagar Bazar and Brak in the upper Khabur basin.

This may be the appropriate moment to inject a comment on the choice of large sites based on our personal experience, particularly since we have chosen since 1976 to resume the work at Brak. In times of increasing financial stringency and escalating costs it is an obvious temptation to devote resources to projects such as survey – where it is politically possible – and to the exploration of small mounds that appear to be characteristic of a particular period or sequence of periods. But in historic times it is obvious that the great focal centres of administration, commerce and culture are both integral to our understanding of any civilization and most likely to produce the documents that immeasurably increase it. Mari and most recently Ebla, in western Syria, are conspicuous examples. Evidence of this precision will never be available for the preliterate periods, but the further our still rudimentary understanding of prehistory extends in time and space, the more clearly evident is the need to explore the larger sites that were the foci of local settlements and nodes in the web of long-distance contacts – contacts that are now known to have existed on a scale and at a date entirely unsuspected even twenty years ago. Some of these centres are irretrievably buried beneath the massive debris of later cities. Aleppo, Nineveh and Erbil, to name but three, will never reveal the significance in prehistory that their geographical situation must have ensured. Tell Brak is a daunting mound – 35 hectares in extent, up to 43 metres high, containing at a rough estimate 7,000,000 tons of stratified occupation material, and by any standards a life sentence for the excavator. But its position in a zone of marginal rainfall apparently inhibited any significant occupation after the mid-second millennium BC. As a result, large settlements of the fourth and third millennia, when it commanded an important metal trade route and must have been a major political centre, remain relatively accessible. The main difference between us and our predecessors lies not in historical motive, but in the improvement of techniques of excavation, the scientific analysis of material, and the concurrent expansion of interest in ecological studies that these have made possible.

One further point demands our attention here. The hiatus in foreign archaeological activity during the Second World War led, notably in Iraq, to the first major field activity by a national antiquities department now staffed by Arab archaeologists trained in the best international tradition. The excavation of Aqar Quf was undertaken for traditional reasons, but it is still our only record of a Kassite foundation, and the Kassite dynasty ruled Babylonia longer than any other in history. The investigation of Hassuna – again a 'problem-oriented' exercise – carried our knowledge of north Mesopotamian prehistory back to the sixth millennium. After the war, the Department's work at the Sumerian holy city of Eridu produced a prehistoric sequence in the south that is still fundamental to our understanding of the earliest settlements there and of Sumerian origins. The experience and expertise thus acquired have been enormously important in the last thirty years. Despite the resumption of conventional large excavations by foreign expeditions since the war, some with spectacular results, the overdue rise in living standards in Near Eastern countries has greatly increased the cost of such work. At the same time there has been a growing national desire for more stringent control and, most conspicuously in the case of the major oil producers, a startling increase in their relative wealth, from which large sums have been devoted directly to archaeology or to development projects which entail archaeological investigation. The wheel of patronage has come full circle.

In recent years the most important advances in archaeological knowledge in the Near East have undoubtedly been in the field of prehistory. Reasons for this shift of emphasis lay in the increasing post-war concern with 'problem-related' fieldwork (not that this was, as we have seen, in any way a new concept), with the New Archaeology's preoccupation with 'culture process' as opposed to 'culture history', and with the introduction of more 'scientific' procedures in the interpretation of archaeological data. Such methodological considerations, combined with ever-escalating costs, served to encourage the investigation of simpler sites with less complex inventories. (A corollary of course is the investigation of less complex problems.)

At the same time the post-war development of techniques of absolute dating, in particular the use of radiocarbon, revolutionized the prehistoric perspective and stimulated a search for 'origins' and early manifestations of such advances in human adaptation as farming and the use of metal. The work of Robert Braidwood was of particular importance at this time, and his multi-disciplinary project in Iraqi Kurdistan (1948–55), with its judicious use of archaeological survey, sounding and excavation provided a model for all subsequent investigation.

Braidwood went to Kurdistan in 1948, and in 1951 Kathleen Kenyon reopened the excavations at Jericho, producing one of the most startling archaeological discoveries of this century: a stone-walled town, some 3–4 hectares in area, of the early eighth millennium BC. The prehistory of the Near East has changed beyond recognition since these pioneering projects. While Jarmo and Jericho still await publication, the hiatus in knowledge that encouraged the somewhat acrimo-

nious exchange between Braidwood and Kenyon in 1957 (*Antiquity*, 31) has begun to be filled with a variety and antiquity of sites unimaginable at the time. Undoubtedly the most spectacular of Neolithic sites is Çatal Hüyük, excavated by James Mellaart (1961–5). Here was a settlement originating in the seventh millennium BC which by the middle of the sixth millennium (uncalibrated dates) covered 13 hectares and boasted numerous ritual structures with extraordinarily elaborate wall paintings and plaster relief sculpture. The pace of discovery can be seen in the fact that only five years before, and despite field surveys on the Anatolian plateau by Mellaart, David French and others from 1951 onwards, it had been possible for a prominent Near Eastern archaeologist to write, 'The greater part of modern Turkey, and especially the region more correctly described as Anatolia, shows no sign whatever of habitation during the Neolithic period' (Lloyd 1956, 53).

The past decade has seen equally surprising if perhaps less spectacular revelations. In north-west Syria survey and rescue excavations along the Euphrates near Tabqa, in an area to be flooded by a new dam, revealed sites such as Mureybet and Abu Hureyra which appear to take the life of the settled cultivator well back into the ninth millennium BC. Even more recently, the excavation by a Russian expedition of the site of Maghzaliyah, to the east in Iraq, provides the possibility of settlement of comparable antiquity on the lowland plains of northern Mesopotamia. In Turkey Braidwood's latest project (1970–   ), carried out together with Halet Çambel, has not only brought to light the early farming site of Çayönü, but provides an early and highly successful example of a joint expedition between foreign and local archaeologists (in this case from the Oriental Institute, Chicago, and the Prehistory Section of Istanbul University). A less happy consequence of the recent escalation of archaeological activity in the Near East has been the generation of almost indigestible quantities of new data, much available only in the most preliminary of reports, if at all. (Summary reports on such excavations can be found in journals like *Iraq, Iran, Sumer, Anatolian Studies, Archiv für Orientforschung*, etc.) One result has been that, with a few notable exceptions, the stream of popular accounts and textbooks that have recently been published on such subjects as the origins of agriculture and the rise of civilization, books that have appeared in response both to public demand and to increasing general theoretical preoccupation with such problems, are already twenty years out of date in their treatment of Near Eastern evidence. This situation is unlikely to improve in the foreseeable future, and is unfortunately exacerbated by increasing special-

31

ization which leaves authorities in one narrow field unable to judge the significance or value of their colleagues' work in others.

A second major focus in the recent archaeology of the Near East reflects the primacy of urban origins in this region and current theoretical interest in the growth of such institutions as the city and the state. At the purely prehistoric level, the Iraqi excavations at Tell es-Sawwan and our own work at Choga Mami have significantly pushed back the earliest stages in the rise of complex settlements and of the intensive irrigation economy that provided the economic basis of urban growth, while the application of neutron activation analysis, perhaps the most useful of the new techniques acquired by archaeology from the physical sciences, has added much to our still very limited understanding of the processes of cultural change in the pre-urban societies of the fifth and fourth millennia BC (*Antiquity*, 51 (1977), 221–34). Basic to these investigations of course are the German excavations at Warka. Work in the impressive Eanna and Anu precincts at this great site still provides virtually our only material illustration from Sumer itself of the growth of the bureaucratic institutions that characterized the Sumerian city-state. However, in recent years new discoveries from the Mediterranean to Central Asia have expanded the investigation of such evidence to a truly international perspective. Proto-Elamite tablets and associated administrative paraphernalia have been found at such sites as Godin Tepe near Kermanshah and Tepe Yahya, 1000 km south-east of Susa, while in north-west Syria sites such as Habuba South/Qannas and Jebel Aruda, both excavated in the course of the Tabqa salvage operations, appear to have been late-fourth-millennium Sumerian mercantile, and possibly administrative, 'colonies', another 1000 km north-west of Uruk and Ur. Indeed it is a paradox of contemporary archaeology that the growing emphasis on 'science' and 'quantification' has caused some fieldworkers severely to narrow their horizons at a time when new discoveries of the sort mentioned above are making it increasingly clear that no Near Eastern phenomenon can be understood in geographical isolation.

The subject of urban development and the international contacts demonstrated by these new discoveries raise a further methodological problem, namely that in Near Eastern archaeology there persists a regrettable lack of communication between anthropologically oriented prehistorians and those scholars who study the written documents of the historic periods. Nowhere else in the world can one study the evolution of society, indeed the 'culture process' beloved of anthropological archaeology, with the

aid of extensive written records over thousands of years. Indeed no modern culture has survived for anything approaching the three thousand years of documented Mesopotamian history. Yet all too commonly anthropologically trained archaeologists turn to ethnographic data from environmentally different areas, eschewing the economic and social sources available within Mesopotamia itself for no better reason than the belief that archaeology is not history. It is much to be hoped that current interest elsewhere in ethnohistory will stimulate a similar concern among prehistorians in the Near East, and that there will emerge a closer cooperation between prehistorian and historian to the mutual benefit of both. Current literature suggests that they are all too often unaware of each other's contributions.

Among the most important and productive archaeological projects of recent years have been the rescue operations mounted in Iraq, Syria and Turkey in areas where dam construction has threatened to flood large numbers of archaeological sites. The consequent cooperation between local antiquities departments and foreign expeditions has led to the recovery of data, both qualitative and quantitative, at levels previously unparalleled. We have already mentioned the discovery at Tabqa in Syria of sites such as Abu Hureyra, Mureybet and Habuba which have totally altered existing views of the development on the one hand of settled agriculture and, on the other, of the level of political and economic achievement of Uruk Mesopotamia. At Tabqa some eleven countries took part in the individual and joint excavation of twenty-four sites, from 1965 over a period of about ten years. The operation benefited greatly from the far-sighted and generous research policy of the Syrian Government, which supported an initial stage of mapping and aerial photography and later (1969) promulgated a special decree which enabled the export of half the antiquities recovered by individual expeditions, a valuable fund-raising gesture. With the cooperation of UNESCO the removal and restoration of certain Islamic monuments was also effected.

Various dam schemes in Turkey have provided similar opportunities. Particular mention should be made of the Keban project, in which not only archaeological but also 'folklore, architectural and ethnographic studies' were carried out, both by Turkish and international groups. The Aşvan Project of the British Institute in Ankara provides a model of what can be achieved in such multi-disciplinary exercises.

More recently, in Iraq, salvage operations in the basin of the Diyala River to the east of Jebel Hamrin (1977–9) have led to the identification of more than seventy archaeological sites, dating from the sixth millennium BC to the twelfth century AD. At the time of writing over two-thirds of the mounds to be flooded have been investigated. Many of the major sites have been excavated by the State Organization of Antiquities itself, and the Iraq Government has generously met the local excavation expenses of foreign expeditions as well as supplying much of their equipment. British, Italian, French, Belgian, Austrian, Japanese and several German and American expeditions have taken part in excavations which have provided particularly valuable documentation of the prehistoric 'Ubaid phase and the relatively little known Early Dynastic I. Most unexpected is the site of Tell Gubba, excavated by the Japanese, at which has been discovered a unique circular building (*c.* 3000 BC) with a round central core and 'fire pit' surrounded by a series of concentric walls, the inner passages of which appear to have been vaulted.

Neither the Tabqa region of the Middle Euphrates nor the Hamrin is particularly inaccessible, but neither had previously been explored. The very important results from these recent salvage operations underline two very basic facts of Near Eastern archaeology: 1) that we are still at the stage of primary exploration and 2) that the information to be gained from concentrated, cooperative ventures in geographically restricted areas is far greater than the sum of its parts. Important too is the new emphasis (in a period of burgeoning nationalism, escalating costs and increasingly limited resources) on cooperation between foreign archaeologists and local antiquities services, surely the future of archaeology in the Near East.

We have seen that the nature and pace of archaeological fieldwork have changed immeasurably in the past twenty years. Whereas in the past there were relatively few foreign expeditions, working with small staffs and employing large numbers of local workmen, both the number of foreign projects and the nationalities participating have increased. Excavations on the scale of Ur are no longer financially viable. At the same time the rush to work while political conditions permit and the increasing number of research students chasing Ph.D.'s has meant a proliferation of small-scale projects, often inadequately published.

The functions and interests of local antiquities services have also changed, in that both major excavations and the restoration, partly for purposes of tourism, of important sites such as Babylon, Nineveh and Ashur, are being undertaken. A growing number of young professionals is being trained both in local universities and abroad. At the same time the winds of nationalism have brought changes in the antiquities laws, in some cases severely restricting certain types of archaeological activity (e.g. survey), and in all cases (except the Tabqa research, noted above), the export of antiquities, once an important source of funding for foreign expeditions. Such restrictions have other effects, in necessitating, for example, on-site completion of all recording. Such pressures, to which are added inadequate finance and thus inadequate staffing, have meant that record-keeping techniques have not always kept pace with other parts of the world where field archaeology can be pursued in a more relaxed fashion. It is indeed a common view that the Near East has lagged behind in the adoption of the methods of the New Archaeology. All too often, however, research designs of great merit are frustrated by restrictions of access not only on the ground but to such essential tools as air photographs and adequate maps. Moreover, the complexities of large mound sites are ill-understood by many proponents of sampling and other quantitative techniques, while modern financial resources have simply not kept pace with the increasingly stringent demands now made of archaeological data. On the other side of the coin, a particularly regrettable consequence of the emphasis on quantification and preoccupation with 'process', especially in situations of limited time and money (and often experience), has been the solemn investigation of 'problems' of the utmost triviality, from which have been inferred such low-level generalizations that they are deservedly dismissed as 'Mickey Mouse Laws' (Flannery 1973). Such misguided applications of the New Archaeology, however, are not confined to the Near East.

It should perhaps again be emphasized that despite the growing archaeological activity of recent years, Near Eastern archaeologists work in an area still demanding basic, primary exploration. Much excellent work has been carried out, most notably surveys by Jacobsen and Adams in the Diyala and Adams and Nissen at Warka, but the blanks on the archaeological map are far greater in extent than those small regions that have to some extent been filled in. And even in areas that have been intensively studied, such as the Hamrin, there are not as yet data of the quality required for the elegant processual studies espoused by archaeologists in better documented (? and less complex) regions. Indeed, Near Eastern archaeologists still lack basic pottery sequences over hundreds of years, and those sequences that do exist do not permit the identification of contemporaneity so vital to the proper application of geographical models. New Archaeologists will rise to such antediluvian sentiments, but the fact remains that without such information locational studies, even indeed the simplest of comparative studies, have no meaning. (At best one can identify but a small proportion of surface materials

33

on any Near Eastern site, and we have more than once walked over tells on which not a single surface fragment could be recognized!)

In a world of ever-rising costs and increasing refinements in archaeological method and technique, qualitative improvements in data retrieval are undoubtedly made at the cost of total information. One key to the future must certainly be to tailor new procedures to the stark reality of Near Eastern complexities. A second key must lie in greater cooperation between local antiquities services and foreign expeditions, especially when we remember that important historical problems can only be investigated by the exploration of important sites, i.e. in terms of large-scale and long-term projects. For the moment one can only remark that while theoretical interpretation has forged ahead, evidence has not kept pace. The challenges and rewards of Near Eastern archaeology remain high, but we must resist the temptation to let interpretation outstrip its factual basis.

Bibliography

ADAMS, R. McC. AND NISSEN, H.J. 1972 *The Uruk Countryside*, Chicago.

Antiquités de l'Euphrate, Exposition des découvertes de la campagne internationale de sauvegarde des antiquités de l'Euphrate, Musée National d'Alep, 1974.

BRAIDWOOD, R.J. AND HOWE, B. 1960 *Prehistoric Investigations in Iraqi Kurdistan*, Studies in Ancient Oriental Civilization, no. 31, Chicago.

FLANNERY, K.V. 'Archaeology with a Capital S', in Redman 1973, 47-53.

FRENCH, D. *et al.* 1973 'Asvan 1968–72' *Anatolian Studies* XXIII, 69-307.

HOLE, F., FLANNERY, K.V. AND NEELY, J.A. 1969 *Prehistory and Human Ecology of the Deh Luran Plain*, Memoirs of the Museum of Anthropology, 1, Ann Arbor.

International Symposium for Babylon, Assur and Hamrin, *Sumer* XXXV, 1979.

LLOYD, S. 1947 *Foundations in the Dust*, Oxford (revised edn, London and New York 1980).

1956 *Early Anatolia*, London.

1978 *The Archaeology of Mesopotamia*, London and New York.

MELLAART, J. 1967 *Catal Hüyük*, London and New York.

1975 *The Neolithic of the Near East*, London and San Francisco.

OATES, D. AND J. 1976 *The Rise of Civilization*, Oxford and New York.

OATES, J. 1979 *Babylon*, London and New York.

OPPENHEIM, A.L. 1964 *Ancient Mesopotamia*, Chicago.

REDMAN, C.L. (ed.) 1973 *Research and Theory in Current Archeology*, New York.

5 Spinden's Archaic Hypothesis

Gordon R. Willey

AMERICAN ARCHAEOLOGY was slower in its formulation of broad historical-development schemes than Old World archaeology. In Europe, C.J. Thomsen offered his Stone, Bronze and Iron Age sequences as early as 1819, and later in that same century this scheme was further refined by the division of the Stone Age era into Palaeolithic and Neolithic segments (Daniel 1950, 1968). Nothing with this same kind of orientation or scope was to appear on the New World scene until the twentieth century. The reasons for this American lag are not altogether clear. To be sure, Old World archaeology had deeper roots. The Stone-Bronze-Iron stages of human history were a part of Classic Greek intellectual speculation; Renaissance humanism had a distinctly antiquarian strain; and scholarly antiquarians of England and Scandinavia provided antecedents for Thomsen's interests and ideas. Still, we must realize that American archaeologists of the nineteenth century were influenced by what had gone on and was going on in Europe and did not begin completely *de novo* in their discipline or avocation. A variety of reasons can be offered. Much of the earliest American field archaeology was carried out in the eastern United States where a sequence comparable to the European Stone-Bronze-Iron scheme was out of the question. Also, early attempts to demonstrate the American presence of 'Palaeolithic' cultures associated with Pleistocene strata were unsuccessful, and this may have retarded the concept of stratigraphy and stratigraphic digging with Americanists. In the most spectacular area of American 'high cultures', Mexico, early research emphasis was on native inscriptions and documents rather than 'dirt archaeological' chronology (Willey and Sabloff 1974, 54-6, 89). But, whatever the explanations, broad generalizing cultural-historical formulations, of inter-continental or hemispheric sweep, did not come along until later. The archaeologist responsible for the first of these was Herbert Joseph Spinden (1879-1967), and his concept has often been referred to as the 'Archaic Hypothesis'. It is the purpose of this brief essay to examine this hypothesis, both in the context of its time and from the perspective of history.

It will be my thesis that Spinden's Archaic hypothesis was the first serious American hemispheric cultural-historical scheme devised for explicating the story of Precolumbian America. By 'serious' I mean not only in the sense in which it was offered but in the sense by which colleagues may be able to accept or, at least, discuss it. As even the most casual student of the history of American archaeology knows, Spinden was preceded by others who propounded theories about the 'Ten Lost Tribes of Israel', 'Hindustanis', mysterious wandering 'Toltecs', and others as the bearers and disseminators of the ancient American civilizations and cultures; but Spinden was the first to attempt to deal with the objective data in an organized geographical-chronological frame of reference. In so doing, Spinden allowed for his scheme to be appraised and criticized–as it was–on the basis of other objectively verifiable archaeological data; thus, at least to my way of thinking, Spinden made a major contribution to American archaeological thought, the influences of which have continued down to the present. Spinden, in his task, had the advantage of a previous build-up of archaeological information – scant though this may have been by modern standards – which his predecessors did not enjoy. In addition, Spinden was also advantaged by being an anthropologist as well as an archaeologist, with the anthropologists' culture-comparative perspective.

Spinden was an American, a westerner, born in South Dakota at a time when the American Indian was still very much a part of the scene in that part of the world. He was first educated in the state of Washington, developing his anthropological interests early. Subsequently, he went to Harvard where he received the A.B. degree in 1906 and the Ph. D. in anthropology in 1909. His first fieldwork and publications were in Plains Indian ethnology (Will and Spinden 1906; Spinden 1908a,b); but at Harvard he came under the influence of the great Mayanist and teacher, Alfred M. Tozzer, and his doctoral dissertation, published in 1913, was the monumental, *A Study of Maya Art: Its Subject Matter and Historical Development*. From that time forward he was primarily devoted to Mayan and Mesoamerican archaeology although he also ranged more widely in Lower Central America and South America. His subject-matter interests were also wide-ranging. He continued with his studies of Maya art (Spinden 1916), established himself as an authority on Maya hieroglyphics and calendrics

(Spinden 1924, 1928a), and conducted field and museum surveys in Central (Spinden 1925) and South (Spinden 1939) America. It was his flair for synthesis, however, that particularly concerns us here. It was manifest, of course, in the Maya art thesis; but shortly after that he gave this talent wider scope. This was in an article, 'The Origin and Distribution of Agriculture in America', which was presented to the 19th International Congress of Americanists, in Washington, D.C., in 1915, and published two years later in the *Proceedings* of that body (Spinden 1917). This now historic article had been preceded and, to a degree, foreshadowed by another paper which Spinden brought out in the *American Anthropologist* in 1915. Entitled 'Notes on the Archaeology of Salvador', it set forth some of his ideas about Mesoamerican-wide cultural relationships from the vantage point of that Central American country; but the 1917 Congress of Americanist paper may be taken as the first full enunciation of the Archaic hypothesis. Later, in his well-known handbook, *Ancient Civilizations of Mexico and Central America* (Spinden 1928b), he further elaborated on the idea (see also Spinden 1933).

Before turning to Spinden's key article and the Archaic hypothesis, it might be well to review the status of American archaeological synthesis or generalization prior to 1915. There had been some very early general statements. The most scholarly of these was by the great French Americanist, the Abbé Brasseur de Bourbourg, who published his *Histoire des Nations Civilisées du Mexique et de l'Amérique-Centrale*, in 1857–9. As the title indicates, he was writing primarily about Mesoamerica. The work is firmly grounded in the ethnohistoric documents. It deals with ethnic and cultural origin theories of the time, but it is essentially a descriptive account of what was known of the archaeology of the area. S. F. Haven's *Archaeology of the United States*, brought out in 1856, is comparable although in treating with North America he lacks the rich ethnohistoric background available to Brasseur. A good bit later Cyrus Thomas' *Introduction to the Study of North American Archaeology* (1898) could be judged the most authoritative summary of that area but is, again, a descriptive treatment. Most pertinent, from the point of view of appraising Spinden's contribution, would be the two volumes by the British Museum scholar, Thomas Joyce, general compendia on South America (1912) and Mexico (1914), with the latter brought out just the year before Spinden presented his Congress paper. Joyce was a master of museum collections and archaeological art styles. Inter–regional and inter–areal relationships of this sort are dealt with at great length in his books, including such possible long–distance connections as may have existed be-

tween Mexico and Peru. He was sensitive to what chronological information there was available. Specifically, he was aware of the Valley of Mexico stratigraphy (Joyce 1914, 188–9) which was to play such an important part in Spinden's Archaic formulation; but he passes over this discovery with only a descriptive mention.

To summarize, it is fair to say the Americanist archaeological establishment, as of 1914, had no synthetic model for bringing order out of the diversity of Precolumbian cultural chaos that confronted them. Spinden's Archaic model was the first important attempt to do this within a typological, geographical, and chronological–developmental frame of reference which also, to a degree, made a first step toward processual understanding.

The triggering event that was to lead to Spinden's hypothesis was the above–mentioned Valley of Mexico stratigraphy. This was carried out by Manuel Gamio (1913; see Willey and Sabloff 1974, 88–9) at the site of Atzcapotzalco. Gamio, in a deep test pit sunk into refuse, encountered superficial levels of Aztec sherds, Teotihuacan pottery in levels below these, and then, in the bottommost levels, pottery and figurines in a then unknown style which was soon to be designated as the 'Archaic'. It was the first important stratigraphic sequence for Mesoamerica – or for the Americas at large – and it obviously made a strong impression upon Spinden.

In his Salvadoran paper (Spinden 1915), Spinden saw similarities between certain pottery and figurine styles in that country and the Valley of Mexico Archaic culture. He also observed that this Archaic stylistic strain was present in other Mesoamerican regions: in West Mexico, Morelos, Puebla, Veracruz, Oaxaca and the Ulua Valley of Honduras. In all these regions he conceived of it as the earliest complex (as, indeed, at that time it was), being succeeded by later regional styles. He speculated that it probably was to be associated with peoples of Nahua speech. This was the kind of archaeological-ethnic identification that was then the primary theoretical or synthetic exercise in American archaeology; the Joyce books are replete with it; and Spinden did not go much beyond this in the Salvadoran paper. But in 'The Origin and Distribution of Agriculture in America' the Archaic archaeological substratum was to be viewed in a different light.

As the title states, a principal theme of this essay is agriculture. This new lifeway was linked to the Archaic culture of Central Mexico, and Central Mexico was the *fons et origo* of both in the New World. The Archaic hypothesis is, thus, strongly diffusionist; but, at the same time, it carries other implications. Although he did not use the term, Mexican Archaic culture was to provide what was, in effect, the 'floor' of an American Neolithic stage. Here, in the Americas, as in other parts of the world, agriculture was seen as the antecedent condition for all high cultures and was generally associated with the beginnings of sedentary life which provided the base for later developments. To Spinden, the Mexican Archaic culture was a nexus of functionally interrelated features – agriculture, sedentary life, and pottery-making; and it was also the first occurrence of such a nexus, or complex, on New World soil. More specifically, the agriculture in question was of a semi-arid upland variety, featuring maize, beans, squash and the chili pepper.

Spinden developed his arguments simply and briefly – the paper is only seven pages in length – along geographic distributional lines. The content or the essential typology of the Archaic culture was never well defined. In the Salvadoran paper he had referred to pottery figurines, hand-made, some small and solid, others large and hollow. They were characterized by various kinds of eye-treatments, including the rather distinctive appliqué 'coffee-bean' pellets, and sometimes turban-like headdresses. Pottery is described as well constructed and decorated with plastic techniques or simple painted ones. Associated stone sculptures were simple and crude, and there is an absence of complex iconography or the deity representations characteristic of later Mesoamerican horizons. Spinden summarizes this in the 1917 paper, and there are some further trait-listings, accompanied by illustrations in the later handbook presentation of the argument (Spinden 1928b, Ch. I). It is obvious, from a present-day perspective, that Spinden was describing the Late Preclassic or Late Formative cultures of the Valley of Mexico, plus other materials from other regions that appeared to him to be related. We know now that he was nowhere near the beginnings of ceramics or sedentary village agricultural life; the succeeding six or more decades since Spinden advanced his ideas have pushed back the Mesoamerican culture sequences to reveal a complexity of origins and growth that he never dreamed of; however, for its time the Archaic concept was a vital and interesting one.

The first map in the 1917 article gives Spinden's idea of the New World distributions of this Archaic cultural complex, and it is reproduced here (ill. 1). The black areas represent what he considered to be the definite evidences of Archaic ceramics and figurines. These include Central and Southern Mexico, upland Central America, and highland portions of Colombia and Venezuela. The stippled areas of the map apparently represent a more doubtful or attenuated presence of Archaic culture; and these include the Maya Lowlands,

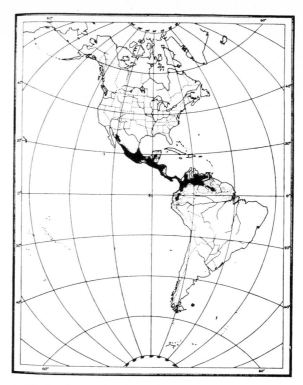

1 *The distribution of Archaic culture in the New World. Black areas indicate definite occurrences, stippled areas less secure or attenuated occurrences. (After Spinden 1917, pl. I.)*

a northern Mexican fringe, Ecuador, Peru, and a large portion of north-eastern South America. It is of interest to note that in the later handbook article (Spinden 1928b, pl. XI) he expanded both the solid black and the stippled areas, with the former going as far south as Peru and the latter reaching up into the south-western United States. Clearly, Spinden was becoming ever more convinced of his hypothesis, and he was painting with a very broad brush.

Spinden's second 1917 map plots the distribution of pottery in the Americas (ill. 2). The trait of pottery clearly outruns that of his Archaic culture although the intensive pottery areas (solid black) do correspond more or less to the Archaic culture distributions – the principal exception being the occurrence of ceramics in the south-eastern United States. But it is clear from Spinden's text that he saw the phenomena as related. He believed that all New World pottery (except for the Eskimoan wares of the far north) had essentially

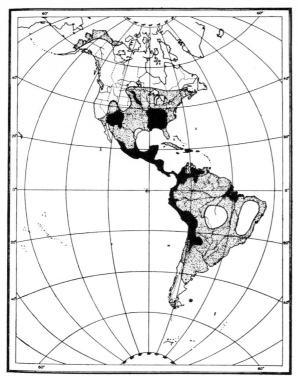

2 The distribution of aboriginal pottery in the New World. Intensive regions in black, less intensive regions stippled; non-pottery regions in white. (After Spinden 1917, pl. II.)

a single origin and that this single origin was in the Mexican Archaic culture and its spread. It is probable that most American archaeologists would agree with the first part of this statement today – although not with the second.

Spinden's third 1917 map is concerned with the distributions of native agriculture (ill. 3). The semi-arid maize agricultural complex is indicated in black, and one notes the close correspondence of this to the distribution of Spinden's Archaic culture. In his opinion, this was the oldest form of American agriculture. He felt that it had developed in an upland and semi-arid environment where cultivation would have been relatively unimpeded by heavy vegetation and where, because of environmental circumstances, 'necessity would have been the mother of invention'. It was his further opinion that the great potential of upland, semi-arid maize agriculture could not have been realiz-ed without irrigation and that, therefore, irrigation

must have appeared early on in Archaic culture development; however, at that time this was sheer speculation as no archaeological evidence for irrigation had yet been found in the Central Mexican highlands. Spinden saw both tropical forest (root crop) and temperate zone farming as being later than the semi-arid zone upland maize tradition. These are shown on the map, respectively, in stippled and hatched areas. He reasoned that the tightly linked maize-beans-squash complex was proof of their common domesticated origins in a single small region; and this region was the Valley of Mexico where these agricultural origins were also linked to the beginnings of pottery and to the rise of the Archaic complex.

Spinden's ideas did not go uncontested for long. S.K. Lothrop indicated his objections to them in several papers dealing with Central American ar-chaeology (Lothrop 1921, 1926, 1933), and G.C. Vaillant joined him in these objections (Vaillant 1934). Most specifically, they rejected the monogenetic theme in Spinden's Archaic theory. They did not see the Archaic culture of the Valley of Mexico as being the progenitor of all other Mexican and Central American early pottery cultures. They noted that in the Guatemalan Highlands, Salvador, the Maya Lowlands, and in the Ulua Valley of Honduras, other complexes which appeared to be as early as the Valley of Mexico Archaic – and which shared some traits with that Archaic – also had traits which could not have been easily derived from that source. Vaillant's 1934 paper, 'The Archaeological Setting of the Playa de los Muerto Culture', is the best summary statement of the Lothrop-Vaillant position. They formulated what they called the 'Q-Complex'. This was a series of traits, often found in association in early contexts in southern Mesoamerica, which were not shared with the Valley of Mexico Archaic. These included spouted vessels, effigy vessels, shoe-form vessels, tetrapodal supports, Usulutan resist-painting decoration on pot-tery, and styles of hand-made figurines and crude stone sculptures differing from those of Central Mexico. What this criticism meant was that other early cultures were being discovered in other parts of Mesoamerica, and the Mexican Archaic, as revealed by Gamio's stratigraphy, was no longer the only early pottery assemblage on record. Subsequent research from then on has filled out this early record, and it has become obvious that Spinden was premature in his selection of a single early culture as the basic root of it all. Indeed, what he, as well as Vaillant and Lothrop were talking about, was the tip of the iceberg, the then exposed upper limits of a long Preclassic or Formative Period developmental stage in the rise of Mesoamerican civilization. We know now that these Late Preclassic or Formative cultures date back, for the most part, no earlier than about 300 BC. Middle Formative and Early Formative antecedents, in the Valley of Mexico and elsewhere, reach back to 2000 BC and maybe even before.

As to ultimate origins, the story is now so complex we cannot say. While it would appear that maize domestication was probably first achieved in Meso-america, although perhaps south of the Valley of Mexico rather than in that valley, other agricultural traditions, such as that of the root crops of the tropical forests, probably had other areas of origin, most likely in the Amazon Basin. We also know now that the American hearth for pottery is more likely to have been in north-western South America than in Meso-america; almost certainly it was not in the Valley of Mexico. And we also know that there was no one monolithic Archaic culture which, in spreading from a single centre, gave rise to all farming and pottery-making in the Americas.

Spinden's Archaic hypothesis, thus, suffers from the monogenetic fallacy of many extreme diffusionistic theories. On these grounds it has been properly criticized; yet the theory had within it something more than diffusionism. Spinden recognized that agriculture, sedentary life, and pottery-making were – or could be – functionally inter-related. He was enough of an anthropologist to know that sedentary living, under certain circumstances, could be achieved without farming and that semi-nomadic peoples may sometimes have pottery. There were ethnographic examples of these exceptions in various parts of the world. But Spinden also knew that on the Mesoamerican scene he was operating within a long, continuous and dense cultural tradition. This was a tradition in which agriculture, sedentary life and pottery-making had long been associated and functionally interlinked; and because of this he felt that he was justified in arguing for the presence of such a functionally inter-related complex from the presence of the early pottery in the deep levels at Atzapotzalco.

And was the presence of settled village life, farming and pottery at a relatively early time unrelated to the Precolumbian appearance of such a trait complex else-where in the Americas? Of course it is not; however, the over-simplified way in which Spinden attempted to make the connections, or to explain a New World Neolithic stage, cannot be accepted. What, then, are the relationships? To what extent are the processes of diffusion, direct migration and local independent invention involved in, for example, the relationships between the Mexican Formative cultures and those of the south-western United States? Along with Philip Phillips, I addressed such questions a number of years

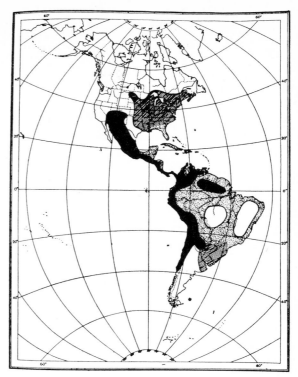

3 *The distribution of native agriculture in the New World. Mountainous and mostly arid regions in black; lowland humid regions stippled; temperate regions hatched. (After Spinden 1917, pl. III.)*

back (Willey and Phillips 1955). With regard to the Mesoamerican-south-western situation – or with regard to any other similar situations – it was clear that we had no definite answers. Where do the factors of diffusion or contact end and those of independent development take over? Was our concept of a New World Formative a diffusionist or an evolutionary construct? Almost certainly the idea and the means of maize cultivation spread, in one way or another, from northern Mesoamerica into the south-western United States. Similarly, the idea of pottery-making must also have spread from south to north. Yet the total cultural configurations in Mesoamerica and in the South-west are quite different. Early Mogollon or Early Hohokam cultures in the latter area are not Mexican Formative cultures in the way that Spinden seemed to be claiming that they were Mexican Archaic cultures.

Or was Spinden making such a claim? Do we take him too literally? Did he really view the Archaic

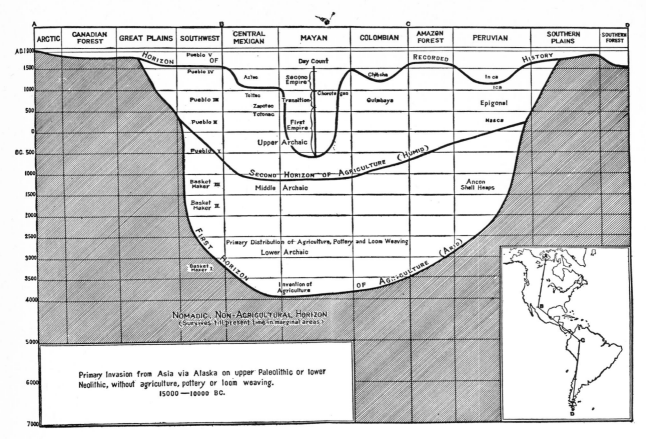

4 Chronological-developmental chart of New World cultures. (After Spinden 1928b, ff. p. 253.)

as a cultural stage rather than as a phenomenon of diffusion? Perhaps he was not altogether clear in his own mind. It must be remembered, though, that in the archaeology of the Americas in 1915 diffusion was about the only process that was ever evoked. Sometimes it was countered by ideas of 'psychic unity' or 'independent convergent invention', but there was really little attention paid to the forces of *in situ* culture development. Such an intellectual climate may have conditioned Spinden's ideas and made them appear more diffusionistic than was his intent. But before we criticize too severely his vagueness and ambiguity, it may be remarked again that we are still often ambiguous in our uses and definitions of the concepts and processes of diffusion and evolution in current archaeological writing. And this applies not only to Americanist studies but to such concepts and reconstructions as the spread of an agricultural economy from the Old World Middle East into Europe.

What has been the value of Spinden's Archaic hypothesis about New World prehistory and culture development as we view it from the perspective of sixty-five years later? As a model for a very precise understanding of the complex lines of region-to-region and area-to-area interaction, it is obviously of little utility. Indeed, its obsolescence was being pointed out by Spinden's contemporary critics a few years after he floated the idea. Spinden defined it rather vaguely. Ironically, this may have been one of the strengths of his concept. At those points where he did try to tie it down to traits, trait descriptions and illustrations of materials he was soon shown to be in error. Yet when we view the Precolumbian story in the large, it is obvious that there is a significant developmental level of the village agricultural threshold, however varied in specifics of content this may be. This level was first attained somewhere in the middle latitudes of the New World, probably not in one but in several places through a variety of *in situ* and interactive processes, and from there its effects were felt in more areas on generally later time horizons.

Spinden himself realized this, and this broader chronological development is expressed in a very remarkable

40

chart which he prepared for his 1928 handbook (Spinden 1928b, ff. p. 253). This chart (ill. 4) represents a transect through the Americas, running from north to south. It shows the rise and spread of arid lands agriculture, a subsequent 'second horizon' of tropical forest or 'humid' agriculture, and the first appearances of Neolithic-type arts of pottery-making and loom-weaving. As far as I am aware it is the first such chart on American prehistory; and while it is incorrect in such things as the United States southwestern sequence dates and, probably, the chronological relationship between 'arid' and 'humid' agriculture, in others it is amazingly close to the mark in the light of recent data and findings. Thus, Spinden shows the beginnings of agriculture in Mesoamerica at *c.* 4000 BC and the primary distribution of agriculture, pottery and loom-weaving at sometime between 3000 and 2500 BC. In this connection, it is to be remembered that Spinden had no real way of estimating the age of his Valley of Mexico Archaic culture, other than that it preceded the beginnings of the Maya Long Count and was, therefore, known to be more or less prior to the beginning of the Christian era. In other words, the *c.* 300 BC date that we can now assign to the Valley of Mexico Late Formative cultures was completely unknown to Spinden in 1928. It is a finding of radiocarbon dating.

This way of looking at the data is the lasting contribution of Spinden's Archaic hypothesis. It still has a value in directing our attention to broad problems in Americanist diffusions and other processes in cultural evolution.

Bibliography

BRASSEUR DE BOURBOURG, C.E. 1857–9 *Histoire des Nations Civilisées du Mexique et de l'Amérique-Central,* 4 vols, Paris.

DANIEL, G.E. 1950 *A Hundred Years of Archaeology,* London.

1968 'One Hundred Years of Old World Prehistory', in J.O. Brew (ed.), *One Hundred Years of Anthropology,* Cambridge, Mass., 57-96.

GAMIO, M. 'Arqueologia de Atzcapotzalco, D.F., Mexico', in *Proceedings, 18th International Congress of Americanists,* London, 180-7.

HAVEN, S.F. 1856 *Archaeology of the United States,* Smithsonian Contributions to Knowledge, vol. 8, art. 2, Washington, D.C.

JOYCE, T. A. 1912 *South American Archaeology,* London.

1914 *Mexican Archaeology,* London.

LOTHROP, S.K. 1921 'The Stone Statues of Nicaragua', *American Anthropologist* XXIII no. 3.

1926 'Stone Sculptures from the Finca Arevalo, Guatemala', *Indian Notes,* Museum of the American Indian, Heye Foundation, vol. 3, no. 3, New York, N.Y., 147–17

1927 'Pottery Types and Their Sequence in El Salvador', *Indian Notes and Monographs,* Museum of the American Indian, Heye Foundation, vol. 1, no. 4, New York, N.Y.

1933 *Atitlan, An Archaeological Study of Ancient Remains on the Border of Lake Atitlan,* Carnegie Institution of Washington, Publication No. 444, Washington, D.C.

SPINDEN, H.J. 1908a 'Myths of the Nez Perce Indians', *Journal of American Folklore* XXI 13–23, 149–58.

1908b *The Nez Perce Indians,* Memoirs, American Anthropological Association, vol. 2, pt 3.

1913 *A Study of Maya Art: Its Subject Matter and Historical Development,* Memoirs, Peabody Museum, vol. 6, Harvard University, Cambridge, Mass.

1915 'Notes on the Archaeology of Salvador', *American Anthropologist* XVII, no. 3, 446-87.

1916 'Portraiture in Central American Art', *Holmes Anniversary of Volume,* 434–50, Washington, D.C.

1917 'The Origin and Distribution of Agriculture in America', *Proceedings, 19th International Congress of Americanists,* Washington, D.C., 269–76.

1924 *The Reduction of Mayan Dates,* Peabody Museum Papers, vol. 6, no. 1, Harvard University, Cambridge, Mass.

1925 'The Chorotegan Culture Area', *Proceedings 21st International Congress of Americanists,* Göteborg, 529–45.

1928a 'Maya Inscriptions Dealing with Venus and the Moon', *Bulletin,* Buffalo Society of Natural Sciences, vol. 14, no. 1, Buffalo, N.Y.

1928b *Ancient Civilizations of Mexico and Central America,* 3rd edn, Handbook Series No. 3, American Museum of Natural History, New York. (First and second editions published 1917 and 1922).

1933 'Origin of Civilizations in Central America and Mexico', in D. Jenness (ed.), *The American Aborigines, Their Origin and Antiquity,* Toronto, 217–46.

1939 'The Archaeology of the Northern Andes', *Transactions*, New York Academy of Sciences, vol. 1, no. 5, New York. N.Y., 83–7.

THOMAS, C. 1898 *Introduction to the Study of North American Archaeology*, Cincinnati, Ohio.

VAILLANT, G.C. 1934 'The Archaeological Setting of the Playa de los Muertos Culture, *Maya Research*, vol. 1, no. 2, New York.

WILL, G.F. AND SPINDEN, H.J. 1906 *The Mandans –*

A Study of Their Culture, Archaeology, and Language, Peabody Museum Memoirs, vol. 3, no. 4, Harvard University, Cambridge, Mass.

WILLEY, G.R. AND PHILLIPS, P. 1955 'Method and Theory in American Archaeology, II: Historical-Developmental Interpretations', *American Anthropologist* LVII, 723–819.

WILLEY, G.R. AND SABLOFF, J.A. 1974 *A History of American Archaeology*, London and San Francisco.

6 Two Hundred and Four Years of African Archaeology

Brian M. Fagan

GENERATIONS of Cambridge-trained archaeologists have made important contributions to African archaeology. To my knowledge, however, no holder of the Disney Chair has paid even a short visit to these favourite Cambridge stamping grounds. This brief essay is dedicated to Glyn Daniel in affectionate thanks for the gift of a lifetime's interest in the history of archaeology. It is written in the hope that he, and his successors, will include Africa in their global travels.

Early Development of Archaeological Research

The earliest recorded archaeological excavation in Africa was carried out by the Swedish naturalist Andrew Sparrman in January 1776 (Robertshaw 1979). With the aid of an iron bar, he dug into a stone mound near the Great Fish River, only to find nothing. He concluded that these mounds were 'irrefragable proof' that a 'more powerful and numerous' population had lived in the area before being 'degraded to the present race of Cafres, Hottentots, Boshiesmen, and savages' (Sparrman 1787).

The Khoi Khoi (ill. 1) and San were the early focus of antiquarian research. Most early observers were more interested in exotic customs than prehistoric remains, and it was not until 1858 that Thomas Holden Bowker of Albany started collecting Middle Stone Age points. He was somewhat surprised when the Curator of the Capetown museum was excited by his discoveries. He claimed he had used identical finds as arrowheads while hunting as a child! Bowker was followed by dozens of other collectors, who ransacked

shell middens and coastal rockshelters for prehistoric artifacts, burials and painted grave slabs. Most of these collecting activities were little more than treasure hunting by people who were on the lookout for 'Bushman relics'. Collecting fever reached new heights after the opening up of the diamond-rich Vaal River alluvial deposits in the 1870s, deposits that yielded thousands of much older Palaeolithic tools. David Livingstone's geologist, Richard Thornton, had found similar artifacts at the mouth of the Zambezi in 1858 (Clark 1959). But most antiquarians were much more interested in the Khoi Khoi and San, who, they realized, were doomed to extinction in South Africa.

Fortunately for archaeology, a number of dedicated people devoted much of their lives to recording the lifeways of southern African hunter-gatherers before it was too late. George Stow excavated in rockshelters and recorded many details of San life in his classic *Native Races of South Africa*, published in 1906. Bleek, Dunn and others documented the hunter-gatherers' desperate struggle for survival and recorded not only rock paintings but the ways in which the San made their stone tools. They laid the foundations of a strong anthropological tradition that persists in African archaeology to this day.

The 1890s saw the beginnings of systematic archaeological research in southern Africa. Geologist J.P. Johnson examined the stratigraphical contexts of Palaeolithic tools in the Orange Free State and Transvaal. Louis Péringuey, Director of the South African Museum in Capetown, concentrated on later prehistory. Péringuey (1911) divided South African prehistory into two broad phases: 'Palaeolithic' implements from river gravels, and 'Bushman relics' from coastal shell middens and rockshelters. By 1910, a wider scholarly audience was beginning to think about three basic issues in African prehistory: had humankind originated in Africa, how long had human beings lived there, and how did the present inhabitants arrive in their homelands?

The Migrations of African Races

The explorers, missionaries and government officials, who were the first to encounter Black Africa's many complex societies, arrived with the assumption that Victorian civilization was the pinnacle of human achievement. It was hardly surprising that they assumed that agriculture, metallurgy and urban life had been introduced to sub-Saharan Africa by the ancient Egyptians and other Mediterranean civilizations. Strongly influenced by Darwinism and doctrines of social evolution, both colonist and scholar considered African societies as inferior cultures at a lower stage of cultural development than even the early Mediterranean civilizations. Thus, any elaboration of African society stemmed from external contacts and diffusion from the Nile or Mediterranean.

Diffusionist views of African history were to persist until the early 1960s, stemming in part from a belief that the present inhabitants of Black Africa had migrated into tropical Africa in very recent centuries. This viewpoint was inadvertently strengthened by the remarkable linguistic researches of Sir Harry Johnson, pioneer colonial administrator, entrepreneur and polymathic writer. Johnson enjoyed a successful career as a colonial administrator and traveller in the Congo, Nyasaland and Uganda (Oliver 1957). He was retired at the early age of forty-three and devoted the remainder of his life to scholarship and writing. Astounded to discover that he knew more about Bantu languages than the leading linguistic authorities of the day, Johnson devoted more than ten years to his *Comparative Study of the Bantu and Semi-Bantu Languages*, completed in 1922. The *Comparative Study* was an astonishing *tour-de-force*, a study of over three hundred Bantu dialects using data collected by Johnson himself and his wide network of correspondents. His most important conclusion is still generally accepted — that the three hundred or so Bantu languages spoken in tropical Africa are so closely related that they are the descendants of a single parent language. So small were the differences between them, argued Johnson, that the Bantu-speaking peoples must have expanded into their present homelands in a remarkably short time, and very recently.

1 *A Khoi Khoi man and woman at the Cape of Good Hope. A sixteenth-century print that gives an impression of the grotesque appearance of non-Western peoples in European minds. The picture bears no resemblance to reality.*

Sir Harry Johnson's Bantu research has proved to be one of the foundations of early African history. He himself was convinced that Africans were capable of remarkable achievements. He believed that the African peoples would play an important role in determining their own future. His political views were advanced for their day, and were not shared by many of his colleagues. Most of them thought of the African, as Johnson himself put it, 'in contemptuous admiration of his big muscles and in satisfaction that they were going to be employed in the White Man's work.' In historical and archaeological terms, we find settler after settler remarking on traces of prehistoric settlement in the far interior that were much too extensive to be the work of anyone as primitive and lazy as the African. There was nothing unique in these views. Many highly respected scholars refused to believe that the American Indians had built the great earthen mounds of the Ohio Valley. They argued that a great Mound Builder civilization had flourished in North America long before the Indians settled among the deserted earthworks (Fagan 1977;

43

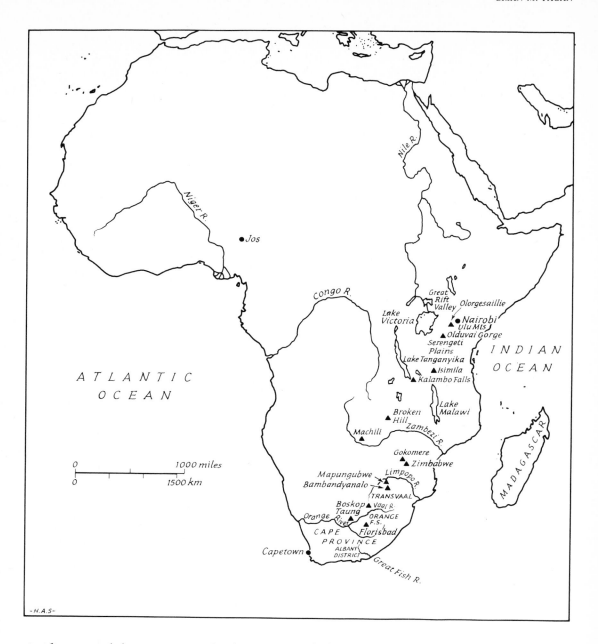

2 African sites and place-names mentioned in the text.

Priest 1833). Such viewpoints stemmed from both ethnocentric attitudes, and from peoples' need to justify the annexation of what they considered undeveloped and wasted territory (Fisher 1977).

The controversies that surrounded, and in some way-out circles continue to surround, the Zimbabwe ruins are a microcosm of these attitudes. Although the Portuguese were aware of the existence of great stone buildings in the far interior, it was not until 1871 that Zimbabwe was described in even outline terms, and then by a German geologist named Carl Mauch, who was convinced that he had found the lost palace of the Queen of Sheba north of the Limpopo. Mauch was strongly influenced by missionaries in the northern Transvaal, who talked of a Land of Ophir in the north, where spectacular ruins awaited discovery. The Rhodesian pioneers took these legends north with them in 1890, prompting the British South Africa

44

3 Theodore Bent. Illustration from his own Ruined Cities of Mashonaland *(1892).*

Company to commission archaeological excavations at Zimbabwe. No less a personage than Cecil Rhodes himself took an interest in Theodore Bent's investigations. He was well aware of the propaganda value of the site as proof of ancient white settlement within the frontiers of his new colony. Theodore Bent (ill. 3), a well known European antiquarian, did not disappoint him. Bemused by a mass of gold objects, imported china and porcelain, and the famous soapstone bird effigies from the Acropolis, Bent concluded that Zimbabwe had been built by Arabian peoples and attempted to date the site by astronomical means (Bent 1892) (ill. 4).

Zimbabwe came under official protection in the early years of the century, when a journalist named Richard Hall was appointed curator. Unfortunately, Hall was not only a disastrous excavator but a facile writer as well. He was convinced of the high antiquity of the ruins, which, he claimed, had been built by Sabaean peoples from Arabia centuries before the present African peoples had settled in the area (Hall and Neal 1904). He concentrated his entire attention on the exotic imports from the site, basing his arguments on the familiar assumption that the local people were incapable of building in stone or crafting gold artifacts.

4 Bent's lithograph of a descent from the Acropolis at Zimbabwe in 1891. From Ruined Cities.

To Hall, and hundreds of Rhodesian settlers, Zimbabwe was the long lost centre of the Phoenician empire, a comforting reminder of ancient white civilization in a remote and strange land. Its very antiquity provided ample justification for white settlement of the region.

The Hall excavations caused concern in European archaeological circles. Several eminent archaeologists, among them Arthur Evans and Flinders Petrie, pressed for a new and impartial investigation of Zimbabwe. They prevailed on the British Association for the Advancement of Science to sponsor some Rhodesian excavations to coincide with their 1905 meeting in South Africa. Randall MacIver, a Flinders Petrie trained scholar who shared his mentor's concern with the dating of small objects, was appointed director of the excavations. These were much more scientific than those of his predecessors, for he dated the ruins with the

5 *Gold beads from Ingombe Ilede, Zambia, a sixteenth-century trading village in the Middle Zambesi valley, Zambia. Beads of this type were found in the Rhodesian ruins and provoked an orgy of treasure hunting in the early years of this century. (Photo Brian M. Fagan.)*

aid of Chinese imported porcelain fragments, which he submitted for analysis to experts at the Victoria and Albert Museum in London. His sober and well-argued report dated Zimbabwe to the sixteenth century AD, or perhaps a few centuries earlier (MacIver 1906). Settler interests, spearheaded by Richard Hall, attempted to rebutt his conclusions (Hall 1905). So vicious was the furore raised by MacIver's work that it was nearly a quarter of a century before anyone could excavate seriously at Zimbabwe again. In the meantime, the Rhodesian government used the 'mystery' of Zimbabwe as a device to attract tourists to the ruins.

The Beginnings of Systematic Research

As early as 1871, Charles Darwin argued that Africa was a likely candidate for the cradle of humanity. He based his arguments on the distribution of African apes and their close anatomical relationships to human beings. Evidence to support his hypothesis was slow in accumulating, partly because Africa was still remote country, and also because most scholars were engrossed in the *Homo erectus* finds from Indonesia and the Piltdown discoveries.

Southern Africa was an early focus of research into human fossils. The Boskop remains were found in the Transvaal in 1913, the Broken Hill cranium north of the Zambezi in 1921 (ill. 6), and the Florisbad skull in 1932 (Clark 1959). In 1924, Raymond Dart was handed the celebrated breccia block from Taung in the

northern Cape that contained the first skull of *Australopithecus africanus*. His description of the Taung child as a 'Man-Ape' was received with scepticism by his European colleagues (Dart 1925). It was not until the redoubtable Robert Broom found further Australopithecines at locations in the Transvaal that Dart's claims were taken more seriously (Pfeiffer 1973). Unfortunately, however, there was no means of dating the sites where they were found.

Between 1900 and 1930, Stone Age research began at isolated locations in eastern and south-central Africa. The geologist J. W. Gregory found stone tools in the Ulu mountains of Kenya in 1893. At first he thought they were gun flints until he came across more palaeoliths elsewhere in the Rift Valley. C. W. Hobley, a government official who started his career with Harry Johnson, collected Stone Age tools throughout East Africa, and published a steady stream of articles on his discoveries. Both Gregory and Hobley recognized that there were several phases of the East African Stone Age, but they were unable to classify their finds with any accuracy.

There matters lay until 1926, when the young Louis Leakey organized his first East African Archaeological Expedition from Cambridge. His researches led not only to the first cultural sequence for eastern Africa, but in the widespread adoption of a succession of pluvials and interpluvials that were widely believed to coincide with the fluctuations of glacial and interglacial periods in northern latitudes (Leakey 1931). Leakey's framework for East Africa continued in regular use until the 1950s.

Both Leakey, and his few pioneer colleagues, like the geologist A. J. Wayland, were seriously handicapped not only by their isolation and lack of research monies and facilities, but the dearth of information on Palaeolithic cultures outside Europe. The Mortillet-like terminology used by French prehistorians was widely applied to sites all over the world, until the sheer complexity of the archaeological record forced archaeologists to develop local cultural terms and labels. It was no coincidence that Louis Leakey acknowledged the assistance of such European luminaries as the Abbé Breuil and Denis Peyrony in his *Stone Age Cultures of Kenya Colony* (1931). His terminology, despite its local associations, still used European terms such as the Aurignacian. Prehistory was just as ethnocentric as African history in the 1920s.

The first lasting continent-wide African terminology came from the hands of two South African archaeologists, A. J. H. Goodwin and C. van Riet Lowe, who took over where Louis Péringuey and others left off (Goodwin 1935, 1946). Both were in close touch with geologists like A. P. du Toit, who

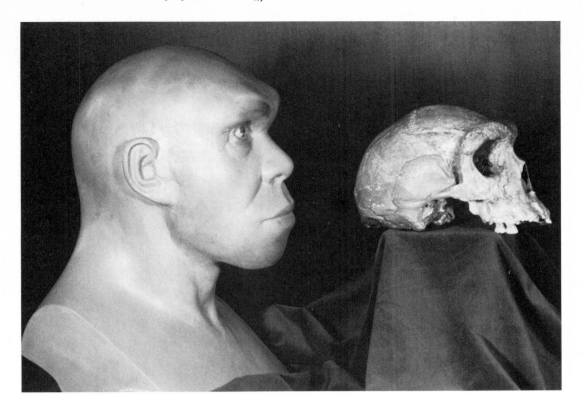

6 Broken Hill skull, compared with a reconstruction. Photograph of a cast of the cranium. (Photo Brian M. Fagan.)

were busy trying to establish the stratigraphic context of early Stone Age cultures in the Vaal River Valley and elsewhere. A geological framework of terraces and down-cutting phases provided a relative chronology for Goodwin and van Riet Lowe's classic synthesis, *The Stone Age Cultures of South Africa*, published in 1929.

The Stone Age Cultures is a remarkable work, written by an uneasy partnership between two great, and independently minded, archaeologists. Much of it, recorded Goodwin in his notes, was written 'in trains'. The geological framework for the earlier cultures is combined with classic descriptions of recent cultures based on rockshelter excavations. Goodwin based much of his analysis of the later cultures on careful analogies from late nineteenth-century ethnographic data, a primitive form of the Direct Historical Method. The two archaeologists developed a tripartite sequence of Early, Middle and Late Stone Age that still remains in general use, despite substantial modification. Their broad, terminological scheme was widely adopted throughout Africa during the 1930s and 1940s. Visits by the Abbé Breuil and Miles Burkitt were an important stimulus to further research, and raised international consciousness of the importance of African prehistory.

Miles Burkitt's *South Africa's Past in Stone and Paint* (1928) was still assigned reading at Cambridge when I was a freshman in the late 1950s. And rightly so, for at the time it was the only widely available account of southern African archaeology for the introductory student. Burkitt brought a wide knowledge of European prehistory to South Africa. He travelled as far north as the Zambezi in search of rock paintings and parallels for South African cultures. Among the pioneers he visited was the missionary Neville Jones, who spent years travelling between the Limpopo and Zambezi collecting stone tools and excavating key sites (Jones 1949). In many respects, the pre-war years were halcyon ones for African prehistory. The few archaeologists on the ground had an outline framework of geological events to work with, a small, but congenial group of colleagues, and a fantastically rich archaeological record to study. One of the fallouts of Burkitt's visit to South Africa was a steady stream of Cambridge-trained archaeologists who entered both the ranks of government service or became professional scholars. They built on the legacy of the pioneers.

The first trained Stone Age archaeologists arrived at a time when European governments were still consolidating their hold on Africa, and committing only minimal funds to territorial development. But the Colonial powers, especially the British, encouraged anthropological research, which gave them useful insights into the peoples they administered. The earliest ethnographic studies were the work of missionaries, later ones by professional anthropologists, some of whom were employed by colonial governments to advise on agricultural and development projects (Brown 1979). Anthropology developed and flourished as a result of colonialism. The success of the early studies, and a widely felt need to preserve traditional crafts, provided the stimulus for the founding of territorial museums. Institutions like the Coryndon museum in Nairobi, the Achimota College museum in the Gold Coast, and the Rhodes-Livingstone Institute in Northern Rhodesia came into being before World War II. At first humble organizations with miniscule budgets, they were lucky in their directors and curators. Newly trained young scholars, such as J. Desmond Clark, Bernard Fagg and others, were soon associated with the new museums, archaeologists who melded the latest advances in European archaeology with the pioneer efforts of local archaeologists. In this sense, modern African archaeology, too, was a product of colonialism.

The Beginnings of Iron Age Archaeology

Nowhere was the link between colonial government and the preservation of Africa's past more direct than in West Africa, where the early years of European rule were noticeable for their muted African resistance to foreign rule. Most Nigerians, for example, were more interested in acquiring the trappings of European culture. Many of them consciously rejected the values and artifacts of their parents and grandparents as being 'uncivilized', this despite Nigeria's great wealth of artistic achievement in wood, bronze and terracotta (Shaw 1978). Almost single-handed, an art teacher named Kenneth Murray set out to preserve Nigeria's indigenous art traditions and to convince people that they were worth studying. Appointed to the Nigerian Education Department as an adviser on the impact of European education on African art in 1927, he fought official apathy for years until the Nigerian Antiquities Service was founded sixteen years later. As first Director of the Service, he was responsible for attracting Bernard Fagg to his staff. Fagg, a Cambridge-trained archaeologist, expanded archaeological research throughout Nigeria. He founded the Jos Museum and several other regional museums that brought traditional art and culture closer to the mainstream of emerging African nationalism.

The passions of the early years had cooled considerably when the British Association for the Advancement of Science met in Capetown in 1929. The Association renewed its interest in Zimbabwe by commissioning Gertrude Caton-Thompson to excavate in Rhodesia. She brought modern methods to bear on Zimbabwe's complex problems. Never one to suffer fools gladly, she filed the correspondence of 'anonymous gentlemen of lively imagination' with strange views about Zimbabwe under the category 'Insane'. Her excavations paid careful attention to the complexities of local stratigraphy, the local pottery industries, as well as the plethora of imported objects that came from her excavations on the Acropolis (Caton-Thompson 1931). She was able to draw on a much wider data base than her predecessors, even studies of imported glass beads carried out by Horace Beck and a young archaeologist named Kathleen Kenyon. So meticulous were her excavations that no serious scholar has ever challenged her general conclusion that Zimbabwe was built by African hands in the early second millennium AD.

The Caton-Thompson research stimulated many less spectacular investigations, among them the work of John Schofield, who devoted the leisure hours of a lifetime to a systematic analysis of southern African glass beads and pottery. It was he who developed the first typologies of southern African Iron Age pottery from such settlements as Gokomere in Rhodesia and Mapungubwe in the northern Transvaal (Fouché 1937). His *Primitive Pottery* (1948) remains a classic study of the subject. But his efforts were hampered by major uncertainties about the chronology of the Iron Age. Imported glass beads soon proved an inadequate means of dating even major sites like Zimbabwe, let alone isolated village sites. Most people assumed that Iron Age peoples had crossed the Zambezi and Limpopo in very recent times. Indeed South African schoolbooks roundly stated that Bantu-speaking peoples crossed the Limpopo at about the same time as Jan van Riebeeck landed at the Cape in the sixteenth century, a myth that is still in the syllabus today. The Mapungubwe excavations were caught up in this controversy, when the physical anthropologists claimed that the burials from both Mapungubwe and Bambanyanalo were of Khoisan type. Thus, it was argued, the sites were first occupied by Khoi Khoi cattle herders rather than Negro, Bantu-speakers. It was not until the 1960s that large-scale studies of South African Negro populations and a reassessment of the archaeological data placed these Limpopo sites in their wider Iron Age context, dating the South African Iron Age at least as early as the tenth century AD, if not before (Fagan 1964).

Iron Age Research lagged far behind that into the Stone Age, partly because of contemporary archaeological preoccupations with earlier cultures. There were few incentives to study cultures that were considered to be 'native', or 'recent'. Almost no historians were concerned with pre-European African history; indeed, many scholars believed that there was no such history to write anyhow. Before the 1950s, nationalistic sentiments, except, perhaps, those of some European settlers, were so muted that the study of African art and Iron Age archaeology was left to amateur enthusiasts and a mere handful of anthropologists.

The Emergence of Palaeoanthropology

One of the catalytic events of archaeology took place that memorable day in 1911 when Professor Wilhelm Kattwinkel stumbled across Olduvai Gorge when searching for butterflies on the Serengeti Plains of Tanzania. The gorge soon came to the attention of the palaeontologist Hans Reck, who claimed that there were no stone tools at Olduvai. Louis Leakey, fresh from his Rift Valley expeditions, realized the enormous potential of the site, and persuaded Reck to accompany him there in 1931. The rest is history, culminating with the Leakeys' triumphant discovery of the *Zinjanthropus boisei* skull in 1959 (Leakey 1951, 1971).

The Olduvai excavations between 1931 and 1959 did not take place in academic isolation. The focus of the investigations changed gradually, as the wider interests of African prehistorians changed from river valley chronologies to the reconstruction of ancient lifeways. One problem surrounded the identity of the earliest toolmakers, and the typology of the earliest artifacts they made. The eolith controversies of the 1930s had shown that the identification of simply flaked artifacts was thwart with difficulties, especially when their geological context was uncertain. When A. J. Wayland and others identified a simple Kafuan chopper tool industry in many African river valleys, it was soon clear that a variety of natural causes could result in the production of perfect pebble tools (Clark 1958). At issue was the precise cultural context of the earliest artifacts. So Leakey and others began to pay increasing attention to early camp sites where the artifacts and food remains of the earliest humans could be found in undisturbed association and precise geological context.

This shift in research interests coincided with a major shift in Palaeolithic studies in the late 1950s, when a series of wide-ranging geological studies showed that Leakey's pluvial and interpluvial scheme was based on very localized evidence (Cooke 1958; Flint 1959). The elaborate correlations of artifacts and river gravels were shown to be of very dubious value, even for local chronologies. Cooke and Flint urged archaeologists to examine living sites where preservation conditions favoured the preservation of fossil pollens and local palaeoenvironmental data.

Louis and Mary Leakey had pioneered living-floor archaeology at Olorgesaillie during the 1940s, and were now focussing their attention on camp sites in the lower beds at Olduvai. Clark Howell and Desmond Clark began long-term excavations at Isimila in Tanzania and Kalambo Falls in Zambia (Howell, Cole and Kleindeinst 1962; Clark 1969), living sites, where both subsistence and climatic data were available in profusion. From these major excavations, with their strong multi-disciplinary emphasis and focus on the surviving remains of human behaviour, came the new specialty known as palaeoanthropology.

The close marriage between archaeology and Pleistocene geology and climatology on the one hand and anthropology on the other has stemmed both from research needs in the field, and from the long roots of African archaeology in both geology and ethnographic research. But interpretations of the archaeological record based on ethnographic analogy alone were inadequate for palaeoanthropologists, who argued that the earliest humans may have enjoyed a way of life that was closer to that of the non-human primates than living hunter-gatherers. The new preoccupation with living-floor archaeology coincided not only with an explosion of information about palaeoenvironments and many new fossil hominid discoveries, but with a rash of studies of baboons, chimpanzees and other non-human primates. These researches have provided a mass of new interpretative data, and remarkable insights into tool-use among apes (Goodall 1973; Pfeiffer 1973). At the same time, anthropologists such as Richard Lee and Irven DeVore (1976) have focussed their attention on San hunter-gatherers, whose cultural ecology is a rich source of comparative information. None of these studies will provide absolutely reliable barometers for the interpretation of early hominid sites, but the palaeoanthropology of the 1970s and 1980s is based on a wide range of data from many different, multidisciplinary sources. Thanks to the strong input of Pleistocene geologists, cultural ecologists and physical anthropologists, as well as massive infusions of American funding and scholarship, Stone Age archaeology has come a long way from the arid typologies and sequences of yesteryear.

Nationalism and Archaeology

As in other parts of the world, perhaps the greatest revolution in African archaeology has been the advent of radiocarbon dating, which began to have an impact on Africa in the late 1950s and early 1960s. Apart from its impact on Middle and Late Stone Age chronologies, radiocarbon samples for Zimbabwe and other Iron Age sites not only confirmed the essential accuracy of Caton-Thompson's dates from imported objects, but showed that iron-using peoples had been living in Africa for very much longer than had previously been suspected. One notable radiocarbon date was that for a find of Early Iron Age pottery at Machili near the Zambezi, which came out at ad 96 ± 220 (Clark and Fagan 1965). This date, and other early Iron Age readings, showed that iron-using peoples had been living in much of tropical Africa for at least two thousand years. Thus, Johnson's Bantu migrations must have taken place very much earlier than hitherto suspected.

Radiocarbon dating came into use at a time when the rising tide of African nationalism had provoked a new and urgent interest in African pre-Colonial history among historians, linguists and anthropologists. The gaps in historical knowledge were startling. No one had attempted a synthesis of early African history since the days of Johnson and Seligman (1930). New methodologies were needed, for written records covered only the most recent centuries of African history. Even as late as 1963, many textbooks used in African schools began with the Victorian explorers. The landmark year was probably 1960, when the *Journal of African History* was founded, and the new, multi-disciplinary field of pre-European African history came into active being.

There was a sense of urgency about African history in the 1960s, for both archaeologists and historians were confronted with an immediate need for new school syllabuses which covered not only recent history, but pre-Colonial times as well. The archaeologist was confronted not only with a practically virgin field of research, but with external pressures to reconstruct African history in a form intelligible to lay people. It was the scholar's responsibility to communicate the results of recently completed fieldwork to a new generation of interested consumers. The muted nationalism of earlier decades was replaced with an ardent interest in African history and traditional culture that could only be satisfied by multi-disciplinary research that helped establish not only a sense of national identity but traced complicated tribal histories and evolving prehistoric societies as well. The recording of oral histories alone has been shown to be a formidable task, since many earlier versions of tribal histories have been shown to be highly unreliable (Ranger 1979). Since the 1960s Iron Age archaeology has become anthropology and history rolled into one, a form of research that draws on data derived both from contemporary and ancient sources. Gone are the ethnocentric and racist stereotypes of earlier years which assumed that African societies had developed in response to nothing but external stimuli. The concerted research efforts of the past quarter-century have shown that prehistoric Africa enjoyed its own distinctive technology and institutions, cultures that were fine-tuned adaptations to one of the richest and most diverse natural environments on earth.

Today, African archaeology is caught up not only in research work that draws on many academic disciplines, but in another development, too, the increasing involvement of African scholars in archaeological research. The pioneer amateurs of the early twentieth century were joined by professional archaeologists trained overseas, who brought new methodologies to African prehistory. They, in turn, are training, and are being replaced by, African scholars, whose academic background is derived partly from African institutions and also from foreign training. The future direction of African archaeology lies in large part in the hands of the Africans themselves, as it should. We can be certain, however, that archaeologists based outside Africa will continue to make important contributions.

The approaches developed by several generations of African archaeologists have been shown to be highly effective both in the field and in responding to nationalistic challenges. The same historical and archaeological methodologies could well be effective in other parts of the world, where there is a need for the writing of unwritten history. One immediate opportunity lies in the pre-Columbian history of the American Indian (Fagan 1977). In this sense, and many others, African archaeology has become a prototype for archaeological endeavours elsewhere in the world. Cambridge-trained archaeologists have played a leading role in placing African archaeology at the forefront of modern prehistoric research. Let us hope that future generations of Downing Street graduates follow the lead of students trained by Dorothy Garrod, Grahame Clark and Glyn Daniel.

Bibliography

BENT, T. 1892 *The Ruined Cities of Mashonaland*, London.

BROWN, R. 1979 'Passages in the Life of a White Anthropologist: Max Gluckman in Northern Rhodesia', *Journal of African History*, XX, 525-42.

BURKITT, M. 1928 *South Africa's Past in Stone and Paint*, Cambridge.

CATON-THOMPSON, G. 1931 *Zimbabwe Culture*, Oxford.

CLARK, J. D. 1958 'The Natural Fracture of Pebbles from the Batoka Gorge, Northern Rhodesia', *Proc. Preh. Soc.* XXIV, 64-77.

1959 *The Prehistory of Southern Africa*, Harmondsworth.

1969 *The Kalambo Falls Prehistoric Site*, Cambridge.

CLARK, J.D. AND FAGAN, B.M. 1965 'Charcoals, Sands, and Channel-Decorated Pottery from Northern Rhodesia', *American Anthropologist* LXVII, 354–71.

COOKE, H.B.S. 1958 'Observations relating to Quaternary environments in East and Southern Africa', *Geological Society of South Africa Bulletin*, Annexure, 60.

DART, R. 1925 '*Australopithecus africanus:* the Man-Ape of Southern Africa', *Nature* 115, 195.

DARWIN, C. 1871 *The Descent of Man*, London.

FAGAN, B.M. 1964 'The Greefswald Sequence: Bambandyanalo and Mapungubwe', *Journal of African History* V, 337–61.

1977 *Elusive Treasure*, London.

FISHER, R. 1977 *Contact and Conflict*, Vancouver.

FLINT, R.F. 1959 On the basis of Pleistocene correlation in East Africa', *Geological Magazine* XCVI, 265–84.

FOUCHÉ, L. 1937 *Mapungubwe*, Cambridge.

GARLAKE, P. 1973 *Great Zimbabwe*, London and New York.

GOODALL, J. 1973 *In the Shadow of Man*, Boston.

GOODWIN, A.J.H. 1935 A commentary on the history and present position of South African prehistory with full bibliography', *Bantu Studies* IX, 291–417.

1946 *The Loom of Prehistory*, Capetown.

GOODWIN, A.J.H. AND VAN RIET LOWE, C. 1929. *The Stone Age Cultures of South Africa*, Capetown.

HALL, R. 1905 *Great Zimbabwe*, London.

HALL R. AND NEAL, W. 1902 *Ancient Rhodesia*, London.

HOWELL, F.C. COLE, G.H., AND KLEINDEINST, M.R. 1962 'Isimila: an Acheulian site in the Iringa Highlands, Southern Highlands Province, Tanganyika', *Actes du IVème Congrès Panafricain de Préhistoire et de l'Etude du Quaternaire*, Tervuren, 43–80.

JOHNSON, SIR H. 1922 *Comparative Study of the Bantu and Semi-Bantu languages*, 2 vols, London.

JONES, N. 1949 *The Prehistory of Southern Rhodesia*, London.

LEAKEY, L.S.B. 1951 *Olduvai Gorge, 1931–1951*, Cambridge.

1971 *Olduvai Gorge* vol. I, Cambridge.

MACIVER, R. 1906 *Medieval Rhodesia*, Cambridge.

OLIVER, R. 1957 *Sir Harry Johnson and the Scramble for Africa*, London.

PÉRINGUEY, L. 1911 *The Stone Ages of South Africa*, Capetown.

PFEIFFER, J. 1973 *The Emergence of Man*, 2nd edn, New York.

PRIEST, J. 1833 *American Antiquities and Discoveries in the West*, New York.

RANGER, T.O. 1979 'The Mobilization of Labour and the Production of Knowledge: The Antiquarian Tradition in Rhodesia', *Journal of African History* XX, 507–24.

ROBERTSHAW, P.T.1979 'The First Archaeological Excavation in Southern Africa?', *South African Archaeological Bulletin* XXXIV, 52–3.

SCHOFIELD, J.F. 1948 *Primitive Pottery*, Capetown.

SELIGMAN, C.G. 1930 *The Races of Africa*, London.

SHAW, T. 1978 *Nigeria*, London and New York.

SPARRMAN, A. 1787 *Voyage au Cap de Bonne- Espérance et autour du monde*, Paris.

7 Gum Leaves on the Golden Bough: Australia's Palaeolithic Survivals Discovered

D.J. Mulvaney

AT THE 1823 Cambridge Commencement, W.C. Wentworth of Peterhouse was runner-up for the Chancellor's Medal. The heroic couplets of his passionate 'Australasia' combined Augustan confidence with the sounds, imagery and aspirations of his 'new Britannia in another world'. Wentworth's great-grandson became the first Minister for Aboriginal Affairs in the Australian Parliament and attempted to grapple with the realities of the racial situation. Poet Wentworth peopled his Australia with untroubled dusky Aborigines, redolent of Rousseauesque nobility:

> Ye primal tribes, lords of this old domain,
> Swift footed hunters of the pathless plain,
> Unshackled wanderers, enthusiasts free,
> Pure native sons of savage liberty,
> Who hold all things in common – earth, sea, air, –
> Or only occupy the nightly lair
> Whereon each sleeps; who own no chieftain's pow'r
> Save his, that's mightiest at the passing hour;
> Say – whence your ancient lineage, what your name,
> And from what shores your rough forefathers came?
> Untutor'd children, fresh from Nature's mould,
> No songs have ye to trace the time of old; –
> No hidden themes like these employ your care,
> For you enough the knowledge that ye are: –
> Let Learning's sons who would this secret scan,
> Unlock its mystic casket if they can –

Despite Wentworth's appropriate reference to academic research possibilities, he lost to W.M. Praed, whose 'Australasia' hastened missionaries to a land of spiritual opportunity, with 'nothing dark except the soul of man'. As in Praed's version, but for different reasons, by 1823 there were no noble savages inhabiting those regions of Australia settled by Europeans. Aboriginal society around Sydney comprised depressed fringe-dwellers, while Tasmanians were within a decade of extinction or banishment to a windy Bass Strait Island. Neither was Praed's vaunted evangelical triumph evident amongst 'that tumultuous horde'. European colonial perception of these diseased and degraded remnants was expressed in art by a style which Bernard Smith (1960, 129) termed 'the comic savage'. The same denigration of humanity was typified in prose by Surgeon Cunningham (1828, 11,

39), neither anthropologist nor Darwinian precursor, who observed of Aborigines:

> How is it that the abject animal state in which they live . . . should place them at the very zero of civilization, constituting in a measure the connecting link between man and the monkey tribe? – for really some of the old women only seem to require a tail to complete the identity.

Noble savage, comic savage – vanishing savage: a survey of sources dating from the first half of the nineteenth century, whose reference to Aboriginal society indicated some appreciation of its scientific value, found few perceptive authors (Mulvaney 1958).

Academic interest in Australian tribes changed dramatically when Charles Darwin turned time back beyond the Garden of Eden. Between 1863, when T.H. Huxley first hinted at the relevance of Australian data for physical anthropology and material culture (in Lyell 1863, 89; Huxley 1906 [1863], 146–50), to the end of the century, when James Frazer (1899, 281) pronounced The Native Tribes of Central Australia 'a document of priceless value for the understanding of the evolution of human thought and society', the Relic Savage or primeval survival, emerged as a scientific phenomenon. Australia's intrusion into European armchair anthropology impinged also upon Palaeolithic archaeology and the interpretation of cave art. A brief review of the chief protagonists is appropriate here. (Further details in Mulvaney 1958, 1966, 1970, 1971a, b, in press.)

The future editor of Antiquity, in writing perhaps the first of his many defences of prehistory as history, observed (Daniel 1949, 132) that 'the study of prehistory quite obviously merges into the study of contemporary preliterate societies, and this is one of the many reasons why prehistoric archaeology and anthropology have grown up together'. This tribute to Glyn Daniel from an historian turned prehistorian originates from such a Department of Prehistory and Anthropology, in a continent where the descendants of the original Australians still constitute 1.2 per cent of the national population.

Model formulation and ethnographic analogy form part of the stock-in-trade of contemporary prehistorians. Models were erected on less solid foundations

a century ago and analogies were simplistic; yet their proponents were no less sure of their validity and universal applicability than are some contemporary ideologues.

Huxley was the first significant builder to invoke Australian parallels, but he proved more cautious than many of his European contemporaries. He also possessed a unique advantage over most of them, because during the 1840s he actually encountered Australian and Melanesian 'savages' in the flesh. Frazer confidently grafted Australian stock on the Golden Bough without any field experience.

In his evaluation of Man's place in Nature, Huxley (1906 [1863], 150) generalized about those surviving 'lowest savages . . . and . . . we have every reason to believe the habits and models of living of such people to have remained the same from the time of the mammoth . . . ' That Huxley was citing the Australian example is evident from his earlier comments on two Neanderthal crania, written for Lyell's *Antiquity of Man* (1863, 86–9). Their implications were profound for both archaeology and comparative ethnography.

The marked resemblances between the ancient skulls and their modern Australian analogues,

1 In the beginning. Aboriginal perception of life in prehistoric Arnhem Land. The central figure in this rock painting is using a spear-thrower; he holds short spears for swamp fowl and a ceremonial fan of magpie goose wing in his other hand. Other ethnographic details include woven dilly-bags or baskets. (Photo Robert Edwards.)

however, have a profound interest, when it is recollected that the stone axe is as much the weapon . . . of the modern as of the ancient savage; that the former turns the bones of the kangaroo and of the emu to the same account as the latter did the bones of the deer and urus; that the Australian heaps up the shells of devoured shellfish in mounds which represent the 'refuse heaps' . . . of Denmark, and . . . that, on the other side of Torres Straits. . . are. . . people who now build their houses on pileworks, like those of the ancient Swiss lakes.

Two years later, John Lubbock (1890 [1865], 429–30) illustrated *Pre–Historic Times* by reference to the 'Manners and Customs of Modern Savages'. 'In fact', he concluded, 'the Van Diemaner and the South American are to the antiquary what the opossum and the sloth

2,3 Noble savage. European perception in the eighteenth century combined ethnographic detail with the canons of Classical art and sentiment.
(Above) 'Two of the Natives of New Holland, Advancing to Combat'. Engraving by T. Chambers after Sydney Parkinson, 1770.
(Below) 'A Family of New South Wales'. Engraving by William Blake after a sketch by Governor King, 1793.

4 Comic savage. 'Hump Back'd Maria, a Female Native Well-known About Sydney'. R. Browne, 1819. (Nan Kivell Collection, National Library of Australia.)

54

are to the geologist.' E.B. Tylor (1865, 195, 371) was on hand simultaneously to compare a single Tasmanian stone scraper in the Taunton Museum, with (Palaeolithic) Drift implements, and to illustrate the uniformity of mankind's mental evolution (psychic unity), by reference to the Australians, 'the most peculiar of the lower varieties of Man'.

By 1893, and with an enlarged sample of Tasmanian tools in Oxford, Tylor (1893) dubbed the Tasmanians 'representatives of Palaeolithic Man'. His discovery of the Relic Savage (in Roth 1899, ix), ensured that 'Man of the Lower Stone Age ceases to be a creature of philosophic inference, but becomes a known reality.' Tylor's evolutionary doctrines of psychic and artifactual unity and stadial progression formed a nexus with the bold world view of his University Museum colleague, W.J. Sollas (1911). His *Ancient Hunters and Their Modern Representatives* equated Lower and Middle Palaeolithic cultures with Tasmanians and Australians, respectively, although he modified some views in later editions.

During the 1870s, Lieutenant-General Pitt-Rivers applied comparable mechanistic ethnographic parallels to technological innovation. Australian wooden implements played a crucial role in confirming laws of evolution which he hypothesized and then 'proved' by his *a priori* selection process and criteria of evaluation. 'In every instance in which I have attempted to arrange my collection in sequence, so as to trace the higher forms from natural forms', he reported (Myers 1906, 11; cf, 37, 139), 'the weapons of the Australians have found their place lowest in the scale, because they assimilate most closely to the natural forms.' One bizarre instance of ethnographic fieldwork occurred at the Kennington Oval during 1868, when the General visited that ground in experimental mood, to watch

5–7 *Vanishing savage.*
(Above) *'Native police dispersing the blacks', western Queensland, c.1882. (C. Lumholtz, Among Cannibals, London 1890, p.348.)*
(Above right) *Alice Springs area, c.1890. Native police and a Mounted Constable, possibly W. Willshire, a notorious 'disperser' of Aborigines who was credited with executing chained men by shooting them in the back.*
(Right) *Prisoners on a 400 mile journey to gaol, photographed by Hermann Klaatsch, near Wyndham, N.W. Australia, 1906. (Australian Institute of Aboriginal Studies.)*

the touring Aboriginal cricket team throw spears and use parrying shields, during their crowd-pleasing diversion, following their defeat by Surrey (Myers 1906, 133, 136–7; Mulvaney 1967).

In the pages of the numerous natural histories of man or studies of comparative social institutions, Australia resembled a supermarket of evolutionary wares, whose fossilized primeval survivals awaited selection according to the taste of the theorist. There is little evidence that these scholars felt sympathy for the Relic Savage as a person, although they regretted his

passing because of the consequent loss to science. Writing of Tasmanians, Tylor (in Roth 1899, vii) expressed these sentiments clearly. 'Looking at the vestiges of a people so representative of the rudest type of man, anthropologists must join with philanthropists in regretting their unhappy fate. . . . We are now beginning to see what scientific value there would have been in . . . a minute careful portraiture of their thoughts and customs.'

Rather than attempt to survey or tabulate the many references to Australian institutions, customs and

55

8 *Aboriginal perception of 'dispersion and pacification'.*
Rock paintings at Innesvale station, Northern Territory.
(Photo Robert Edwards.)

artifacts which were used to illustrate, substantiate or
disprove theories paraded by the grand European syn-
thesizers, it is appropriate to examine the web of intellectual kinship linking most prominent Australian
fieldworkers, both with each other and with patrons
overseas.

Late Victorian and Edwardian anthropology was
represented in Australia chiefly by A.W. Howitt,

Lorimer Fison, W.E. Roth and the Spencer and Gillen
team. It is remarkable to what extent their intellectual
ambience and social contacts overlapped. They benefited also from the patronage of currently eminent
overseas anthropologists or social theorists, who proposed projects, praised, cajoled and found publication
outlets. Their links with E.B. Tylor were direct in
every instance, while J.G. Frazer, Lewis Henry
Morgan, Andrew Lang and A.C. Haddon, amongst
others, either forged personal contacts or influenced
them indirectly along firm research pathways. In their
turn, these Australian workers stimulated further

fieldwork, either by the emulation of their methods, or by deliberate moves to disprove their offending theories.

Australian fieldworkers proved rather individualistic and jealously guarded their data from others whom they considered rivals or plagiarists. In most cases, however, disharmony was provoked by mischievous European theorists, determined that their views should prevail. At first consideration, some disputes appear as legitimate differences of interpretation between workers in kindred fields, but deeper factors were involved. For example, both Howitt and Spencer were involved in controversies with R.H. Matthews and the elder Strehlow. The Strehlow episode was interpreted by some authorities as undermining the validity of findings by Spencer and Gillen. In fact, behind the scenes Andrew Lang was provoking trouble. He was concerned to assail James Frazer's reputation by discrediting his Australian sources. Concerned to 'prove' his theories of totemism, it was necessary to eliminate conflicting interpretations. Consequently, he busily stirred and manipulated the European scene, transmitting letters and gossip. In modern times, his activities would be termed character assassination (Mulvaney and Calaby, in press).

Lorimer Fison, then a missionary in Fiji, was the first anthropologist of this region whose amateur interest was stimulated by the intervention of a distant patron, who provided him with an attractive research design. It is well known that he received a printed questionnaire on kinship terminology from Lewis Henry Morgan, during 1869. His mind proved receptive and he made important contributions to Morgan's comparative research. Following his return to Australia, Fison advertised in the press in 1872, seeking correspondents and collaborators. He succeeded in recruiting Howitt as his eastern Victorian agent. However, Howitt proved much more than a passive collector of local data. During the next decade they worked actively as a team, with Morgan's encouragement. Their research culminated in *Kamilaroi and Kurnai*, dedicated to their sponsor, which was published in 1880.

A.W. Howitt was one of the major figures in Australian intellectual history. That he responded so enthusiastically to Fison's advertisement was no chance. He was the well-educated son of the English literary figures, William and Mary Howitt. By that time he was a distinguished explorer and respected district administrator. He had embarked upon a series of regional geological and botanical studies which retain permanent value. At the request of Brough Smyth, compiler of *The Aborigines of Victoria*, during 1871 Howitt completed some miscellaneous notes on the Aborigines

of Cooper's Creek, whom he encountered during his explorations. These notes are lacking in any perspective or theoretical cohesion and formed a marked contrast to all his subsequent writings, including a section in the same volume which he wrote shortly after his 'conversion' to Morgan (Smyth 1878, *11*, 300–9; cf. 323–32).

Howitt was introduced to evolutionary thought over the previous few years, when he read seriously and became a convinced Darwinian. Tylor and Lubbock also influenced him deeply on social evolution. He even read *Pre-Historic Times* while crossing the mountains on horseback, during an administrative tour (Mulvaney 1971a, 291).

The intellectual excitement experienced by this isolated bush scholar upon reading Fison's advertisement and learning of Morgan's evolutionary kinship systems, may be comprehended by the enthusiasm with which he espoused Morgan's cause. In that same year, Morgan wrote encouraging words to Fison, who passed them on (Mulvaney 1971a, 295). They provided Howitt with a model and a purposeful drive to study Aboriginal customs that never faltered during the remainder of his long life.

> I am more impressed, each communication I receive from you, with the vast importance of your present field of research. We know a good deal of the barbarous nations in all their shades of development, but of the savage nations our correct and thoroughly worked knowledge is still limited. In Australia and Polynesia you are several strata below barbarism into savagism, and nearer to the primitive condition of man than any other investigator. You have in their institutions of consanguinity, marriage and tribal organization far reaching and intelligent guides, not only as to their present, but also to their past, condition. When all the facts are ascertained through all the shades of savagery and barbarism in the different nations of the earth, we shall recover the thread of man's progress from the first to the last clearly and accurately defined, with the chief agencies and instrumentalities by which the progress has been made.

Over the next decade, Fison and Howitt produced the first major Australian anthropological studies. Their data were collected as systematically and as rigorously as their spare-time, limited funds and remote situations allowed. They adapted a questionnaire on the terms of consanguinity and affinity, drawn up by Morgan and the Smithsonian Institution, and issued it during 1874 (ill. 9). Although widely circulated, it met with an indifferent response. However, Howitt issued several further questionnaires on various themes and set a

The Rev. Lorimer Fison and Mr. Alfred W. Howitt, F.G.S., have undertaken to make enquiries respecting the terms of consanguinity and affinity in use among the Australian Aborigines, and to prepare a report on the subject; and it is hoped that the high scientific importance of such investigations will prompt those who possess information to contribute facts in the form desired.

R. BROUGH SMYTH.

Office of the Board for the Protection of Aborigines,
Melbourne, 31st July 1874.

Sir,

In the prosecution of certain Ethnological enquiries, it has become necessary to multiply as much as possible the sources of information relating to the systems of kinship obtaining among the Aborigines of Australia. The only means of doing so is by asking the aid of those who, in various parts of the continent, are in a position to obtain that information. This circular we now forward to you, trusting that you will kindly assist in the enquiry, which is of great moment in a scientific point of view; and any information furnished will be received with thanks, and duly recorded in your name.

It would still further add to the value of the information if a number of genealogical tables could be obtained from the same tribe, which would explain and correct each other.

We have the honor to be,
Sir,
Your most obedient servants,

LORIMER FISON,
A. W. HOWITT.

The Returns should be forwarded by post to

The Reverend Lorimer Fison,
Care of R. Brough Smyth, Esq.,
Collins street east,
Melbourne.

INSTRUCTIONS FOR ASCERTAINING THE TERMS OF CONSANGUINITY AND AFFINITY IN USE AMONG THE AUSTRALIAN ABORIGINES.

1. Ascertain the family relations of some one aborigine.

2. Construct a Family Tree with the names of his father, mother, all his relations, and his connections by marriage, as in the annexed Genealogical Table (or Family Tree), taken from one of the Gippsland tribes.

3. Affix a number to each name.

4. After the figure preceding each name, insert M or F, as the person named is male or female.

5. In any case where the name of a person cannot be ascertained, it will be sufficient simply to distinguish the sex, and to affix a number. Thus, if in annexed table the names of Nos. 14 and 15 had been unknown, the entry would have been—14. Daughter; 15. Son—and would have answered every purpose.

6. In all cases, arrange brothers and sisters in order of seniority. Thus, in the table annexed, Sophy being placed before Edward, it is taken for granted that she is his elder sister. So also it is taken for granted that Bembinkel is older than Bruthen. This is a point of the greatest importance. Inaccuracy here would seriously impair the value of the information supplied; and cause endless difficulty.

fashion which was copied by lesser compilers, such as E.M. Curr (Mulvaney 1971a, 299–302). The correspondence prompted by Howitt's persistent postal anthropology included much indifferent material. But, some replies provided detailed ethnography. They possess great significance today for prehistorians seeking to reconstruct the 'ethnographic present' of different regions.

During this period, Howitt worked closely under Morgan's supervision, as his long and laborious handwritten letters and diagrams sent to Morgan show. When Morgan sent him a copy of *Ancient Society*, Howitt expressed his gratitude and inspiration, while giving his intellectual assent to its thesis. His comments illustrate vividly the patron's role of positive direction and encouragement (Stern 1930, 262):

> I am now going to reread your book, and note everything that requires investigation here. Several new directions for inquiry have suggested themselves. I have already commenced on the food question, and I find that the distribution of food among the family group is regulated by strict laws, as are also the positions of the camps of the individuals living in the camp. A wide vista has opened itself to me.

Prehistorians may regret that such a discerning scientist devoted his energy to the classification of kinship tables and 'proving' the custom of group marriage, under the misleading tenets of social Darwinism. However, so many of his papers and letters have been preserved and they contain such quantities of incidental information, that they allow reinterpretation. For example, they provide economic data, possibilities for examining settlement pattern, and detailed comments on ceremonial exchange systems, decades before geographic models or social reciprocity were understood. In this context, Grahame Clark (1952, 244) used Howitt's published reference to the Mt William stone quarry to illuminate European prehistory; Howitt's notes provide further details.

Although such information was assembled incidental to questioning on the subject of clan relationships and individual rights, it remains unique information. No anthropologist of more recent times, with the exception of Donald Thomson, made such full references to quarries, ceremonial exchange and other material aspects. Some years ago an attempt was made

to plot the distance covered by traditional Aborigines who fulfilled ceremonial obligations. It was ironic that more precise details were provided on the location of ceremonies, the number of people involved, the nature of the goods exchanged and their place of origin, by nineteenth-century ethnographers, than by eminent modern anthropologists (Mulvaney 1976, 74).

One remarkable instance of Howitt's modern relevance was provided during 1979. In 1883 he attended an initiation ceremony in a forest near Bega, in southeastern New South Wales. His record of that event is sufficiently detailed for the Aboriginal descendants of those participants to use them today to substantiate their tenuous oral traditions that the place was spiritually significant. Howitt may yet save the area from being reduced to woodchips. After a century, Howitt and some of his distant correspondents from tropical Australia have become important sources, also, in the determination of claims by Aboriginal groups to legal title to their lands.

By the date of the Bega ceremony, L.H. Morgan had died and Howitt and Fison turned to E.B. Tylor as their mentor and publication agent. That ceremony eventuated largely because Tylor prompted Howitt to the point where he used his influence with tribal elders to set events in motion (Mulvaney 1970). The manner in which Morgan's two disciples first contacted Tylor warrants explanation, because it illustrates the intellectual kinship of the small band who pioneered anthropology.

Fison returned to Fiji during the 1870s. He sent an anthropological paper from there to London's Anthropological Institute, but for some reason it was never received. Because his submission was unacknowledged, however, Fison assumed that he had been snubbed by British opponents of Morgan. Fison mentioned the matter with some bitterness to the Governor of Fiji, Sir Arthur Gordon. Gordon knew Pitt-Rivers, so he wrote to him in 1879, evidently praising Fison's research and deploring the presumed attitude of the Anthropological Society. Pitt-Rivers promptly contacted Tylor, telling him that 'there must have been some miscarriage'. A few weeks later, Fison received a tactful letter from Tylor. Within that same year, Tylor offered to publish two of Fison's articles (Pitt-Rivers to Tylor: 6 June 1879; Fison to Tylor: 17 Aug 1879 – Pitt-Rivers Museum, Oxford, Tylor Coll. Box 6/1).

At Fison's request, Howitt wrote to Tylor subsequently, and a productive collaboration resulted. Howitt might have corresponded with Tylor in any case, because his sister met him on a social occasion during 1880. She reported Tylor's interest in obtaining a specimen of an Australian 'bull-roarer'. Howitt

9 (Opposite) Postal anthropology. The first page of the 1874 questionnaire adapted by Fison and Howitt from Lewis Henry Morgan and sent to police, postal officials and others. (Mitchell Library, Sydney.)

items of their kind from nineteenth-century Australia. They constitute a precious component of the Aboriginal heritage. It is interesting to reflect that they resulted from Tylor's remote control and were the consequence of his interest in the origins of religion and ritual. 'What makes it the more interesting', he told Howitt's sister (Mulvaney 1958, 51), 'is that Mr Lang has noticed a passage by a scholiast to Clement of Alexandria, which seems to prove that just such an instrument was used in ancient mysteries.' Well before Frazer's *Golden Bough*, therefore, Aboriginal religion was assumed to reflect survivals of archaic minds.

Baldwin Spencer arrived at Melbourne University in 1887, to take the foundation chair of biology. His career profoundly influenced European theories on the origin of religion and artistic expression. His role within Australia in conditioning thinking on many issues was equally important and archaeology and material culture were amongst them. At Oxford from 1881, his formal teacher was H.N. Moseley, Linacre Professor of Human and Comparative Anatomy; another examiner and mentor was Ray Lankester, later Director of the British Museum (Natural History). Moseley had sailed on the *Challenger* expedition, and he conveyed his enthusiasm for ethnography to Spencer.

Moseley was a fine teacher and an informal host to his distinguished group of students – Spencer often visited his home and was taken by him to hear Huxley lecture at the Royal Society. Not surprisingly, the stamp of ethnography was on that student body. W.E. Roth was a fellow student, while another was Spencer's lifetime friend and future curator of the Pitt-Rivers Museum, Henry Balfour. Spencer attended Tylor's lectures on anthropology in company with another close student associate, Halford Mackinder. Mackinder pioneered geographic concepts and it seems likely that Spencer's original thesis of zoogeographic regions within Australia owed something to this association.

Lieutenant-General Pitt-Rivers donated 15,000 ethnographic pieces to form the nucleus of the museum which bears his name, but the material had to be transferred from London. During the summer of 1885, Moseley employed Spencer to assist Tylor and himself to label the whole collection before it was transported. Back in Oxford Spencer and Balfour unpacked this store of material culture. Spencer therefore received a remarkable ethnographic schooling, as he spent weeks in the company both of an eminent evolutionary biologist and the founding figure of British social anthropology, while he worked on the collection designed by Pitt-Rivers to demonstrate technological evolution.

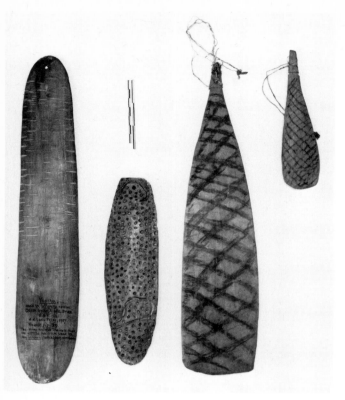

10 *'Primeval survivals': ceremonial items collected by A.W. Howitt in 1883 for E.B. Tylor. The three right-hand objects were used in the 1883 ceremony arranged near Bega by Howitt. (Pitt-Rivers Museum, Oxford.)*

collected some examples of these sacred ceremonial objects and eventually they arrived at the Pitt-Rivers Museum (ill. 10). It was through Howitt's knowledge of these ritual items and his use of them in an appropriate manner in the presence of tribal elders, that he secured their goodwill. They proceeded to arrange the Bega ceremony as a consequence.

A report on that event was within Tylor's hands within a few months, together with some ritual items used during the ceremony. Tylor sponsored the publication and he may have startled members at the next Anthropological Institute meeting, when he exhibited the wooden bullroarers 'and whirled them' (Mulvaney 1958, 51–2; 1970; Howitt to Tylor: 21 Aug 81, 23 Aug 82, 18 June 96 – Pitt-Rivers Museum, Tylor Coll. Box 6/1).

These objects have been housed in the Pitt-Rivers Museum since that time. They are possibly the earliest well-documented ceremonial items to have been collected in Australia and are amongst the few surviving

Spencer was twenty-six years of age when he was appointed to the Melbourne post; three future Fellows of the Royal Society, all his senior, also applied. Huxley was a member of the selection committee. As Spencer's referee, Tylor prophesied 'that if you hold an Australian appointment you will come in contact with interesting questions of local Anthropology'. Spencer was selected just ahead of A.C. Haddon, soon to become identified with Torres Strait (Mulvaney and Calaby, in press).

Other duties at first prevented Spencer from developing his latent anthropological interest. However, he warmed to the companionship of Fison and Howitt, both of whom now lived in Melbourne. He later dedicated a book to them, and frequently acknowledged his debt for their interest and advice, while Howitt exerted great influence on his approach to Aboriginal anthropology. The direct line of descent from Tylor by now ran to all three men; schooling in L.H. Morgan's concepts passed easily to Spencer. Apart from these elders, however, Spencer found few interested in anthropology. When Tylor wrote to him on 23 May 1889 urging the appointment of Fison to a university post, Spencer replied wryly: 'Anthropology is scarcely "Practical" enough for the Australian mind.'

In 1894, Spencer visited Central Australia, while zoologist on the Horn Expedition. At Alice Springs he met the genial head of the telegraph station, F.J. Gillen. He returned there in 1896, this time as anthropologist (ill. 11). The first Spencer and Gillen volume, *The Native Tribes of Central Australia*, was published within three years. Its impact was profound. Social theorists had quarried facts on social organization, technology and discrete examples of the ceremonial life of primeval savages. For the first time, a trained biologist had focussed his expertise on a tribal group. Through an evolutionary filter he presented what like-minded social scientists accepted as a rounded explanation of archaic religious behaviour. Haddon praised it 'as being the best book of its kind about any people' (Haddon to Spencer: 5 May 1902 – Pitt-Rivers Museum, Spencer Coll. Box 1). Even before its publication, J.G. Frazer pronounced its authors 'immortal', surpassing Tacitus in their ethnographic virtues. They succeeded, he explained (1899, 281), in providing evidence for 'understanding . . . the evolution of human thought and society'.

It had been Fison, in this instance, also, who urged Spencer to contact Frazer. Spencer took his advice and wrote to him in July 1897. The result was an immediate

11 Relic savages. Baldwin Spencer with tribal elders on the ceremonial ground which supplied the basis of Native Tribes of Central Australia, *at Alice Springs, 1896.*

and friendly response, and Frazer offered to find a publisher for their research and to assist with editorial work. He acted positively in these matters, and achieved more than Tylor, who was concerned about the 'unsavoury' nature of their findings.

Their subsequent friendship paralleled the manner in which Fison and Howitt developed reciprocal relationships with Morgan and Tylor. It is difficult to disentangle the priorities between the formulation of a theory and its assumed field validation. Even the crucial initial contact between Frazer and Spencer cannot be set in an intellectual vacuum. For example, during 1896, before he even knew Frazer, Spencer first conceived the possibility that Aboriginal totemic ceremonials, in which the totemic food was eaten, were magical increase rites intended to ensure the perpetuation of species. Frazer always acknowledged Spencer's priority in this, although it became a hallmark of Frazer's theory of totemism.

However, as Spencer had read the first edition of *The Golden Bough* and was in intellectual agreement with its thesis, it may have sparked his imagination. The concept was not new, as Frazer indicated in his tribute to Spencer and Gillen in the preface to the 1900 edition of *The Golden Bough*: 'the long-looked-for rite' had been found in ideal circumstances, amongst 'the most primitive totem tribes as yet known'. Spencer advanced some relevant observations about his research methodology, in his first letter to Frazer (Marett and Penniman 1932, 9–10).

> I need hardly say that the *Golden Bough* has been most useful to me. Of course Gillen and I have worked a great deal together up in the Centre, but most of the actual finding out of things has of necessity to be done by him. I send him up endless questions and things to find out, and by mutual agreement he reads no one else's work so as to keep him quite unprejudiced in the way of theories.

Unfortunately, both Frazer and Spencer retained their 'unprejudiced' research models for the remainder of their lives. The amalgam of evolutionary biology and social Darwinism which formed the philosophical mould of Spencer's first major anthropological study was held steadfastly as late as 1927. The preface to *The Arunta*, dedicated to 'Our Master Sir James Frazer', opened as follows:

> Australia is the present home and refuge of creatures, often crude and quaint, that have elsewhere passed away and given place to higher forms. This applies equally to the aboriginal as to the platypus and kangaroo. Just as the platypus, laying its eggs and feebly suckling its young, reveals a

mammal in the making, so does the Aboriginal show us, at least in broad outline, what early man must have been like before he learned to read and write, domesticate animals, cultivate crops and use a metal tool. It has been possible to study in Australia human beings that still remain on the culture level of men of the Stone Age.

In France at the turn of the century, as in Britain, social scientists were receptive to the first two Spencer and Gillen volumes of 1899 and 1904, together with the summation of Howitt's life study, published in 1904. His *The Native Tribes of South-East Australia* was published by Macmillan, publishers to Frazer and Spencer and Gillen; it was titled in deference to their classics; it was only completed because of Spencer's selfless encouragement and advice.

Emile Durkheim would have been unable to expound *The Elementary Forms of the Religious Life* without the evidence of these authors (1915, cf. 90–2, 96). Their influence was equally direct on Salomon Reinach. In the late 1880s, Reinach was 'full of doubts and reservations' about the authenticity of Palaeolithic cave art (Daniel 1950, 131). By 1903, he was championing its reality and emphasizing its symbolic and totemic nature. He stressed the role of sympathetic magic, both in relation to success in the hunt and to fertility rites. The manner in which the theories of both Durkheim and Reinach were taken up by the Abbé Breuil, and incorporated into the canon of the aesthetics of Palaeolithic cave art, has been examined by P.J. Ucko and A. Rosenfeld (1967, 123–30).

It is interesting to reflect that half a century of prehistoric art studies were conditioned by field interpretations of Australian social behaviour. Yet the intellectual ambience in which the Australians sought data and explained it was derived from Tylor and Frazer, the pre-eminent theorists of totemism. In their turn, these men used Australian facts to bolster their theories. It also provided the context for W.J. Sollas, whose 'modern representatives', exemplars of his *Ancient Hunters*, reflected Howitt, Spencer and Gillen. Not only was his text dependent upon them, but he reproduced eighteen of Spencer's illustrations.

Spencer became Honorary Director of the National Museum of Victoria in 1899, a post which he filled for three decades. Under his control it developed into a major ethnographic museum, while his prestige made it the focus for much activity early in the century. Numerous European museums contain extensive exchange collections arranged by Spencer, including many items which Spencer and Gillen obtained in the field. Less than two years after assuming office, Spencer had written a *Guide to the Australian Ethno-*

graphic Collection (1901), over half a century before any other Australian museum attempted such a venture. It expressed sentiments and arranged artifacts in a manner that would have given satisfaction to Pitt-Rivers and Tylor. Not surprisingly, the public learned that the Aborigines were 'a relic of the early childhood of mankind left stranded . . . in a low condition of savagery' (1901, 12).

Under the influence of associates whose hobby was collecting and classifying stone tools, Spencer developed a thesis which had repercussions for future research. He arranged museum displays of stone artifacts to demonstrate that form and type were merely functions of raw material (1901, 78). Change through time, cultural preference, or functional adaptation, were left out of the equation.

The British Association for the Advancement of Science assembled in Melbourne in 1914. A museum gallery exhibited 10,000 stone tools and provided a *Guide* (Kenyon and Mahony 1914), to convince the delegates that there were no significant differences in implement type anywhere across Australia which could not be explained by geology. Presumably the overseas visitors remained unconvinced. Several years later, the authors of the exhibition guide deplored the dead hand of the prehistorian: 'in all discussions . . . into primitive man's history as revealed to us by the artifacts left behind him, the inquirer finds himself hampered, to a distressing extent, by the evil influence of the European archaeologist' (Kenyon, Mahony and Mann 1924, 467).

The Relic Savage, whose simple mind was bound by custom and confused by superstition and who inhabited a Stone Age world in which the very stones predetermined the form of his artifacts and his response to economic needs, was a timeless and timeworn concept. It satisfied the needs of a generation for whom evolution provided a simplistic key to comprehending man's physical, material and mental processes. Australian data stimulated European prehistorians and social theorists to seek ethnographic parallels amongst its presumed elemental survivals. It seems ironic that while they used Australian models to clinch their explanation of phenomena ranging from technological progress to religious origins and the purpose of Palaeolithic cave art, the local Australian scene remained so negative. Even the university in which Spencer held a chair and Howitt served as a member of council still lacks a department of anthropology. Sydney achieved Australia's first department of anthropology in 1926, but the centenary of *Origin of Species* had been celebrated before it or any other anthropology department taught prehistory. It has been argued (Mulvaney 1971b, 1977) that the concept of the Relic Savage

In the presence of His Excellency
Sir George Sydenham Clarke.

Town Hall,
Melbourne.

**Monday Evening
7th July,**
1902.

Lecture on

Aboriginal Life
In Central Australia
By
Professor Baldwin Spencer, M.A., F.R.S.

The slides illustrating the Lecture have been prepared by Mr. J. W. LINDT, from negatives taken by Professor Spencer and Mr. F. J. Gillen, during their recent expedition to Central Australia.

❧ ❧ Synopsis. ❧ ❧

The Lecture is designed to give an idea of the nature of the life led by a Central Australian Aborigine, and for this purpose a brief account will be given of scenes and ceremonies which have been selected as typical of savage life. The various ceremonies will be illustrated by lantern slides, cinematograph views, and phonograph records.

1. Nature of the country illustrated by views of the Stony Desert, Macdonnell Ranges, Mulga Scrub and White Ant Hills.

2. The Natives, their physical structure and appearance at different ages.

3. The ordinary life of the Natives ; their Dances or Corrobborees illustrated by cinematograph views and phonograph records of the Tchichingala Corrobboree, as performed by the Arunta tribe.

4. The social organisation of the tribes. The division of the tribe into two or more classes, so that every native has a class name. The further division of the natives into totemic groups named after some material object, such as a kangaroo, emu, hakea plant, grub, etc. The way in which each individual acquires his class and totemic name.

5. The sacred bull roarer or Churinga.

6. Ideas with regard to totemic ancestors, of whom the living natives are the reincarnations.

7. The sacred ceremomies associated with the totems and totemic ancestors of which a great snake totem called the Wollunqua, in the Warramunga tribe, and the Witchetty grub totem, in the Arunta tribe, will be described as typical examples. The ceremonies will be illustrated by slides, cinematograph views, and phonograph records.

8. Death and Mourning Ceremonies, illustrated by slides.

9. The organisation of a party to avenge the death of a man, illustrated by cinematograph views and slides.

10. The final burial ceremonies as carried out in the Warramunga tribe.

Lanternist : Mr. Alex. Gunn.

Box Plan at Allan's.   **John H. Tait,** Manager.

12 *Innovation in anthropology. Relic savages portrayed on movie film and wax cylinder sound recordings for a Melbourne audience in 1902. After A.C. Haddon, Spencer was the first to attempt such field documentation.*

encouraged intellectual contempt, matching popular denigration of Aboriginal culture, and so inhibited the development of archaeology.

For whatever reasons, until the last decade or so, Australians had to study overseas in order to learn how to apply prehistoric research in their own country. This was my experience in 1951. In my Australian isolation, I convinced the newly founded Australian National University authorities who awarded me a scholarship, that Cambridge offered the appropriate courses. My arguments were products of my reading of prehistory during the previous year. I was excited by Grahame Clark's innovative articles on economic prehistory and by the humanity and wisdom of Glyn Daniel's *A Hundred Years of Archaeology*.

Bibliography

CLARK, J.G.D. 1952 *Prehistoric Europe The Economic Basis*, London.

CUNNINGHAM, P. 1828 *Two Years in New South Wales*, 2 vols, London.

DANIEL, G.E. 1949 'A defence of Prehistory', *Cambridge Journal* III, 131–47.

1950 *A Hundred Years of Archaeology*, London.

DURKHEIM, E. 1915 *The Elementary Forms of the Religious Life*, London.

FRAZER, J.G. 1899 'Observations on Central Australian totemism', *J. of Anth. Inst.* XXVIII, 281–6.

HUXLEY, T.H. 1906 *Man's Place in Nature*, London.

KENYON, A.S. AND MAHONY, D.J. 1914 *Guide to the Stone Implements of the Australian Aborigine*, Melbourne.

1923 'Evidence of outside culture innoculation', *Australasian Association for the Advancement of Science*, 17, 464–7.

LUBBOCK, J. 1890 *Pre-Historic Times as Illustrated by Ancient Remains, and the Manners and Customs of Modern Savages*, London.

LYELL, C. 1863 *The Antiquity of Man*, London.

MARETT, R.R. AND PENNIMAN, T.K. 1932 *Spencer's Scientific Correspondence*, Oxford.

MULVANEY, D.J. 1958 'The Australian Aborigines 1606–1929: Opinion and Fieldwork', *Historical Studies — Australia and New Zealand* VIII, 131–51, 297–314.

1966 'Fact, fancy and Aboriginal Australian ethnic origins', *Mankind* VI, 299–305.

1967 *Cricket Walkabout: The Australian Aboriginal Cricketers on Tour 1867-8*, Melbourne.

1970 'The anthropologist as tribal elder', *Mankind* VII, 205-17.

1971a 'The ascent of Aboriginal Man: Howitt as anthropologist', in Walker, M.H. *Come Wind, Come Weather*, Melbourne.

1971b 'Prehistory from Antipodean perspectives', *Proc. Preh. Soc.* XXVII, 228–52.

1976 'The chain of connection', in Peterson, N. (ed.), *Tribes and Boundaries in Australia*, Canberra.

1977 'Classification and typology in Australia', in Wright, R.V.S. *Stone Tools as Cultural Markers*, Canberra.

MULVANEY, D.J. AND CALABY, J.H. in press *'So Much That is New': Sir Baldwin Spencer 1860–1929*, Melbourne.

MYERS, J.L. (ed.) 1906 *The Evolution of Culture*, Oxford.

ROTH, H.L. 1899 *The Aborigines of Tasmania*, Halifax.

SMITH, B. 1960 *European Vision and the South Pacific*, Oxford.

SMYTH, R.B. 1876 *The Aborigines of Victoria*, 2 vols, Melbourne.

SOLLAS, W.J. 1911 *Ancient Hunters and their Modern Representatives*, London.

SPENCER, W.B. AND GILLEN, F.J. 1899 *The Native Tribes of Central Australia*, London.

1904 *The Northern Tribes of Central Australia*, London.

SPENCER, W.B. 1901 *Guide to the Australian Ethnographical Collection in the National Museum of Victoria*, Melbourne.

STERN, B.J. 1930 Selections from the letters of L. Fison and A.W. Howitt to L.H. Morgan', *American Anthropologist* XXXII, 257–79.

TYLOR, E.B. 1865 *Researches into the Early History of Mankind*, London.

1893 'On the Tasmanians as representatives of Palaeolithic Man', *J. Anth. Inst.* XXIII, 141-52.

UCKO, P.J. AND ROSENFELD, A. 1967 *Palaeolithic Cave Art*, London and New York.

8   The Progress of Archaeology in China

William Watson

GLYN DANIEL has rendered particular service to his subject by ever insisting on the wider perspectives of history against which archaeological data are criticized and validated. For him as for some others of his generation archaeology has been an essential component of history, a history pursued by special means. None more than he has been aware that means taken for ends are the main threat to the effectiveness of the research. In the People's Republic of China the specialization which tends to part archaeologist from historian has been held in check by the persistence of an inherited model of historical evolution, to which Marxist ideas have been adapted (where any adaptation has been attempted at all) only incompletely or incongruously. The Chinese archaeologist finds himself deeply engaged in affirming historical and social views, while meantime he must adapt methods of European origin to an environment and to a dialectic of change for which they were not at first intended. To the occidental observing this process familiar problems are set in fresh relief by the exotic terms in which they present themselves, and in Chinese solutions he may discern a critique of his own experience.

After the advent of the communist regime in 1949 many factors, practical and ideological, contributed to an expansion of archaeological work with speed and scope unprecedented in any Asian country. The main impulse survived from the previous period of nationalist government, but with rare exceptions the men who had launched research on Bronze Age and Neolithic sites under the auspices and control of Academia Sinica had departed to exile in Taiwan, taking with them the near totality of their excavated material and records. On the mainland their work waited to be done again and there was now a nationwide organization and an urgently felt need to establish the ancient identity of Chinese culture in material forms, free alike of the taint of Confucian doctrine and foreign intervention.

The early finds made at Chou-k'ou-tien which led to the recognition of Peking Man had been mostly dispersed and lost during the war. But work was resumed at Chou-k'ou-tien soon after 1949, the lost specimens replaced and exceeded, while discoveries made at Lan-t'ien in Shensi established a new human type which appears to rank just prior to *Sinanthropus*

pekinensis and to be comparable to the Javanese *Pithecanthropus robustus*. More than the Palaeolithic, however, research in Neolithic culture attracted the new generation of archaeologists, for that could throw light on the virtually unexplored gap between the earliest Neolithic and the Shang Bronze Age, and might serve to correct westward-thinking theory which had made China appear tributary to developments elsewhere. This had been the conclusion drawn often in the west from Andersson's publication of the painted-pottery Neolithic cultures of Kansu, whose ceramic undoubtedly bears a general resemblance to the painted potteries of Central and Western Asia. In Bronze Age matters also trade-minded theorists and those preoccupied with tribal origins and migration (both can be seen as intellectual offshoots of the Afghanistan-centred politics of the great western powers at the beginning of the century) had created the impression, even if they had not explicitly advocated the view, that Bronze Age civilization in China was a latter-day reflex of the high Bronze Age cultures of the Fertile Crescent of the Near East. This concept too had to be corrected.

The correction had begun before 1949, but in the case of the Neolithic with the acceptance of a principle whose validity in the Chinese context calls for revision and to the present time is only partly revised. This is the classification of cultures too exclusively in terms of the pottery they carried. The basic text was G.D. Wu's *Prehistoric Pottery in China*, published in London in 1938, and its equivalent in papers issued in China, the fruit of the author's participation in the Academia Sinica's excavations in the halcyon pre-war days, and of his adherence to the prevailing archaeological philosophy of the west. But what fitted the circumstances of prehistoric temperate Europe, with its fringe-characteristics in regard to Mediterranean culture and its quasi-migratory settlement and agriculture, did not necessarily provide the best model for interpreting cultural growth and spread on the loessic uplands of north-west China and on the great plain of the middle Yellow River. The scheme of central-and-western Yangshao culture and subsequent central-and-eastern Lungshan culture which Wu set up was discarded in China under the influence of the founder of post-1949 Neolithic research, Liang Ssŭ-yung. A single line of descent was now proposed for the Neolithic, with Lungshan as merely the later stage of the Yangshao, developing as the Yellow River delta was occupied by its first farmers. Observations made at the west-Honan site of Miao-ti-kou are claimed to show an intelligible succession from the one to the other, with a transitional stage, a view now adopted by Chinese exponents; but a theory of total cultural continuity is not to be argued from the stratigraphy, for in that there is a division already corresponding (say the critics of the unitary theory) to technical distinctions in the two traditions. Yangshao continues alone in West China, showing affinity ultimately with Western Asia in the pottery; while the Lungshan, in some ceramic and non-ceramic aspects, has rather an affinity with the north-east, the Maritime province of East Asia and the eastern seaboard. It is easy to show that the division of ceramic tradition need not imply cultural cleavage of the kind which earlier theorists were suspected of advocating, and which would be belied by all subsequent history. But the centralist view, in which advance in pre-metal culture is seen to radiate from Honan and east Shensi in a diffusionist sense, remains the official one. Pottery is still the criterion, and if G.D. Wu's scheme is abandoned, the principle of his analysis is retained.

Apart from this controversy, however (though hardly now a controversy in China itself), Chinese archaeologists concentrate on the excavation and rescue of sites, and on detailed recording, leaving some larger aspects of interpretation to their foreign observers. The conclusions of the latter are governed strictly by the content of Chinese reports, since thus far no foreign archaeologists have excavated or even witnessed an excavation in progress in the People's Republic. The outstanding achievement in Neolithic research to date is still the excavation in the later 1950s of a large part of the moated village at Pan-p'o, on the second terrace above the Wei River in Shensi: much utilitarian pottery, stone and bone tools, house foundations with traces of wooden structures allowing convincing reconstruction, signs of segregated activities and types of burial allowing significant speculation on the order of society, which is argued to be matriarchal, of settled farmers and fishermen, and peaceable. It is only in recent years that work in Sinkiang has expanded, with the promise that the nagging problem of western ceramic connections may be resolved on a stratigraphic basis. It is already shown that the painted pottery of Kansu is later in date than that of Honan, to that extent giving encouragement to a theory that Chinese influence extended westwards through Central Asia. But the influence through Asia of early Chinese cultures has received little attention in China itself, as

regards either the Neolithic or, as will be mentioned below, the Bronze Age. Radiocarbon dating has put the division between Yangshao and Lungshan in the third millennium BC. It gives no grounds yet for competing with the six-to-eight-millenary antiquity claimed for pottery by some Japanese archaeologists in their own country, but one may think it unlikely that the ceramic art should have arisen earlier in Honshu Japan than on the continent, any more than in Britain it preceded the development in Europe.

There can be little in the history of Bronze Age archaeology that equals the drama of the discoveries made at Hsiao-t'un, near Anyang in Honan by Li Chi and his colleagues of the Institute of History and Philology of Academia Sinica during the decade from 7 October 1928; ten years which shook the scholastic establishment (for were not oracle texts found that confirmed and amended the historical king-list capable of threatening the authority of textual tradition?) and riveted the attention of historians the world over. The trials of the excavators, which included local official obstruction and even sniping, are legendary, and the outbreak of the China Affair in June 1937 put an end to the work. The great shaft graves, the pits with human sacrificial victims accompanied by bronze vessels astonishing to all students of the late Bronze Age for their technique as much as their art, the burials of chariots with their drivers, the finds of bones inscribed with oracular questions – all of this has become well known. The men who conducted these excavations were the archaeological wing of the ill-fated May 4 Movement, whose aim was a cultural and technical accommodation to western tradition which should exclude the imperialist excess that industrialization had induced in Japan. In the summer of 1949 the majority of these founding members took sad farewell of Academia Sinica and of colleagues who decided to remain when Peking fell to the communist forces, and retreated to Taiwan. There they continued to work on the material they had transported with them, in droll isolation from their mainland colleagues, whose work they were obliged to ignore.

At Hsiao-t'un were uncovered the *pisé* foundations of large buildings, whose wooden superstructure could be visualized to some extent from the position of stone pillar bases which remained in place. A large symmetrical complex of foundations in Sector C at Hsiao-t'un (symmetrical, that is, if allowance be made for the part of the site destroyed by the encroachment of the Huan River) embraces at its centre the immolated charioteers, soldiers and menials (possibly a whole squadron of the army) and bids fair to be interpreted as a temple with its annexed buildings. The earth podium designated *beta* 20 becomes in reconstruction an 80-metre long south-facing terrace approached by seven flights of stairs, the largest of these in the middle, and carrying towards either end a small further foundation suggesting the 'drum towers' of later palaces. The whole may even be thought to foreshadow the Altar of Heaven at which emperors officiated.

Forty years have added little to the list of artistic and technical discoveries made at Anyang in the course of the first decade of excavation; but work undertaken there since 1949, now under full technical control and with a display of skill in exploiting the properties of the encasing loessic soil that is equalled elsewhere only by such feats as the Sutton Hoo excavation, have added most significant detail. The shaft grave at Wu-kuan-ts'un, comparable in size to the 'royal' tombs excavated before 1937, preserved earth impressions making clear the nature of the wooden funeral chamber, and on the wide ledge around this were laid the bodies of human victims who are now pronounced to have been slaves. Elsewhere some chained victims were taken as further evidence of the correctness of the designation of the Shang territories as a 'slave state', imposed by the metal-using dynasts on the peaceable matriarchal farmers of the earlier period. Unfortunately it has not proved possible by further excavation of building foundations, of the drainage system etc., to throw decisive light on the unresolved problem of the stratigraphic sequence at Hsiao t'un, but at Chengchou, a hundred miles or so to the south and across the Yellow River, a vast new vista on Shang affairs has been opened in excavations conducted from 1953.

At Chengchou, now proposed as the site of the Shang city of Hao, large sectors of a rectangular earth wall may still be followed above ground or traced by its foundations. It measures 2 km from north to south and 1.7 km from west to east. Its orientation is close to the cardinal directions and at least one south-facing gate has been identified. To meet some unexplained circumstance the north-east corner is cut off; on the other hand such *pisé* foundations as could be traced within the perimeter (all of which is included in the built-up and northern suburban area of the existing city) suggest that the Shang city was divided into insulae along the directional axes. The wall has been dated from low-placed layers of its *pisé* to 620 ± 135 bc and 1595 ± 135 bc. Outside the wall one site has initial-Shang material judged to ante-date the building of the wall, and another (Erh-li-kang), situated about a kilometre to the south-east of the wall, has in its lower level pottery the like of which could be shown to lie also along the inner face of the wall. The Erh-li-kang material must therefore represent the occupation of Chengchou at its *floruit*, and date to about 1600 bc or a

few decades later. Outside the wall, and at varying short distances and in some cases against the outer face of the wall, were industrial sites, burial places and other scattered signs of occupation in the Shang period. The outstanding contrast with the Hsiao-t'un settlement is the existence of the wall itself, whose regulated lines and height of an estimated 10m (the base measuring 20m) must destine it for defence; whereas even the extended search made at Hsiao-t'un since 1949 has failed to locate the trace of a wall at that city.

The results of the Chengchou investigation, combined with finds of bronzes decorated in the Shang style of Anyang at places as far afield as Hunan (i.e. south of the Yangtze) and Shantung, afford a much enlarged picture of the scope of Shang rule and the cohesiveness of its cultural attributes. The first theory, promulgated by Tsou Heng in 1956, regarded both the Shang cities as the seats of rulers, invoking the historical record of a northward move by King P'an Keng in about 1300 bc: on this view the earlier dynasts reigned from Chengchou, and moved to a new foundation north of the Yellow River towards the middle of the dynasty's life. The question of the fate of the southern city after its abandonment was left in abeyance, and no explanation was offered why the move should be made from a walled capital to an undefended site. As to the succession of dynasties, Chinese archaeologists had their confidence in the tradition of written history so well confirmed by the coincidence of the Hsiao-t'un oracular king-list with the list preserved in writings, that they have been reluctant to abandon the concept of an earlier dynasty than that of Shang, the Hsia dynasty of the histories. The latter has never been identified archaeologically, and receives no mention in the Hsiao-t'un oracular sentences. Outside China the Hsia kings were either regarded as minor rulers, contemporary with Shang and occupying the lower Yangtze region (the Kaizuka school in Japan), or were suspected of being a pure invention of annalists intended to bridge the gap between culture heroes designated sovereigns of remote antiquity, and the fully historical Shang. When the Peking Institute of Archaeology presented the results of field research and excavation in Burlington House in 1973, the Hsia dynasty was listed in the chronological table and given its traditional dates, but no exhibits were attributed to it. The gap is now being remedied by an increasing tendency to suggest that Bronze Age material found south of Anhui province, when it does not measure up to the Shang standard, should be attributed to the Hsia period. In China itself the claim made for the dynastic status of Chengchou is apparently maintained, as it must be if the radiocarbon dating is to be brought even approximately into line with the dates preserved in written tradition. Meanwhile excavated evidence, which must mean epigraphy, cannot be cited for identifying Hsia remains, and perhaps in the nature of the case no such evidence can ever be forthcoming. But the notion of cultural and political centralism which is thus tacitly brought to bear on these questions should be considered, for it has its influence on the interpretation and even reporting of archaeological evidence from other periods besides the High Bronze Age.

Beyond conforming to the concepts of matriarchy, primitive communism, and the slave state, Chinese archaeologists have shown little interest in Marxist interpretations, preferring to document technological advance and a process of acculturation proceeding from the inventive centre of Honan and east Shensi. Concurrently they seek to match the archaeological picture with the verbal one of the annals and the historians. Whatever model of interpretation is adopted, the leading function of this region must inescapably be acknowledged, but much argument can be brought against the view that it was uniquely a diffusion from Honan and Shensi of material culture and institutions which eventually produced the uniform culture of the Iron Age. The fusion of Chinese western and eastern elements in the late Neolithic of the central plain demonstrates the attraction this region of rapid and productive change exercised on neighbouring cultures. Similar criticism can be brought against the customary interpretation of the role of the Shang centre, in which no politico-cultural distinction is made between the two cities. As soon as the oracular records excavated at Hsiao-t'un were identified as Shang royal archives, the site was designated the capital of the dynasty, a status which the splendour of its buildings and sacrifice pits confirmed. But it is difficult to avoid the conclusion that occupation at Chengchou must have continued to the end of the Shang dynasty, for if not the very site of this Shang city, at least one in its vicinity has always been indispensable to the ruler of the central plain, and the modern city at the place can be traced back before the Han period. If a walled city continued as an important bastion of Shang rule, the settlements at Hsiao-t'un must have had another function, and its remains point abundantly to a ceremonial and political role. There are signs among the objects excavated at and around Hsiao-t'un of contacts with the Shensi uplands and with faraway south Siberia (both notably connected with the chariots and their drivers), such as have not yet come to light at Chengchou. These are indications of influences drawn in upon the Shang city, rather than of influence which has radiated outwards. But such is not the present Chinese view, or rather it should be said that such implications of the excavated

material are not commented on. Moreover the artistic styles of the ritual bronze vessels associated with the two Shang cities are distinct, pointing to difference of local tradition, in the case of Hsiao-t'un a local tradition much developed and enhanced by the demands which the ceremonial in which the vessels were employed placed upon the artists and bronze-casters who produced them. Thus Chinese reluctance to consider incoming influence upon their high culture is matched by indifference to influence which proceeded outwards from Shang beyond the frontiers to Siberia – an influence which on one view of the facts would be responsible for conveying a form of socketed axe, a Chinese invention treated in Hsiao-t'un style, into the Zabaikalye and on to the Ural region.

To dwell on the achievements of post–1949 archaeology in the People's Republic would be to call the roll of several hundred excavated sites of all periods which have at last provided a framework of typology and dating permitting a satisfactory classification of Han and earlier material. The discoveries presented to attract tourist attention and most bruited in the press – the Manch'eng tomb with its princely treasure of the late second century BC, the Ma Wang Tui with the almost perfectly preserved corpse and abundant grave goods of a noble lady of a slightly earlier time, the life-size clay soldiers and horses from one of the ceremonial pits at an approach to the tomb of the first Ch'in emperor – are not necessarily those most useful in providing wider means of historical interpretation. The survey of the contents of some thirty-five tombs in the Chung-chou-lu district near to Loyang is unsensational but yet the very grist to the archaeologist's mill, and this work is typical of much enterprise. One gains the impression of a strict control of resources: regional surveys take precedence over, for example, the exploitation of the myriad Han tombs whose locations are known; sites are chosen for complete excavation where the results are most telling, as recently in the case of P'an-lung-ch'eng in Hupei, where a large foundation permits the reconstruction of a large building comparable to the great hall at Hsiao-t'un; or the tomb at Ch'i-shan in Shensi where a north-western sequel to Shang culture is well illustrated. All of this is credited to the growth of central power and the expansion of the culture of the men of Han. A site where the centralist philosophy and the claims of provincial independence clash most significantly is the necropolis of the kings of the Yunan state of Tien, on a hillock near to the shore of the Kunming lake. A palpable dynastic fiction recorded by the Han historian explains the singularly flourishing culture of this small state to the fact that a Chinese army, cut off from retreat, had settled there in the fourth century BC. In fact the

Chinese connection, where it exists apart from a few obvious contemporary imports, requires complex explanation, for in Yunan west-China weapon-forms of the eighth century BC still survived in use six centuries later, while the animal sculpture and *genre* village scenes cast in bronze on a small scale introduce us to an aesthetic and a technique utterly different from those of the men of Han, akin rather to the Central Asian animal style and of a quality unsurpassed in the Chinese metropolitan tradition. This site near Kunming lake, excavated in 1955–60 and lavishly published a short time afterwards, provides a new point of departure for the understanding of the entire Bronze Age of South-East Asia, the so-called Dongson culture. Among other things it resolves the problem of the date, origin and further cultural context of the earliest class of the celebrated bronze drums of South-East Asia which had sorely puzzled students since they were made known to the west at the beginning of the present century. It is a measure of the hysteria created by the notorious Gang of Four and attaching no less to archaeological interpretation than to forms of expressive art, that the author of this review was declared, verbally, an 'enemy of the Chinese people' for having, on one count, quoted the Han historian on the independent character of the Tien culture and people.

The many regional surveys have made clear the areas in which future work will be specially revealing. Sinkiang is among the most important of these, and here evidence already appears for a tradition of bronze metallurgy distinct from that of the central plain. The question of metallurgical origins remains in abeyance: while it is proven that bronze-casting methods in the metropolitan region are of independent growth, it is possible that bronze technology in Sinkiang may prove to be allied to that of western Turkestan. Owing to the sparseness of remains the prehistoric and Bronze Age cultures of Inner Mongolia are still ill-defined, and the enclaves of microlithic tradition which characterize the Neolithic of Shansi and Hopei and distinguish it from the Yangshao/Lungshan of the central plain and the east coast await further investigation. But the dimmest part of the prehistoric map is the region of the middle Yangtze and all the territory to the south. The concept of a 'south-eastern Neolithic' formulated soon after the beginning of modern research has been little elaborated, and it remains uncertain how far the spread of Neolithic techniques in the trans-Yangtze zone is to be associated with food production. On the other hand, the results of excavation in the south illustrate the advance to the southern seaboard of the techniques and art of the metropolitan Han culture, furnishing a further chapter of the diffusionist account, although little can be said of the

cultures which this advance of unified Chinese tradition superseded. There are indications that the earliest bronze products of the southern zone link with those of South-East Asia as part of the conglomerate termed Dongson culture. The Chinese contribution to the latter becomes more apparent.

The most superficial observer of the results of Chinese archaeological work in the last thirty years is acquainted with some spectacular sites, more and more of which are now being included in a tourists' circuit. Among the grandiose tombs are those of the Princess Yong-t'ai and of Prince Yi-tê, constructed in the first decade of the eighth century AD. Here the mural painting and the abundant funerary figurines throw light on the realistic sculpture and painting of the T'ang period, much as the figure drawing and perspective treatment of later Han painting is recorded on the engraved stone gateways and pillars of the Yi-nan tomb in Shantung. The Buddhist cave-temples at Yunkang and Lungmen, and now those at Tunhuang in the far western tip of Kansu, near to the beginning of the Silk Route, are accessible to tourists, well repaired and maintained. Unfortunately other Buddhist antiquities are less well protected, and these monuments perhaps most of all suffered from the vandalism of the Cultural Revolution. In reshaping Peking some temples have unhappily been demolished, along with large sections of the palace wall, and the precincts of the imperial altars annexed to the palace have been put to other uses. Inevitably the impact of modern development on urban antiquities has been particularly sudden in China, and in a country where existing cities have occupied their sites for millennia excavation on key economic sites has generally been more hampered than at equivalent places in Europe and in Mediterranean lands. But progress in archaeological research in China is to be measured not in terms of the fortunes of rescue digging or the questionable wisdom of the immensely expensive conservation of spectacular excavated sites (Pan-p'o and the Gate Guard of the Ch'in emperor), but judged rather by the success of systematic recording, the steady stream of publication, and the increasing application of scientific method. Only since 1949 has prehistoric and early historic China been placed on the world-wide archaeological map.

Bibliography

Literature in western languages on the pre-Han archaeology of China is limited, particularly regarding the theory which has guided research and interpretation.

Some of the following are comprehensive accounts, in English or Chinese, of work completed after 1949. The most accessible review of the periodical literature is to be found in the bibliography to the exhibits of the Burlington House exhibition of 1973–4, included in the catalogue, *The Genius of China*.

INSTITUTE OF ARCHAEOLOGY, PEKING 1962 *Archaeology in New China* (Hsin Chung-kuo ti k'ao-ku shou-huo).

1959 *Collected Archaeological Essays of Liang SSǔ-yung* (Liang SSǔ-yung k'ao-ku lun-wen-chi).

CHENG TE-KUN 1959–63 *Archaeology in China* vols I-III, Cambridge.

LI CHI 1977 *Anyang*, Washington.

1957 *The Beginnings of Chinese Civilization*, Seattle.

WATSON W. 1966 *China before the Han Dynasty*, London and New York.

1971 *Cultural Frontiers in Ancient East Asia*, Edinburgh.

1979 'The City in Ancient China' in P.R.S.Moorey, (ed.) *The Origins of Civilization*, Oxford.

WEN-WU CH'U-PAN-SHÊ ('Cultural Publishers') 1979 *Thirty Years of Archaeological Work* (Wen-wu k'ao-ku kung-tso san-shih-nien) Peking.

WU, G.D. 1938 *Prehistoric Pottery in China*, London.

PART II : RUDE STONE MONUMENTS IN EUROPE

9 Introduction: The Megalith Builders of Western Europe

Colin Renfrew

And I remember after dinner walking down to the great Carnac alignments and in the moonlight wandering along those miles of serried, large stones, their dark shadows a reminder of their darker past and our ignorance of their makers and builders. For me that was a great and personal moment, and I knew then what I know even better now: that these megalithic monuments of western Europe would exercise an irresistible fascination for me for ever. . . . The past was alive. It was no archaeological manifestation which specialist scholars could study and argue about. It was something real which everyone could understand or try to understand, something which was the beginning of their own cultural past in western Europe.

Glyn Daniel (1963, 25–6)

IN THESE words, taken from that most admirable archaeological *vade mecum*, *The Hungry Archaeologist in France*, and in the introduction to his less personal yet more systematic volume *The Prehistoric Chamber Tombs of France*, the author of *The Megalith Builders of Western Europe* described the undergraduate holiday in 1934 which made him for life 'an *aficionado* of megaliths'. They convey some of the enthusiasm and of the keen sense of problem, as well as the Celtic eloquence with which generations of undergraduates at Cambridge have been introduced to this subject. No-one who has read archaeology at Cambridge over the past forty years or who has seen the television programmes which he has done so much to encourage can altogether have escaped its fascination, as a number of the succeeding chapters reflect. I count myself fortunate to have first visited those Carnac alignments and the other great monuments of the Morbihan in the company of Glyn and Ruth, together with a number of his students and of my own.

Interpretations may change, and chronologies, but the attraction of these structures, which we may recognize not only as 'the first surviving architectural monuments in north-western Europe' (Daniel 1958, 13) but of the world, does not diminish. It is appropriate, then, that as a tribute to the scholar who has contributed so much to their understanding, and to the teacher who has consistently promoted an aware-

ness of their problems, we should review the *status quaestionis* as it rests today, some four decades after his first substantial contribution to the subject. Succeeding chapters will take a regional approach – as is entirely necessary, since we all now realize that the megaliths were not a unitary phenomenon, and that the very use of the term 'megalith' to class together such a disparate variety of monuments, of several independent origins, is to impose a classification which owes more to our own assumptions than to any inherent unity in the material. Yet to adopt a cross-cultural approach is very much in harmony with current archaeological thought – to compare phenomena which appear to us as similar, irrespective of limitations of space and time, and to look for broader regularities of culture process. Surely there can be little doubt that these megalithic constructions, however independent their origins may be, *do* strike the eyes of the modern observer as in some ways similar? This, I shall argue, is because they fulfilled a similar function, or many of them did, as territorial markers of segmentary societies. So indeed did some of the comparable monuments in other parts of the world – in Polynesia, for instance, as well perhaps as some of those of India or Japan – which earlier generations of scholars sometimes linked together with those in the West as part of a unitary phenomenon, sharing a common origin, just as they did the monuments of western Europe until the past decade.

This shift in opinion, which owes much to the development of radiocarbon dating and its tree-ring calibration, need not be surveyed in detail here. It is admirably reviewed in successive editorials in *Antiquity*, the one international journal (other than *Radiocarbon* itself) which from the outset showed an acute awareness of the problems and results of radiocarbon dating, and their bearing upon the prehistory of Europe, including the stone monuments. I well remember, in the early 1960s, the Editor in his gown, entering the lecture room in Downing Street, on many an occasion clutching a letter from some eminent European scholar, and proclaiming the latest radiocarbon date with all the triumph (or sometimes the consternation) with which others might announce the racing results from Newmarket. Their significance was debated at many a supervision, sometimes over a restoring glass of Muscadet.

The now traditional view, which owed much to the 'modified diffusionism' (Daniel 1962, 95) of Gordon Childe, was set out afresh, with several useful insights in 'The Dual Nature of the Megalithic Colonisation of Europe' (Daniel 1941), and reviewed more comprehensively in *The Megalith Builders of Western Europe* (Daniel 1958). In one of the earliest considerations of the impact of radiocarbon dating upon the whole scene, 'Northmen and Southmen' (Daniel 1967), the alternative case was argued for the independent development of the monuments in several areas 'due to the separate traditions of the Northmen and the Southmen in the fourth and third millennia BC'. The new, independent view has recently been stated still more trenchantly (Daniel 1978):

> It should now be clear to all serious and unbiased students of megaliths that these structures of great stones came into existence in many separate societies: Malta, the toe of Italy, Bulgaria, Almeria, the Algarve of Portugal, Brittany, the northern European plain of NW Germany and Denmark, southern Britain and Scotland. Whether to these nine areas we should add Ireland is a matter for discussion.

These regions, with the exception of Bulgaria, are indicated in ill. 1, drawn by Ruth Daniel (Daniel 1958, 26), a map which today serves to illustrate the variety and the inhomogeneity of the megalithic phenomenon in Europe as elegantly as it once suggested their unity and affinity.

There is little more that need be said at a general level about their origin. I have recently set out one outline explanation (Renfrew 1976), and the authors of the chapters which follow have their own views and arguments for each region in turn. Instead I wish to turn to the inferences about society which we may hope to make on the basis of a study of the megaliths. It is my belief that some more coherent theoretical base is required for this purpose than has yet been propounded. In approaching these remaining indicators of Neolithic activity in north-western Europe there are assumptions which have to be made, and which I think are justifiable.

The first is that the construction of these monuments represents *a serious, coherent, indeed patterned activity*. We may not know the precise motivation of their builders, or have direct insight into the content of their beliefs. But that does not condemn us to regard them as irrational, eccentric, unpredictable manifestations by some manic sect: in the words of the Revd George Barry (1805, 102) writing of the chamber tombs of Orkney, 'inflamed almost to madness by the peculiar genius of their religion'.

1 *Distribution of the megalithic tombs of Europe, drawn by Ruth Daniel.*

The evidence is clear that many of them relate to the disposal of the dead, but we need not assume that this was their primary purpose. One can, if one wishes, dispose very readily of the dead without building great tombs for them. We need not assume that they all had the same purpose, or functioned in the same way. If the megaliths do not represent a unitary phenomenon, they can hardly be approached with a single, specific explanation.

Monuments in Space

A convenient initial approach is a spatial one. It need not involve any very elaborate locational analysis, but does require the consideration of the way in which various kinds of activity take place in space.

It is a commonplace in archaeology today to adopt a systems approach, and for heuristic reasons to speak of different subsystems of the culture system. One may consider the spatial patterning of different kinds of activity in a rather similar way. In that sense it can be meaningful to speak of *ritual space* – referring to the way people divide up the countryside as far as ritual and symbolic categories are concerned, and the manner in which they use space for ritual activities. *Locality space* simply refers to the everyday spatial behaviour of the inhabitants of a particular locality, conceived as the minimum settlement unit, be it homestead or village. *Kinship space* implies a two-dimensional map of the kin-relationships of the individual, which is clearly crucially determined by residence rules. *Political space* maps territorial aspects of the exercise of power. *Burial space*, with which we shall be particularly concerned, reflects spatial aspects of the burial process, relating place of life to place of death and place of burial in a structured way.

To consider such things in spatial terms is not at all to imply that they are spatially *defined*. The formal group, which is generally both the effective reproductive unit and the effective local political unit, may well be defined in kinship terms. But it will still have a territorial behaviour. In some cases, particularly when sedentary agriculture is practised, the local group – that is to say the people who occupy a given tract of land or locality – is effectively much the same as the formal group.

Langness, quoted by Brookfield and Hart (1971, 230–2), has examined the intersection of 'local' and 'formal' groups in the East New Guinea highlands, and found a high degree of overlap. Moreover he has suggested that the ideology of patrilineal descent there, patrilocal residence and group exogamy, is a cognitive model, conceived by the community, an *a posteriori* explanation of a reality in which the sheer *fact* of residence in a locality can determine so-called 'kinship'.

As an example of a particular and perhaps special kind of patterning in burial space, one may take the famous case of the Merina of Madagascar, as described by Maurice Bloch (1971). The Merina, however far they live from the old, traditional heartland of their country, the Imerina, trace back their descent to ancestors originally resident there in localities which they call *tanindrazana* – which one might translate roughly as 'old ancestral home'. They join in the maintenance of communal tombs in this place. On death they are first usually buried locally, where they lived, for a short space of time. Then at a ceremony at least two years afterwards, the *famadihana*, the remains are, with great expense and with the participation of a wide group of kinsfolk, and many guests, solemnly translated to the family tomb. This is an interesting example, not because it offers a supposed 'parallel' for any specific archaeological case, but because it exemplifies the potential difference between life space and burial space in some communities.

In working back from the archaeological remains, there are of course many difficulties, often hard to foresee. For instance, among the LoWiili of the Voltaic-speaking peoples of the Niger area, the actual burial of the dead is not carried out by the close kinsmen of the deceased, but by immediate neighbours who must not be members of the same lineage as the dead (Goody 1967, 100). These complementary funeral groups are usually patrilineages. Burial is generally in the courtyard of the deceased's home (*idem*, 92). The archaeologist must accept the likelihood of various counter-intuitive patternings of this kind. But the behaviour *is* nonetheless patterned – and in this case the spatial outcome is not altered.

Settlement and Burial

One further point which we need to consider in the case of many of the European monuments, is the lack of settlement remains. Only occasionally, for instance in the admirably thorough researches by Strömberg (1971) at Hagestad in Skåne, have settlements associated with megalithic tombs been adequately documented. In many cases they have not been found because they were scanty, and in particular because settlement was dispersed, in scattered household units, rather than aggregated in villages, as reflected in the tell communities of south-east Europe or the villages of the LBK people. Marshall Sahlins has remarked that 'Maximum dispersion is the settlement pattern of the state of nature' (Sahlins 1972, 97).

The choice between aggregation and dispersion is not a casual one. As Brookfield and Hart (1971, 226) noted:

> Why should people tolerate distance when they can virtually eliminate it by living in scattered and if need be mobile homesteads. People aggregate because there are advantages in so doing, whether for common work, co-ordination of efforts in the raising of prestations, in defence, or for the company and social security enjoyed in a group. Such benefits will increase up to a certain group size, but in the absence of division and specialisation of labour will not continue to increase in direct proportion to growing group size. If we can conceive of a 'curve of benefits' arising from aggregation, the point at which this curve peaks represents optimal group size. If while still rising it intersects a curve expressing toleration of distance, the intersection will represent a sub-optimal maximum size.

Thus the documentation of a dispersed settlement pattern, if we can document it, will tell us not only something of the organization of society, but by implication the constraints operating on it, which are in part ecological and in part related to the way the land is exploited. We are at once introduced into a consideration of environmental questions, and of agricultural intensification. Let us now look at some hypothetical arrangements indicative of life space (locality space) and death space (burial space), which cover a number of relevant possibilities. These are set out in ill. 2.

The first (ill. 2, 1a) is the case of an aggregated village settlement with a dispersed burial pattern. (If we were concerned with ritual space, the crosses could indicate shrines or other ritual foci.) One possible example is given by late medieval churches in Greece, for instance in the Greek islands. In some instances settlement is nucleated, in villages, yet the lands of individual families are often accompanied by a small church, effectively a rural family chapel, in which the dead were traditionally buried. This may be a case, like the Merina one, where a former locality space (in this case a former pattern of dispersed settlement) is formalized and retained in ritual or burial space, while a new locality space (centred on the village settlement) is established. It may be that such ritual lag is a very common phenomenon, which we must expect to see often in burial arrangements.

This case of the village with its own accompanying cemetery (ill. 2, 1b) is very much more frequent, pertaining probably to the majority of farming villages both today and in the past. The cemetery can occasionally contain monumental tombs, sometimes for family use. This is perhaps the explanation of the chambered tombs comprising the cemetery in the small fortified township of Los Millares in Spain.

In some cases (ill. 2, 1c) the village has a single, communal tomb. An archaeological example may be offered by the tombs of Mesara in Crete (although sometimes these come in pairs). It has, however, also been suggested that in some cases they served an essentially dispersed settlement pattern.

Intramural burial within village settlement (ill. 2, 1d) is rarely monumental, and is sometimes restricted to children. The Early Neolithic village of Nea Nikomedeia in northern Greece offers a well-known example.

A similar, if perhaps somewhat arbitrary division may be made out for the various spatial modes of burial associated with dispersed settlement. The first is dispersed burial (ill. 2, 2a), where the burial facility is adjacent to the homestead, or at least to the land cultivated. This is exemplified by the custom in some Polynesian islands, for instance the Tuamotus, and some of the smaller marae of Tahiti.

Cemeteries are not, of course, restricted to nucleated populations, and can accompany a dispersed

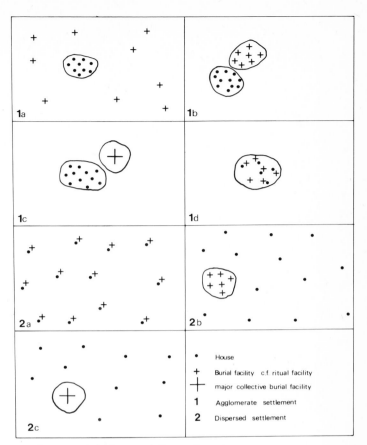

2 Life space and death space: different relationships between settlement pattern and the location of burial facilities.

pattern of settlement (ill. 2, 2b). The cemeteries of many mobile communities are comparable here, for instance the barrow cemeteries of some Iron Age groups in eastern Europe, as well, perhaps, as some of the Bronze Age barrow cemeteries of Europe.

Communal burial within a single burial facility is also logically possible for the dispersed population of a region (ill. 2, 2c). This seems to have been the practice at the larger image ahus of Easter Island. It is tempting also to suggest that the great hypogeum of Hal Saflieni in Malta represents a pattern of this kind.

This treatment of the possible conjunctions of settlement pattern and burial practice leads naturally to the consideration of the circumstances in which a given burial configuration may imply a specific settlement pattern. In particular in what circumstances does a dispersed pattern of monumental tombs reasonably imply dispersed settlement, a configuration approximating to that of pattern 2a, and the existence of what may be termed a segmentary society?

Segmentary societies (Renfrew 1976, 205) 'are small-scale societies, and frequently non-literate. In particular, they display segmentary organization, which implies the repetition of equivalent groups. They are cellular and modular: cellular in that the groups are clearly defined and operate in many ways independently, and modular in that they are of approximately the same size. The segments are autonomous, economically and politically, and usually number between 50 and 500 persons. In segmentary societies the primary functioning unit – normally a residential unit, whether a village or an association of dispersed houses – is the primary segment, a self-sustaining perpetual body, exercising social control over its productive resources.'

This definition as it stands is a very general one but, if it can be shown to be appropriate in a particular archaeological case, it can certainly be informative. It can lead to inferences about the social organization in question, some of which may be opened to testing by other categories of evidence.

When confronted by a dispersed pattern of burial, as so often is the case for megalithic monuments, it is clearly relevant to ask at once whether the settlement pattern may be an agglomerate one (pattern 1a). One is therefore led to look for village settlement. Its absence may carry some of the dangers of negative evidence, yet an intensive field survey of the local region should, in the absence of pronounced geomorphological change, be capable of documenting the presence or, it is hoped, absence of nucleated villages.

Secondly, the term segmentary society is only appropriate when the groups in question are not subordinate parts of an effective and larger unity. It is

3 Socio-spatial hierarchy in Neolithic Wessex. Henges replaced causewayed camps in the Late Neolithic period, c.2500 BC.

therefore relevant to search for a hierarchy, which in this case will presumably be revealed, if at all, in the burial monuments themselves. Inevitably some will be larger than others. One appropriate procedure, in the absence of rich grave goods, is to calculate the approximate man-hour input required to construct the monument. If a real hierarchy of monuments exists, the levels in the hierarchy may be expected to differ by a factor of about 10 in their labour requirement in man-hours. An order of magnitude difference of this kind may well reflect a real, social hierarchy, while a difference by a factor of only 2 is less impressive or persuasive.

Such a hierarchy may be argued for the Neolithic field monuments of southern Britain (ill. 3; see Renfrew 1973), where the long barrows represent a labour investment of some 10^4 man-hours, the causewayed camps 10^5 man-hours, the great henges 10^6 man-hours, and the two prime monuments – Stonehenge and Silbury Hill – an investment well in excess of 10^7 man-hours.

The analysis so far is not a rigorous one. Nor have we yet formulated precise spatial criteria for recognizing *dispersed* monuments. Of course, they do not have to be regularly dispersed, in a lattice. There may be cases where two or three are together. But evidently they should not show close bunching.

There is, however, an independent test of these ideas, in terms of the availability (to the territories defined by the dispersal of the monuments) of resources adequate for survival, especially arable land. A dispersed pattern of monuments in mountain highlands might have very different connotations. The distribution of megalithic cairns in the Scottish island of Arran, in relation to arable land, is a case in point. Considered in their own right in the light of the foregoing discussion, they might well be taken as suggesting a segmentary society in Neolithic times. The presence of a convenient area of arable land within the territory of nearly every cairn, as simply if rather crudely defined by the construction of Thiessen poly-

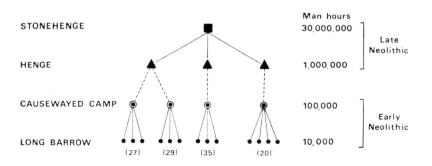

gons (ill. 4) constitutes a positive response to the test.

A thorough consideration of the relation between burial and settlement along the lines indicated could doubtless lead to a series of inferences and alternatives, which particular burial arrangements might offer concerning the social structure of the parent populations. One such is certainly, as argued above, the *hypothesis* that a dispersed pattern of monumental tombs, in the absence of agglomerate settlement, would lead to the inference of a segmentary society, as defined earlier. An independent test of the hypothesis is suggested in terms of the land use potential of the different territories, defined on the basis of the distribution of monuments.

4 Distribution of the chambered cairns of Arran, with notional territorial divisions indicated by means of Thiessen polygons, and with modern arable land shown by stippling. (Contours at 100 m intervals.)

Orkney and the Boyne

The megalithic tombs of two areas of Europe have recently been investigated in a manner relevant to our discussion. The first is Orkney, at the extreme north of the British Isles, where the great concentration of chambered cairns has for long excited the attention of scholars. I had the privilege of directing there a programme of researches, of which the main activity was the excavation of the chambered cairn at Quanterness. The distribution of such monuments in the Orkney islands in general leads to the hypothesis set out above. Only the celebrated monument of Maes Howe, together with the two henge monuments with their stone circles, the Ring of Brogar and the Stones of Stenness, represent a substantially greater input of man-hours, suggesting the possible inference that a hierarchy in scale of monument may here reflect some hierarchy within the society.

One important result of the project was to demonstrate through radiocarbon dating that Maes Howe was probably constructed some centuries after Quanterness. Moreover the radiocarbon dates obtained by Dr Graham Ritchie for the Stones of Stenness during his excavations there suggest that both that monument and the Ring of Brogar are the contemporaries of Maes Howe, and thus later than Quanterness and its sister cairns. During the period of the construction of Quanterness and its earlier use, there is no evidence to suggest a hierarchy of monuments, such as becomes apparent later.

The other important result at Quanterness, within the context of the present discussion, was the recovery of much human skeletal material, which permitted an estimate of the size of the group served by the tomb. This lent valuable confirmation to the original hypothesis. Further details of the project are available in the final report. Here it may be sufficient simply to set out the summary of conclusions as reached there (Renfrew 1979, 218–19):

1. At the time of its early use the cairn at Quanterness was not stratified in a hierarchy above or below monuments of different scale.
2. Quanterness was an equal access tomb, with balanced representation of both sexes and all ages (despite a low average age).
3. No prominent ranking is indicated among the tomb occupants, either by disparity in grave goods or difference in funerary practice (although three grave inhumations were noted).
4. Elaborate burial practices were documented; inhumation within the chambered cairn was among the last stages in the treatment of the deceased.
5. The chamber was in use for at least five centuries.
6. The size of the group using the cairn may have been of the order of twenty.
7. The labour required for the construction of the monument, about 10,000 man-hours, could without difficulty have been invested in the space of just a few years by such a group, perhaps with the assistance of neighbouring groups.
8. Quanterness is just one of a number of similar Orcadian cairns of comparable scale.
9. The distribution of these cairns is fairly dispersed, suggesting that the corporate group using each was largely a locality group, although it could at the same time have been formally organized as a descent group.
10. A subsistence base of mixed farming is inferred (although reference to the settlement site at Skara Brae is necessary to document the cereal component), with the exploitation of game (deer – not necessarily wild), birds and fish.
11. Vegetation was open and treeless, and the environment much like that of today (with little geomorphic change).
12. Late in the period in question just a few monuments of larger scale were constructed in a single central area, implying the emergence of some form of centralized organization.

The conclusion therefore is that the data from Quanterness do firmly support the notion of a segmentary society in Orkney at this time. The development late in the Neolithic of monuments of greater scale, suggesting a measure of centrality, is interesting in view of the comparable pattern of development in southern Britain.

It is interesting to compare the development towards a more centralized society in Orkney and in Wessex with the somewhat different pattern in Ireland demonstrated by Darvill (1979). He has shown graphically (ill. 5) how the court cairns represent a dispersed pattern, while the passage graves show a marked tendency to congregate in groups. He argues that in general the court cairns represent an earlier stage in Ireland than the passage graves, although with some evidence for a chronological overlap. In terms of the model developed above, the court cairns would represent pattern 2a of ill. 2, while the passage graves would represent pattern 2b. The court cairns may perhaps be interpreted as the territorial markers of segmentary societies, within the perspective adopted here. But just as in the case of the unchambered long barrows of Wessex, this need not imply that all the dead were ultimately deposited there: the scarcity or lack of human bones reported from them suggest the contrary. At Quanterness, on the other hand, there is the clear suggestion that the entire group was destined for deposition in the tomb, although the process of excarnation after death has resulted in the loss of much skeletal material.

On the other hand, the passage graves of Ireland show an altogether different pattern, well exemplified by the most famous of the cemeteries, on the Boyne River. For here the development did not lead to just

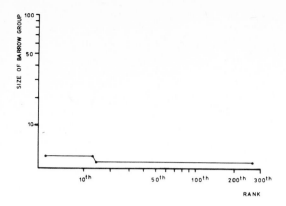 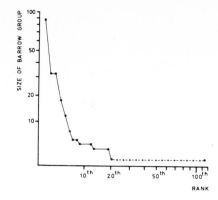

5 *Dispersed versus agglomerate distribution: rank-size plots for clusters of court cairns (left) and passage graves (right) in Ireland. Monuments are said to cluster if they lie within 800 m of each other. (From Darvill 1979.)*

one or two major monuments, analogous with Brogar/Stenness or Stonehenge/Silbury, but to a concentration of no fewer than 32 tombs, a figure itself surpassed by the 89 passage graves at the Carrowmore cemetery.

The Boyne case therefore exemplifies something very different from the Orkney one. In a certain, objective sense it may be seen as the formation of a 'hierarchy', but let it be stressed that the implications of a 'hierarchy' in terms of funerary monuments in this way is something whose social correlates remain to be explored.

Clearly a single 'collective' tomb – and by collective in this case we mean for multiple burials, occurring successively over a long time period – does of itself *define* a social group, in the strict objective sense of those persons who are buried within it. Behind it must lie a *real* social group, in the sense of a community or lineage or whatever, of persons – some corporate body, whose membership is a necessary criterion for burial in the tomb, although not necessarily a sufficient one.

A cemetery of such tombs, whether at Los Millares or the Boyne, is therefore a group of groups – that is where the objective hierarchy comes in. At Los Millares that might mean simply an agglomerate settlement whose population may be divided into a number of burial groups, which may in fact represent lineages. An Irish passage grave cemetery, where there is no corresponding agglomerate settlement, must again, in the larger sense, represent a burial group – those persons who were buried there. Behind that lies a corporate body, whose membership is presumably a necessary criterion for burial in the cemetery.

Such burial is therefore tribal behaviour, if we may use the term 'tribe' in this loose way. But already the emergence of a centre – for surely the cemetery is at least in ritual and burial terms a centre – hints at something beyond the symmetrical and mechanical solidarity of the tribe. It is the essence of a chiefdom society

that it is centred, asymmetrical, and has some elements of organic solidarity. The emergence of a centre is one criterion here, although another is that of personal ranking, which has not been established in this analysis, although it could be for the Boyne cemetery. Other criteria include the mobilization of manpower, as reflected in southern England by Stonehenge, Silbury Hill etc., and to a lesser extent by the Ring of Brogar. The Irish passage grave cemeteries thus hint at some measure of group, of centralization, in the society of the time.

The simple demonstration of a 'group of groups' (although a hierarchy in the strict spatial sense) does not, however, of itself document or even suggest a hierarchy of persons. Nor has any systematic study yet been undertaken of the scale of monuments (in man-hour terms) *within* an Irish passage grave cemetery. So to speak of a chiefdom in the Irish case would appear premature – even if the term be accepted for the Wessex of Stonehenge or for the Orkney of the Ring of Brogar and Maes Howe. The Irish passage grave cemeteries appear to document a different and distinctive configuration, pattern 2b of ill. 2. That is a feature of particular interest.

I would like finally to return to the dispersed settlement pattern which is sometimes implied by the dispersed burial pattern with which we began. Why does this burial pattern occur? Art Saxe (1970, 119) was the first archaeologist to offer a coherent answer:

To the degree that corporate group rights to use and/or control critical but restricted resources are

79

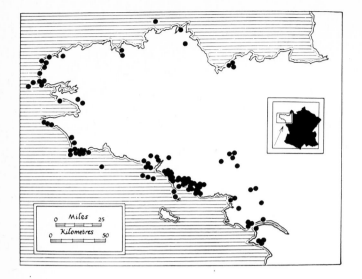

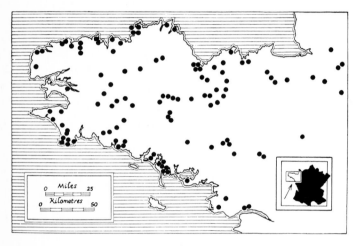

6 Contrasting distributions of the passage graves (above) and allées couvertes (below) of Brittany, drawn by Ruth Daniel. (From Daniel 1960.)

attained and/or legitimised by means of lineal descent from the dead (i.e. lineal ties to ancestors), such groups will maintain formal disposal areas for the exclusive disposal of their dead and conversely.

Here 'formal disposal areas' for the dead are implicitly linked with lineal descent groups. We have seen earlier that this is not a necessary linkage, but it is a frequent and a plausible one. Saxe goes on to equate the use of such formal disposal areas with the control, by such lineages, of crucial but restricted resources, of which

the most obvious is arable land. Grahame Clark in a recent paper (1977) has drawn attention to a different resource, notably in Bohuslan in western Sweden, where the rationale of the pattern may be access to maritime resources. This may well be a non-arable instance of the phenomenon Saxe describes.

Chapman (in press) has recently examined this notion for prehistoric burial in Europe as a whole – naturally including non-megalithic cemeteries within his scope – and finds that it works well. In general, for instance, one does not expect swidden agriculturalists, for whom land itself is not the critical resource, to use formal disposal areas in this way.

The question as to why the formal disposal should be megalithic takes us further. I have already suggested (Renfrew 1976) that these monuments are intended as territorial markers, conspicuous signalling devices in relation to land, to territory, to the most frequent critical resource. This suggestion is in harmony with, although it goes beyond, Saxe's hypothesis. There may be sound demographic reasons why the resource in question – land – became critical first along the Atlantic façade.

There is room, of course, for much more work to follow up these ideas. But if their general drift is accepted, we have a new insight into an important period of European prehistory. The Neolithic of western Europe, far from being extremely poor in settlement data, is seen instead as exceptionally rich in information bearing upon land use, settlement pattern and population. For while it remains true that preserved domestic, residential structures are in general rare, and likely to remain so, the chambered tombs – under the conditions which we have discussed – offer us as comprehensive a pattern of settlement data as we can expect to obtain from prehistoric times. The signalling devices were built to last, and in many cases they continue to signal.

A whole series of survey techniques has recently been developed or adapted to archaeology, some of them springing from the initial insights of the 'site catchment analysis' of Eric Higgs and Claudio Vita-Finzi. Now of course burial facilities are not residential sites, and the same locational constraints do not hold between tomb and field as between homestead and field. But while the relationship may not be direct or invariable, there is reason to suggest, as stressed in the assumption made at the outset, that it is patterned.

Much work remains to be done, indeed it is only beginning, with the detailed surveys like those in Arran by Roger Mercer, and in Rousay by my colleague the geomorphologist Donald Davidson. Environmental variables have to be taken into account. I forecast, however, that the megaliths will be found to be capable of revealing to us some of the best archaeologically documented segmentary societies of any period anywhere in the world.

Chronological problems will persist, whenever spatial distributions are studied, until the far-off day when every monument under consideration can securely be dated by means of radiocarbon. Yet already the broad sequences now available open up new perspectives in terms both of land use and social organization. Ruth Daniel's elegant maps (ill. 6) contrasting the distributions of the Breton passage graves and the *allées couvertes* (Daniel 1960) can be seen in this way, in the light of the useful ascription by Giot and L'Helgouach (1979, 172 and 293) of the former to the earlier fourth millennium BC, and the latter to the third millennium BC. The Breton passage graves no longer document, by their coastal distribution, the path of some colonists from Iberia: their pattern of location has, on the contrary, much to teach us of the economy

of their builders, as well as of their society. The inland distribution of the *allées couvertes* testifies, among other things, to the wider distribution of agricultural practice in the Armorica Peninsula at the later time.

The archaeological potential of these remarkable structures is far from exhausted, and each generation of archaeologists will no doubt find new ways of looking at them, and obtain fresh insights from them. The young traveller of today would do well to heed the sage advice of that young Celtic traveller of forty-seven years ago, who has since done so much to encourage and stimulate their study (Daniel 1963, 187):

> But wherever your last meal in France, take back with you the memory of the great painted caves and the great megaliths – archaeological vestiges of a time when France was young, when Western Europe was young, and when neither Frank nor Anglo-Saxon had been heard of.

Bibliography

BARRY, G. 1805 *History of the Orkney Islands*, Edinburgh.

BLOCH, M. 1971 *Placing the Dead*, London.

BROOKFIELD, H. C. and Hart, D 1971 *Melanesia, a Geographical Interpretation of an Island World*, London.

CHAPMAN, R. W. (in press) 'Emergence of formal disposal areas and the "problem" of megalithic tombs in prehistoric Europe', in Chapman, R. W. (ed.), *The Archaeology of Death*, Cambridge (forthcoming).

CLARK, J. G. D. 1977 'The economic context of dolmens and passage-graves in Sweden', in Markotić, V. (ed.), *Ancient Europe and the Mediterranean, Studies Presented in Honour of Hugh Hencken*, Warminster, 35–49.

DANIEL, G. E. 1941 'The dual nature of the megalithic colonisation of Europe', *Proc. Preh. Soc.* VII, 1–49.

1958 *The Megalith Builders of Western Europe*, London.

1960 *The Prehistoric Chamber Tombs of France*, London.

1962 *The Idea of Prehistory*, London.

1963 *The Hungry Archaeologist in France*, London.

1967 'Northmen and Southmen', *Antiquity* XLI, 313–17.

1978 Review of S. J. De Laet (ed.), *Acculturation and Continuity in Atlantic Europe: Papers Presented at the IVth Atlantic Colloquium*, in *Helinium* XVIII, 268–9.

DARVILL, T. C. 1979 'Court cairns, passage graves and social change in Ireland', *Man* XIV, 311–27.

FERGUSSON, J. 1872 *Rude Stone Monuments in all Countries: their Ages and Uses*, London.

GIOT, P-R., L'HELGOUACH, J. AND MONNIER, J-L. 1979 *Préhistoire de la Bretagne*, Rennes, Ouest-France.

GOODY, J. 1967 *The Social Organisation of the LoWiili*, Oxford.

RENFREW, C. 1973 'Monuments, mobilisation and social organisation in neolithic Wessex', in Renfrew, C. (ed.), *The Explanation of Culture Change: Models in Prehistory*, London, 539–58.

1976 'Megaliths, territories and populations', in De Laet, S. J. (ed.), *Acculturation and Continuity in Atlantic Europe, Papers Presented at the IVth Atlantic Colloquium*, Brugge, De Tempel, 198–220.

1979 *Investigations in Orkney*, Reports of the Research Committee of the Society of Antiquaries of London, 38, London.

SAHLINS, M. 1972 *Stone Age Economics*, Chicago.

SAXE, A. 1970 *Social Dimensions of Mortuary Practice* (Ph.D. Dissertation, University of Michigan) Ann Arbor, University Microfilms.

STRÖMBERG, M 1971 *Die Megalithgräber von Hagestad*, Acta Archaeologica Lundensia, ser.8,no.9, Lund, Gleerup.

10 The Megaliths of France

P.-R. Giot

ARCHAEOLOGISTS are usually aware of how artificial and risky it is to separate megaliths from their total cultural and chronological contexts. 'Rude Stone Monuments' do certainly present a few specific problems of their own, which can be studied in isolation, but there are great dangers in this. It provides scope for the 'lunatic fringe', who seem to be purveying their nonsenses ever more successfully around the world – even if some of them do from time to time have a brilliant idea or observe an interesting detail which had escaped the notice of the professionals. As they are a permanent nuisance to archaeologists, it is often difficult to give them due credit for the few ideas one owes them. Enough said; Professor Glyn Daniel, as a most distinguished editor of *Antiquity*, has had to fight many a fine battle against the lunatics and false druids.

Because most of us are drawn to those clearly visible piles of stone called megalithic monuments, we may be giving them – or those forms that have resisted destruction – undue importance. Conditions of conservation or preservation induce a differential destruction and can obliterate whole blocks of evidence. Perhaps archaeologists working in countries with no visible megaliths – or only a few, or unimportant ones – are spending their time more profitably in not getting involved in absorbing and exacting megalithic enquiries.

One great truth arises from recent excavations in France. Besides the most prominent types of megaliths and para-megalithic structures one has known about for a long time, there exist quite a range of other monuments, which appear nowadays to be unique or exceptional probably only because all the other examples have vanished. We are not even sure that the monuments we consider characteristic constitute an adequate sample of those built during their time, or even that they don't simply represent a collection of more durable chance survivals. At least we now know that beside them once stood an array of wooden or part-wooden-and-part-earthern structures which were perhaps just as important as – or more important than – the stone ones. Megaliths, like icebergs, may always have features or characteristics hidden from view.

Twenty years ago or so Professor Glyn Daniel wrote a book about the prehistoric chamber tombs of France. It gave a useful although sometimes partial summary of the evidence available up to the 1950s. It was, however, conceived and constructed in pre-radio-carbon days and for this reason did not have the impact which it might otherwise have deserved, nor of course could it anticipate the results (and the radiocarbon datings) which were to emerge from subsequent excavations in Brittany and elswhere (Daniel 1960). This was the time when the maximal contraction of the chronological concertina was in fashion and inevitably with its subsequent expansion, many concepts have had to be changed. This being said we should acknowledge how stimulating to further work was this summary statement of the position – even if the stimulation has sometimes been in reaction rather than in agreement.

Statistics and Surveys

Last century, people were very enthusiastic in France about the idea of counting for each *département* or province the total number of recorded monuments of different types, as if it were a competition, and on this basis they would produce elaborate density distribution maps. Counting the stones of alignments as menhirs and then adding the result to the dolmens could distort the statistics. Because of the amount of destruction, even with present information one should be very careful about utilizing these figures for districts which have been densely populated for a long time – subject to agricultural disturbance, urbanization, quarrying for building and road-making materials, or massive alterations in the Dark Ages.

Some recent detailed toponymic studies, such as those of B. Tanguy in Brittany (Tanguy 1976, 1979), have shown how numbers of presumed monuments may have left their names to fields, names recorded at the beginning of the last century in the original rolls. Districts without monuments today may have had nearly as many as other places less ravaged. Of course, in poorly populated areas such as the Causses plateaux of southern France one would not expect such devastation.

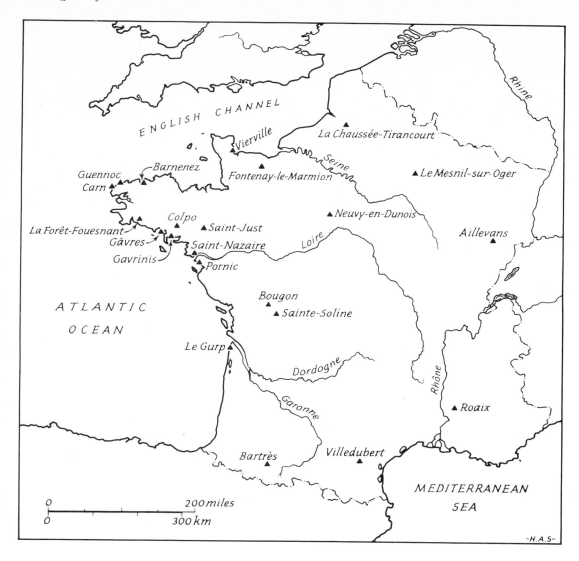

1 French sites and place-names mentioned in the text.

Megaliths, or any visible antiquities, are not popular with farmers practising modern methods of agronomy. One could multiply unhappy stories such as the following: recently an archaeologist was to re-excavate the well-known monument of Le Pouy de la Halliade, at Bartres (Hautes-Pyrénées). He had obtained a written agreement from the owner and the official licence from the authorities; possibly it was the monument scheduled as a 'dolmen' in that commune since 1887. A few days before this archaeologist was to begin his dig, a bulldozer was ordered and destroyed the site (Clottes 1975). Peasants are politically very powerful through their trade associations. Destroying a megalith, especially if the monument interests tourists or ramblers, even if the action is of no agricultural benefit, is a prerogative of independence and a clear manifestation of property rights. To go and show interest in a megalith can sometimes be fatal for the monument.

There have been many unhappy examples – especially after the operations of the *Remembrement*, the compulsory redistribution of the land, when amalgamations were taking place and all 'obstacles to the rational exploitation of the land' were being eliminated. The Ministry of Agriculture always seems to take note, sincerely or not, when it is told that an antiquity has been destroyed. But giving them in advance lists of monuments or sites to be respected and preserved has proved sometimes to be provoking martyrdom. The peasants are induced to bribe the bulldozer drivers and contractors and to pay for the additional work which will permit them to get a clean open space.

The administrative protection of megaliths by scheduling them as Historical Monuments has not always prevented destruction either. And even monuments bought by the state have escaped from public ownership through usucaption – the acquisition of right to property by uninterrupted possession – and are now again in private hands.

During the last century, the need for regional archaeological surveys eventually became apparent. These were initiated locally in some places at first, and then received official encouragement, although it never brought about a complete and uniform coverage of the country. Megalithic monuments were often incorporated in general archaeological inventories, or occasionally in special lists, some more detailed and descriptive than others. The fewer monuments there were in a district, the more precisely were they located, described and illustrated.

Some thirty years ago, an ambitious programme of inventories of French megaliths was proposed by Professor R. Vaufrey (Vaufrey 1943). It took a long time to become a reality and to find volunteers. At present the special volumes for some *départements* have been published in the collection of supplements to *Gallia-Préhistoire*: *Indre-et-Loire* (Cordier 1963), *Maine-et-Loire* (Gruet 1967), *Loir-et-Cher* (Despriée and Leymarios 1974), the *départements* of the Paris region (Peek 1975), *Lot* (Clottes 1977). The *Deux-Sèvres* (Germond 1980) has just been published. The work of Dr J. Clottès, being a doctoral thesis, has a more synthetic aspect; it concerns a southern *département* with very few menhirs and many 'dolmens' (498, although in fact the number now recognized is 500). Most of the other *départements* covered by the survey are moderately rich in megaliths, and some devoted research worker or other has managed to find the time and the resources to study each one. For all those involved it has been a heavy voluntary burden. Having to deal with so many menhirs can become monotonous after a while. But it is a matter for regret that some people who began work on the scheme, in Brittany for instance, have had to give up because of other pressing commitments.

In fact general synthetic works on the Neolithic cultures of whole provinces or groups of provinces, such as the Paris Basin (Bailloud 1964, 1974), Provence (Courtin 1974), the Centre-Ouest (Burnez 1976), give quite a lot of information about the megaliths,

and still more is to be found in the regional synthetic works on megalithic tombs, such as in the standard and classic one for Brittany (L'Helgouach 1965), which can now be supplemented by different revisions and general works (Giot, L'Helgouach and Monnier 1979; Giot, Briard and Pape 1979). There has been a huge amount of regional research in the same sense: in the North and Pas-de-Calais (Piningre 1980), in Normandy (Verron 1976), in Vendée (Chaigneau 1965, and Joussaume, in preparation), in Poitou (Germond and Joussaume), in the Charentes (the same and Gauron, and Mohen), in Aquitaine (Roussot-Larroque), in the Côte d'Or (Joly 1965), the Franche-Comté (Pétrequin and Piningre 1976), the Massif Central (G.E.M.A. 1973), the Grands Causses (Lorblanchet 1965, Maury 1967), the Lodévois (Arnal 1979), the Aveyron (Galtier 1971), the Gard (Audibert 1958 and 1962, Roudil since), the Hérault (Arnal 1963), Provence (Sauzade, in preparation), the Roussillon (Abelanet 1970), the Aude (Guilaine), etc. And we have probably not heard about all the unpublished doctoral dissertations and master dissertations involved either.

Recent Excavations

To obtain an idea of the number of modern excavations that have taken place over the past twenty years or so we have drawn on the information reports collected in *Gallia-Préhistoire*, amended by some other documents.

There have been approximately 250 small rescue excavations (before or after destruction), or cleaning up operations of already emptied tombs which can involve the sifting of spoil tips from older or clandestine excavations, a procedure very rewarding in the south of France. And in addition there have been 60–80 excavations of considerable importance, some very large-scale digs concerning complex multiple-chambered monuments or even groups of them. If we take into account the individual chambers we might arrive at about 120–140 monuments excavated or re-excavated minutely and on a large scale. If one also considers the amount of money involved (including the funds needed to conserve some of the major sites) the conclusion must be that never before has such an effort been expended on megaliths, even in the era of private amateur digging, which was always a quick affair. A possible total of about 400 monuments have thus been explored.

This research can be divided into two distinct but not mutually exclusive categories. On the one hand we have the large and complex megalithic structures of the Atlantic façade, from the Charentes to Normandy, where problems of architecture and of the antiquity of the structures have been highlighted. On the other hand we have the tombs in the limestone, chalky or calcareous areas, where the good or better preservation of bone makes the delicate dissection of the contents of the tombs very profitable. (In those monuments where the bones have been leached out, some settling of the in-fill will have occurred at the least, and less precise information on burial rites will be available.)

Chronology

We are much better informed about megaliths than we have ever been, now we know that they were built over a span of at least 2,500 years (more probably 3,000 years), and that quite a lot of them are nicely linked by a series of complementary cross-datings through time.

The first megalithic chamber tomb to be radiocarbon dated (in 1959) was the central one of the Ile Carn cairn, at Ploudalmezeau (Finistère), and in fact from some material from my own first excavation there. The result caused a small sensation at the time, truly without any justification, as already quite a few dates were available from different Neolithic cultures in Europe which demonstrated the need to open up the chronological concertina. Of course some conservative scholars went on arguing for the old dates because they were obsessed by problems of origins and of beginnings. Cultures have no beginning and no end. They emerge gradually and spontaneously out of the mists of time. We are still living in a culture which is to an extent 'megalithic' in its inheritance.

In Central Europe particularly we still encounter scholars who seem uneasy about the early dating of the big monuments of the Atlantic façade of Europe. They consider them to be – from a comparative archaeological point of view – typically 'Chalcolithic' or 'Eneolithic' achievements. They are very annoyed by the many 'early' radiocarbon dates from Western European monuments, especially if these are calibrated. One should not forget that these radiocarbon dates, more and more numerous every year, are supported by corresponding TL dates, palynological evidence, geological evidence (sea-level variations for instance), and so on. Details may be made more precise by the new methods of the future, at least if they provide more precise dating, but now we can consider the principal lines of our chronological system to be good enough, at least if we assume that an approximation within five-to-ten per cent of the correct ages is sufficient.

At present we have about twenty-five radiocarbon dates or so of 5000 years BC or older for monuments of

the Western façade, and probably a good hundred of later Neolithic or Chalcolithic date from megalithic and para-megalithic sites in all parts of the country.

Chronological Distribution of Collective Tombs

If we briefly synthesize this chronological information in a geographic model, we find a decrement when we progress from the Armorican Atlantic seaboard towards eastern or southern France.

Middle Neolithic collective graves (4000–2700 BC approximately) are found in Brittany, western Normandy, Poitou, Charentes, possibly Anjou and Touraine. A unique case is possibly a site on the coast of Aquitaine (Le Gurp). In the old typological language, these monuments would belong to the passage graves and their derivatives.

Late Neolithic collective graves (from 2700 BC onwards) are to be found in the Paris Basin, eastern Normandy, Champagne, Burgundy, Jura, the Massif Central, Aquitaine and the Pyrenees. In the traditional typological terminology, these monuments would fit into the categories of the gallery graves, the trenches and the rock-cut tombs.

Chalcolithic collective graves (from about 2200 BC onwards) can be found in Provence, the Alps, Languedoc and the Causses. They correspond to the meridional dolmens, to the rock-cut hypogea and the natural caves used as ossuaries. There is a small overlap since in these southern and south-eastern districts the Chalcolithic begins earlier than farther north, where the Late Neolithic tombs have been more often re-used in the Chalcolithic than really built anew, though this has certainly happened.

These chronological simplifications and their presentation may not be taken too seriously. The distribution pattern thus revealed is nevertheless remarkable. Ignoring contacts with Iberian megaliths through the Pyrenees, the apparent picture is that of a diffusion from the older monuments of the Atlantic façade towards the interior. Even if we don't want to use a diffusionist model, we can't get away from this fact.

We should not forget either that the Danubian Neolithic cultures buried their dead in single graves, as did also the principal Middle Neolithic culture of continental France, the so-called Chasséen (and its regional variants). The Chasséen tombs of southern France are quite often in small cists.

Typology

The greatest preoccupation of many megalithic scholars over the last thirty to fifty years has been with typological subtleties.

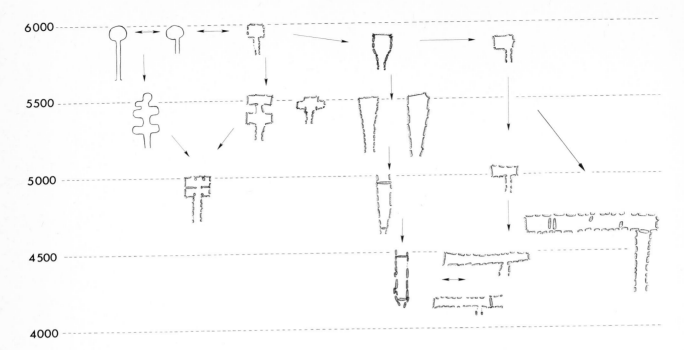

6000

5500

5000

4500

4000

2 Chronological (years before the present) and typological relationship of the main types of megalithic tomb plan in Brittany, in a tentative chart of complete regional development.

In spite of its diffusionist flavour, Glyn Daniel's 1941 paper on the 'Dual Nature of the Megalithic Colonisation' has provided illumination for many megalithic-lovers over a number of years. Its principal merit was to reduce the different regional or local variants to two main successive types. Of course this paper did also dwell on the problem of 'origins'. As I have said above, these sorts of phenomenon may have no definite origins. They may appear spontaneously at about the same moment in quite separate population groups under approximately the same conditions, the societies being at about the same stage of development. Even if such an hypothesis is false, it has at least a provisional value, in exorcizing those questions which ask about the earliest megaliths.

The tendency today is to study typological problems in regional or local groups of monuments which are definitely linked. If ancient people in the past could reach most megaliths in a group on foot within a few days, one can assume that knowledge of some kind about the megaliths would spread. Elements from nearby populations might meet together on certain grand occasions, the most obvious even being for the transport of the biggest stones, so that plenty of men could have had the opportunity to see monuments in the course of construction. These contacts will have been the most likely means by which regional types became standardized, with of course the possibility that 'masons', 'architects' or 'engineers' moved about to give technical help or advice. One can't very well imagine 'academies' of megalithic architecture!

Even if information only circulated between distant communities through chance contacts or at best through the movement of middlemen, these people are likely to have been allowed to see the interiors of tombs in each community, or at least to have heard precise descriptions. But since most monuments were probably covered up under mounds, barrows or cairns there will have been great difficulty in obtaining an accurate idea of their dispositions from only an outside view – unless it proved possible to get inside that is. We are so accustomed to see exposed the inner skeletons of the megalithic monuments that we rather tend to forget when discussing typological or structural niceties that the interiors were no doubt hidden to the profane.

At least as a game or an exercise, one can tentatively build up phyletic trees with types of megalith from a region. As an example we present one for Brittany (ill. 2), which ties in with all the chronological evidence currently available, although some aspects are speculative. It shows that all the main types of tomb-plan known in that region can be fitted into such a chart. Of course the lay-out of tombs is only part of the definition of each type – if types exist other than as ideas in the minds of modern scholars.

Mortuary Practices

Reading old publications leads one to doubt the accuracy of many observations of burial ritual, such as the practice of cremation in some instances, or more often the idea that megalithic chambers only contained secondary interments, as if they were used only as bone-houses after a *décharnement pré-sépulcral* in another place. But some nineteenth-century antiquaries did correctly observe cremated bones. And at least in northern Europe, modern excavations have proved that some megalithic tombs were utilized as repositories or charnel-houses.

Some descriptions of cremation actually concern inhumed bones which have been secondarily scorched by accident, either by torches, or when during a much later intrusion in a tomb a fire may have been lit.

The collective tomb of Neuvy-en-Dunois, Eure-et-Loir (Masset 1968), has produced an early but definite case of incineration. It was not a true megalithic structure, but simply a sub-rectangular pit, measuring 2.60 m by less than 2 m, with a depth of 1.20 m. It contained the remains of 22 to 24 individuals of both sexes and of all ages. All had been cremated, on a small hearth not very far away, positioned on their backs, with half-open arms. Earth and stones were laid over the bones, and there were a very few grave-goods. A radiocarbon date of 3300 ± 140 BC has been compared with that of the cases of cremation known from some of the very large barrows of the Morbihan.

At a later period, a very curious cremation trench was cut into the side of the cairn of La Hoguette, at Fontenay-le-Marmion, Calvados (Caillaud and Lagnel 1972). Of a total length of 12 m, 3 m cut into the already dilapidated cairn, leaving the greater part outside. The trench's mean breadth was 1.30 m, its depth more than 0.50 m. At least 16 corpses were represented, with some Seine-Oise-Marne (SOM) style pottery and other grave-goods. A radiocarbon date from the associated charcoal of 2350 ± 120 BC gives the best fit out of four dates. Apart from a few cases of incineration associated with inhumations in

3 The gallery grave of La Chaussée-Tirancourt (Somme) in the process of being excavated by C. Masset, in 1974. The photograph shows the oldest burial layer in a central compartment. The interruption to the left is due to an earlier excavation. In the right half of the picture are two incomplete primary burials, somewhat disturbed. In the left half, the bones are still more disconnected. (Photo C. Masset.)

4 The hypogeum of Roaix (Vaucluse) during the excavation by J. Courtin, in 1966: the most recent burial layer, eastern part. A massive inhumation of piled up bodies. (Photo J. Courtin.)

the Paris Basin, the tomb of Stein in the Netherlands is a good counterpart.

The same cairn of La Hoguette has given excellent information on the practices of the passage-grave builders. It contained 7 or 8 chambered tombs, the last being destroyed. Two chambers presented rather mixed up bones from 8 and 9 people respectively, in the first chamber with some protection of the skulls, in the second some partly connected bones; another disturbed chamber yielded the remains of 14 individuals, some bones still being joined together. Three other chambers produced bones of 14, 6 and 5 persons re-

spectively, most of them being crouched on their sides, with flexed limbs. This excellent excavation has shown clearly the importance of the flexed position. To keep an eight-month-pregnant woman as crouched as possible, her calcanea had been bored after her death.

In the second cairn of Vierville, Manche, also in the calcareous area of western Normandy, but less well preserved, at least one contracted skeleton lying on its right side has been discovered (Verron 1977). In an intact chamber of La Hogue, Fontenay-le-Marmion, Calvados, six skeletons were found dispersed; the early digs had encountered a protected skull.

The cairn of Le Montiou, Sainte-Soline, Deux-Sèvres (Germond and Joussaume 1978) has chiefly produced disordered bones, although there were indications among the older burials that the bodies were lying prone, bent knees towards the abdomen. In the celebrated group of cairns at Bougon, Deux-Sèvres (Mohen 1977), where tomb A had yielded about 200 skeletons in 1840, the first chamber of cairn E contained 5 or 6 people, the skulls against the walls, with a radiocarbon date of 3850 ± 230 BC. The bottom of chamber O contained 10 skeletons, bones still partly linked in a huddled position; half were children and radiocarbon dates of 3850 and 3650 BC are available.

Thus a very coherent picture of the mode of deposition of the dead comes out of this survey. In all the older types of megalithic tombs we have primary burials in a lateral and crouched position. New burials often dispersed the bones of the first occupants, and sometimes the skulls received greater attention. No case of specific removal of certain bones has yet been noticed.

If we pass on to the later monuments, similar conclusions also emerge from modern excavations. The *allée couverte* of La Chaussée-Tirancourt, Somme, the most northerly of its type (Masset 1972), contained well over 350 burials (ill. 3). The later burials greatly disturbed the earlier ones, but happily a few of the latter did at least partly survive intact. The first inhumations were distributed in compartments, the later ones in smaller cells or boxes. The compartments were divided off by lines of stones and possibly by wooden planks. This very meticulous dig, extending over eight years, has given a lot of information about the way the bones were treated and disposed of some time after their deposition. For instance, they could be packed so as to take up less space, sometimes when the flesh had decayed but the ligaments were still extant. At the beginning of the use of the monument, the corpses lay on their left side, with flexed legs; later, they may have been placed flat on their backs. At one period heads were turned towards the entrance of the tomb, at another towards the back.

The famous excavation of the rock-cut hypogeum of Les Mournouards, Mesnil-sur-Oger, Marne (Leroi-Gourhan, Bailloud and Brézillon 1962), provided a lot of details, including the relationship of the grave-goods to the burials. About 40 adults and 20 children had been inhumed there, although only about 20 had bones still connected, and in fact only 6 had not been displaced at all. The corpses had been placed in a supple shroud or bag not covering the head. This made it easier to move the bodies about at a later stage, the skulls being piled in corners. The arms were often folded on the chest. Burying a body thus bagged was a rapid operation, possibly not taking more than a minute.

The remarkable excavation of what was left of half the rock-cut hypogeum of Roaix, Vaucluse (Courtin 1974), gives a dramatic picture of the same sort of tomb for the south of France, also from a Chalcolithic culture (ill. 4). This site has not received the attention it deserves. In an upper layer one hundred corpses or so had been deposited or rather – extraordinarily – piled up one on top of the other, stretched out, sometimes with legs bent; the arms were folded over the chest, the feet often crossed, so that here again one can think of a bag or shroud. The bodies had clearly been buried all together at one moment, men, women and numerous children mixed up, often head to foot. Fierce fires had been lit on top of the last corpses. This massive burial may have been the result of some tragic event. A radiocarbon date of 2090 ± 140 BC is associated with this upper layer. The lower series, separated by a metre of sterile sand, was more normal, with the usual disorder of earlier skeletons. Some bones which still remained linked proved that the bodies had been placed in a crouched position, as was usual in the caves used as ossuaries in the south of France. Here the radiocarbon date is 2150 ± 140 BC.

A current theory is that the megalithic tombs of southern France were only secondary burial places, containing heaped bones from skeletons which had been discarnated elsewhere. No modern excavation has provided any evidence for this; on the contrary, convincing traces of at least parts of connected limbs survive. During the reshuffling to make room for new bodies, the skulls were usually stacked in corners or against the walls. A very precise excavation from this point of view has been conducted for six years in the dolmen of Les Peirières at Villedubert, Aude (Duday, forthcoming) (ill. 5). Sealed in and abandoned after the Beaker period, the monument offered an excellent opportunity to conduct a methodological test in an undisturbed deposit. Six yearly digging seasons have been devoted to the excavation of the upper level of burials of the Chalcolithic, and about forty groups of

5 The dolmen of Villedubert (Aude) during the excavation by H. Duday, in 1977: upper layer of Beaker period burials, with the lower limbs of an adult still joined together. (Photo H. Duday.)

bones have been discovered anatomically connected. This upper level was in use over quite a long period of time; the corpses were not strictly buried, but left on top of the sepulchral deposit. The dissection of the earlier level of burials under a pavement of stones will also probably be the scrupulous work of many years to come. The minuteness of this procedure, with the recording of the most infinitesimal details, is beyond description in a few words.

If we sum up these results, we see that except when bodies were dragged into a rock-cut tomb through a narrow aperture, corpses were generally deposited in a contracted position. In megalithic monuments with portholes we should also possibly expect the use of some kind of shroud.

Architectural Convergence

The best demonstration that there is something wrong in envisaging distant correlations between monuments of similar form baptized by the typologists with the same names, is given by a chronological comparison between some monuments in the British Isles or Ireland and those on the Continent. If we are to believe even the most recent textbooks (such as Megaw and Simpson 1979), the so-called 'passage graves' of Ireland or of Scotland came into existence some time after the building of 'passage graves' of more or less similar plan had been abandoned in Brittany. In the same way it is absurd to think that in calling the monuments of the Causses *dolmens à couloir* or 'passage graves' there is anything other than a purely verbal similitude.

It is more interesting to compare technologically monuments built out of the same sort of rocks, from stones with the same sort of characteristics, or in the same sort of topographical or morphological location. Similar conditions quite naturally tend to produce similarities in the solutions chosen by the different 'architects'. For instance, monuments made out of schist usually possess a whole host of detailed similarities. The number of obvious methods for solving technological problems is limited. Perhaps quite a lot of similarities on a broader scale arise from such parallelisms.

The Complex Structure of the Great Cairns

Until recently both small and large cairns were considered to have been created by the casual piling up of stones over and around monuments, with little or no method in the process. Certain excavators, such as Z. Le Rouzic in the Morbihan, had noticed traces of internal walling in some cases. But the great lesson of Barnenez, twenty years ago, was that the outer walls were built to be seen. Also, that when a concentric series of walls existed, their tops were graduated so that the upper parts of all the internal walls would be partly visible, in a series of steps. The appearance of a heap of stones was only the result of collapse and time. In fact probably for hundreds of years cows at Barnenez had walked to the fields along a narrow lane, on one side of which was a large exposed part of the innermost original facing. It was not only the internal aspects of megalithic architecture that could be grandiose – the façades were intended to be impressive as well.

Another practical lesson we learnt at Barnenez was that these facings could be excavated, exposed, strengthened and restored if necessary in the best preserved monuments. Everyone began hunting for façades in the large cairns of the Atlantic fringe.

Outer wallings at least have been found everywhere: for instance, in Normandy at La Hogue and at La Hoguette, Fontenay-le-Marmion. Concentric or successive walls, or walls with buttresses are known at Bougon (Mohen 1977), at Le Montiou (Germond and Joussaume 1978), at Les Mousseaux, Pornic (L'Helgouach 1977), at Dissignac, Saint-Nazaire (L'Helgouach 1976, 1977, 1979), at Larcuste I, Colpo (L'Helgouach and Lecornec 1976), at Kerleven, La Forêt-Fouesnant (Le Roux and L'Helgouach 1967), and at Carn (Giot 1980).

The large cairns containing more than two passage graves have quite often been built in a series of phases, by accretion and by modification. Clear cases are those of Barnenez, Carn, Guennoc III (Giot 1980), and on a different scale, Kerleven. The important cairn of Dissignac, with its two chambered tombs, has given a very clear and interesting case of remodelling, with lengthening of the passages. Good evidence for such a lengthening is also evident at least in the first phase at Barnenez, where the process may even have been quite general. Rebuilding of some kind may be suspected in many large megalithic tombs which have lost their cairns or barrows; the presence of dry-stone walling in a cairn helps one detect such reconstructions.

The re-use of stones and slabs from earlier stages of the same monument may have been more frequent than we tend to suspect. The abnormal position of ornamental stones, as at Barnenez and also at Gavrinis, is a good indication of this.

The closing in or the blocking of passages must have been a common practice. We found intact transversal walls in the passage of the central chamber at Carn, and large accumulations of stones blocking some of the passages at Barnenez. Evidence for the closing of the lateral cells of the monument of Larcuste II at Colpo has also been quite clear (L'Helgouach and Lecornec 1976). In some cases there were real doors of stone, such as between the chamber and the passage of the angled monument of Gâvres, Morbihan (L'Helgouach 1970), and a half-door at the entrance to the chamber of Barnenez A. Wooden doors are thus possible.

From many points of view, the outside of the monuments was quite as important as the inside. The Atlantic cairns do not present typical forecourts, but one can speak of a parvis. Recent excavations have shown that important events or ceremonies took place in front of the entrances to the tombs or on the lower buttress-like masses of stone-walling between them.

90

Often quite large quantities of sherds of pottery have been found there, coming sometimes from ceremonial sorts of pots.

Many other indications or hints have emerged from the more careful and methodical excavations of the large cairns. The ethical problem is sometimes to decide whether some parts should be completely stripped and taken down, or if it is more essential to preserve the maximum number of undisturbed structures. Archaeologists have a tendency to overdo investigation, and architects and contractors to overdo restoration!

Wooden Structures

The importance of associated wooden buildings for some later types of megalithic monument has been brilliantly demonstrated in Franche-Comté, especially for the site of Aillevans, where a trapezoidal house was set over the chamber (Pétrequin and Piningre 1976).

My personal impression is that the more frequent occurrence of these types of structure has been overlooked. Post-holes indicating structures of the same sort have been observed in the low long barrows of Brittany. The low barrows built around the later megalithic tombs of gallery-grave type are so similar to the low long barrows without a true megalithic structure that we would certainly expect wooden houses adjoining some of the western *allées couvertes*.

R. Joussaume (1977b) was obliged to postulate a covering of perishable materials for the curious megalithic tomb at Xanton-Chassenon in the Vendée.

Standing Stones

Menhirs have long been neglected and rather unpopular among professional archaeologists. A renewed interest is developing, however, quite apart from the problems and questions raised by the geometrical and astronomical theories.

Recent rescue excavations at Saint-Just, Ille-et-Vilaine (Le Roux 1979), on one of the small alignment sites, have shown the existence of post-holes interspersed with the stone menhirs. And beside the row of standing stones five post-holes seem to indicate the position of a small hut-like structure.

There were probably many more curious things in the megalithic world than we can ever imagine. Unhappily most of these types of sites are in places where the depth of soil is thin because of erosion, and only a very limited part of any one structure survives.

Megalithic Experimental Archaeology

The various popular media have demanded experiments in megalithic building for a long time. But they usually proposed that an authentic monument should be uprooted and then rebuilt, a procedure which could only be refused. At Bougon in July 1979, however, Dr J. P. Mohen was able to conduct a most interesting test. Amongst other achievements, a concrete block of 32 tons, equivalent to one of the capstones from the local monuments, was moved by about 200 people, 170 pulling ropes and 30 moving wooden rollers and using tree-trunks as levers to ease their efforts.

The experiment worked very well, and confirmed all the calculations which demonstrate that megalithic building was technically quite feasible for the types of society involved in it.

Many new facts have come to light and many theories have been proved or disproved during the last twenty years of work on the French megaliths. Undoubtedly during the next twenty years our information will improve at least as much, and many aspects of the subject which today seem 'mysterious' will have been explained rationally.

Bibliography

ABELANET, J. 1970 'Les dolmens du Roussillon', *Les civilisations néolithiques du Midi de la France*, Carcassonne, 74–9.

ARNAL, G.B. 1979 *Les mégalithes du Lodévois*, Lodève.

ARNAL, J. 1963 'Les dolmens du département de l'Hérault', *Préhistoire* XV.

AUDIBERT, J. 1958 'Les civilisations chalcolithiques du Gard', *Mémoires de la Société Préhistorique Française* V, 233–305.

1962 *La civilisation chalcolithique du Languedoc oriental*, Institut international d'études ligures, Bordighera-Montpellier.

BAILLOUD, G. 1964 'Le Néolithique dans le Bassin Parisien', *II° supplément à Gallia-Préhistoire* (2nd edn, 1974).

BURNEZ, C. 1976 'Le Neolithique et le Chalcolithique dans le Centre-Ouest de la France', *Mémoires de la Société Préhistorique Française* XII.

CAILLAUD, R. AND LAGNEL, E. 1972 'Le cairn et le crématoire néolithiques de la Hoguette à Fontenay-le-Marmion (Calvados)', *Gallia-Préhistoire* XV, 137–97.

CHAIGNEAU, P.R. 1966–7 'Les dolmens vendéens', *Société d'émulation de la Vendée*, 17–31.

CLOTTES, J. 1975 'Informations', *Gallia-Préhistoire* XVIII, 619.

1977 'Inventaire des mégalithes de la France, Lot', *I° supplément à Gallia-Préhistoire* V.

CORDIER, G. 1963 'Inventaire des mégalithes de la France, Indre-et-Loire', *I° supplément à Gallia-Préhistoire* I.

COURTIN, J. 1974 'Le Néolithique de la Provence', *Mémoires de la Société Préhistorique Française* XI.

DANIEL, G.E. 1941 'The Dual Nature of the Megalithic Colonisation of Prehistoric Europe', *Proc. Preh. Soc.* VII, 1–49.

1960 *The Prehistoric Chamber Tombs of France*, London.

1966 'The Megalith Builders of the SOM', *Palaeohistoria* XII, 199–208.

DESPRIEE, J. AND LEYMARIOS. C. 1974 'Inventaire des mégalithes de la France, Loir-et-Cher', *I° supplément à Gallia-Préhistoire* III.

GALTIER, J. 1971 'Les sépultures mégalithiques du Sud de l'Aveyron', Ph.D. Université de Paris I.

G.E.M.A. (BARBIER, L. et al.) 1973 'Répertoire préliminaire à un inventaire des monuments mégalithiques du Cantal, de la Haute-Loire et du Puy-de-Dôme', *Revue Archéologique du Centre* XII, 253–79.

GERMOND, G. 1980 'Inventaire des mégalithes de la France, Deux-Sèvres', *I° Supplément à Gallia-Préhistoire* VI.

GERMOND, G. AND JOUSSAUME, R. 1978 'Le tumulus du Montiou à Sainte-Soline (Deux-Sèvres)', *Bulletin de la Société historique et scientifique des Deux-Sèvres* (2), XI, 129–88.

GIOT, P.R. 1980 *Barnenez, Carn, Guennoc*, Rennes.

GIOT, P.R., L'HELGOUACH, J. AND MONNIER, J.L. 1979 *Préhistoire de la Bretagne*, Rennes.

GIOT, P.R. BRIARD, J. AND PAPE, L. 1979 *Protohistoire de la Bretagne*, Rennes.

GRUET, M. 1967 'Inventaire des mégalithes de la France, Maine-et-Loire', *I° supplément à Gallia-Préhistoire* II.

GUILAINE. J. 1972 *La nécropole mégalithique de la Clape (Aude)*, Carcassonne.

JOLY, J. 1965 'Les tombes mégalithiques du département de la Côte-d'Or', *Revue archéologique de l'Est et du Centre-Est* XVI, 57–74.

JOUSSAUME, R. 1972 'La préhistoire en Vendée, point des connaissances', *Société d'émulation de la Vendée* CXIX, 7–74.

1977a 'Les architectures mégalithiques particulières du Sud de la Vendée', *Bulletin de la Société Polymathique du Morbihan* CIV, 125–42.

1977b 'Le mégalithe de la Pierre-Virante à Xanton-Chassenon (Vendée)', *L'Anthropologie* LXXXI, 5–65.

LEROI-GOURHAN, A., BAILLOUD, G. AND BREZILLION, M. 1962 'L'hypogée II des Mournouards, Mesnil-sur-Oger, Marne', *Gallia-Préhistoire* V, 23–133.

LE ROUX, C.T. 1979 'Informations', *Gallia-Préhistoire* XXII, 526–30.

LE ROUX, C.T. AND LECERF, Y. 1977 'Le dolmen de Cruguelic en Ploemeur et les sépultures transeptées armoricaines', *Bulletin de la Société Polymathique du Morbihan* CIV, 143–60.

LE ROUX, C.T. AND L'HELGOUACH, J. 1966 'Le cairn mégalithique avec sépultures à chambre compartimentée de Kerleven, La Forêt-Fouesnant (Finistère)', *Annales de Bretagne* LXX, 7–52.

L'HELGOUACH, J. 1965 *Les sépultures mégalithiques en Armorique, dolmens à couloir et allées couvertes*, Rennes.

1970 'Le monument mégalithique du Goërem à Gâvres (Morbihan)', *Gallia-Préhistoire* XIII, 217–61.

1976 'Le tumulus de Dissignac à Saint-Nazaire (Loire-Atlantique)', *Dissertationes archaeologicae gandenses* XVI, 142–9.

1977 'Le cairn des Mousseaux à Pornic (Loire-Atlantique)', *Bulletin de la Société Polymathique du Morbihan* CIV, 161–72.

1979 'Informations', *Gallia-Préhistoire XXII*, 562–8.

L'HELGOUACH, J. AND LECORNEC, J. 1976 'Le site mégalithique Min Goh Ru près de Larcuste à Colpo (Morbihan)', *Bulletin de la Société Préhistorique Française* LXXIII, 370–97.

LORBLANCHET, M. 1965 'Contribution à l'étude du peuplement des Grands Causses', *Bulletin de la Société Préhistorique Française* LXII, 667–712.

MASSET, C. 1968 'Les incinérations du Néolithique ancien de Neuvy-en-Dunois (Eure-et-Loir)', *Gallia-Préhistoire* XI, 205–34.

1971 'Une sépulture collective mégalithique à la Chaussée-Tirancourt (Somme)', *Bulletin de la Société Préhistorique Française* LXVIII, 178–82.

1972 'The megalithic tomb of La Chaussée-Tirancourt', *Antiquity* XLVII, 297–300.

MAURY, J. 1967 *Les étapes du peuplement sur les Grands Causses*, Millau.

MEGAW, J.V.S. AND SIMPSON, D.D.A. 1979 *Introduction to British Prehistory*, Leicester.

MOHEN, J.P. 1977 'Les tumulus de Bougon', *Bulletin de la Société historique et scientifique des Deux-Sèvres* n° 2–3, 48.

PEEK, J. 1975 'Inventaire des mégalithes de la France,

Région parisienne', *I° supplément à Gallia-Préhistoire* IV.

PETREQUIN, P. AND PININGRE, J.F. 1976 'Les sépultures collectives mégalithiques de Franche-Comté', *Gallia-Préhistoire* XIX, 287–394.

PININGRE, J.F. 1980 'Dolmens et menhirs du Nord — Pas de Calais', *Atlas archéologique Nord — Pas de Calais* III.

SAUZADE, G. 1978 'Les sépultures du Vaucluse du Néolithique à l'Age du Bronze', Ph.D. Université d'Aix-en-Provence.

TANGUY, B. 1976 'Toponymie et peuplement', in Calvez, L. (ed.), *La presqu'ile de Crozon, Histoire, Art, Nature*, Paris, 61.

1979 'Toponyme et peuplement', in Dilasser, B. (ed.), *Un pays de Cornouaille, Locronan et sa région*, Paris, 70–2.

VAUFREY, R. 1943 'Projet d'Inventaire des monuments mégalithiques', *Bulletin de la Société normande d'Etudes préhistoriques* XXXII, 121–8.

VERRON, G. 1976 'Acculturation et continuité en Normandie durant le Néolithique et les âges des Métaux', *Dissertationes archaeologicae gandenses* XVI, 261–83.

1977 'Un type de monuments funéraires classique dans le Néolithique de Normandie', *Bulletin de la Société Polymathique du Morbihan* CIV, 187–219.

11   The Megalithic Tombs of Iberia

Robert W. Chapman

NEARLY A decade ago a reviewer of David Clarke's *Beaker Pottery of Great Britain and Ireland* gibed at Cambridge prehistorians, who, he claimed, believed that Africa began at the Pyrenees. Whatever the roots of this gibe, no such myopia can be attached to Glyn Daniel. Throughout his long career he has devoted consistent attention to the Iberian cultures and megalithic tombs which form the subject of this paper. Between hard covers there is his *Megalith Builders of Western Europe* (1963), which formed a worthy successor to earlier syntheses by James Fergusson (1872) and Eric Peet (1912) and gave due attention to the tombs from Spain and Portugal. Their position in the origins and development of Neolithic and Copper Age monumental tombs in western Europe and the Mediterranean was also discussed in a series of papers, ranging from the dual colonization model of his early career (1941) to the affirmation of multiple centres of megalithic genesis (e.g. 1966, 1967, 1970, 1973) in more recent years. This move from a predominantly diffusionist model to one of multilinear evolution nicely mirrors the thinking of European prehistorians in the last forty years. Debate over the origins of megalithic monuments depends fundamentally upon the adoption of different theoretical frameworks such as 'evolution' and 'diffusion', as Glyn Daniel also recognized in his contribution to the volume of the

Proceedings of the Prehistoric Society dedicated to Grahame Clark (1971). Given the priority of theory in the successful pursuit of archaeology (a statement with which Professor Daniel may feel slightly less sympathy!), it seems appropriate to view the megalithic tombs of Spain and Portugal in terms of theory and approaches to culture change and to specify those dimensions of study which require close scrutiny.

Orientalists, Occidentalists and Culture Theory

The 'classic' theories of origins for Iberian megalithic tombs have been summarized too clearly elsewhere to require more than cursory repetition (see Daniel 1963; Almagro and Arribas 1963). The local development or 'occidentalist' position was formulated initially by Cartailhac (1886), who argued for an evolutionary sequence, beginning with the polygonal chambers in the upland areas of northern Portugal (Beira, Tras-os-Montes) and then spreading south and west, evolving into passage graves and 'tholoi'. This thesis was followed and developed by Wilke (1912), Leeds (1918–20), Obermaier (1919) and Aberg (1921) in the first two decades of the present century, although it should be noted that Wilke and Obermaier modified this position to allow for the introduction of corbelled passage graves into Iberia from the east Mediterranean.

But it was Bosch-Gimpera who built upon this foundation and integrated Iberian megalithic origins into a masterly synthesis of the peninsula's later prehistory (1932, 1944). He maintained this position throughout his career (e.g. 1967), defining stages in the evolution of megalithic architecture. But even at his most evolutionary he still acknowledged the existence of contact between Iberia and the central and eastern Mediterranean, with its implications for cultural development. Other prehistorians preferred to give this 'contact' greater weight and pursue an 'orientalist' argument (Forde 1929, 1930; Peake and Fleure 1930; Childe 1932), by which corbelled tombs and rock-cut tombs were introduced into Iberia and subsequently diffused and devolved into megalithic passage graves and single chambers. Glyn Daniel's paper on the dual nature of megalithic colonization in western Europe (1941) finds its context among the works of these orientalist proponents in the 1930s and 1940s. But it was the monumental syntheses of George and Vera Leisner which crystallized the debate over megalithic origins by providing the comprehensive treatment of the data which had been lacking in earlier analyses (1943, 1951, 1956; Leisner 1965; Márquez, Leisner and Leisner 1952). Now it would be rather facile to refer to them simply as orientalists or occidentalists, since their arguments for separate south-east and south-west Iberian origins for corbelled tombs and megalithic passage graves respectively were integrated within a context of wide Mediterranean contacts (e.g. 1943). In a similar vein one should also note the position adopted by Savory (e.g. 1968, 1977), who follows the Leisners' arguments regarding south-east and south-west Iberia, but finds an underlying unity of origin for megalithic culture(s) in the diffusion of communal burial from the east Mediterranean (cf. Blance 1960, 1961).

This East-West conflict was established before the development of radiometric dating techniques. So before we look in detail at the effects of radiocarbon and thermoluminescence dating on our knowledge of the chronology and genesis of Iberian megalithic tombs, let us pause to outline the basic assumptions and culture theory behind the debate. A good starting point here lies in Glyn Daniel's statement of the main questions asked by students of megalithic tombs (1963, 39):

who were the builders, where did they come from, how and where did they live, why did they spread over western Europe and what contributions, if any, did they make to the future heritage of prehistoric Europe?

The basic unity of megalithic tombs and monuments is affirmed in terms of the defining characteristic of using large stones and, more particularly for the tombs, in terms of collective burial, which was 'a complicated and religious idea' (1963, 78). Given this unity we are witnessing 'the spread of styles of funerary architecture, with certain basic patterns on which regional and local variations are made' (1963, 45). This practice of communal burial in chamber tombs, attaining impressively monumental proportions (e.g. Cueva de Menga, Antequera – Leisner and Leisner 1943), seemed internally coherent and diverged from preceding mortuary practices in western Europe, which, where known, were characterized by individual inhumation. Thus the fundamental assumption made was that changes in mortuary practices of this kind reflected changes of culture and population. The pursuit of megalithic enquiries then became the pursuit of an area of origin and the plotting of the diffusion of the megalith builders through progressive changes in the form and dimensions of the individual tombs.

Whatever the favoured area of origins, it was assumed that formal similarities in mortuary practices reflected interaction between groups of megalith builders. Regular change in mortuary practices signified continuity, irregular change signified a break of population. Nuclear areas formed the focus of culture change, with diffusion as the process by which change was conveyed to increasingly wider areas. Now within the wider context of European prehistory and indeed of archaeology in the first half of this century, this approach and these assumptions were widespread. They reflect what has been called the normative and historical-distributional approaches to the study of culture (Binford 1965, 1971). Such assumptions were characteristic particularly of Iberian prehistorians. The identification of cultural assemblages with 'peoples' can be witnessed before Gordon Childe's work in the pioneering publications of Louis Siret in south-east Spain (1913). The seven successive chronological periods which he defined for the post-Pleistocene were argued to represent a series of separate 'couches ethniques'. Culture change was to be explained in terms of ethnic movement and survivals. The demonstration of movement and contact depended upon the formal comparison of cultural traits (e.g. Siret 1913, fig.3). With the subsequent development of models of Iberian prehistoric culture change based upon processes of diffusion, colonization or influence from the central and eastern Mediterranean, nuclear areas of contact and development were defined (e.g. south-east Spain, southern Portugal). The detailed discussion of this culture theory has already beeen presented elsewhere (Chapman 1975) and will be published (Chapman, forthcoming). Suffice it to say

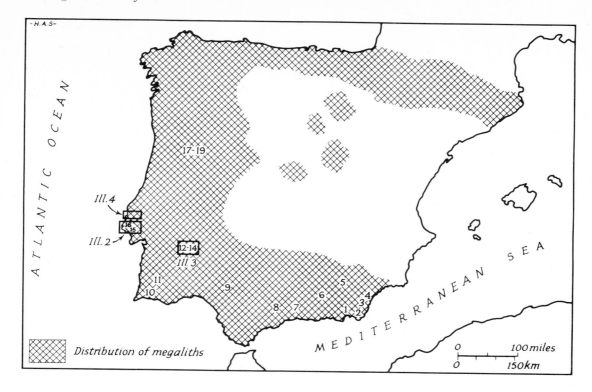

1 *Schematic distribution of megalithic tombs in Iberia. Main sites mentioned in text: 1 Los Millares 2 El Barranquete, 3 Cerro de Nieles, 4 Almizaraque, 5 Cerro de la Virgen, 6 Gorafe group, 7 Pantano de los Bermejales, 8 Antequera group, 9 Dolmen de Matarrubilla, 10 Alcala, 11 Anta dos Tassos 1, 12 Poço da Gateira, 13 Anta dos Gorginos, 14 Herdade de Farisoa, 15 Carenque, 16 Praia das Maças, 17 Carapito 1, 18 Orca dos Castenairos, 19 Seixas. Location of ills 2–4 is indicated.*

here that megalithic tombs represent just one type of cultural trait which was studied through normative theory and that the assumptions mentioned here applied to both orientalists and occidentalists (for an example of the latter, see Bosch-Gimpera 1932, 1944, 1967). My apologies to readers for this predominance of assertion over detailed argument, but time and space require brevity and we must move on rapidly to look at absolute chronology.

The Absolute Chronology of Iberian Megalithic Tombs

An independent chronology for Iberian megaliths was absent before the advent of radiocarbon and TL dating. Colin Renfrew has published a list of both radiocarbon and TL dates for the tombs (1976) and has discussed the implications of the new chronology in several publications (e.g. 1970, 1973), while the TL dates are published in full by Whittle and Arnaud (1975). What I wish to do here is to discuss these dates in more detail than has been attempted on previous occasions.

The dating of megalithic passage graves and single chambers in inland areas of northern Portugal now extends back to at least 3000 bc (*c*.3900 BC). From 1964 to 1967 Schubart, Ribeiro and Vera Leisner surveyed

and excavated tombs in the province of Beira Alta, between the rivers Mondego and Douro, over 600 m in altitude. Only the radiocarbon dates and the Carapito excavations have been published so far (Leisner and Ribeiro 1968). The dates come from three sites: Orca dos Castenairos – 3110 ± 50 bc (GrN 4924) from the bottom of the chamber fill overlying the natural weathered granite and 2660 ± 50 bc (GrN 4925) from a layer of black organic earth stratigraphically above the other sample in the chamber; Carapito 1 – 2900 ± 40 bc (GrN 5110) from the floor of the chamber, associated with microliths, flint blades, polished stone tools, callais and amphibolite beads, and 2640 ± 65 bc (GrN?) also from the chamber floor but nearer a gap in the chamber wall where the entrance/passage may have been; and Orca de Seixas – 2950 ± 40 bc (GrN 5734) from wood charcoal from a lower level (no more precise information available). The last of these tombs is described as a 'dolmen', but although one may suppose that this refers to a single chamber, the Carapito sites (three passage graves and the dated tomb, which is now a single chamber) are referred to as 'die dolmen' by Leisner and Ribeiro (1968), thus creating confusion.

The single chambers and megalithic passage graves of Beira Alta have been included by Savory (1968, 105–7) within a group of such tombs in the north-west of Iberia supposedly later than, and derived from, the collective tombs of the Upper Alemtejo. This follows the views of the Leisners, Heleno and other Portuguese archaeologists as to the development of collective tombs in the south-west from earlier oblong or oval megalithic cists covered with circular mounds and initially containing single burials, axes, adzes and microlithic tools. Bosch-Gimpera, on the other hand, argued that the single round megalithic chambers of the north-west (Beira Alta, Tras-os-Montes) evolved first (c.4000 bc – period 1 of his Portuguese megalithic culture) and the passage graves of the Upper Alemtejo did not develop until his period 3, over a thousand years later (c.3000 bc – see Bosch-Gimpera 1967).

There are no radiocarbon dates from the Upper Alemtejo, but the programme of TL dating provided interesting results. The earliest dates come from the group of tombs studied by the Leisners around Reguengos de Monsaraz (Leisner and Leisner 1951). Poço da Gateira 1 has a polygonal chamber and a short passage and contained polished stone axes, adzes, flint blades, microliths and undecorated pottery which yielded a date of 4510 ± 360 BC (OxTL 169b). Anta dos Gorginos 2 is a similar type of tomb with similar grave goods and a date of 4440 ± 360 BC (OxTL 169c). Thus comparison of these dates with the calibrated radiocarbon dates given above from Beira Alta suggests that the tombs of the south-west in the Alemtejo evolved before those of the north-west. As Renfrew has pointed out, these dates also demonstrate that the Iberian tombs, with an origin by c.4500–4000 BC, begin before their alleged Aegean prototypes (1970, 1973, 1976).

The construction and use of passage graves with dry-stone walling and corbelled roofs seems to have begun by 2400 bc and continued in some areas until the middle of the second millennium bc. In calendar years this would be from before c.3000 BC down to c.2000 BC. There are eight dates from five sites in Almería and southern Portugal. From Los Millares 19 (Almagro and Arribas 1963) comes a date of 2430 ± 120 bc (KN

72) for one of a local series of tombs with side-chambers and a triple segmented passage, supposedly late in the evolution of the passage grave. Unfortunately the context of the charcoal sample is not known. A closely similar date (2345 ± 85 bc – H 204) was obtained from a sample at the inner foot of the settlement wall at Los Millares, but its position in relation to the duration of occupation on the site lacks clarity (Sangmeister, pers.comm., 1974). However, tomb 7 in the cemetery at El Barranquete (M.J. Almagro Gorbea 1973a), some thirty kilometres to the south-east of Los Millares, has also given comparable dates: 2330 ± 130 bc (CSIC 81) and 2350 ± 130 bc (CSIC 82) from wood samples from the central pillar in the chamber. Dates in the last quarter of the third millennium bc have also been obtained from contemporary settlements at Tabernas and Tarajal (M.Almagro Gorbea and Fernández-Miranda 1978).

In southern Portugal we have TL as well as radiocarbon dates (Whittle and Arnaud 1975; Arnaud 1978). Anta dos Tassos 1 (Alamo, Ourique, Bajo Alemtejo) has a dry-stone chamber and a short orthostatic passage (Viana, Veiga Ferreira and Freire de Andrades 1961, 9 – 12; Leisner 1965, 146) and two published dates – 1850 ± 200 bc (Sa?) and 1370 ± 200 bc (Sa 199) – though there are no details of their spatial/stratigraphical relationships to each other or to the period of construction. There has also been confusion as to the authenticity of the dates (M. Almagro Gorbea 1970, 20), both of which have been published as *the* date for the tomb (Leisner and Veiga Ferreira 1963, 364; Delibrias, Roche and Veiga Ferreira 1967). Savory (1968, 150) confuses the laboratory numbers. Clearly even the earliest of these dates is rather late compared with our expectations based on the Millares and Barranquete tombs. This is the case also with the TL date of 2675 ± 270 BC (OxTL 169j) from the 'tholos' of Herdade da Farisoa (Reguengos de Monsaraz, Leisner and Leisner 1951), which is almost indistinguishable from the date of 2405 ± 260 BC (OxTL 169i) from sherds in the primary passage grave at this site. Further north near Lisbon, there are radiocarbon dates from a primary rock-cut tomb – 2300 ± 60 bc (KN?) and BS 2210 ± 110 bc (H?) – and a secondary partly rock-cut passage grave with dry-stone walling and a corbelled vault – 1700 ± 100 bc (H?) and 1690 ± 60 bc (KN?) – at Praia das Maças (Sintra). On the basis of the grave goods Savory (1968, 122, 152) suggests that the dates for the primary tomb relate to disturbance when the secondary tomb was constructed and similarly that the dates for the secondary tomb are the result of later Beaker burials. This would mean in calendar years that the secondary tomb was built by c.3000 BC (in accordance with expectations) and the primary tomb earlier. Support for this view may be derived from the TL date of 3930 ± 340 BC (OxTL 169h) from the rock-cut tomb Carenque 2, although this is much earlier than either of the two dates from the settlement nearby (Whittle and Arnaud 1975).

What conclusions may we draw about the absolute dating of Iberian megaliths? First the good news. The use and construction of collective tombs spans at least two thousand five hundred calendar years, from the middle fifth to the late third millennia BC, compared with a maximum of one thousand years allowed by the pre-radiocarbon and pre-TL chronology. There is now a basis for supporting the evolutionary development of tomb forms, with megalithic passage graves appearing by 4500–4000 BC in the north-west and south-west of the peninsula and the so-called 'tholoi' by 3000 BC in the south-east and the south-west. But what about the bad news? Unfortunately this comprises a lengthy bulletin. As the reader will notice there are pitifully few dates available given the numbers of tombs published for the peninsula. Leaving aside a small number of anomalous dates (M. Almagro Gorbea and Fernández-Miranda 1978), there are only twenty dates from twelve sites! This represents a very low coverage both temporally and spatially. For the south-east the dates given above are for two tombs out of over 350 in Almería (Leisner and Leisner 1943). We have no dates for tombs in the north and north-east of the peninsula. We have no dates for the primary *rundgräber* in the south-east nor the single chambers/cists excavated by Heleno (and still unpublished) in the south-west. For the dates that we do possess too many are either single dates or of ambiguous or unknown context. Given continued access to such tombs over at least a generation, if not several, then what phases of activity are being dated? Is a radiocarbon date from a charcoal sample on the floor of a chamber necessarily dating the construction or primary use of the tomb? A related point may be made about the dating of pottery sherds by TL – what relation do they bear to the lifespan of the tomb's use? It is noticeable also that the location of some of the sherd samples dated by TL (e.g. Carenque – Whittle and Arnaud 1975) was unknown. All these are important problems, but they are not insoluble. Much now depends upon the excavation of contemporary settlement sites, as has already begun in southern Portugal (see below). Given the highly variable stages of publication and destruction afflicting Iberian megaliths (as those of other areas of western Europe), excavation of settlements and the analysis of change through cultural sequences offers us a better means of organizing the data on megalith forms and grave goods. We may then begin to approach an understanding of regional variation in the construction and use of tombs which is not solely dependent upon typology (e.g. Chapman in press, a).

Beyond Chronology: a Theoretical 'Knee-Jerk'

In spite of the bad news, we have seen that radiocarbon and TL dating have given us the basis of an independent chronology for megalithic tombs and cultural development within Iberia. This is also the case throughout western Europe (e.g. Renfrew 1973, 1976). With longer chronologies we lose the necessity for the 'catastrophic' explanations conditioned by pre-radiocarbon schemes (Clarke 1973). For megaliths in particular Glyn Daniel's writings witnessed a rapid change in his earlier views, now denying their unity within western Europe (1966, 201):

'I think it is fair to say nowadays that most archaeologists are prepared to accept several independent origins for megaliths and to realise that the phrase "megalith monument" does not mean specifically structures formally, constructionally and functionally identical and therefore historically connected.'

Iberia became one area of megalithic origins (cf. Daniel 1967, 1973; Renfrew 1973, 1976). However, among prehistorians concerned with Iberia reaction ranged from acceptance (e.g. Arnaud 1978) to cautious appraisal (e.g. M.J. Almagro Gorbea 1973b, 333; Balbín-Behrmann 1978) and disbelief. It is worthy of note that radiocarbon dating has been slower in its adoption in Iberia for all periods of prehistory than in other areas of western Europe.

Another reaction has been to accept broadly the new chronology but to maintain the mode of interpretation (e.g. Savory 1968, 1975, 1977; MacKie 1977). This reminds us that chronology does not constitute explanation. Time like space is but a dimension of archaeology. In order to explain we have to invoke a body of theory and move beyond chronology. Here I disagree with the assumptions underlying traditional culture theory in the discussion of megalithic origins. Formal similarities in mortuary practices do not necessarily reflect interaction between communities of builders. Indeed this would be a dubious assumption for any cultural studies, as Renfrew was arguing in his paper on supposed links between the eastern Mediterranean and prehistoric Iberia (1967) and has been discussed in other more recent case-studies (e.g. Hodder 1978). The sole identification of change within mortuary practices with religion or beliefs and hence with population change has also received criticism (e.g. Binford 1971; Chapman 1977, in press, b; Chapman and Randsborg in press). The social correlates of mortuary practices are now in the ascendant. Irregular change in mortuary practices, as in other cultural traits, does not necessarily imply any disjunction in human populations. Given periods of comparatively rapid social change, it is surely not surprising that our archaeological time-scales may be too coarse to plot the essentially continuous development. Changes in the form of mortuary practices may conceal continuity in the processes of social change.

Given assumptions such as these and a more anthropological approach to social change, more recent 'explanations' of megalithic origins are found wanting. The role of diffusion is central to the work of Savory (1968, 1975, 1977), Clark (1977) and MacKie (1977). For Savory it is the rite of collective burial which is the most important characteristic of megalithic tombs and which diffused westwards from the Levantine Near East (e.g. the Natufian culture c.8000 bc) to Iberia and then up the Atlantic façade (or 'corridor' as Savory refers to it) to the rest of western Europe. For Savory communal burial was 'more fundamental than tomb morphology'(1977, 162). But what is not explained is why communal burial should have been the result of monogenesis, what is symbolized that was different from individual or family burial and how it could diffuse through the length of the Mediterranean and up Atlantic Europe? In other words what is lacking is an explanation based on coherent, testable social theory. The unity of the megalith builders and their religious orientation is also assumed by Clark, who considers the role of fishermen in the exploration of 'remoter territories as well as helping to feed the builders and even themselves assisting in the new cult' (1977, 43). One wonders whether they were also 'fishers of men'! Certainly MacKie's megalith builders were (1977). Collective burial again forms the unifying factor, but MacKie is much more explicit about the nature of the diffusion process. In place of social evolution he presents an argument based upon ethnocentric attitude and genetic reductionism: following Darlington he claims that 'numerous recorded examples appear to show quite clearly that periods of innovation and rapid development in the past have coincided with hybridization between hitherto separate populations or classes' (1977, 139). The appearance of megalithic tombs in Iberia and western Europe is then reduced to the 'talents' and 'skills' of travelling 'theocrats'. With this untestable hypothesis based upon genetic rather than social theory MacKie then proceeds to a series of unwarranted assertions: for example 'the emergence of the rite of collective burial almost certainly means that a new class of dominant people had arrived or developed in Iberia' (1977, 158) and the existence of Copper Age water control in south-east Spain rein-

forces the existence of a 'well-organized governing class served by specialist professions' (1977, 161: for a contrary view, Chapman 1978).

In contrast there have been recent examples of testable theory which may be applied to megalithic tombs (Renfrew 1976, 1979; Chapman in press, b). Elsewhere I have argued as follows (Chapman in press, b):

> Interment in cemeteries or monuments will emerge in periods of imbalance between society and critical resources. Such imbalance may arise in many ways, but in all cases society perceives the spatial and/or temporal variation in important resources to have approached a critical level and devises new mechanisms to regulate access to these resources. The emergence of territorially based descent groups . . . is a response to this process and the new social order may be symbolized to the community at large by the use of formal disposal areas, through which a permanent claim to the use and control of critical resources is established by the presence of the ancestors.

The difference between cemeteries and monuments (whether megalithic or not) lies in the fact that the former are bounded in two dimensions while the latter are bounded in three dimensions. The emphasis here is upon processes of sociocultural change and their reflection in archaeologically discernible human behaviour. Furthermore the 'problem' of megalithic tombs dissolves and in each area where they occur attention is focussed upon patterns of variation within local cultural systems. The remaining sections of this paper consider Iberian megalithic tombs in this light.

Regional Distribution and Representation

We begin at the regional level and in subsequent sections move down to local areas, cemeteries and individual tombs. The aim here is to provoke thought on the regional distribution of tombs in Iberia and the degree to which it is fully representative of the original distribution in the fifth to third millennia BC. Such assessment is essential when analysing the intensity of prehistoric settlement and the relative importance of megalithic tombs in different regions of the peninsula. The map in ill 1 gives a schematic representation of tomb distribution. From this can be seen the overwhelming focus upon the northern, western and southern edges of the peninsula, with the central and eastern areas containing few, if any, tombs (for more detailed maps, see Savory 1968, Figs. 23, 32, 37, 41 and 44). Corpus volumes have been published for the tombs of Andalucia and the south-east (Leisner and

Leisner 1943), Huelva (Márquez, Leisner and Leisner 1952), Reguengos de Monsaraz (Leisner and Leisner 1951), southern Portugal (Leisner and Leisner 1956; Leisner 1965) and Catalonia and the Pyrenees (Pericot 1950). Further publications are awaited, for example on Beira Alta, while in the north-west publication has been supplemented by the volumes of the *Corpus de Sepulcros Megaliticos* and by distribution maps and a corpus of tombs for the province of Alava (Apellániz 1973; Ciprés, Galilea and Lopez 1978).

Work on a number of areas of southern Iberia encourages the conclusion that the main distribution of tombs as published by the Leisners is an accurate reflection of the survival of tombs, although there are one or two interesting exceptions. In the south-east there have been two cemeteries published since the 1940s, at El Barranquete (at least thirty tombs – M.J. Almagro Gorbea 1973a) and Cerro de Nieles, La Huelga (again at least thirty tombs – Algorra Esteban 1953). Elsewhere there have only been three further tombs published in lowland Almeria. Moving over into Granada, in the east there have been occasional finds of single or small numbers of tombs (e.g. Cerro de la Virgen – Schüle and Pellicer 1966), while the main change in our knowledge occurred within the confines of an already existing group at Gorafe, where García Sánchez and Spanhi (1959) increased by a quarter the number of tombs excavated by the Sirets. To the west the only sizeable number of recently published tombs occurred at Pantano de los Bermejales (Arenas del Rey – e.g. Arribas and Sánchez de Corral 1970). Moving into Seville and Huelva provinces the basic frequency and distribution of tombs has remained unaltered in the last thirty years.

The estimation of tomb destruction, even in modern times, is a difficult process. For the present century García Sánchez and Spanhi (1959) calculated that some forty tombs in the Gorafe area has been destroyed. This amounts to a quarter of those excavated by the Sirets and one-sixth of the total number known.

The central plateau, the Meseta, presents problems of interpretation when looking at prehistoric human occupation in any period, especially when one considers the nature of the environment and the low density of the contemporary human population. The main concentration of tombs is to be found on the western side (e.g. around Salamanca: Losada 1976) and seems to represent the extension of settlement and megalith building up the valleys of the main rivers (Guadiana, Tagus and Duero). More isolated tombs extend to the east to Guadalajara and through the provinces of Burgos, Palencia and Logrono (discussion in Savory 1975). The north-western and south-eastern Meseta

are devoid of tombs. How do we interpret these distributions? Savory (1977) suggests that we do not know the extent of tomb destruction and that fieldwork may yet change our knowledge of tomb distribution. In this light it is certainly true that new tombs have been discovered in the last two decades, as Savory discusses elsewhere (1975). New sites have been discovered for other prehistoric periods. For the Lower Palaeolithic the need for more systematic survey was highlighted by the concentration of new sites found on the southern Meseta around Calatrava (Santonja Gómez 1976). The same point was made by the distribution of Bronze Age 'motilla' sites on the south-east Meseta: recent publication shows just how many of these highly visible sites had escaped previous attention (Molina and Najera 1978). On the other hand the low density of occupation on the north-west and south-east Meseta is noted even in the Lower Palaeolithic and is repeated in the Upper Palaeolithic (Davidson 1980) and in the distribution of Beaker culture material (Delibes de Castro 1977; Harrison 1977). In one area where fairly intensive survey has been undertaken recently, in the north of Burgos, no new tomb finds were noted (Clark 1979). What is interesting here is that the authors concluded that the main human exploitation of this area did not begin until the second and first millennia bc. Prior to this there was a low population density and a mainly pastoral exploitation is favoured. Given the severe climatic extremes and higher altitudes of the Meseta, it is a logical hypothesis that the main initial centres of prehistoric populations in the peninsula were around the lower coastal fringes and that the last two millennia bc represented periods of more substantial colonization (e.g. the period of the Beaker finds, including grave goods in megalithic tombs, and of the 'motillas' in the south-east) of the plateau. However, this should not be taken as support for the proposition that the distribution of megalithic tombs in the Meseta and in the peninsula as a whole could be accounted for by the pattern of medieval and modern transhumance (e.g. the Mesta – Higgs 1976). The distribution of tombs is not identical to that of the transhumance routes and the medieval flock movements were directed and determined by political and economic pressures (Chapman 1979).

Groups, Cemeteries and Settlement: the Spatial Dimension

Moving down from the broad regional level, we must now focus on the spatial patterning of tombs and groups of tombs within the settlement landscape. What patterns can be defined? How do they relate to

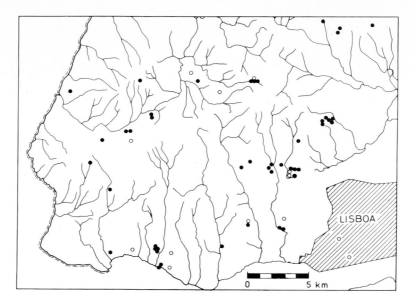

2 Tombs and Copper Age settlements in the Lisbon peninsula. Closed circles: all tombs (megalithic, rock-cut etc.). Open circles: settlements. (After Leisner 1965.)

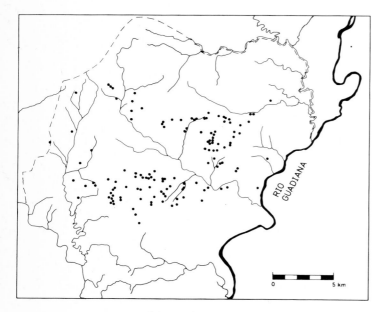

3 Megalithic tombs in Reguengos de Monsaraz. (After Leisner and Leisner 1951.)

settlements and resource distribution? Ultimately our interest here lies in the relationship between the settlement landscape of the living and the funerary landscape of the dead (Chapman and Randsborg in press). To put it another way, what factors govern the spatial location of megalithic tombs in relation to the everyday activities of the surviving members of the local community? On this level the archaeologist can approach the question of territorial definition and resource control raised in recent theoretical discussions (Renfrew 1976; Chapman in press, b).

Our knowledge of spatial patterning for megalithic tombs is rather poor for south-east Spain. The tombs published by the Leisners (1943) for Almeria are divided into groups 1–40, but no large-scale plans of their locations have been published, with the exception of the tombs at Almizaraque (Leisner and Leisner 1943, taf. 165, top; also M.J. Almagro Gorbea 1965) and Mojácar (Leisner and Leisner 1943, taf. 165; cf. Arribas 1955–6). More recently we have seen the plans of the cemeteries from Los Millares (Almagro and Arribas 1963) and El Barranquete (M.J. Almagro Gorbea 1973a). It is a matter of debate whether the Leisners' groups represent coherent cemeteries as opposed to more dispersed arrangements: certainly their groups 32 (Tabernas) and 20 (Nijar) do not form single cemeteries. We also have a poor knowledge of the internal chronology of the cemeteries of the Copper Age (Chapman in press, a) and of the association of all the tombs with settlements (although note the exceptions of Los Millares, El Barranquete (M.J. Almagro Gorbea 1977), Cerro de la Virgen (Schüle and Pellicer 1966), Almizaraque and Mojácar.

Further to the west in Granada there are plans of the groups at Gorafe and Alicún (García Sánchez and Spanhi 1959), Laborcillas and Fonelas (Leisner and Leisner 1943, tafs. 167–8), with the latter examples showing more localized, nucleated patterns.

In the south-west of the peninsula there are more maps of megalith distributions (e.g. Leisner and Leisner 1951, 1956; Leisner 1965). For the Alto Alemtejo and the Lisbon peninsula there is a much surer basis for analysis of spatial patterning. In addition more Neolithic and Copper Age settlement locations have been published. Ill. 2 shows the distribution of megalithic tombs and rock-cut tombs in relation to Copper Age settlements in the Lisbon peninsula. For Alto Alemtejo Arnaud (1971) has published a list of a dozen Neolithic-Copper Age settlements which were known from surface collections and has subsequently excavated at Castelo do Giraldo, from which a date of *c*.3100 BC was obtained on pottery (Whittle and Arnaud 1975). To the south, in the Algarve, excavation has begun on the settlement located within 200 m of the famous group of tombs at Alcalar (Arnaud and Gamito 1978).

The nature of spatial patterning in the south-east and the south-west has aroused interest. It has been suggested that there is an important contrast between the nucleated cemeteries of the south-east and the dispersed examples of the south-west. The distribution of tombs at Reguengos de Monsaraz (ill. 3) and near Torres Vedras (ill. 4) (to the north of Lisbon) could be contrasted with that in the cemetery at Los Millares (ill. 5). It is certainly true that a dispersed pattern of tomb distribution is visible in the south-west and there is no cemetery like Los Millares. On the other hand Millares is exceptional in the south-east, with its eighty to one hundred tombs. With the exception of the Gorafe tombs as well, only two other

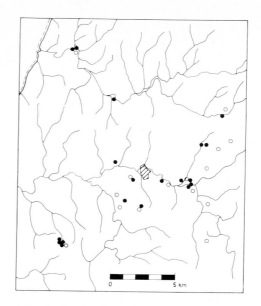

4 Tombs (closed circles) and Copper Age settlements (open circles) near Torres Vedras (shaded). (After Leisner 1965.)

5 Cemetery of tombs at Los Millares (Almeria).

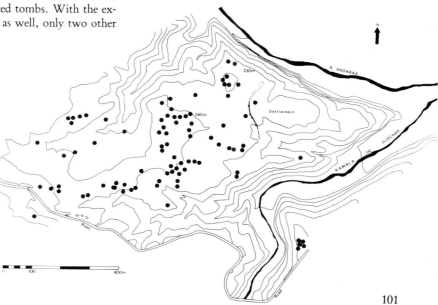

cemeteries or groups have at least thirty tombs and the overwhelming majority only have between one and five tombs in each group. Thus it can be argued that the contrast between the large, nucleated cemeteries of the south-east and the smaller or dispersed groups of the south-west has been overemphasized. Which all goes to raise further questions about the conditions under which nucleated cemeteries appear, in particular the parts played by social development and increased settlement hierarchization and the control of critical resources (Chapman, in press, b; Renfrew 1979).

6 Examples of structural differentiation within megalithic tombs in Iberia. Top left, Fonelas 10. Top right, Fonelas 9 Bottom left, Los Rurialillos 2. Bottom right, Los Millares 17. (All after Leisner and Leisner 1943.) Scale 1:100.

Tombs, Formation Processes and 'Megalithometry'

The last level of analysis relates the form, dimensions, internal division and contents of individual tombs to their design and the sequence of activities which took place within them. As with other levels it has its difficulties: if the analysis of spatial patterning is affected by tomb destruction, then individual tombs are subject to robbing and many an indecent assault in the name of excavation! In most cases we have to work with tombs through such filters (e.g. Chapman, in press, c). Basically all tombs share the common factor of providing an enclosed space for a series of activities relating to the disposal of the dead, or rather, to follow Kinnes (in press) the preservation and utilization of the dead. Their morphology may be seen as the result of what Fleming has referred to as 'a process of problem-solving' (1973). Both Fleming (1972, 1973) and Kinnes (1975, in press) have focussed upon the factors which lie behind tomb morphology, with (in Fleming's case) the use of metrical indices to distinguish the

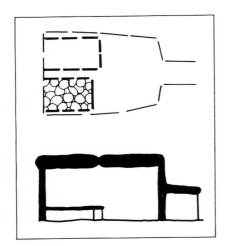

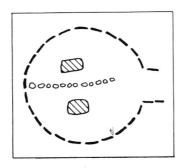
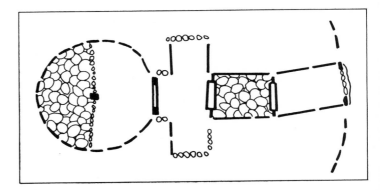

relative importance of tomb and mound. This study of 'megalithometry' has yet to be pursued for Iberian tombs, although an initial attempt was published by Ruiz (1973). Note might also be made of the relationship between the increased enclosed space provided by later tombs in some areas and the increase in the range and frequency of activities carried out within them. This would reflect the distinction between earlier burial 'crypts' and later 'charnel houses', as discussed by James Brown (nd) for the middle Woodland period in the Eastern United States.

Given differential preservation and destruction, one cannot be sure that a sufficient sample of tombs with internal structural differentiation is available. In the Leisners (1943) publication one can find examples of tombs with segmented passages and others with divisions of the chamber area, including stone slab divisions, walls, stone paving, and slab compartments (e.g. ill. 6). In some cases (e.g. the Fonelas tombs) there are even details of the presence of skeletal material and grave goods associated with these divisions. But as a whole there are only a few tombs in Almería and Granada for which we have any knowledge of the spatial distribution of skeletal parts, and grave goods. For the cemetery of Los Millares we only have the plan of tomb XXI (Almagro and Arribas 1963), with its evidence for the differential treatment and arrangement of crania, long bones and vertebrae. With the exception of an old sketch of Luis Siret's of the Encantada I tomb at Almizaraque, the only other plans from Almería come from the more recent excavations at El Barranquete: the excavator noted clusters of crania, piles or bundles of bones and in a few cases more completely articulated skeletons, as well as distinct layers of deposits (M.J. Almagro Gorbea 1973a). In addition it should be noted that further evidence was found which supported the conclusion that the size of such tombs was not simply determined by the number of individuals to be accorded final interment within them. In the Guadalquivir valley, tombs such as the Cueva del Vaquero, Cañada Honda and the Dolmen de Matarrubilla have preserved evidence for depositional sequences and spatial arrangements of skeletal remains and grave goods (Leisner and Leisner 1943; Collantes de Teran 1969). The best evidence from southern Portugal comes from Praia das Maças (Leisner 1965), while in the north we may note the Carapito tombs (Leisner and Ribeiro 1968). It is upon such few tombs as these that attention will have to be focussed, as well as any future excavations.

Conclusion

In 1970 Glyn Daniel wrote that 'the question now before earnest megalithic enquirers is this: what ancient peoples built megalithic tombs in which ancient places in Europe, and why?' (1970, 267). In this paper I have considered Iberian megalithic tombs and have argued that the 'ancient peoples' were indigenous to the peninsula. How do we explain the tomb development? The answer lies in the development of coherent theory which links change in mortuary practices to the wider sociocultural setting. Above all else we now seek to understand these tombs in a context and not as isolated entities. As a contribution towards this aim I have considered three levels of analysis which might be pursued: the regional level, the local settlement landscape level and the individual tomb level. At each level we are concerned with different problems and scales of analysis. If this paper serves no other purpose than to demonstrate the inadequacy and futility of pursuing the megalithic 'problem', then a step will have been taken in the right direction.

Acknowledgments

I would like to thank Jan Chapman for typing this paper, and for her general support during the writing of it. Ills 2–4 and 6 were kindly prepared by Averil Martin-Hoogewerf.

Bibliography

ABERG, N. 1921 *La Civilisation Enéolithique dans la Péninsule Ibérique,* Leipzig.

ALGARRA ESTEBAN, R. 1953 'Cerro de Nieles', *Noticiario Arqueológico Hispánico* I, 37.

ALMAGRO, M. AND ARRIBAS, A. 1963 *El poblado y la necropólis megalíticos de Los Millares,* Madrid.

ALMAGRO GORBEA, M. 1970 'Las Fechas del C–14 para la Prehistoria y la Arqueología Peninsular', *Trabajos de Prehistoria* XXVII, 9–44.

ALMAGRO GORBEA, M. AND FERNÁNDEZ-MIRANDA, M. (eds.) 1978 *C–14 y Prehistoria de la Península Ibérica, Reunión 1978,* Madrid.

ALMAGRO GORBEA, M.J. 1965 *Las Tres Tumbas Megalíticas de Almizaraque,* Madrid.

1973a *El Poblado y la necrópolis de El Barranquete (Almeria),* Madrid.

1973b *Los Idolos del Bronce I Hispano,* Madrid.

1977 'El recientemente destruido poblado de El Tarajal', *XIV Congreso Nacional de Arqueologia,* 305–18.

APELLÁNIZ, J.M. 1973 'Corpus de materiales de las culturas prehistoricas con ceramica de la poblacion de cavernas del Pais Vasco meridional', *Munibe* suplemento 1, 7–366.

ARNAUD, J.M. 1971 'Os povoados "Neo-Eneoliticos" de Famao e Aboboreira (Ciladas, Vila Viçosa)'. Noticia Preliminar, *II Congreso Nacional de Arqueologia,* 199–221.

1978 'O Megalitismo en Portugal: Problemas e Perspectivas'. *Actas das III Jornadas Arqueológicas,* 91–112.

ARNAUD, J.M. AND GAMITO, T.J. 1978 'Povoãdo Calcolítico de Alcalar. Notícia de sua identificaçao', *Anais do Município* VIII, 3–10.

ARRIBAS, A. 1955–6 'El sepulcro megalítico del Cabecico de Aguilar de Cuartillas (Mojácar, Almería)', *Ampurias* XVII–XVIII, 210–14.

ARRIBAS, A. AND SANCHEZ DEL CORRAL, J.M. 1970 'La necrópolis megalitica del Pantano de los Bermejales (Arenas del Rey, Granada)', *XI Congreso Nacional de Arqueologia,* 284–91.

BALBÍN-BEHRMANN, R. DE 1978 'Problematica actual de la cronologia radioactiva en relacion con la tradicional durante el megalitismo y el eneolítico', in Almagro Gorbea, M. and Fernández-Miranda M. (eds), *C-14 y Prehistoria de la Península Ibérica, Reunión 1978,* Madrid.

BINFORD, L.R. 1965 'Archaeological systematics and the study of culture process', *American Antiquity* XXXI, 203–10.

1971 Mortuary practices: their study and potential, in Brown, J.A. (ed.), *Approaches to the social dimensions of mortuary practices,* Memoirs of the Society for American Archaeology no.25.

BLANCE, B.M. 1960 *The Origins and Development of the Early Bronze Age in the Iberian Peninsula,* Ph.D. dissertation, University of Edinburgh.

1961 'Early Bronze Age colonists in Iberia', *Antiquity* XXXV, 192–202.

BOSCH-GIMPERA, P. 1932 *Etnologia de la Península Ibérica,* Barcelona.

1944 *El poblamiento antiguo y la formación de los pueblos de España,* Mexico.

1967 'Civilisation mégalithique portugaise et civilisations espagnoles', *L'Anthropologie* LXXI, 1–48.

BROWN, J.A. n.d. 'Charnel houses and mortuary crypts: disposal of the dead in the Middle Woodland Period.'

CARTAILHAC, E. 1886 *Les âges préhistoriques de l'Espagne et du Portugal,* Paris.

CHAPMAN, R.W. 1975 *Economy and society within later prehistoric Iberia: a new framework,* Ph.D. dissertation, University of Cambridge.

1977 'Burial practices – an area of mutual interest', in Spriggs, M. (ed.) *Archaeology and Anthropology. Areas of Mutual Interest,* Oxford.

1978 'The evidence for prehistoric water control in south-east Spain', *Journal of Arid Environments* I, 261–74.

1979 'Transhumance and megalithic tombs in Iberia', *Antiquity* LIII, 150–2.

in press (a) 'Los Millares and the relative chronology of the Copper Age in south-east Spain', *Trabajos de Prehistoria* XXXVII.

in press (b) 'The emergence of formal disposal areas and the 'problem' of megalithic tombs in prehistoric Europe', in Chapman, R.W., Kinnes, I.A. and Randsborg, K. *The Archaeology of Death,* Cambridge.

in press (c) 'Archaeological theory and communal burial in prehistoric Europe', in Hodder, I., Isaac, G. and Hammond N. (eds) *Pattern of the Past: studies in honour of David Clarke,* Cambridge.

forthcoming *Autonomy and Social Evolution: the later prehistory of the Iberian peninsula,* Cambridge.

CHAPMAN, R.W. AND RANDSBORG, K. in press 'Approaches to the archaeology of death', in Chapman, R.W., Kinnes, I.A. and Randsborg, K. (eds) *The Archaeology of Death,* Cambridge.

CHILDE, V.G. 1932 'Scottish megalithic tombs and their affinities', *Transactions of the Glasgow Archaeological Society,* 120–3.

CIPRÉS, A., GALILEA, F. AND LÓPEZ, L. 1978 'Dolmenes y tumulos de las Sierras de Guibijo y Badaya. Plantamiento para su estudio a la vista de los ultimos descubrimientos', *Estudios de Arqueologia Alavesa* IX, 65–125.

CLARK, G. (ed.) 1979 *The North Burgos Archaeological Survey. Bronze and Iron Age Archaeology on the Meseta del Norte (Province of Burgos, North-Central Spain),* Arizona.

CLARK, J.G.D. 1977 'The economic context of dolmens and passage graves in Sweden', in Markotic, V. (ed.), *Ancient Europe and the Mediterranean,* Warminster.

CLARKE, D.L. 1973 'Archaeology: the loss of innocence', *Antiquity* XLVII, 6–18.

COLLANTES DE TERÁN, F. 1969 'El Dolmen de Matarrubilla', in *Tartessos y sus problemas, V Symposium

Internacional de Prehistoria Peninsular, Barcelona.

DANIEL, G.E. 1941 'The Dual Nature of the Megalithic Colonisation of Prehistoric Europe', *Proc. Preh. Soc.* VII, 1–49.

1963 *The Megalith Builders of Western Europe,* 2nd edn, London.

1966 'Megalith builders of the SOM', *Palaeohistoria* XII, 199–208.

1967 'Northmen and Southmen', *Antiquity* XLI, 313–17.

1970 'Megalithic Answers', *Antiquity* XLIV, 260–9.

1971 'From Worsaae to Childe: the models of prehistory', *Proc. Preh. Soc.* XXXVII, part II, 140–53.

1973 'Spain and the problem of European megalithic origins', in *Estudios dedicados al Prof. Dr. Luis Pericot,* Barcelona, 209–14.

DAVIDSON, I. 1980 'Transhumance, Spain and ethnoarchaeology', *Antiquity* LIV, 144–7.

DELIBES DE CASTRO, G. 1977 *El Vaso Campaniforme en la Meseta Norte Española,* Valladolid.

DELIBRIAS, J., ROCHE, J. AND VEIGA FERREIRA, O.da 1967 'Chronologie absolue d'un monument énéolithique du Bas Alentejo (Portugal) par la méthode du carbone 14', *Comptes Rendus Academie des Sciences de Paris* 265, serie D, 245–6.

FERGUSSON, J. 1872 *Rude Stone Monuments in all Countries, Their Age and Uses,* London.

FLEMING, A. 1972 'Vision and design: approaches to ceremonial monument typology', *Man* VII, 57–73.

1973 'Tombs for the living', *Man* VIII, 177–93.

FORDE, C.D. 1929 'The Megalithic culture sequence in Iberia', *Liverpool Annals of Archaeology and Anthropology* XVI, 37–46.

1930 'Early Cultures of Atlantic Europe', *American Anthropologist* XXXII, 19–100.

GARCÍA SÁNCHEZ, M. AND SPANHI, J.-C 1959 'Sepulcros megalíticos de la región de Gorafe (Granada)', *Archivo de Prehistoria Levantina* VIII, 43–113.

HARRISON, R.J. 1977 *The Bell Beaker cultures of Spain and Portugal,* Cambridge, Mass.

HIGGS, E.S. 1976 'The history of European agriculture: the uplands', *Philosophical Transactions of the Royal Society of London,* B, 275, 159–73.

HODDER, I. (ed.) 1978 *The Spatial Organisation of Culture,* London.

KINNES, I. 1975 'Monumental function in British neolithic burial practices', *World Arch.* VII, 16-29.

in press 'Dialogues with death', in Chapman, R.W., Kinnes, I.A. and Randsborg, K. (eds) *The Archaeology of Death,* Cambridge.

LEEDS, E.T. 1918–20 'The Dolmens and Megalithic Tombs of Spain and Portugal', *Archaeologia* LXX, 201–32.

LEISNER, G. AND LEISNER, V. 1943 *Die Megalithgräber der Iberischen Halbinsel: Der Süden,* Berlin.

1951 *Antas do Concelho de Reguëngos de Monsaraz,* Lisbon.

1956 *Die Megalithgräber der Iberischen Halbinsel: Der Westen,* Berlin.

LEISNER, V. 1965 *Die Megalithgräber der Iberischen Halbinsel: Der Westen,* Berlin.

LEISNER, V. AND RIBEIRO, C. 1968 'Die Dolmen von Carapito', *Madrider Mitteilungen* IX, 11–62.

LEISNER, V. AND VEIGA FERREIRA, O. DA 1963 'Primeiras datas de rádiocarbono 14 para a cultura megalítica portuguesa', *Revista de Guimaraes* LXXIII, 358–66.

LOSADA, H. 1976 'El Dolmen de Entreterminos (Madrid)', *Trabajos de Prehistoria,* XXXIII, 209–26.

MACKIE, E.W. 1977 *The Megalith Builders,* Oxford.

MÁRQUEZ, C.C., LEISNER, G. AND LEISNER, V. 1952 *Los Sepulcros Megalíticos de Huelva,* Madrid.

MOLINA, F. AND NAJERA, T. 1978 'Die Motillas von Azuer und Los Palacios (Prov. Ciudad Real)', *Madrider Mitteilungen* XIX, 52–74.

OBERMAIER, H. 1919 *El Dolmen de Matarrubilla,* Madrid.

PEAKE, H.J.E. AND FLEURE, H.J. 1930 'Megaliths and Beakers', *Journal of the Royal Anthropological Institute* IX, 47–72.

PEET, T.E. 1912 *Rough Stone Monuments and their Builders,* London.

PERICOT, L. 1950 *Los Sepulcros Megalíticos Catalanes y la Cultura Pirenaica,* Barcelona.

RENFREW, C. 1967 'Colonialism and megalithismus', *Antiquity* XLI, 276–88.

1970 'The tree-ring calibration of radiocarbon: an archaeological evaluation', *Proc. Preh. Soc.* XXXVI, 280–311.

1973 *Before Civilisation,* London.

1976 'Megaliths, territories and populations', in De Laet, S.J. (ed.), *Acculturation and continuity in Atlantic Europe,* Bruges.

1979 *Investigations in Orkney,* London.

RUIZ SOLANES, J. 1973 'Para el estudio estadistico de los sepulcros megalíticos', *XII Congreso Nacional de Arqueologia,* 201–10.

SANTONJA GÓMEZ, M. 1976 'Industrias del Paleolítico Inferior en la Meseta Española', *Trabajos de Prehistoria* XXXIII, 121–64.

SAVORY, H.N. 1968 *Spain and Portugal,* London.

1975 'The role of the Upper Duero and Ebro basins in megalithic diffusion', *Boletin del Seminario de Estudios de Arte y Arqueologia* XL–XLI, 159–74.

1977 'The role of Iberian communal tombs in Mediterranean and Atlantic prehistory', in Markotic, V. (ed.), *Ancient Europe and the Mediterranean,* Warminster.

Schüle, W. and Pellicer, M. 1966 *El Cerro de la Virgen, Orce (Granada)*, Madrid.

Siret, L. 1913 *Questions de Chronologie et D'Ethnographie Ibériques*, Paris.

Viana, A., Veiga Ferreira, O. da and Freire de Andrade, R. 1961 'Descoberta de dois monumentos de falsa cúpula na regaio de Ourique', *Revista de Guimarães* LXXI, 5–12.

Whittle, E.H. and Arnaud, J.M. 1975 'Thermoluminescent dating of neolithic and chalcolithic pottery from sites in central Portugal', *Archaeometry* XVII, 5–24.

Wilke, G. 1912 'Sudwesteuropäische Megalithkultur', in *Mannus Bibliothek* VII.

12   Megaliths of the Central Mediterranean

Ruth Whitehouse

This essay discusses the peninsula and island zones of the central Mediterranean, excepting only Malta which is the subject of a separate article by David Trump. The main regions covered are peninsular Italy, Sicily, Sardinia and Corsica. In this region we find a great variety of monuments: rock-cut tombs, megalithic chamber tombs, menhirs and statue–menhirs, and tower-like structures of cyclopean masonry (*nuraghi* and *torri*). All these diverse monuments have at times been labelled megaliths and have been considered part of a megalithic complex or movement. Work in the last twenty years has done much to establish the dates and relationships of the various groups of monuments of all these types. However, not all the information has yet percolated through to the general literature and much misunderstanding persists. I feel, therefore, that the most useful thing I can do in this paper is to devote most of it to a straightforward description of what we can establish about the distribution, function and dates of these monuments. I shall deal with all the funerary monuments and the menhirs and statue-menhirs, but shall not consider the *nuraghi* or *torri*, which are beyond the scope of this discussion. I shall make no attempt to present a full bibliography, which would be truly vast, but under each heading I shall list a few important references. Almost all these themselves contain a useful bibliography.

Rock-cut Tombs

Of all the monuments described in this paper, the rock-cut tombs are the most widespread in the central Mediterranean; they also start earliest and last longest. Moreover they demonstrate no obvious connection with any of the other types of monuments: although there is *some* chronological and geographical overlap, the rock-cut tombs occurred initially before any of the other monuments existed and they occurred in areas where the other types of monuments were never built. In 1972 I published a paper in which I drew attention to these facts and argued that rock-cut tombs developed independently in the central Mediterranean and were not part of an intrusive megalithic complex (Whitehouse 1972). Indeed there is no reason to see them as part of a megalithic complex of any kind, whether indigenous or intrusive. I do not wish to rehearse all the arguments here, but shall outline briefly the salient facts about the tombs.

Distribution (ill. 1) Rock-cut tombs occur throughout the central and southern part of the Italian peninsula, in Sicily and in Sardinia. They are not found in Corsica or in Italy north of Tuscany.

Typology (ill. 2) On Sicily and the Italian mainland the most common tomb form in use in the early phases was the *a forno* or oven-shaped type, entered usually from a shaft, sometimes from a cliff face, occasionally through a hole in the roof. Most commonly these tombs have a single chamber, though two- and even three-chambered examples occur. In the Bronze Age there was a tendency to more regularly-made tombs, often rectangular in plan. Other forms also occur, for example a tomb with a kidney-shaped chamber and bulbous passage at Altamura in south-east Italy (late Copper Age/Early Bronze Age); or the tomb with a long passage and lateral niches on the island of Ognina, in south-east Sicily (Middle Bronze Age). In Sicily

tombs on the Early Bronze Age site of Castelluccio have blocking slabs decorated with carved spirals (once compared to those of Mycenae). In the Middle Bronze Age Thapsos culture some tombs with more elaborate architecture occur, including one with a four-pillared ante-chamber and another with a façade with sham pillars.

By far the most elaborate tombs in our area, however, are found on the island of Sardinia. Here more than 1,100 tombs have been recorded. These are entered either directly from a cliff face or through long entrance passages descending from the surface. The chambers are oval or rectangular, or, occasionally, round, and there may be many of them, often clustering round a large central chamber. Skeuomorphic wooden architectural features, such as beams, lintels and gables, are characteristic of these tombs. Other decoration occurs quite commonly: schematic bulls'

1 Distribution of rock-cut tombs in the central Mediterranean.

heads and other stylized designs executed in red paint or sculpted in relief.

Burial Rite It has generally been assumed that rock-cut tombs are invariably associated with the practice of collective burial, but this is not the case in the central Mediterranean. In the earliest tombs, both in Italy and Sicily, single or double burials only occur. Good examples are Final Neolithic tombs at Serra d'Alto and Arnesano in south-east Italy and thirty-three out of thirty-six tombs in the Copper Age cemetery at Sciacca (prov. Agrigento) in southern Sicily. In this cemetery the other three tombs had been used for collective burial and these were, on the basis of the pot-

107

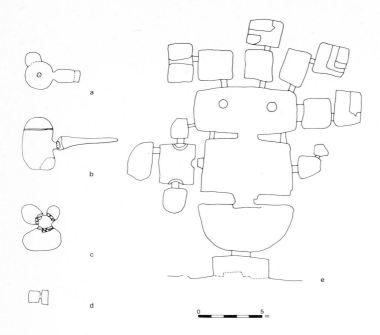

2 Plans of rock-cut tombs. a *San Vito dei Normanni (after Lo Porto);* b *Casal Sabini, Altamura (after Biancofiore);* c *Cellino San Marco (after Lo Porto);* d *San Francesco, Matera (after Rellini);* e *Sant' Andrea Priu (after Lilliu). (Drawn by Philip Howard.)*

tery they contained, later in date. On this site at least single burial was the rule initially, with collective burial coming in at a later stage. In the third millennium BC and later collective burial seems to have been the general rule everywhere. Skeletons are often found disarticulated, with only the last interment complete. Pottery, flint and metal weapons and ornaments commonly occur as grave goods.

Chronology There is some controversy over the date of the earliest rock-cut tombs in the central Mediterranean. The earliest dates actually from rock-cut tombs occur in the south-west Italian cemetery at Buccino, in association with artifacts of the Copper Age Gaudo group. A series of six radiocarbon dates from this site fall between 2580 and 1970 bc, correcting to c. 3350–2500 BC (all radiocarbon dates are listed with full details in the Appendix). However, the earliest tombs are certainly earlier than this. In 1972 I claimed that rock-cut tombs were used first in Italy not in the Copper Age, as had always been claimed, but in the Neolithic (Whitehouse 1972, 276). In support of this claim I quoted two damaged examples of probable fifth millennium BC (Middle Neolithic) date

– Fonteviva on the Tavoliere plain and Pizzone near Taranto – and an undamaged example of early fourth millennium BC (Final Neolithic) date at Serra d' Alto near Matera. At a conference held in Foggia in April 1973 (Tinè 1975), my view came under attack from David Trump and Santo Tinè, both of whom claimed that the structure at Fonteviva was not a true rock-cut tomb and that the date and nature of the Pizzone example were not established. These criticisms I accept to some extent. The Pizzone example is certainly unsatisfactory and there are also some problems about the Fonteviva structure. However, this latter structure *was* Neolithic, *was* cut in the rock (though apparently from the side of a village ditch) and *was* used for burial. If not a true cut tomb, it makes a good prototype for the real thing. There has been no challenge to the validity of my third Neolithic example: the tomb excavated by Rellini at Serra d'Alto. Moreover, since then another rock-cut tomb of indisputably Final Neolithic date, at Arnesano near Lecce, has been published (Lo Porto 1973). This tomb, of the *a forno* type, was used for the burial of a single individual, who was interred with pottery of Bellavista type (Whitehouse 1969, 300–3). This tomb should be approximately contemporary with the Serra d'Alto one, dating to c. 3950–3750 BC (C14 dates 3200–2900 bc; Whitehouse 1978, 81). It is clear that rock-cut tombs were in use in the first half of the fourth millennium BC in Italy; they may have begun in the fifth millennium BC.

Some of the Sardinian rock-cut tombs may be almost as early. We have no radiocarbon dates from the tombs themselves, but we have dates for the Ozieri culture, with which many of the tombs are associated, from the Grotta del Guano and from Bonu Ighinu of 3140–2880 bc (3950–3650 BC)

In the peninsula rock-cut tombs became common in the Copper Age, c. 3300–2300 BC (Whitehouse 1978, 84–5), and it is to the same period that we should probably assign many of the rock-cut tombs in Sardinia and Sicily; tombs on both islands have yielded sherds and occasional complete vessels of Beaker pottery, in keeping with the chronology just suggested. The main cultural groups of the Copper Age with which rock-cut tombs are associated are: Rinaldone, Gaudo and Laterza in peninsular Italy (Whitehouse and Renfrew 1975), Ozieri in Sardinia, Conca d'Oro, San Cono and Malpasso in Sicily.

After the third millennium BC rock-cut tombs went out of fashion in most of peninsular Italy; they continued in use, however, in south-east Italy, in Sicily and in Sardinia. In Sicily indeed they continued to be the main tomb form throughout the Bronze Age and into the Iron Age, and until and beyond the Greek col-

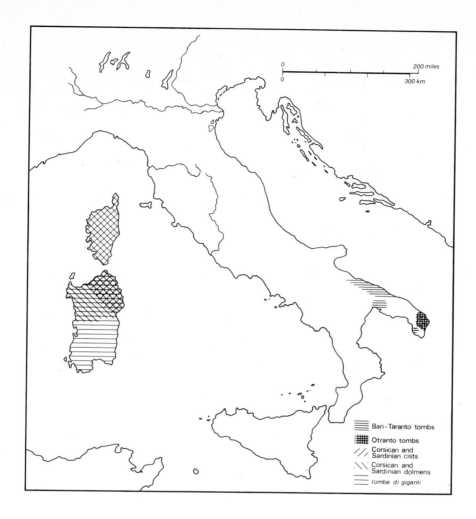

Bari-Taranto tombs
Otranto tombs
Corsican and Sardinian cists
Corsican and Sardinian dolmens
tombe di giganti

3 Distribution of megalithic tombs in the central Mediterranean.

onization of the island. Huge cemeteries of thousands of tombs characterize the Sicilian Iron Age, e.g. the Pantalica North and Caltagirone cemeteries. Late Bronze Age and Iron Age examples are found also in south-east Italy and in the extreme south-west (southern Calabria). In Sardinia they continued in use well into the Nuragic period, in the second millennium BC. In central Italy their use was reintroduced by the Etruscans in the seventh century BC.

Relationships In the central Mediterranean, rock-cut tombs are not generally associated with megalithic chamber tombs as they are in Portugal. Megalithic tombs indeed are not found at all in Sicily or in much of peninsular Italy. In those areas where rock-cut and megalithic tombs *are* both found – south-east Italy and Sardinia – the rock-cut tombs begin earlier, though they continue in use alongside the megaliths.

In both areas also some rock-cut tombs (including examples of both early and late types) are associated with menhirs.

In 1972 I expressed the view that there was no reason to believe that the rock-cut tombs of the central Mediterranean represented an intrusive feature. I based this on the fact that central Mediterranean tombs are at least as early as, and perhaps earlier than, hypothetical prototypes in the east Mediterranean (Cyprus and the Cyclades). Moreover the earliest tombs in mainland Italy and Sicily are simple in form and were used for single or double burial only. They appear in the context of local Neolithic cultures and cannot be seen as part of an intrusive Copper Age complex. The

109

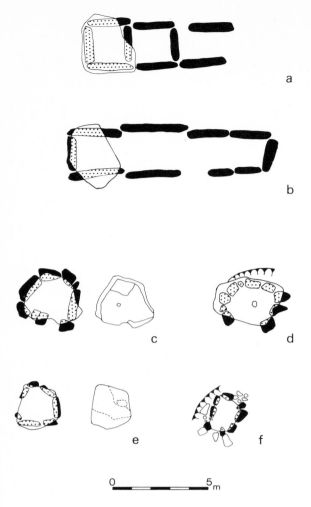

4 Plans of megalithic tombs in Italy. a Corato (after Gervasio); b Bisceglie (after Gervasio); c Quattromacine; d Scusi; e Placa; f Gurgulante. (Drawn by Philip Howard.)

simplest explanation is to see a local development within the central Mediterranean from the simple Neolithic tombs to the more elaborate Copper Age and later ones.

References Bernabò Brea 1957, Chapter III; Bray 1963: Guido 1963, Chapter II; Lilliu 1975, Chapter IVa, 2; Whitehouse 1972.

Megalithic Chamber Tombs (ill. 3)

True megalithic chamber tombs occur in three separate areas within our region: south-east Italy, Corsica and Sardinia. 'Sub-megalithic' tombs such as small stone cists also occur, both within these areas and else-

where, but I shall exclude these in general from the present discussion. I shall deal, however, with those examples that have been claimed as ancestors of the true megalithic tombs: the stone cists of southern Corsica and northern Sardinia and the group at Pian Sultano on the Tyrrhenian coast of mainland Italy just north of Rome.

I shall deal separately with the three main areas in which megalithic tombs occur.

South-east Italian Megalithic Tombs

The south-east Italian megalithic tombs, always known as dolmens, fall into two clearly defined groups, to which Evans gave the names Bari-Taranto and Otranto groups (Evans 1956, 85). I employed these names in my account of the Apulian megaliths in 1967 (Whitehouse 1967).

Distribution The Bari-Taranto tombs number ten, all found within 15 km of the sea, seven near the Adriatic coast, three near the Ionian Gulf. There is also a possible megalithic tomb near Vieste on the northern coast of the Gargano promontory. The Otranto group consisted formerly of at least sixteen tombs (of which only five were extant in 1965 when I visited them); they are concentrated on the eastern side of the Terra d'Otranto (the 'heel' of Italy) and eleven of them are clustered round the village of Giurdignano.

Typology (ill. 4) The Bari-Taranto tombs are either simple rectangular chambers (e.g. Acetulla, Taviano and Trani) or larger gallery graves. They vary in length from c.3 to c. 17 m. They are built of stone (usually limestone) slabs, supplemented at Giovinazzo by a stretch of drystone walling. The tombs at Corato and Giovinazzo were subdivided into segments. Two other tombs –Bisceglie and Leucaspide – were closed at both ends and were also divided into a distinct chamber or *cella* at one end, separated from the main gallery. The exceptional Giovinazzo tomb has a damaged circular structure at one end, which appears to be original and is interpreted by the excavator as an *anticella* or lobby. This tomb was also unusually long and the passage/chamber was divided into several segments. Traces of a 'port-hole' can be seen in one slab, but this appears not to be in its original position. Six capstones survive at Giovinazzo; elsewhere only one or none at all survive. Most of the tombs have, or had when discovered, traces at least of earth or earth and stone mounds, oval or rectangular with rounded corners, sometimes revetted with drystone walls. Many tombs are aligned east-west, with the entrance facing east.

The Otranto tombs are quite different from those of the northern group. They are much smaller and lack the rectangular form and regular slab construction that characterize the Bari-Taranto group. Instead they are oval, polygonal or sub-rectangular in plan and are built in what I have called the *block-and-boulder* style. The supports for the capstones vary in number from two to eight and may be rough slabs, monolithic blocks, pillars made of several superimposed stones, projecting blocks of bedrock or even, in one case, a section of dry-stone walling. Several tombs were built over shallow hollows in the bedrock. The tombs are rarely more than 1 m high and vary from *c.* 2 to 4 m in length. Unlike the Bari-Taranto tombs, they lack any regular orientation; they also lack any surviving traces of mounds (though this may be an accident of preservation). Interesting features of these tombs are various markings on the upper surfaces of the capstones; two tombs had perforated capstones and another three had shallower holes, while two tombs had incised grooves.

Burial Rite No finds – neither skeletal material nor artifacts – have ever been recorded from tombs of the Otranto group, which are generally open and have often been used as tool stores or pigsties by the local *contadini*. Indeed, we have no direct evidence that these monuments were tombs at all, though their similarity to definite funerary structures elsewhere (see below) makes it likely that they were.

The Bari-Taranto monuments were certainly tombs. Many of these too had been robbed along ago, but several have yielded both human remains and artifacts. The Bisceglie tomb contained the remains of at least thirteen individuals; most of the skeletons were disarticulated, but a few survived intact and these had been buried in the contracted position. In the Giovinazzo tomb human bones were found only in one section, marked off by septal slabs; the bones, fragmentary and in a state of complete disorder, represented the remains of at least nine adults, two youths and two children.

Chronology We have no radiocarbon dates for any south Italian megalithic tomb, so for discussion of dating we are dependent on the typology of artifacts found within them or – with due caution – on the typology of the tombs themselves.

Until 1967 it was customary to date the Bari-Taranto tombs to the Middle or Late Bronze Age or even the Early Iron Age (Puglisi 1959,43; Trump 1966, 145–8). Certainly material of the Apennine culture of the later second millennium and early first millennium BC has been found in several tombs (Bisceglie, Albarosa). However, in 1967 I pointed out that some of the material from one tomb – Leucaspide – belongs to the very beginning of the Bronze Age, to

the phase sometimes called Proto-Apennine (Lo Porto's Protoappenninico B (Lo Porto 1963, 363)). Moreover, the material from Giovinazzo, published in the same year, also belongs to the Proto-Apennine B phase (Lo Porto 1967). There is also full Apennine pottery from Giovinazzo and one sherd of painted ware, which may come from an imported vessel of Late Helladic I/II type, suggesting that the tomb was still in use in the sixteenth century BC. We have no radiocarbon dates for Proto-Apennine material, but we should expect this phase to fall in the range 1800-1400 bc, between the Copper Age and the full Apennine culture (Whitehouse 1978, 84–7). This chronology, corresponding to *c.* 2300–1750 BC in calendar years, is consistent with the discovery of imported sherds of Middle Helladic type (datable to *c.* 2000–1600 BC) in Proto-Apennine levels at Porto Perone, Leporano (Lo Porto 1963). If the Bari-Taranto tombs *were* built during this period, they would overlap the main period of megalith construction elsewhere in the Mediterranean, rather than being very much later.

The Otranto tombs can only be dated – very speculatively – by comparative typology. Evans pointed out in 1956 that the Otranto tombs were very similar to those of Malta, which share the hollows beneath the tombs, the holes and grooves in the capstones, as well as the general block-and-boulder style of building. The Maltese dolmens are associated with the Tarxien Cemetery Culture, which has radiocarbon dates ranging from *c.* 1900 to 1350 bc (*c.* 2400-1650 BC). The evidence is flimsy, but as far as it goes it suggests a late third-early second millennium BC date for the initial construction of monuments of both groups.

Relationships South-east Italy has, as well as megalithic tombs, both menhirs and statue-menhirs (see below). The distribution of the menhirs is very similar to that of the chamber tombs. In the Terra d'Otranto there seems to be a specific association between menhirs and some megalithic tombs (as well as rock-cut tombs): two tombs – Scusi and Chiancuse – have in their immediate vicinity small rectangular holes in the rock, exactly like those in which surviving menhirs stand. It seems likely that these originally held menhirs, which were used as stelae marking tomb positions.

The relationship between the two groups of tombs themselves has been a matter of controversy in the past. Whereas most Italian archaeologists have always regarded them as closely related (e.g. Puglisi 1959, 43 and, by implication, Peroni 1967, 85, fig. 18), the English archaeologists Evans (1966, 90–3) and Trump (1966, 87–9, 145–7) have regarded them as entirely separate. This arose from the divergent dating for the two groups (Copper or Early Bronze Age for the Otranto group, Late Bronze or Early Iron Age for the Bari-Taranto group) and, in view of the apparent contemporaneity of the two groups on recent evidence, now seems less likely. In 1967 I regarded the two groups as related, with the Otranto tombs as derivatives of the – intrusive – Bari-Taranto group. Now I think of them as varying manifestations of the same phenomenon, much as the Italian scholars do (though I favour an earlier date and a different origin).

Parallels for both types of tombs have been sought in other parts of the central and west Mediterranean. Evans pointed out the similarities between the Otranto dolmens and those of Malta (Evans 1956), while other scholars (e.g. Guido 1963, 82–8) have pointed to similarities also with some of the Sardinian dolmens. In the case of the Bari-Taranto tombs, the best parallels are to be found in the southern French gallery graves, especially those of the Aude group (Daniel 1960, 146–54), though similar tombs occur elsewhere in France and in Iberia. The Sardinian gallery graves (*tombe di giganti*) discussed below, also have some features in common with the Bari-Taranto tombs.

The parallels for both groups of Apulian tombs are to the south or west: indeed the Apulian tombs represent the easternmost occurrence of a west European phenomenon. As the tombs are also relatively late compared to those of west and north-west Europe, it seems reasonable to look for a western origin for the Italian tombs. However, I do not believe in the route proposed by Puglisi (1959, 43), which brings them first to the Tyrrhenian coast at Pian Sultano (where there is a group of small megalithic cists), then across the Apennines (where there is nothing) to the Gargano promontory (where there is a monument of doubtful type and function). Nor indeed do I now feel convinced, as I did in 1967, that there was an actual intrusion of French megalith builders by sea to southern Italy (Whitehouse 1967, 360–4). When all is said and done, the Italian tombs are of very simple forms; it may simply have been the idea of megalithic tombs that spread, through maritime trade and other contacts, within the central Mediterranean in the third millennium BC. This will be discussed further in the final section.

References Evans 1956; Gervasio 1913; Jatta 1914; Lo Porto 1967; Palumbo 1956; Whitehouse 1967.

Corsican Megalithic Tombs

There are two types of megalithic tomb in Corsica: slab cists set into the ground, known as coffres, and above ground chamber tombs, known as dolmens.

Distribution The stone cists occur singly, in small groups and in larger cemeteries. Grosjean (1966, 24–5) lists six major groups, all in the south of the island, but isolated examples are found in other regions also. Grosjean claims there are 'tens' of these cists known, presumably fewer than one hundred. The dolmens occur all over the island, but the greatest concentration is in the south. About one hundred are known.

Typology The stone cists measure up to 3 m in length and are built of large stone slabs, often of granite. They are set into the ground, sometimes up to 2 m deep. They are frequently surrounded by stone circles, which mark the perimeter of a low mound. No coffres have been found with surviving capstones; it is not known whether they were originally roofed or not.

The dolmens are either simple rectangular chambers or, rarely, have a chamber approached by a separate short passage. The Corsican tombs are all built of large slabs and not in the block-and-boulder style sometimes found in south-east Italy, Malta and Sardinia. Three tombs – Settiva (Petreto-Bicchisano), Cardiccia (Giunchetu) and Taravu (Sollacaro) – have 'portholes' in the upper part of the entrance slab. Two other tombs – Capu-di-Logu (Campo Moro) and Pagliaiu (Sartène) – have simple incised decoration. Traces of mounds survive in a few cases. The Settiva dolmen has a 'horned' facade like the Sardinian *tombe di giganti* (see below).

Burial Rite Neither the stone cists nor the dolmens are normally found intact: as in Italy and in other areas legends that they contain treasure have made them the objects of *clandestini* or *chercheurs de la nuit*. However, fragments of bone and artifacts sometimes survive. Grosjean believes that the cists were used for individual burial, but claims also that they were reused for centuries. They may, perhaps, never have held more than one body at any one time. The artifacts found include tools of Sardinian obsidian, ground stone axes, stone beads and, in one case, a perforated stone macehead. Most of the dolmens have been robbed, but one – Settiva (Petreto-Bicchisano) – has yielded the remains of at least five individuals, indicating that collective burial was practised.

Chronology Grosjean assigns the stone cists to his Megalithic I period, which he believes began in the late fourth or early third millennium BC and lasted through much of the third millennium. The only direct evidence comes from one cist at Pagliaiu (or Palaggiu), which had only been partially robbed; this yielded material of Beaker type (Peretti 1966), which suggests a third millennium BC date. The only other – indirect

– dating evidence is the similarity to the cemetery of circular tombs excavated at Li Muri (Arzachena) in north-east Sardinia. If this parallel is valid, it may indicate a date as early as the early fourth millennium BC (see below).

The above-ground megalithic chamber tombs – the dolmens – are assigned by Grosjean to his Megalithic II period, on the grounds of their association with menhirs of this phase. This period he dates from late third to late second millennium BC. There is a radiocarbon date for this period, not from a dolmen, but from a presumed cult site at Castello d'Alo (Bilia). This date, which belongs to the middle phase – IIB – of the period, is *c.* 1870 bc, which corrects to *c.* 2350 BC. The dolmen of Settiva (Petreto-Bicchisano) produced in its primary level twenty single-handed conical cups, for which Grosjean has sought parallels in Copper and Bronze Age material from elsewhere in the central Mediterranean; this would fit with a late third or early second millennium BC date (Grosjean 1974).

Relationships There is a close association in Corsica between megalithic tombs and menhirs of all kinds. The coffres are associated with small menhirs of Grosjean's stage 1 (see below), which are found in the immediate vicinity of the tombs. The dolmens are associated with the menhirs and statue-menhirs of Grosjean's stages 2–5; these are often found in alignments or in other groupings and may be a few metres or tens of metres away from the tombs. Grosjean believes that the dolmens developed out of the earlier coffres and indeed that they represent simply above-ground versions of the same tomb type. This is difficult to demonstrate, but seems plausible and there are some tombs, which are partly sunk into the ground, which would make a plausible half-way stage in this hypothetical sequence.

For external relationships, the closest parallels for the stone cists are the ones at Li Muri (Arzachena) already mentioned, and others in the same area of northern Sardinia. However, rather similar monuments are found in many parts of the Mediterranean and parallels have been claimed, both to the west (e.g. the round tombs of Almeria) and to the east (e.g. the cemetery of cist tombs excavated by Dörpfeld on the island of Levkas).

For the dolmens parallels can be found among the simpler tombs in most areas where megaliths occur; they are particularly common in southern France, in the Pyrenees and in Catalonia. They are also like some of the Sardinian dolmens (those not built in the block-and-boulder style).

References Grosjean 1966a, 1966b, 1967, 1974; Jehasse and Grosjean 1976.

Sardinian Megalithic Tombs

Sardinia has three main varieties of megalithic tomb: stone cists, known as *circoli megalitici* or *dolmenici;* **simple rectangular chambers known as** *dolmens;* **and large and elaborate gallery graves known as** *tombe di giganti.* There are also a number of long cists, some of which are built in a megalithic manner; these are known as *tombe a poliandro,* because of the large number of bodies they contain.

Distribution The fifty or so known stone cists occur only in the Gallura, the north-east part of Sardinia, close to Corsica. The dolmens are found in the northern half of the island; about forty are known. The *tombe di giganti* are found all over the island. Lilliu (1975) claims 321 of these monuments, but Castaldi regards only 219 of these as true *tombe di giganti*, characterized by forecourts and stelae (Castaldi 1969, 251-6, Appendix I). She regards the other 102 monuments as megaliths of simpler type. There certainly are in Sardinia megalithic tombs that do not fit very comfortably into either the dolmen or the *tombe di giganti* category; these include some of the *tombe a poliandro.*

Typology (ill. 5) The stone cists of the Gallura (Lilliu's *circoli dolmenici*) take the form of a cist of stone slabs in the centre of a round mound made of earth and stone, which is surrounded by a peristalith of stone slabs set on end. The cists themselves measure from 1.2 x 1.6 m to 2 x 2 m; three sides are made of large slabs, while the fourth, usually that facing south or south-west, either has no slab or one much smaller than the others. The diameters of the mounds range from 5.3 to 8.5 m. Associated with the mounds, but outside them, are smaller cists perhaps used to hold funerary offerings, and vertical stone menhirs, used as stelae.

Lilliu divides the dolmens into two groups. The first group have a mound and surrounding peristalith, usually elliptical in shape; the second group has neither. Many dolmens have simple rectangular chambers 3–4 m long, e.g. Elcomis (Buddoso) or a larger chamber, divided into two, e.g. Perdalonga (Austis). One dolmen at Motorra (Dorgali) has a polygonal chamber approached by a short passage – a true passage grave in fact. As well as regular slab-built dolmens, there are also tombs consisting of a rectangular, oval or polygonal chamber, roofed by a large capstone which is supported on a number of uprights, varying from three to seven (or perhaps even more originally). In this respect these dolmens resemble the block-and-boulder-style dolmens of Apulia and Malta, though other features of these, e.g. pillars made of superimposed stones or pierced or decorated capstones, do not occur in Sardinia.

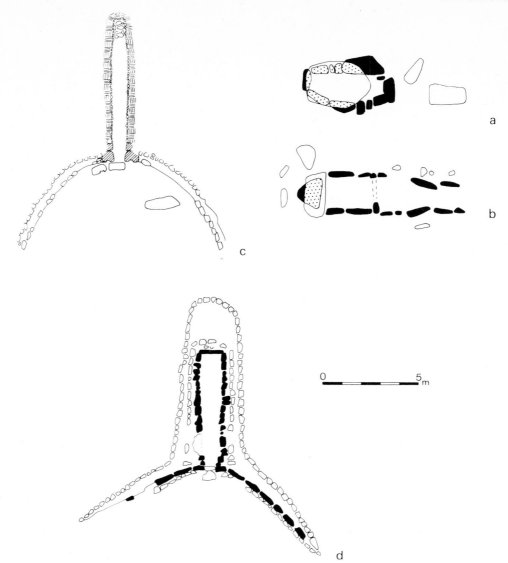

5 *Plans of Sardinian megalithic tombs. a Maone (after Guido); b Perdalonga (after Guido); c Oridda (after Castaldi); d Li Mizzani (after Castaldi). (Drawn by Philip Howard.)*

The *tombe di giganti* are the most elaborate of all the megalithic tombs in the central Mediterranean. The distinguishing features of these tombs are their long chambers, entered through the centre of a façade, which frames an apsidal, semi-circular or occasionally almost circular forecourt. The chambers may have walls of orthostats roofed with slabs or be made of coursed masonry, inclining inwards to form the roof.

The mounds that cover these chambers, sometimes surrounded by a peristalith, are long, rounded at the far end and often expand out in two long 'horns' behind the wings of the façade at the entrance end. This feature has in the past provoked some inappropriate comparison with the 'horned cairns' of the Irish Carlingford group. The chambers range from a few metres to *c.* 15 m in length and the monuments as a whole may exceed 20 m (the longest, Li Lolghi near Arzachena, is *c.*27 m long). In the centre of the façade, closing the entrance to the chamber, is often a tall carved slab – described as a stele – which has a small arch-shaped opening at the base, often no more than 50 cm high, giving access to the chamber.

Recent meticulous work on four *tombe di giganti* in

114

the province of Sassari has demonstrated that, like many British tombs, they were rebuilt many times and used over a very long period. The final plans are sometimes complex with double chambers, changes in level and other features. Interesting connections with the rock-cut tombs are evident. Both Lilliu (1975, 311) and Castaldi (1969, 242–50) believe that the stelae of the *tombe di giganti* copy the carved features found above the entrances to earlier rock-cut tombs in the Sassari area, e.g. one at Molafa. The chronology of the finds from the tombs favours this view, rather than that of Guido (1963, 91) who believes that the rock-cut tomb carvings copy the *tombe di giganti*. 'Hybrid' tombs also occur. One, at Oridda, is actually a rock-cut tomb, but the rock-cut chamber is long, narrow and rectangular, like that of the *tombe di giganti*, and the entrance is flanked by stone 'horns', enclosing a semi-circular forecourt. The entrance itself is closed by a stele, shorter than that commonly closing the *tombe di giganti*, but otherwise very similar and with the customary small opening in the bottom.

Yet another kind of megalithic tomb is the long stone cist, of which examples have been found in many parts of the island. These tombs are sunken, rectangular, trapezoid or boat-shaped, lined with slabs or drystone walling, and may be several metres long. Some had one or more capstones.

Burial Rite Lilliu suggests that only some of the fifty or so circular structures were used for burial: others may have been used for cult purposes. Indeed only three tombs have actually yielded skeletal material: one of the tombs at Li Muri, Li Muracci and San Pantaleo. The first two tombs had a single burial each; the third contained two skeletons, an adult and a child.

Most of the dolmens, long exposed to the elements and to man, have yielded neither skeletal remains nor artifacts, though occasionally fragmentary material survives. We do not know whether the dolmens were intended for single or collective burial.

The *tombe di giganti* have fared a little better than the dolmens; although undisturbed tombs are rarely found, many have yielded material. These tombs were undoubtedly used for collective burial. The tomb of Preganti (Gergei) produced remains of about fifty individuals, that of Las Plassas about sixty, while the hybrid tomb of Oridda (Sennori) produced remains of at least twenty-seven bodies. Pottery, stone and metal artifacts have been retrieved from some of these tombs, presumably representing original grave goods.

The long cists were also used for collective burial, from which they derive the name *tombe a poliandro*. One tomb at Ena' e Muros (Ossi) had more than thirty skeletons, while one at San Giuliano (Alghero) contained some fifty-four. Pottery and other artifacts also occur in these tombs.

Chronology We have no radiocarbon dates for the construction of Sardinian megalithic tombs, any more than for Apulian or Corsican ones, but we do have some chronological information from the artifacts found in the tombs, and one radiocarbon date for later material from one.

For the circular tombs with their cists the best information comes from the goods found at Li Muri. As well as flint and obsidian flakes and sherds of coarse pottery these cists yielded a number of polished stone objects: axes, perforated maceheads, beads and a carinated cup with spool handles, made of steatite. Parallels for this vessel have been sought in third millennium BC Egypt and Crete, but the form is very close to that found in pottery in the Final Neolithic Diana culture of Lipari. As already mentioned, the Diana Culture has radiocarbon dates which correct to calendrical dates of *c*. 3950-3750 BC. So, if we accept this geographically much closer parallel, we should perhaps think of a date much earlier than usually envisaged for the Sardinian stone cists, and perhaps for the Corsican ones as well.

Some information about the date of the dolmens comes from the one at Motorra (Dorgali), which has produced a stone wristguard, stone beads, flint and bone flakes and potsherds which apparently have parallels in the Ferrières-Fontbouisse cultures of the south French Chalcolithic. These cultures, traditionally dated to the early second millennium BC, should now, in the light of the tree-ring calibration, be dated to the first half of the third millennium BC.

The *tombe di giganti* have long been recognized as the main burial places of the people of the Nuragic culture, producing characteristic Nuragic pottery and metal artifacts. Radiocarbon dates for this culture run from *c*. 1500 bc to *c*. 700 bc (*c*. 1900–900 BC) and we know that *nuraghi* continued to be built and used still later, indeed into the third century BC in the northern part of the island (outside the area of Carthaginian domination). The beginning of the culture must go back into the third millennium BC: the 'protonuraghe' of Brunku Madugui has yielded a radiocarbon date of *c*. 1820 bc (2300 BC). The earliest *tombe di giganti* may even be earlier than this. Castaldi suggests that the tomb of Coddu Vecchiu was built in the Early Bronze Age, which she dates to *c*. 1800 BC, but which should now be pushed back into the third millennium BC. Earlier still is the 'hybrid' tomb at Oridda, which has produced Copper Age and Early Bronze Age material, suggesting a date early in the third millennium BC. The *tombe di giganti* were used over very long periods of

6 Distribution of menhirs.

time: Li Lolghi was still in use in the Late Iron Age, having been built in the Middle Bronze Age (indicating use for more than a thousand years). Some tombs have even yielded Roman sherds, suggesting use into the third century BC.

The long stone cists also seem to have a long date range. San Giuliano (Alghero) is attributed by Lilliu to the Early Bronze Age Bunnanaro culture and others are attributed to the succeeding Monte Claro culture (late third to early second millennium BC). Others belong to the full Nuragic culture.

To summarize, it seems that the earliest 'megaliths' in Sardinia, the slab cists, may have been fourth millennium BC in date, perhaps contemporary with the earliest rock-cut tombs. To the early third millennium BC may belong the dolmens, as well as many of the rock-cut tombs. The more elaborate megaliths, the *tombe di giganti*, as well as the long stone cists were probably first built in the later third millennium BC and continued to be constructed and used throughout the second millennium BC and much of the first also.

Relationships Menhirs are found in association with most of the types of tombs (see below). As far as relationships between the different groups of tombs themselves are concerned, the circular tombs with their slab cists seem to be separate, but it is difficult to make hard and fast distinctions between the other groups: tombs intermediate between simple dolmens and *tombe di giganti* exist, as do forms intermediate between *tombe di giganti* and rock-cut tombs. Also, as we have seen, there is probably considerable chronological overlap in the use of the different types of monuments.

As far as external relationships are concerned, for the slab cists and the dolmens, similar parallels are sought

116

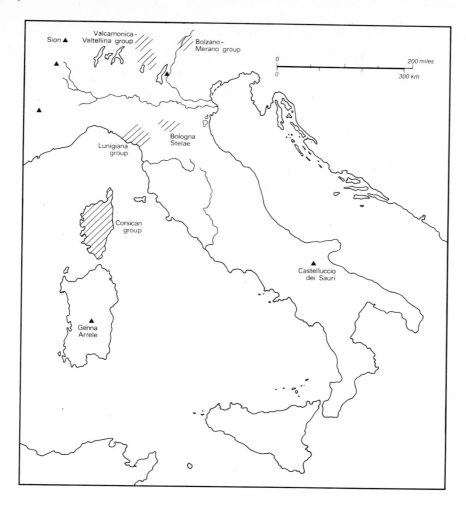

7 *Distribution of statue-menhirs.*

as for the Corsican tombs. For the slab cists, the similarities with the Corsican coffres themselves are close, other parallels (whether eastern or western) more remote. Among the dolmens, some are very like those found on Corsica; others more closely resemble the block-and-boulder-style dolmens of Malta and the Otranto group in southern Italy.

For the *tombe di giganti* there are no plausible parallels outside the island. The most reasonable hypothesis derives them from the dolmens by a process of local evolution.

References Castaldi 1969; Guido 1963, Chapter III; Lilliu 1975, 98–105, 319–16; Puglisi 1941–2.

Menhirs and Statue-Menhirs (ills 6 and 7)

In the central Mediterranean standing stones, both unadorned examples known as menhirs and an-

thropomorphic ones called statue-menhirs are found in all the areas where megalithic tombs occur and also in parts of northern Italy. The area in which this particular form of megalithism was most highly developed was undoubtedly the island of Corsica. I shall describe the different groups separately.

Southern Italy (ill. 8)

There is a single group of statue-menhirs in southern Italy, found at Castelluccio dei Sauri on the southern edge of the Tavoliere plain. Three small stone slabs (none more than 1 m high), one very fragmentary, were carved to indicate breasts, necklaces and other features. The breasts are in relief with an incised outline, the rest incised. A fragment of a possible

117

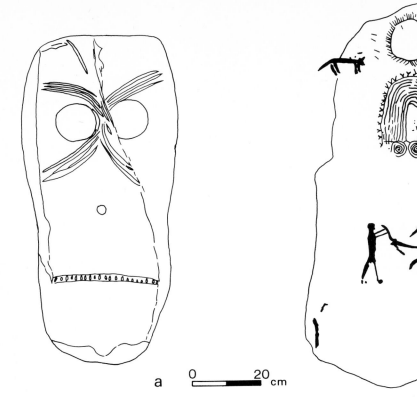

a   0   20 cm

8 Italian statue-menhirs. a Castelluccio dei Sauri; b Bagnolo II, Val Camonica (after Anati). (Drawn by Philip Howard.)

fourth statue-menhir shows a dagger with a triangular blade and rounded pommel. This group of menhirs is isolated and there is no associated dating evidence. On typological grounds they are usually assigned to the Copper Age.

The undecorated menhirs occur in much the same areas as the megalithic tombs of Apulia. A sparse group of twenty-eight known menhirs (not all surviving) occur in the province of Bari. Most of these are isolated but two groups at Sovereto, one of four stones and one of three, are said to form alignments, the first *c.* 2 km long, the other much shorter. A much larger group of menhirs, numbering about sixty today, but formerly at least 101, occurs in the Terra d'Otranto. These menhirs, known locally as *pietrefitte*, are narrow stone pillars of rectangular section, ranging in height from *c.* 2 m to more than 4 m. They are made of soft local limestone, carefully shaped and tend to be aligned north-south (i.e. with the longer sides facing east and west). Alignments are not recorded in this group.

These *menhirs* are sometimes found in association with tombs. These may be rock-cut tombs, both early (Copper or Early Bronze Age) and late (Iron Age) examples; there is some evidence that they may be associated with *dolmens* of the Otranto group also (see above).

References Gervasio 1913; Ornella Acanfora 1960; Palumbo 1955; Whitehouse 1967.

Northern Italy (ill. 8)

In northern Italy undecorated menhirs do not occur, but several groups of statue-menhirs are known. One group is found in various parts of the central Alps: at least seven in the upper Adige valley, about ten in the Val Camonica (famous for its rock carvings) and another seven in the neighbouring valley of Valtellina. Most of these menhirs have no clear heads and are identifiable as human figures through the depiction of collars and belts and, in one case, breasts. These figures are sometimes provided with incised axes and daggers (triangular with crescentic pommels) and some have carts or ploughs pulled by oxen. These are all like

118

similar artifacts depicted in the Val Camonica rock carvings and assigned to the Copper or Early Bronze Age. The best dating evidence, however, comes from the site of Sion, over the border in Switzerland. Here a very similar statue-menhir with a dagger had been reused in the side of a Bell Beaker cist burial (suggesting a date no later than the early third millennium BC for the menhir).

Another numerous group of statue-menhirs occurs in north-west Tuscany and is known as the Lunigiana group. Trump (1966, 98, 166) suggests a two-fold division of this group. The first sub-group is named after the site of Pontevecchio. Menhirs of this group have faces indicated schematically and arms more clearly; some have breasts and no weapons; other have no breasts indicated, but are provided with triangular daggers with crescentric pommels like the Alpine examples. This group Trump regards as Copper or Early Bronze Age like the Alpine statue-menhirs. The other component of the Lunigiana group is named after the site of Filetto. These are more elaborate. They appear to be male figures, with face, arms and legs all shown clearly and equipped with weapons which include long swords, spade-shaped axes and lances. Trump suggests a Late Bronze Age or Early Iron Age date for this group and believes that a long gap intervened between the Pontevecchio group and the Filetto group. To me this seems unlikely; there may have been a continuous and very long-lived tradition of erecting statue-menhirs of increasing complexity in this area, just as there was in Corsica (see below). None of the statue-menhirs of the Lunigiana group is associated with a tomb. Nor are alignments recorded.

The last group in northern Italy is of the same period as the Filetto group – Late Bronze Age to Early Iron Age – but these *are* associated with tombs. They are the stelae set over late Villanovan and Etruscan tombs in the Bologna area, which are carved to suggest the head and shoulders of a human form.

References Anati 1973; Barfield 1971, 65–7; Formentini 1972; Ornella Acanfora 1952–5; Trump 1966, 98–100, 166–7.

Sardinia

About fifty menhirs survive in Sardinia, distributed all over the island. These are usually made of basalt or granite and vary both in height (from less than 1 to 6.5 m) and in the amount of dressing they have received. Only one true statue-menhir has been published. This figure, at Genna Arrele (Laconi), is 1.45 m high.

It appears to be a male, with facial features indicated schematically by a T-shape in relief; he is equipped with a dagger below the waist and a trident-shaped object on his chest, both in relief also. The dagger is like Copper Age examples and suggests a fourth or third millennium date. A few other menhirs have simple decoration, which may be anthropomorphic in intention. Perda Fitta (Serramanna) has a vertical row of ten carved hollows down one side and several have multiple breast-like protuberances, e.g. Is Araus (S. Vero Milis), which has four.

The Sardinian menhirs are often associated with tombs: rock-cut tombs, the slab cists of the Gallura, dolmens in the same area, and also *tombe di giganti*. No alignments are recorded, but the menhirs are often found in groups; thirteen pairs have been recorded and six groups of three. To judge by the dates of associated tombs, it seems likely that the Sardinian menhirs were erected from the Copper Age (fourth millennium BC), right through the Bronze Age and into the Iron Age (mid-first millennium BC).

We should perhaps consider here the marble statuette, of the type often labelled 'Cycladic' (though now widely thought to be of local origin) from Senorbi. This female figure, 44 cm high, had been set into the ground; while hardly monumental, this figure is larger than the smaller idols of similar type found in the rock-cut tombs of the Ozieri culture.

References Atzeni 1972; Guido 1963, Chapter III: Lilliu 1957, 20–5, 92–5; Lilliu 1975, 129–36.

Corsica (ill. 9)

While Corsica cannot compete with its neighbouring island Sardinia in the number or splendour of its megalithic tombs or its cyclopean towers, in the production of menhirs and statue-menhirs the northern island is undisputed leader. Some 450 menhirs and statue-menhirs are known in Corsica, most of them in the south of the island. Alignments and groups of various sorts are the rule rather than the exception in Corsica and the largest group at Pagliaiu (or Palaggiu) consisted originally of no fewer than 258 menhirs in seven distinct groups. Groups of this size do not occur elsewhere in the Mediterranean and are reminiscent of the great alignments of Brittany.

All but five of the Corsican menhirs are made of granite, and they vary in form from small undecorated stones less than 1 m in height to elaborately ornamented statues several metres high. On typological grounds Grosjean has divided the Corsican menhirs and statue-menhirs into six stages which he believes represent a real sequence of development.

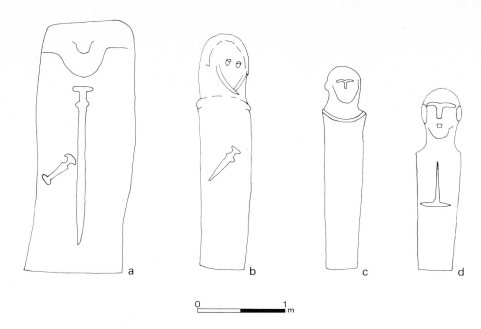

9 Corsican statue-menhirs. a *Filitosa V;* b *Nativu, Barbaggiu;* c *Tavera;* d *Filitosa IV. (Drawn by Philip Howard.)*

Stage 1 consists of small stones, normally associated with tombs. They are usually less than 1 m high and may be triangular, round or oval in section.

Stage 2 menhirs are described by Grosjean as 'proto-anthropomorphic', by which he means that the sculptors intended to indicate the human form (though sometimes very schematically). These menhirs are 2–5 m high, well shaped, thin and rectangular, semi-circular or oval in section.

Stage 3 has anthropomorphic menhirs with the head clearly separated from the body. No features are shown on these menhirs, which are rarely more than 2 m high. Sections may be rectangular, semi-circular or oval.

Stage 4 consists of statue-menhirs with facial features shown. These menhirs have no weapons. They are 2–3 m high, rectangular, oval or semi-circular in section. They occur only in the south of the island.

Stage 5 consists of statue-menhirs with weapons. Twenty-three of these are known, all from the south of the island and many of them from Filitosa. They are of similar height and shape to those of Stage 4. On most of the statue-menhirs the weapons are shown in bas relief, but on three examples from Pagliaiu and one from Rinaiu they are engraved. The weapons shown include daggers, long swords, corselets and helmets of

various sorts (including ones that Grosjean thinks were originally equipped with horns).

Stage 6 consists of statue-menhirs found only in the north of the island (north of the area in which the Torrean culture is found). These statue-menhirs have no weapons; they are thinner and narrower than those of the other stages.

Grosjean's interpretation of the development is as follows. The sequence begins with the introduction from further east of the 'megalithic idea', which included the erection of small menhirs, associated with the slab cists. After this the whole development was a local phenomenon. Grosjean believes that all the menhirs, including the undecorated ones, represent dead individuals and all represent males (certainly there are no specifically female figures in Corsica: breasts are never shown). Grosjean's interpretation of the armed figures of his Stage 5 is particularly interesting: he sees these as portraits of dead enemies, who invaded Corsica at this time. He claims that the people of the megalithic culture were not metal-using and that the undoubtedly metal weapons portrayed on the statues are closely comparable with those of the 'Peoples of the Sea', especially the Shardana, as portrayed in particular on the famous reliefs on the Temple of Medinet Habu, Thebes, of the early twelfth century BC. He believes that the Shardana invaded Corsica at about this time, destroyed the megalithic culture and established the culture of the Torri in the south of the island. The statue-menhirs of Stage 6 represent the phase following the establishment of the Torrean culture in the

120

south, when the defeated megalith builders fled to the north of the island.

Such independent chronological evidence as there is does not entirely support Grosjean's interpretation. There is one early radiocarbon date associated with menhirs – *c.* 1870 bc (*c.* 2400 BC) – from the cult site of Castello d'Alo (Bilia), which is associated with fragmentary menhirs of Stage 2 type. Other evidence comes from Filitosa, where statue-menhirs of several stages, including Stage 5, had been broken transversely and the fragments incorporated into the construction of the Torrean period, which has radiocarbon dates of *c.* 1430 and 1200 bc (*c.* 1750–1500 BC), as well as some later ones. If Grosjean is right, this date should represent a *terminus ante quem* for the main development of the megalithic culture on the island, only those menhirs of Stage 6 being later. However, there are dates later than this associated with two alignments of

statue-menhirs of earlier stages (Stantare: dates of *c.* 1000, 170 and 130 BC; Pagliaiu, or Palaggiu: 730 and 700 BC). The second-century dates presumably represent later activity on the site and the other dates *may* not represent primary use either; this must remain an open question at the moment.

On the oft-debated subject of the Shardana I do not wish to say much except that radiocarbon dates indicate that both the Torrean and the Nuragic cultures were in existence by *c.* 1800 BC; moreover proto-nuragic structures were being built before 2000 BC. These dates are far too early to allow either of these cultures to be the work of Sea People warriors fleeing to the central Mediterranean after their defeat by the

121

Egyptians. The alternative hypothesis – that Sardinia and/or Corsica was the original *homeland* of the Shardana – remains possible at least on chronological grounds, but further discussion of this topic is beyond the scope of the present paper.

References Grosjean 1966a, 1966b, 1967; Jehasse and Grosjean 1976.

Discussion

I do not feel qualified, nor have I space here, to discuss the origins and relationships of the various monuments described in this chapter in any detail. I shall confine myself to taking a quick look at how the evidence from the central Mediterranean relates to some of the major topics of discussion about megaliths, both current and perennial. The topics I shall look at are the existence or otherwise of a 'megalithic complex'; diffusion or independent invention, and the 'mother-goddess'.

The Megalithic Complex It has been customary to regard rock-cut tombs, megalithic tombs, menhirs and statue-menhirs, circles and alignments and, often enough, also stone temples, as part of a total megalithic complex (e.g. Daniel 1963, 27). In the central Mediterranean, as we have already seen, it seems unjustified to regard the rock-cut tombs as part of such a complex. They begin earlier than the other types of monument and they occur in many areas where no megalithic tombs or standing stones are found; moreover they may well have been developed locally by indigenous Neolithic groups (Whitehouse 1972). It is true that in the central Mediterranean rock-cut tombs are sometimes associated with menhirs, but these may represent a feature which was added later in some areas only.

As for the other types of monuments, within our area they *do* on the whole seem to belong together. All areas with megalithic tombs also have menhirs and there are many examples of specific associations between menhirs and tombs. In Corsica the statue-menhirs are equally clearly associated with megalithic tombs, though this is not the case with any of the statue-menhirs on the Italian mainland, with the exception of the stelae from the Bologna cemeteries.

Diffusion or Independent Invention?
Traditional views derived the whole megalithic complex of Europe from the east Mediterranean. In this interpretation it would have been logical if scholars had regarded the central Mediterranean as crucial in the transmission of megalithism from east to west. In

practice, although rock-cut tombs were sometimes claimed as evidence for such a role (e.g. Childe 1957, 234–42; Daniel 1963, 81), there were always chronological difficulties to contend with in pursuing such an interpretation. In the case of the megalithic tombs and standing stones, the chronological problems were greater still and it was always difficult to claim that the central Mediterranean monuments could have been ancestral to those of west and north-west Europe. In 1963 Glyn Daniel recognized (89–94) that the Italian and Sardinian tombs must be later than those of France and Iberia. This fact has been made crystal clear by the subsequent publication of the early radiocarbon dates for north-west European megaliths, which are now so well known.

It is certainly impossible to see the central Mediterranean megaliths as transitional between hypothetical east Mediterranean ones and well known west European ones. However, an external origin for the central Mediterranean megaliths remains a possible interpretation and indeed the one favoured by most scholars working within the area, such as Puglisi, Lilliu and Grosjean. There is no agreement, however, about the source of the megalithic inspiration, with parallels being chased round almost the entire shoreline of the Mediterranean basin!

Both Lilliu (1975, 100) and Grosjean (1966a, 23–8) believe that it was only the simplest forms of megaliths (the slab-cists, perhaps simple dolmens and small plain menhirs) that were introduced to their respective islands. The more complex monuments – the Sardinian *tombe di giganti* and the elaborately decorated statue-menhirs of Corsica – are seen as the products of long processes of local development on the islands. In the case of the Apulian megaliths there is general agreement that these must have been introduced from the west, for the simple reason that there are no megalithic tombs further east.

Whether one accepts the view that megaliths were introduced from outside or believes that they developed locally is largely a matter of personal prejudice, since it is impossible to demonstrate conclusively on chronological or other grounds, that either of these views is untenable. I cannot resist taking the opportunity here, in an article that has otherwise been devoted largely to description, of airing – briefly –my own prejudices on this issue. I tend to favour a local origin, for the following reason. If the complex monuments are demonstrably the result of local development, we are left with small and unimpressive monuments – simple stone chambers, small undecorated standing stones – as the 'introduced' megaliths. And yet these are just the types of monument that might well have developed locally, particularly in the geological regions in question, where stone was an easily available building material and natural outcrops might suggest the form of chamber or standing stone.

Having said that, it seems to me unlikely that the various areas with megaliths in the central and west Mediterrranean were completely unconnected. We know from analyses of obsidian that trade, both maritime and overland, had been established since the sixth millennium BC in the central Mediterranean (at least between Sardinia and Corsica) and we have evidence for increasing connections in the subsequent millennia. I imagine the spread of megalithic ideas taking place in this context of increasing contact, but without significant movements of people. In any case, all the more remarkable manifestations of megalithism in Sardinia and Corsica, as in the case of the Maltese temples, seem to be the products of largely isolated insular traditions.

The Mother Goddess The 'mother goddess' can be disposed of more quickly. Fleming (1969) has argued cogently against the interpretation of all megalithic art (and indeed of anything decorated that comes out of a megalith) in terms of a universal mother goddess cult. The case for a female deity in the area we have been considering is particularly thin. Only a handful of all the hundreds of statue-menhirs in this region have breasts and many carry weapons and these in all probability represent males (unless we have an Amazon mother goddess!). The whole complex of decorated statue-menhirs of Corsica does not include one single example that is clearly, or even probably, female. The only clearly female figures are the few statue-menhirs with breasts from the Italian mainland and the Senorbi 'Cycladic' type statuette in Sardinia, as well as the related small idols from the rock-cut tombs. They are certainly female but none the less may not represent a mother goddess; there are other possibilities, as Ucko has pointed out in the case of figurines from Egypt, western Asia and Greece (Ucko 1968, 427–44).

The central Mediterranean megaliths when looked at from afar and as a whole, as through the wrong end of a telescope, appear as a clear-cut and coherent group. When the telescope is reversed and the monuments looked at in detail, the group dissolves into a number of separate elements, with differing typologies, differing dates, differing associated artifactual material and, in some cases, possibly different functions as well. The apparent coherence is the product of generalization. Such generalizations may, of course, be both valid and helpful, but in the case of megalithic monuments, they have dominated interpretation too long. The detailed analysis of individual monuments and groups of monuments in their local context should now be the aim of research in the central Mediterranean. Much valuable work of this kind has already been done; more work in the future will, I hope, bring to this region the kind of enlightenment that recent studies have brought to the megaliths of the north and north-west.

Bibliography

BPI   *Bullettino di Paletnologia italiana*
BSPF   *Bulletin de la Société préhistorique française*
NSc   *Notizie degli scavi di antichità*
PPS   *Proceedings of the Prehistoric Society*
RSP   *Rivista di Scienze preistoriche*

ANATI, E. 1973 'Le Statue Stele di Bagnolo', *Origini* VII, 229–83.
ATZENI, E. 1972 'Notiziario', *RSP* XXVII, 476.
BARFIELD, L. 1971 *Northern Italy before Rome*, London.
BERNARBÒ BREA, L. 1957 *Sicily before the Greeks*, London.
BRAY, W. 1963 'The Ozieri Culture of Sardinia', *RSP* XVIII, 155 ff.
1964 'Sardinian Beakers', *PPS* XXX, 75–98.
CASTALDI, E. 1969 'Tombe di Giganti nel Sassarese', *Origini* III, 119–274.

CHILDE, V. G. 1957 *The Dawn of European Civilization*, 6th edn, London.
DANIEL, G. 1960 *The Chambered Tombs of France*, London.
1963 *The Megalith Builders of Western Europe*, Harmondsworth.
DRAGO, C. 1947 'Sepolcreto del Pizzone', *RSP* XI, 333.
EVANS, J. D. 1956 'The 'dolmens' of Malta and the origins of the Tarxien cemetery culture', *PPS* XXII, 85–101.
FLEMING, A. 1969 'The myth of the mother-goddess', *World Archaeology* I, 247–61.
FORMENTINI, U. 1927 'Statue stele della Lunigiana', *Studi etruschi* I, 61.
GERVASIO, M. 1913 *I dolmen e la civiltà del bronzo nelle Puglie*, Bari.

GIORGI, C. DE, 1912 'Censimento dei dolmens di Terra d'Otranto', *Apulia* III, 99.

GROSJEAN, R. AND LIEGEOIS, J. 1964 'Les coffres mégalithiques de la region de Porto-Vecchio', *l'Anthropologie* LXVIII, 527–48.

1966a *La Corse avant l'Histoire*, Paris.

1966b 'Recent Work in Corsica', *Antiquity* XL, 190–8.

1967 'Classification descriptive du Mégalithique Corse, *BSPF* XLIV, 707–42.

1974 'Le complexe dolmenique de Settiva', *Gallia préhistoire XVII*, 707–9.

GUIDO, M. 1963 *Sardinia*, London.

JATTA, A. 1914 *La Puglia preistorica*, Bari.

JEHASSE, J. AND GROSJEAN, R. 1976 *Sites préhistoriques et protohistoriques de l'Ile de Corse*, UISS IX Congress, Nice 1976. Livret-guide de l'Excursion C4.

LILLIU, G. 1957 'Religione della Sardegna prenuragica', *BPI* LXVI, 7–96.

1968a II Dolmen di Motorra (Dorgali-Nuoro)', *Studi Sardi* XX, 74–128.

1968b 'Rapporti tra la cultura 'torreana' e aspetti pre e **protonuragici della Sardegna'**, **Studi Sardi XX, 3–47.**

1975 *La Civiltà dei Sardi*, 2nd edn. Turin.

LO PORTO, F. G. 1961 'Notizie', *RSP* XVI, 270.

1963 'Leporano (Taranto) – la stazione preistorica di Porto Perone', *NSc*, Ser. 8, 17, 280–380.

1967 'Il "dolmen a galleria" di Giovinazzo', *BPI*. LXXVI, 137–80.

1972 'La tomba neolitica con idolo in pietra di Arnesano (Lecce)', *RSP* XXXVII, 357–72.

ORNELLA ACANFORA, M. 1952-5 'Le Statue Antropomorfe dell'Alto Adige', *Cultura Atestina* VI, 1952–5.

1960 'Le stele antropomorfe di Castelluccio dei Sauri', *RSP* XV, 95–123.

PALUMBO, G. 1955 'Inventario delle pietrefitte Salentine', *RSP* X, 86–147.

1956 'Inventario dei dolmen di Terra d'Otranto', *RSP* XI, 84–108.

PERETTI, G: 1966 'Une sepulture campaniforme en rapport avec l'alignement des menhirs de Palaggiu (Sartène, Corse)', *Actes du XVIIIe congrès préhistorique de France*, Ajaccio 1966, 230–42.

PERONI, R. 1967 *Archeologia della Puglia preistorica*, Florence.

PUGLISI, S. M. 1941-2 'Villaggi sotto roccia e sepolcri megalitici nella Gallura', *BPI* V–VI, 123–41.

1950 'Le culture dei capannicoli sul promontorio Gargano', *Atti Accad. naz. Lincei. Memorie,* ser. 8, 3–57.

1959 *La civiltà appenninica*, Florence.

RELLINI, U. 1925 'Scavi preistorici a Serra d'Alto', *NSc*, ser. 6, 1, 257–95.

TINÈ, S, (ed.) 1975 *Cilità Preistoriche e Protostoriche della Daunia*, Atti del Colloquio Internazionale di Preistoria e Protostoria della Daunia, Foggia 1973, Florence

TRUMP, D. H. 1966 *Central and Southern Italy before Rome*, London.

UCKO, P. J. 1968 *Anthropomorphic Figurines of Predynastic Egypt and Neolithic Crete*, London.

WHITEHOUSE, R. 1967 'The megalithic monuments of south-east Italy', *Man* II, 347–65.

1969 'The Neolithic Pottery Sequence in Southern Italy', *PPS* XXXV, 267–310.

1972 'The rock-cut tombs of the central Mediterranean', *Antiquity* XLVI, 275–81.

1978 'Italian Prehistory, Carbon 14 and the Tree-ring Calibration', in H. Mck. Blake, Potter, T. W. and Whitehouse, D. B. (eds), *Papers in Italian Archaeology I: the Lancaster Seminar*, Brit. Arch. Reports, S 41, 71–91.

WHITEHOUSE, R. AND RENFREW, C. 1975 'The Copper Age in Peninsular Italy and the Aegean', *Annual of the British School in Athens* LXIX, 343–90.

Appendix

List of relevant C14 dates

Site	Culture	Lab. no.	C14 date 5568 half-life bc	Corrected date BC, to nearest 50 years
MAINLAND ITALY				
Grotta della Madonna, Praia a Mare, prov. Cosenza	Diana	R–283	3160 ± 70	3950 ± 110
Lipari acropolis prov. Messina	Diana	R–180	3050 ± 200	3850 ± 210
Contrada Diana, Lipari, prov. Messina	Diana	R–182	2935 ± 55	3750 ± 110
Buccino, prov. Salerno	Gaudo	St–3627	2580 ± 100	3350 ± 115
	Gaudo	St–3620	2370 ± 120	
	Gaudo	St–3632	2155 ± 120	
	Gaudo	St–3628	2075 ± 100	
	Gaudo	St–3634	2060 ± 100	2600 ± 115
	Gaudo	St–3631	1970 ± 360	2500 ± 365
Riparo La Romita, Asciano, prov. Pisa	Rinaldone	Pi–100	2298 ± 115	2950 ± 130
Grotta dei Piccioni, Bolognano, prov. Pescara	Rinaldone	Pi–50	2356 ± 105	3050 ± 120
Luni sul Mignone, prov. Viterbo	Rinaldone	St–2043	2075 ± 100	2650 ± 115
	Rinaldone	St–2042	2005 ± 200	
	Rinaldone	St–1343	1850 ± 80	2350 ± 110
Grotta del Pertusello, Val Pennavaira, prov. Savona	Beakers	R–155	2440 ± 70	3150 ± 110
Monte Covolo, prov. Brescia	Beakers	Birm–471	2000 ± 320	2550 ± 325
	Beakers	Birm–470	1860 ± 210	2350 ± 215
Riparo Arma di Nasino, prov. Savona	Beakers	R–309	2270 ± 70	2950 ± 110
	Beakers	R–311	1815 ± 70	2300 ± 110
MALTA				
Tarxien	Tarxien Cemetery	BM–141	1930 ± 150	2400 ± 160
	Tarxien Cemetery	BM–711	1404 ± 76	
	Tarxien Cemetery	BM–710	1336 ± 72	1600 ± 110

Site	Culture	Lab. no.	C14 date 5568 half-life bc	Corrected date BC, to nearest 50 years
SARDINIA				
Grotta di Sa 'Ucca de	Bonu Ighinu	R–882	3730 ± 160	4550 ± 170
su Tintirriolu, Bonu Ighinu,	Ozieri	R–884	3140 ± 50	3950 ± 110
prov. Sassari	Ozieri	R–883a	2980 ± 50	3800 ± 110
	Ozieri and Bonu Ighinu	R–879	2900 ± 50	3700 ± 110
Grotta del Guano	Ozieri	R–609a	2950 ± 50	3750 ± 110
or Gonagosula, Oliena,	Ozieri	R–609	2880 ± 50	3700 ± 110
prov. Nuoro				
Sa Turricula, Muros, prov. Sassari	Bunnannaro	R–963a	1510 ± 50	1850 ± 110
Brunku Madugui, Gesturi, prov. Cagliari	Monte Claro	Gif–243	1820 ± 250	2300 ± 255
Grotta d'Acqua Calda, Nuxis, prov. Cagliari	Monte Claro	R–677	1740 ± 60	2150 ± 110
Barumini, prov. Cagliari	Nuragic	K–151	1470 ± 200	1800 ± 210
Albucciu, prov. Sassari	Nuragic	Gif–242	1220 ± 250	1500 ± 110
Oridda, Sennori, prov. Sassari	Nuragic	R–1060	1220 ± 50	1500 ± 110
Ortu Commidu,	Nuragic	P–2401	1130 ± 60	1450 ± 110
Sardara, prov.	Nuragic	P–2402	1020 ± 50	1300 ± 110
Cagliari	Nuragic	P–2400	960 ± 250	1150 ± 255
	Nuragic	P–2399	960 ± 220	1150 ± 230
Genna Maria, Villanovaforru, prov. Cagliari	Nuragic	P–2403	970 ± 50	1150 ± 110
Sa Mandra 'e Sa	Nuragic	R–1094a	1100 ± 50	1400 ± 110
Giua, Ossi, prov	Nuragic	R–1096	860 ± 50	
Sassari	Nuragic	R–1097	850 ± 50	
	Nuragic	R–1092a	790 ± 50	
	Nuragic	R–1093a	740 ± 50	
	Nuragic	R–1098	720 ± 50	
	Nuragic	R–1095a	640 ± 50	850 ± 70
Su foxi 'e S'Abba,	Nuragic	R–1074a	960 ± 50	1150 ± 110
Lecorci, prov.	Nuragic	R–1065a	720 ± 50	
Nuoro	Nuragic	R–1065	700 ± 50	900 ± 70
Grotta A.S.I. or	Nuragic	R–492	820 ± 60	1000 ± 110
Piroso, Santadi, prov. Cagliari	Nuragic	R–492a	730 ± 60	900 ± 80

Site	Culture	Lab. no.	C14 date 5568 half-life bc	Corrected date BC, to nearest 50 years
CORSICA				
Basi, Serra-di-Ferro	Basien 'Chalcolithic'	Gif–1849 Gif–1850 Gif–1848	3300 ± 120 3250 ± 120 3250 ± 120	4100 ± 135 4050 ± 135 4050 ± 135
Curacchiaghiu, Lévie	'Late Neolithic'	Gif–1960	2980 ± 140	3800 ± 150
Araguina-Sennola, Bonifacio	'Late Neolithic' 'EBA' 'MBA' 'LBA'	Gif–779 Gif–778 Gif–777 Gif–776	2030 ± 140 1600 ± 120 1350 ± 120 1090 ± 110	2550 ± 150 2000 ± 135 1650 ± 135 1350 ± 125
Curacchiaghiu, Lévie	'BA' 'IA'	Gif–1959 Gif–1958	1280 ± 130 660 ± 110	1550 ± 145 850 ± 120
Basi, Serra-di-Ferro	Torrean Torrean	Gif–1847 Gif–1846	1620 ± 110 1400 ± 110	2000 ± 125 1750 ± 125
Tappa II, Porto-Vecchio	perhaps pre-Torrean	Gsy–94B	1915 ± 125	2450 ± 140
Tappa I, Porto-Vecchio	Torrean	Gsy–94A	680 ± 200	850 ± 205
Castello d' Alo, Bilia	pre-Torrean	Gif–480 Gif–479 Gif–478	1870 ± 200 1550 ± 120 1150 ± 110	2350 ± 210 1900 ± 135 1450 ± 125
Castello de Caccia 3, Porto-Vecchio	Torrean	Gsy–120	1345 ± 110	1650 ± 125
Filitosa, Sollacaro	Torrean Torrean Torrean Torrean	Gif–2399 Gsy–58 Gif–2398 Gif–150	1430 ± 110 1200 ± 150 1130 ± 110 600 ± 170	1750 ± 125 800 ± 175
Cucuruzzu 3, Lévie	Torrean	Gif–241	880 ± 150	1050 ± 160
Cucuruzzu 1, Lévie	Torrean	Gif–239	600 ± 150	800 ± 160
Stantare alignment, Sartène	? ? ?	Gif–1396 Gif–1397 Gif–2103	1000 ± 110 170 ± 110 130 ± 110	1250 ± 125 170 ± 120 130 ± 120
Palaggiu, Sartène, funeral chest A	?	Gif–476	700 ± 150	900 ± 160
Palaggiu alignment, Sartène	?	Gif–477	730 ± 150	950 ± 160

13 Megalithic Architecture in Malta

David Trump

COMPARED WITH the other regions of Europe being considered–Iberia, Scandinavia, even the British Isles–the Maltese islands are minute and would hardly seem to merit a chapter to themselves in a work such as this. The evidence which has survived there, however, is out of all proportion to the islands' size, and no study of megalithic architecture, particularly as regards origin and function, would be complete without them. Further, it gives me the opportunity to contribute to this volume, and to record my profound thanks to Glyn Daniel for directing my interest towards both the Mediterranean and megaliths many happy years ago.

Malta and Gozo together have a surface area of only 320 sq. km and lie nearly 100 km from the nearest other land, Cape Passero in south-east Sicily. There is unequivocal archaeological evidence throughout prehistory for contact with the larger island and beyond in the form of imported raw materials, notably a good brown flint from the Monti Iblei and obsidian, from Lipari and, to a lesser extent, Pantelleria (Cann and Renfrew 1964). But equally clear is the minimal extent of cultural dependence during the period of the temples, 4000–2500 BC; the number of sherds of foreign manufacture so far recovered in Malta is barely a score, against many millions in local wares.

1 Skorba, the 'shrines' of c.4000 BC, possible ancestors of the Maltese temples. Lengths 8.40 and 5.60 m.

Although overseas influences on temple architecture cannot be excluded, there is little to suggest that they in any way explain its introduction to the islands. Closer study reinforces the argument by failing to reveal any but a few superficial details of similarity with architecture elsewhere. Some of these details are too generalized to carry much weight, others lose all significance when radiocarbon dating places them substantially earlier than their suggested prototypes.

Megalithic architecture in Malta, then, is an indigenous phenomenon, and its origins and function must be sought in the purely local context. The account given here follows closely that suggested by J. D. Evans (1959, 84–134), expanded but not materially altered by details discovered subsequently. I would freely admit that it is not the only possible interpretation of the recorded facts, but it seems easily the most convincing, given the evidence at present available.

The use of stone masonry in Malta is attested from the time of the earliest known inhabitants, immigrant farmers of the Ghar Dalam phase (Trump 1966, amending and dating Evans 1953, 1959), deriving immediately from Sicily and bringing a variant of that island's Stentinello culture with them. Associated radiocarbon dates at Skorba gave readings of 4190 ± 160 bc (BM 378) and 3810 ± 200 bc (BM 216). Unfortunately, a single 11 m length of straight stone wall, a footing for one of mudbrick, is the only structure that has yet been located (Trump 1966, 10), so nothing can be said of building plans. By the end of this first cycle of cultural development in the Red Skorba phase, 3225 ± 150 bc (BM 148), a building of two oval chambers, 5.60 and 8.40 m long, had appeared nearby (ill. 1). It had much more substantial walls, still for upward continuation in mudbrick. The absence of a reasonable floor surface, easy access or any hearth, and the presence of a number of figurines, tentatively suggested that the rooms were shrines, but this cannot be pressed. The masonry was of uncoursed but in no sense megalithic stonework.

The immigrants who initiated the second cycle of cultural development *c.* 3200 bc brought with them, in the Zebbug phase, a material culture recognizably related to that of the San Cono-Piano Notaro culture

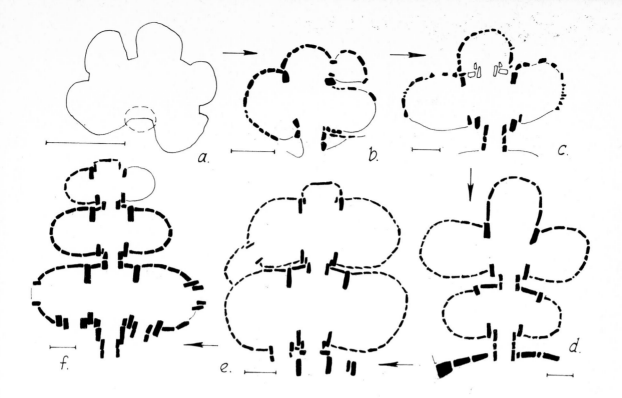

2 The evolution of the Maltese temples. a rock-cut tomb,
Xemxija 5; b lobed temple, Mgarr East; c trefoil temple,
with later cross-wall, Skorba West; d 5-apse temple,
Ggantija South; e 4-apse temple, Mnajdra Central; f
6-apse temple, Tarxien Central. The scale measures 3 m.

of Sicily, probably including the practice of excavating rock-cut tombs for their dead (Whitehouse
1972). This seems more likely than that they
invented this burial rite in the islands independently.

The rock-cut tombs call for a digression, the relevance of which will become apparent shortly.
Though they are not themselves megalithic, it has
long been recognized that, at least in western Europe,
there is some sort of relationship with megalithic
tombs, if only one of parallel development. There
would be some truth in the view that both are artificial substitutes for natural caves, and could arise
wherever caves are found inadequate as chambers to
accommodate collective burials (Whitehouse 1972).
I leave it to colleagues writing on other areas to
explore possible relationships there, and look forward
to seeing the results of their latest thinking, but must
myself confine my attention to the Maltese temples.

The earliest of these known are the group of five at
Ta Trapna, Zebbug (Baldacchino and Evans 1954;
Evans 1971, 166), which are, however, of little relevance here since their orignial form is unclear. At the
time of discovery they consisted of no more than oval
depressions in the rock, but whether these were the
surviving remains of chambers entered from a shaft, or
of simple shafts, or are exactly as first constructed cannot now be determined. With one very notable exception, the other tombs are of the more characteristic

shaft-and-chamber form, the latter simple oval or
kidney shaped (Nadur, Xaghra, Xemxija tombs 3, 4
and 6), or more elaborately lobed (Xemxija 1, 2 and
particularly 5). All contained material of the Ggantija
and later phases, Xemxija having in addition a little
going back to Zebbug. It seems, then, that rock-cut
tombs were coming into use in Malta early in the
fourth millennium BC.

It was early in the Ggantija phase of pottery development in Malta, around 2800 bc (3500 BC) that the
islanders began to build massive stone monuments of
Cyclopean or orthostatic masonry, the famous prehistoric temples. They can best be explained as the
result of a decision to build a copy of a lobed rock-cut
tomb of the Xemxija 5 type above ground. Some
change of function is also implied, and it could well
have been this, elaboration of ceremonies before the
tomb, which produced the need for a more appropriate
setting than the shaft in bare rock offered. The small
eastern temples at Kordin III and Mgarr show the sort
of structures that would result, though excavation at

129

the latter in 1960 (Trump 1966, 17-19) showed that this building probably belonged in the succeeding Saflieni phase. If the lobed temple/rock-cut tomb link is not accepted, the similarity of plan must be explained as later convergent development of the two classes of monument, or else complete coincidence. This would make the trefoil temples, to be considered next, the earliest form, with no antecedents since the Red Skorba 'shrines' five centuries earlier. Apart from traces of simple huts at the Skorba site, no above-ground buildings dating to the Zebbug and Mgarr phases have been located. A derivation of the lobed temples from the tombs, already a considerable intellectual leap, must surely appear more likely.

Perhaps before proceeding further, we should justify the use of the term 'temple'. There is fortunately strong supporting evidence. The complete absence from the built structures of contemporary burials excludes a funerary function, the internal chambers would seem too small for assembly, and though a domestic use cannot be quite so categorically denied, it is hardly more convincing. Their interpretation as places of worship, temples, does not depend solely on negative evidence. In the ceramic repertoire, one vessel shape which occurs in extraordinary numbers and often in both enormous and minute sizes, equally clearly non-functional, has been plausibly recognized as an offering bowl. Handsome decorated blocks in the temples seem better fitted to serve as altars than tables. Numerous statues, again one at least greater than lifesize, look like cult figures. Holes far too small for passages connecting separate chambers have been interpreted as oracle holes, though the exact nature of their use cannot now be recovered. All these indentifications are clearly matters of assumption rather than proof, but all are reasonable and mutually consistent.

In the trefoil temples we see the first formalized plan, and can recognize the prototype of the later forms. Already present are the concave and monumental façade, trilithon entrance passage, paired lateral and single terminal chambers (somewhat misleadingly described in the literature as 'apses'), and the use of both orthostatic and megalithic blocks. Surviving examples include the western temples in the Mgarr, Kordin III and Skorba groups. If we do not need to look outside the islands for the form of the temples, nor do we have to for the constructional techniques. With stone so readily available in Malta, as is immediately apparent to any visitor, its use, even in exceptionally large blocks, occasions no surprise. There can be few areas in the world where the incentives to megalithic building were greater.

Subsequently the trefoil temples were all altered by having the large central chamber closed off with a substantial cross wall, apart from a central lintelled doorway. There are perforations in the jambs apparently to support some form of door or screen of wood or leather, and bar holes by which it could be secured. It was investigations at Skorba which proved this cross wall to be a later addition, as is very probably the case at the other two sites.

This stage of development, with its division between an inner area which could be securely closed off and the more public outer chambers, can be convincingly recognized again in those temples with five apses. The same result is achieved here by the addition of an extra pair of apses between the façade and the lateral apses of the trefoil plan. Seating for a door is again provided in the central passage between the two pairs, and serves the same purpose as the closing wall across the terminal apse, which is therefore not needed. The five-apse plan is represented at the Ggantija South, Hagar Qim North and, probably, Ta Marziena. All these temples, note, were shown by material in their floors to be still of the Ggantija phase. In other words, we are dealing so far with a typological seriation. It must be frankly admitted that this sequence is unsupported by (though in only one, possibly unimportant, respect (at Mgarr East, referred to above) contradicted by) the evidence of associated pottery. Further, there are a number of sites, or elements of compound sites, which do not fit into the classification, either because they do not follow a regular apsed plan, or because they have been too damaged for their original form and affiliation to be determined.

The final stage, excepting the six-apse temple of Tarxien Central, includes all the temples whose underfloor and wall deposits include material of the Tarxien phase, a terminus post quem for their construction. Their distinguishing feature is the reduction in size of the central apse of the five-apse plan to a mere niche. Perhaps the three-apse-with-closed-terminal chamber was felt to be clumsy, and the five-apse-with-three-closed too roomy in its inner parts. Be that as it may, all Tarxien phase temples in the main line of development are of this four-apse-and-niche form. One example, the Ggantija North, yielded only material of the Ggantija phase in the areas sampled, but since this gives, as already mentioned, only a terminus post quem, it is possible that it could fall in the later phase, making the correlation lobed/three/five apses – Ggantija phase, four apse – Tarxien phase, complete. Tarxien Central is unique, though clearly only a variant on the four-apse plan, in having an additional pair of apses making six in all. Associated pottery places it in an advanced stage of the Tarxien phase and so later than the four-apse temples on either side of it at this complex site.

The description of this sequence may seem a little laboured, but is designed to stress the progressive advances made by the designers of these buildings. This shows in many other ways. All the early temples were built of rubble masonry, and were probably originally plastered to a smooth surface internally and painted. Only at the Ggantija and Skorba could this be demonstrated. In these, only the external walls and the doorways and passages were of truly megalithic construction, of carefully selected or well-tooled orthostatic blocks. Later, all walls were so constructed, giving a much more impressive result. For one thing, tooled blocks, meeting along the whole of their adjacent faces, gave much greater stability, and successive courses could be over-sailed as horizontal arches, allowing the roof opening to be appreciably narrowed before it was closed with a beam and thatch ceiling. At Mnajdra South (ill. 8), Hagar Qim and Tarxien Central, this over-sailing is shown in the surviving walls, together with the inward slope of the blocks which proves the horizontal arch – as opposed to the corbel – principle of construction. Nowhere outside Malta is this principle known at such an early date, probably well before 2500 BC: indeed the horizontal arch has rarely been used elsewhere at any period.

Unfortunately, though fragments of wall plaster covered in red paint were found at both the Ggantija and Skorba, we do not know if this was applied in patterns or as an all-over wash. The walls of the Hypogeum demonstrate both. Certainly altar blocks and other internal fittings within the temples had their surfaces decoratively carved in three successive styles. In the first flat surfaces were relieved by being sparsely pitted. Then the pitting, by either pecking or drilling, was much more closely spaced and framed within a relief border. Later still, spiral designs were carved in relief like the borders, the pitting being relegated to the background or suppressed altogether. A fragment from Wiel Filep suggests that this background was painted red, the relief designs being reserved, and this may well have been general practice. More ambitious designs were occasionally attempted, particularly at Tarxien (animal friezes, repeat curves; see ill. 4), and there is a notable piece from Bugibba portraying two fish. This could be contemporary with the third style or constitute a fourth: we do not have chronological evidence as we certainly do for the earlier ones. For example, the central altar in Tarxien South shows a fragment of a style 2 panel left as a result of the floor level having been raised when the rest was cut away to take style 3 relief spirals. Artistically too, then, there is evidence for progress and innovation, paralleled in the case of the spirals in the decoration of the pottery.

Technically the remains testify to the introduction

3 The Hypogeum, the rock-cut temple at the heart of the site. Height of doorway 1 m.

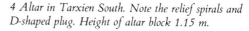

4 Altar in Tarxien South. Note the relief spirals and D-shaped plug. Height of altar block 1.15 m.

of two constructional aids, one probably very generally spread, though rarely so clearly demonstrated as here, the other apparently unknown outside Malta. Many orthostats show a prominent notch in the middle of a long side, the clearest examples being visible in Tarxien East. This notch must have been deliberately cut to take the tip of a sizeable lever with which the final adjustment of the block into position could be effected. The value of such an aid is obvious when one remembers that individual blocks could reach a weight of 19 tonnes. A stone roller beneath a massive threshold slab in Tarxien Central demonstrates the use of cannon-ball-like spheroids frequently found on temple sites. Timber rollers have long been postulated as aids to the moving of megalithic blocks, but we have no other records of 'ball-bearings' until several thousand years later.

All this builds up to an impressive record of the highly ingenious designers, engineers, architects even, who were responsible for the development of the Maltese temples (Trump 1980). The title 'architect' perhaps needs further substantiation, but this is not far to seek. There are a number of well-known contemporary illustrations of temples, both two-dimensional engravings and three-dimensional models. With many of them, we cannot demonstrate that they were other than artists' views of buildings already erected. For example, though the temple façade beautifully carved on a limestone slab from Tarxien (ill. 5) strongly suggests an architect's elevation, prepared in advance to show what was required, this is now unprovable.

But the terracotta model from Hagar Qim (ill. 6) shows a five-apse temple in the form of wall stumps, a form in which no temple could have physically appeared even during the course of construction. It is an abstract plan, presumably drawn up before building (of Hagar Qim North?) was commenced. Even more intriguing is the stone fragment from Tarxien (ill. 7) showing a complex building of rectangular rooms on an ashlar podium, intriguing because no building remotely like this is known in Malta of that period. It would seem that a plan was prepared but never put into effect – the Planning Committee turned down so revolutionary a design, and the architect was required to submit a more traditional, and more acceptable, scheme in keeping with the apsed structures already

5 *The limestone façade model from Tarxien. Width as restored 39 cm.*

6 *The terracotta temple plan from Hagar Qim. Width of larger fragment c.12 cm.*

7 *The limestone rectilinear building model from Tarxien. Length surviving 29 cm.*

standing on the site. It is very difficult here not to speculate beyond the material finds, to reach out to the people behind the objects. Even if we regard the Planning Committee and its decisions as too hypothetical to be taken seriously, we certainly seem to have an individual, the architect, inherent in that physical evidence.

We need to remind ourselves of the antiquity of the period we are talking about. The span of the Maltese temple development covered 2800–2000 bc, *c.* 3600 –2500 BC. In comparison with Mesopotamia, it began about the same time as the mudbrick temples of Eridu and Uruk, though Tepe Gawra is older, and it ended around the time of the Royal Cemetery at Ur. As regards Egypt, its end overlapped by only a century or so the building of the pyramids (Renfrew 1972). Imhotep, who is honoured as the world's first architect for his introduction of stone masonry in the Step Pyramid of Sakkara, could have been a contemporary of that other nameless architect who worked on

8 Mnajdra South, interior of the first apse. Note the trilithon doorway, porthole slab, two oracle holes, and the over-sailing and inward slope of the upper blocks in the wall. Width of apse 6.20 m.

Tarxien Central. He in turn was a thousand years later than his predecessor who had designed and built the first of the Maltese temples.

This might be a suitable moment to return to the subject of the Hypogeum (ill. 3) (Evans 1971, 44). We suggested that the temples began with an imaginative leap, surely by an individual – let us build a copy of a rock-cut tomb above ground, where it will be so much more conveniently accessible for us to carry out communally the associated rites and ceremonies. Long after, it was asked why, when the underground cemetery of interconnecting rock-cut tomb chambers under what is now Hal Saflieni had grown so large, a temple along the lines of those being built at the time

133

9 The giant statue in Tarxien. Width of skirt as restored c.1.60 m.

was not carved out of the solid rock as part of that site. The suggestion was acted on. At the centre of the Hypogeum can still be seen the chambers carved in close imitation of the above-ground architecture, with such details as trilithon door-frames, pierced door slabs ('porthole' entrances), wall courses projecting in order to narrow roof openings, together with ochred spirals and wash decoration, all preserved by being cut and painted deep below ground. This part of the site, if we interpret the often inadequate excavation reports aright, did not contain burials, so was probably in function as well as form more closely related to the temples than to the rock-cut tombs from which the Hypogeum sprang. The great water cistern at one end of the site would seem also to fit better into a religious context than a funerary one. The revolutionary decision to construct, or rather excavate, a temple below ground must once more imply an individual initiative, even if it was effected by that individual's society.

The contrast between this and the situation with all other ancient megalithic architecture, indeed prehistoric architecture of any kind, hardly needs spelling out. Elsewhere, the great majority of monuments are so firmly rooted in the tradition of the society that erected them that there seems no room for individual architects, rather a long line of architects, each trying *not* to make innovations. Even where a particular structure stands out as a masterpiece – the Cueva de Romeral, Gavr'inis and Maes Howe might be instanced – our only evidence on the designer is what can be read directly from his architecture, and that is usually but little. It is not surprising that study, if it extends beyond the monuments themselves, does so in the direction of the societies they were meant to serve, or in the efforts of the labourers who raised them, but very rarely, and then often controversially, to the designers, the architects. Thanks to their technical innovations, and above all their models, we can approach much more closely to those of Maltese temples.

Such a discussion leads us on naturally to a consideration of the role these temples played among the communities who built them. The evidence that they really were places of worship has been already briefly reviewed, though a little more should be said on what can be recovered of the religious beliefs and practices of the time. There is here little to imply connection with megalithic sites elsewhere, whether funerary, astronomical or religious, unless the Maltese 'mother goddess' of fertility and death can, as an act of faith rather than proof, be equated with the much more shadowy 'dolmen deity' of western Europe. The evidence is as follows.

The deity of the temples is presumably to be recognized in the above-lifesized statue in Tarxien (ill. 9). Despite the loss of its upper half, this can be equated iconographically with similar standing figures, though of smaller size, from Hagar Qim (ill. 10) and Ta Silg, and seated ones from Tarxien and, in a slightly different posture, Hagar Qim. All these represent a grossly corpulent figure, skirted or nude, on which, however, sexual characteristics are noticeably lacking. That should immediately advise caution in the use of terms like 'mother goddess' or, less flattering, 'fat lady'. When figures of the same proportions are clearly female, as with the 'sleeping lady' from the Hypogeum, they are on a much smaller scale and no longer necessarily divine. Another terracotta from Hagar Qim is a delightful female figure with none of the grossness of the others, but again not necessarily a goddess.

But despite that hesitation, the underlying idea of fertility symbolism remains probable, and receives unequivocal support from other finds, particularly from Tarxien. There a wall relief shows a very male bull and a very female sow, with no less than fourteen piglets at suck, immediately adjacent. This site has, too, produced several indubitable carved phalli.

Suggestive but less explicit is the link between the temple deity and death, probably implied by the tomb-to-temple development, more certainly by the funerary temple within the Hypogeum.

Practices should be more easily recoverable by archaeology than beliefs. Animal sacrifice is well attested. The flint knife and goat horn core from the 'cupboard' in the decorated altar in Tarxien South, and the dove skeleton in the central niche of Skorba East, are but two examples. Animal bone was frequent on many sites, and the rows of animals carved in relief at Tarxien hint at the same. The forecourts so apparent at most sites must have been designed for open-air ceremonies before the shrines, but the content of those ceremonies is now quite irrecoverable.

Two pieces of evidence suggest the presence of a priesthood of some kind – and I do not include the so-called 'priest' figurine from Tarxien, whose sex and calling are alike matters of conjecture only. The distinction in the temples between 'public' outer parts, in which the decorated blocks are concentrated, and 'private' inner parts, with doors which could be barred only from the inside, indicates that access to those inner parts was restricted to a small and in some way privileged group of people. Whatever passed through the 'oracle holes', they too imply two classes of person, one positioned in the inner, even secret, chamber in contrast to the other in the outer or public part of the building. The 'oracular' reverberation of a deep voice in one chamber of the Hypogeum cannot be considered conclusive unless it can be shown to have been deliberately planned, which seems unlikely. It is tantalizing how far the evidence will take us before it gives out, with so many questions still unanswered.

But if the specific functions and even more beliefs are so difficult to recover, the general ones of displaying and stressing a community's existence and separateness from other communities are much more readily apparent. Renfrew broke new ground when he pointed out (1973, 147–67) that the distribution of the temples could be interpreted as mirroring a social or political grouping of the population of Malta at the time. While his criterion for the 'really big' temples was both somewhat arbitrary and inconsistently applied, the pattern changes little when all known buildings of the temple period are added in. The only danger comes

10 Limestone seated figure from Hagar Qim. Height 23.5 cm.

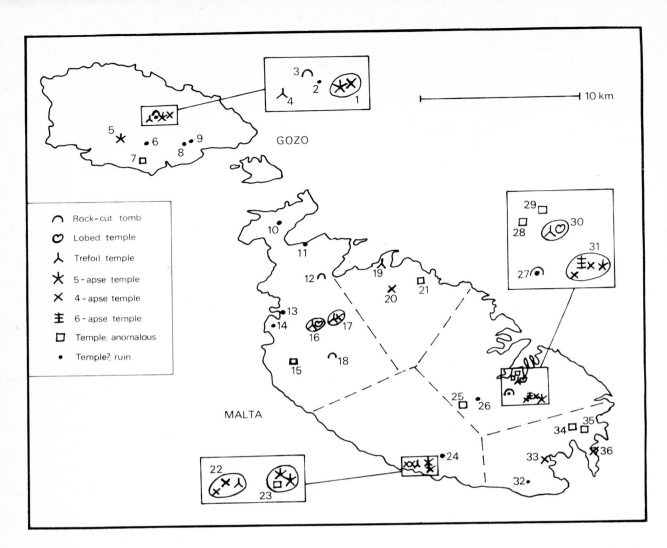

11 The distribution of the Maltese temples, with suggested territories. (After Renfrew 1973, with additions.) 1 Ggantija, 2 Ghar ta Ghejzu, 3 Xaghra tomb, 4 Santa Verna, 5 Ta Marziena, 6 Xewkija, 7 Borg li Mramma, 8 Li Mrejsbiet, 9 Borg il Gharib, 10 Armier, 11 Ghajn Zejtuna, 12 Xemxija 1–5, 13 Ta Lippija, 14 Ras il Pellegrin, 15 Li Mdawwar, 16 Ta Hagrat, Mgarr, 17 Li Skorba, 18 Bengemma, 19 Bugibba, 20 Tal Qadi, 21 Il Maghtab, 22 Mnajdra, 23 Hagar Qim, 24 Sqaq il Bal, Qrendi, 25 Debdieba, 26 It Tumbata, 27 Hal Saflieni, 28 Kordin I, 29 Kordin II, 30 Kordin III, 31 Tarxien, 32 Hal Far, 33 Borg in Nadur, 34 Hal Ginwi, 35 Ta Silg, 36 Xrobb il Ghagin.

from the possible complete disappearance of other temples of which we know nothing, and against this we have no defence. But using what evidence has come down to us, we could reasonably argue for six 'tribal' territories in the islands, each responsible for the erection and maintenance of the major and minor temple sites therein contained (ill. 11).

The new map might suggest a further possibility, that the pattern is of three territories rather than six. There is, of course, no reason why territories of human groups should necessarily be of equal size, like those of a single pair of nesting birds, since the numbers within the groups could vary. The gap across central Malta, despite just as appropriate areas as elsewhere in the island for the survival of monuments, around Naxxar and Rabat in particular, remains very clear, whereas the boundaries between Renfrew's three eastern territories have become rather more blurred. In either case, the monuments presumably served as foci for the ceremonies which marked off tribe from tribe. What we cannot explain is the multiplication of temple sites within each group, but this is hardly more of a problem than that long recognized, the reason for the multiplication of temples on each site.

One crucial piece of evidence seems to have been consistently undervalued. The stone trough in Kordin III (ill. 12) was, as recognized by Evans (1971, 73), an integral part of the temple into which it was built, though he had doubts whether the grooves worn into it were contemporary with the temple occupation. The fact that it is the only block of coralline limestone to be used on the site, having been transported at least a kilometre for the purpose, implies that it was chosen for some particular need, surely the grinding that was undoubtedly carried out on it. The substance ground, therefore, is likely to have been grain, as Ashby (Ashby *et al.* 1913, 42) originally suggested. The number and depth of the grooves, seven and at least 18 cm deep, in turn suggest a very considerable quantity of grain, probably over a long period of time. It would be interesting to speculate what proportion of limestone grit in the flour was considered acceptable. To me the implication seems clear that it was the community's grain being brought into the temple to be ground

under the immediate protection of the community's deity. There was almost certainly also a strong social element in this communal grinding of the daily flour. While the case would be greatly strengthened if every temple, or at least one in each territory, had its public quern, no other explanation seems to explain the facts from Kordin III so satisfactorily.

On the matter of the political organization of temple-period Malta, and the likelihood of some sort of chieftainship, I can add nothing useful to those points Renfrew has already advanced, and refer readers to his work *(op. cit.).*

A consequence of this patent link between the temples and the society which produced them is that the collapse of the one around 2400 BC can be regarded as prime evidence for the breakdown of the other. Despite the considerable body of information which has been recovered on these events, however (Trump 1978), its interpretation has so far produced no clear answers. The end of the temples is even more mysterious than their beginning. There is a hint of decline

12 The communal quern of coralline limestone in the Kordin III temple. Length 2.66 m.

13 The Wied Znuber dolmen. Length 3.70 m.

at Skorba, where the east temple went out of use before the west temple, to be used for rubbish dumping. Otherwise the collapse seems to have been sudden and complete, as if the whole population of Malta and Gozo had abandoned everything and fled the islands. So far, none of the many possible explanations, singly or collectively, is clearly preferred by the recovered evidence. It remains only to be hoped that future research, probably environmental and not necessarily within the temples themselves, will eventually allow us to suggest what really happened to destroy such remarkable buildings, their culture and their people.

It could be argued that Malta and Gozo's very isolation, giving us almost laboratory conditions so little affected by extraneous influences, automatically reduces their value for comparative purposes. This is not so, since no claim is being made, or can be made, that any one set of circumstances will provide answers for application elsewhere. On the contrary, although the islands allow us to advance a powerful argument for Maltese temple architecture being the result of a remarkable indigenous development, the product of not only a human community but of a few gifted individuals within that community, we have already noted in the appearance of agriculture in the Ghar

Dalam phase, and of new pottery styles and tomb forms in the Zebbug phase, equally clear examples of cultural diffusion, invasion even, however unfashionable that term now is.

Following the temple period, we have another example of massive overseas influence on the Maltese islands, which must represent an immigrant population. The use of megalithic architecture again comes into the story, though in a very different form. The culture of the Tarxien Cemetery demonstrates a total break with the tradition built up over the preceding millennium and a half. It owed nothing to the earlier inhabitants of its new home, its antecedents all lying elsewhere (Evans 1956). Only one of its cultural elements need be pursued here, that of building with large blocks of stone.

Some sixteen dolmens have been recorded from the Maltese islands, though the exact number is uncertain by reason of their often ruinous state. One at least, at Ta Hammut near the north coast, has produced an archaeological deposit of the Tarxien Cemetery phase, *c*.2500–1500 BC. Several of them are distinctive, if not exactly distinguished, monuments, Wied Znuber (ill. 13), Safi, the Misrah Sinjura and Wied Filep, to name only the four finest. These share characteristics in general and in detail with the Otranto group in the Salentine peninsula, the heel of Italy. They consist of a slab of limestone up to 4.40 x 3.80 m poised on stone supports. The Misrah Sinjura has a groove cut around its margin on the upper surface, and this and the Safi and Bidni dolmens have vertical perforations through the slab. The suggestion that both are connected with libation rites is tempting, if speculative. Both these features can be paralleled in the Otranto area, implying some meaningful connection. Admittedly this takes us very little further in explaining how either group is affiliated to the mainstream of western European megalithic tombs. There is effectively nothing to suggest that they appeared independently in either of these areas, but hardly more to indicate how they could have reached either from further west.

Even the function they served amongst the Maltese communities which raised them is uncertain. The associated material at Ta Hammut included broken pottery but no bone, and the small size of the chamber implied that any interment there may once have been must have been by cremation, as in the Tarxien Cemetery itself. All other dolmens had been stripped bare before discovery, so it is only an assumption, based on evidence from other parts of Europe, that the dolmens of Malta were burial chambers at all. In consequence, they offer us little help in the wider enquiry we are here pursuing.

Several menhirs have been recorded from the islands (Evans 1971, 198–9), but only two seem to be rightly so called. These are the well-squared pillars at Kirkop and Kercem. Being without association of any kind, they are undatable, and one can only note that similar pillars are known around Otranto, in the area which yields the best parallels for the Maltese dolmens. Other examples from Malta are unshaped and have scatters of temple-period pottery around them. They are probably, as that at Skorba was demonstrated to be, surviving blocks of temple-like buildings otherwise destroyed.

Malta and Gozo, then, have offered us excellent examples of both local evolution and diffusion from an external source in their megalithic architecture, their geography allowing us to trace both processes more clearly than is possible in many other areas. They serve to remind us that if a coin falls head-side-up on one occasion, or even on many consecutive occasions, that does not in the least alter the chances of its falling heads or tails on the next toss, provided only that the coin has not been mischievously given two heads. The origins of any group of megalithic monuments, or indeed of any other cultural trait, will be determined only when all the available evidence is assembled and weighed dispassionately.

Acknowledgments

All objects illustrated are in the National Museum of Malta, Valletta. Ill. 10 is by courtesy of the Malta Government Tourist Board; all other illustrations are by the author.

Bibliography

ASHBY, T., BRADLEY, R. N., PEET, T. E., TAGLIA-FERRO, N. 1913 'Excavations in 1908–11 in various megalithic buildings in Malta and Gozo', *BSR* VI, 1.

BALDACCHINO J.G. AND EVANS, J.D. 1954 'Prehistoric Tombs near Zebbug', *BSR* XXII, n.s.IX, 1.

CANN, J. R. AND RENFREW, C. 1964, The Characterization of Obsidian and its application to the Mediterranean Region', *Proc. Preh. Soc.* XXX, 111.

EVANS, J. D. 1953 'The Prehistoric Culture Sequence in the Maltese Archipelago', *Proc. Preh. Soc.* XIX, 41.

1956 'The "Dolmens" of Malta and the Origins of the Tarxien Cemetery Culture', *Proc. Preh. Soc.* XXII, 80.

1959 *Malta*, London and New York.

1971 *The Prehistoric Antiquities of the Maltese Islands*, London.

RENFREW, C. 1972 'Malta and the calibrated radiocarbon chronology', *Antiquity* XLVI, no. 184, 141–5.

1973 *Before Civilization*, London.

TRUMP, D. H. 1966 *Skorba*, Oxford.

1972 *Malta, an archaeological guide*, London.

1978 'The collapse of the Maltese temples', in Sieveking, G. de G., Longworth, I.H. and Wilson, K. E. (eds), *Problems in Economic and Social Archaeology*, London.

1980 'I primi architetti del mondo, i costruttori dei templi maltesi', in Fontana, M. J., Piraino, M. T. and Rizzo, F. P. (eds), *Miscellanea di Studi Classici in Onore di Eugenio Manni*, Rome.

Appendix

Catalogue of Temples and Rock-Cut Tombs

No. on map	Site	Form	Length (m)	Breadth (m)	Earliest material	Orientation
1	Ggantija North	4-apse	18.75	17.50	Ggantija?	133°
	South	5-apse	26.25	23.75	Ggantija	128°
2	Ghar ta Ghejzu	ruinous			Ggantija	
3	Xaghra tomb	r.c.t.	1.73		Ggantija?	
4	Santa Verna	3-apse?	16.90?	16.15?	Ggantija	120°?
5	Ta Marziena	5-apse	17?	16.80?	Ggantija	180°?
6	Xewkija	destroyed				
7	Borg li Mramma	anomalous		37.50 max.		
8	Li Mrejsbiet	ruinous				
9	Borg il Gharib	ruinous				
10	Armier	ruinous				
11	Ghajn Zejtuna	destroyed				
12	Xemxija 1–5	r.c.t.'s		5.65 max.	Zebbug	
13	Ta Lippija	ruinous				
14	Ras il Pellegrin	ruinous			Tarxien	
15	Li Mdawwar	anomalous			Tarxien	
16	Ta Hagrat, Mgarr W.	3-a	14	12.55	Ggantija	135°
	E.	lobed	7.25	8.90	Saflieni?	176°
17	Li Skorba West	3-apse	14.20	18.30	Ggantija	139°
	East	4-apse	16.15	14.20	Tarxien	170°
18	Bengemma	r.c.t.			Ggantija	
19	Bugibba	3-apse?	?	13.45?	Tarxien	200°
20	Tal Qadi	3-apse?	10.50?	18.30	Tarxien?	78°
21	Il Maghtab	anomalous				
22	Mnajdra South	4-apse	15.15	13.65	Tarxien	103°
	Central	4-apse	18.05	16.60	Tarxien	148°
	East	3-apse	7.05	9.25	Ggantija	218°
23	Hagar Qim Central	4-apse, anom.	17.10	20	Ggantija	132°
	North	5-apse	16	7.30	Ggantija	184°
24	Sqaq il Bal, Qrendi	ruinous				
25	Debdieba	anomalous	23 max.		Tarxien?	
26	It Tumbata	ruinous				
27	Hal Saflieni	r.c.cem. ruinous	29.40 max.	22.50 max.	Zebbug	
28	Kordin I	anomalous	20			
29	II	anomalous	25.50			
30	III West	3-apse	15.45	13.65	Ggantija	149°
	East	lobed	9.10	12.25	Ggantija	203°?
31	Tarxien West	4-apse	22.80	18.30	Early Tarxien	204°
	Central	6-apse	23.10	18.60	Tarxien	230°
	East	4-apse	15.60	12.60	Early Tarxien	200°
	Far East	5-apse	12	6?	Ggantija	176°
32	Hal Far	destroyed				
33	Borg in Nadur	4-apse	8.45?	8.45	Tarxien	108°
34	Hal Ginwi	anomalous	10.60 max.		Ggantija	
35	Ta Silg	anomalous	15.50			106°
36	Xrobb il Ghagin	4-apse	13.50	9.10?	Ggantija	135°

14   Megaliths of the Funnel Beaker Culture in Germany and Scandinavia

Lili Kaelas

SINCE THE Second World War, Professor Glyn Daniel has been the vanguard figure in megalithic tomb research. His field of studies has covered major areas of Atlantic Europe. To collaborate in a work of tribute to my colleague Glyn is like continuing a dialogue, both one which took place at a personal level and one which sprang from the reading of his many investigations and surveys. Nothing could be more inviting.

Fifteen years ago I wrote a survey of megalithic tombs in southern Scandinavia. In this survey I discussed their architecture and building technique as well as their functions as graves and cult-centres. I concentrated on chronology, migration and cultural influences. This approach was in no way unique to Scandinavian research. Similar questions were regarded as central by scholars in other parts of Europe where megalithic tomb research has been done.

Since this study was published (1966/67) I have been mainly involved with administrative work. A great deal has happened in megalithic research since then. The evidence is more solid now. When my article was written, few monuments in Scandinavia had been totally examined by modern field-methods. During the 1960s and 1970s many such examinations were conducted in Denmark and southern Sweden (Scania). However, the most comprehensive ever to be carried out were those in Mecklenburg, East Germany. Under the guidance of Evald Schuldt, 106 megalithic tombs were investigated and the results recorded in the course of six and a half years. As a result, Mecklenburg is the best-recorded area in Europe. But in West Germany (Lower Saxony) too, new investigations and findings have extended the evidence for theoretical judgment.

What can we learn from Recent Investigations?
First and foremost we have gained increased knowledge of the architecture and techniques of tomb-building in these areas. The finds and observations made during the numerous investigations have partly substantiated previous conclusions, and also provided new information about ritual and cult observances. It is now for example possible to compare the Mecklenburg tombs with the southern Scandinavian ones in terms of age with much greater certainty, and to include them in the chronological scheme used by Scandinavian scholars.

In addition, the new evidence provides a better basis for understanding the megalithic-tomb society's economic structure, a problem which has now become more relevant than when I wrote my earlier paper.

I shall first give a survey of some of the new evidence of the architecture of the tombs and related problems.

The Tomb Monuments

Dolmens Interest in the origin of Nordic dolmens has not slackened. It has kept scholars busy almost continuously for over a hundred years, since the time of Montelius. The simple rectangular dolmens, the so-called 'urdolmens', and their development have always attracted the greatest attention and still do. I shall not dwell on the details of design and construction of different local dolmen types since the evidence is well known, but briefly compare differences and similarities.

German and Scandinavian scholars had long regarded the rectangular and polygonal dolmens as generically connected forms. The polygonal were treated as a development via several typologically related links from the 'urdolmens'. Becker's interpretation (1947, 266–9) of the small rectangular southern Danish dolmens was therefore welcomed as a turning point in the discussion. He characterized these as a local counterpart of the subterranean human-length stone cists found in the continental Funnel Beaker Culture, i.e. similar to the Funnel Beaker Culture people's characteristic early stone tombs. This view rests on the assumption that some of the oldest southern Danish dolmens are subterranean, which is not proven. His view is still accepted, especially in Denmark.

However, some objections have been raised (Kaelas 1956, 11). The dating of these subterranean southern Danish dolmens presents difficulties. According to known finds they are from the beginning of the Middle Neolithic. New arguments have recently emerged which dispute Becker's interpretation.

The subterranean stone cists are single graves. The small dolmens have also been regarded as such up till now. Recent German research, however, has begun to question the plausibility of this theory. It has been possible to establish that also in the small rectangular dolmens, with a few exceptions, skeletal fragments from more than one individual as primary interments can be found and consequently they cannot be considered as single graves (Raddatz 1979, 130). The question of the origin of the rectangular dolmens has therefore become more complicated.

Long barrows without stone chambers

Rectangular dolmens *in* long barrows (ill.1) are typical of southern Scandinavia. Rectangular dolmens *without* long barrows appear for example in France, Scotland and Portugal. Some of these are very like the Nordic 'urdolmens'. In addition, long barrows *without stone chambers* exist both in Scandinavia and elsewhere.

The fact remains that the Nordic rectangular dolmens in long barrows have no counterpart anywhere, as has been previously maintained (Kaelas 1966/67, 229). Long barrows without stone chambers appear in the west of France, mainly in the Department of Morbihan in Brittany. In southern England, they occur between Portland and Eastbourne and on the coastline of Lincolnshire and Yorkshire. Within the cultural area of the Funnel Beaker

Culture – that is, in Denmark, northern Germany and Poland – they are to be found in Jutland and Schleswig-Holstein, western Mecklenburg, western Pomerania and in Kujavia (north-western Poland) (ill.2).

Within this large area the long barrows are not uniform either in shape or chronology. Within the Funnel Beaker Culture area rectangular long barrows dominate up to the Oder, but are not found east of the river (although a few trapezoid long barrows occur in western Pomerania). In Kujavia at Weichsel Knie, triangular barrows with a blunt end, often very extended, predominate (see ills 3–4). The River Oder forms a border in another sense as well: east of the river there appear no megalithic tombs proper within the Funnel Beaker Culture groups. All the passage graves found in barrows there are secondary and built within already existing barrows (Jazdzewski 1973, 65 with references). In western Europe trapezoid long barrows predominate.

In all the above areas long barrows appear sometimes in groups, sometimes singly, usually in areas without megalithic tombs. In Jutland and Mecklenburg, however, single long barrows are found within groups of megalithic tombs.

There are great similarities between the Funnel Beaker Culture 'chamberless' earthen long barrows and long barrows with stone chambers (= dolmens). There are also similarities between the Funnel Beaker Culture and western European 'chamberless' long barrows. What is common to both types of long barrow is that they are usually surrounded by a frame of erratic

1 View from the west of long barrow (22 x 8 m) at Araslöv in Vinslöv, Scania, surrounded by megalithic blocks. The gaps between the boulders were originally sealed with slab-shaped stones and similar material in a dry-masonry technique, enclosing the barrow with a continuous wall. There are two rectangular dolmens within the 'wall'. (Photo Skanes Hembygsförbund/Carin Bunte.)

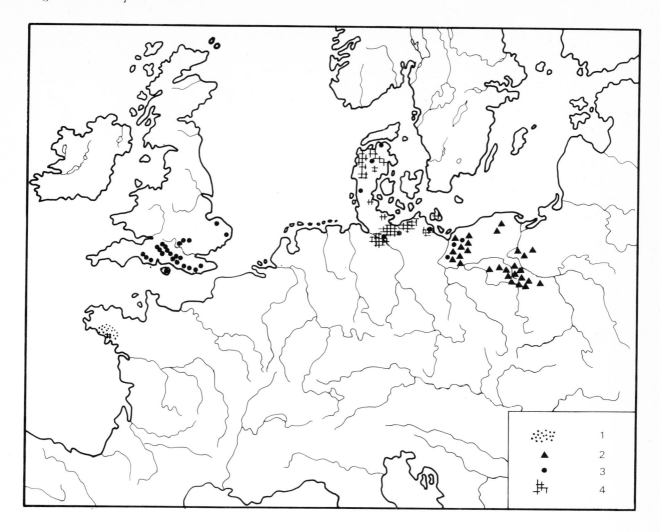

2 *'Chamberless' earthen long barrows in Europe: 1 and 3 barrows of general trapezoid shape; 2 triangular barrows (i.e. Kujavian barrows); 4 rectangular barrows. (Poland, England and Brittany after Jazdzewski 1972, with revisions; northern Germany after Schuldt 1972; Denmark after Madsen 1979, with revisions.)*

boulders (ills 1 and 3–4) and with dry masonry between the stones (– a closed stone wall). In Britain and Poland ditches are usually found along the barrows – that is to say, quarries from which the earth was taken for the barrow. In both Britain and Denmark traces of a timber façade in the eastern end of the barrow have been discovered. In both areas there are palisade enclosures and transverse rows of poles sectioning the barrows (probably remainders of hurdle fences, according to Madsen 1979, 318).

So many features in common cannot depend merely on chance. This led Stuart Piggott, who also brought in the evidence of pottery and causewayed camps, to put the question: 'Windmill Hill — East or West?'(1956). His conclusion that there was probably contact between the primary Neolithic cultures of Britain and the northern European Funnel Beaker Culture

seemed bold and at that time rested on slender evidence. Ten years later (1966) he again took up the question of a common northern European tradition for 'chamberless' long barrows from a British point of view. Since then the evidence has increased considerably – also on the question of causewayed camps – through well-documented studies from both the northern German and Danish areas (Schuldt 1972, 31, 102–5; Jazdzewski 1973, 65–72: Madsen 1979, 317–19 with references).

3,4 Kujavian barrow at Wietrzychowice, province of Wloclawek: above, after excavation; below, after reconstruction. (Photos Muzeum Archeologiczne i Etnograficzne, Lodz, Poland.)

The similarities between the northern German and Polish tombs and those described above are less tangible. Burnt mortuary houses appear but are exceptional. Tombs in northern German and Kujavian barrows are largely simple earth graves. In Kujavia these have also been found around the barrows.

Consequently one can no longer question the existence of a common tradition for northern European and British 'chamberless' long barrows, a tradition first argued by Piggott and recently convincingly proved in Denmark by Madsen (1979, 302, 318). In addition to the formal similarities there is also a chronological agreement between the Funnel Beaker Culture 'chamberless' long barrows and long barrows with stone chambers. There can appear in one and the same long barrow earth graves as well as megalithic tombs

and the tombs are not necessarily the last to have been constructed (Madsen 1979, 315). The construction of 'chamberless' long barrows continued during the Middle Neolithic as well, contemporary with passage graves and sometimes close by them (Schuldt 1972, 104).

The difference between the two types of long barrows would seem to be that single graves – one or more in succession – commonly appear in 'chamberless' long barrows whereas in long barrows *with* stone chambers the skeletal remains of several individuals appear collectively.

The new investigation results are suggesting now that dolmens were being used primarily as graves for more than one individual even during the Early Neolithic (Raddatz 1979, 130–2, cf. however, Jörgensen 1977, 177). Surprisingly enough similar observations have been made in long barrows without stone chambers in Jutland (Madsen 1979, 311). This means – if the observations are valid – that in the 'chamberless' long barrows besides single graves there were also earth graves which were used for several successive interments. This suggests that the same burial ritual was practised in long barrows of both types, at least locally.

Which type of long barrow is the oldest within the Funnel Beaker Culture? Is the megalithic tomb a wooden construction transferred into stone, as a number of archaeologists claim (most recently e.g. Madsen 1979)? Or is it the other way round? The question is relevant for western Europe too, but cannot be answered in general terms.

In Denmark almost all known 'chamberless' long barrows are found in Jutland. The oldest rectangular dolmens – 'urdolmens' in long barrows – have their nucleus on Zealand where they begin to appear around the middle of the Early Neolithic (phase C). Although they are found during this period in Jutland too the great majority there were built at the beginning of the Middle Neolithic. Generally speaking, both types of long barrow are of equal antiquity within the Nordic Funnel Beaker Culture area. According to a more recent, and more fashionable, theory 'the megalithic graves involved no functional change, only an architectural one, which may or may not have its background in foreign influences' (Renfrew 1976, 200; Madsen 1979, 317). It can thus be established that the great similarities between the two types suggests a common tradition. Where this common tradition has its origin from a European perspective – North or East or West – is still an open question.

Polygonal dolmens Polygonal dolmens (ill. 6) present a different problem. Once the idea of a common origin

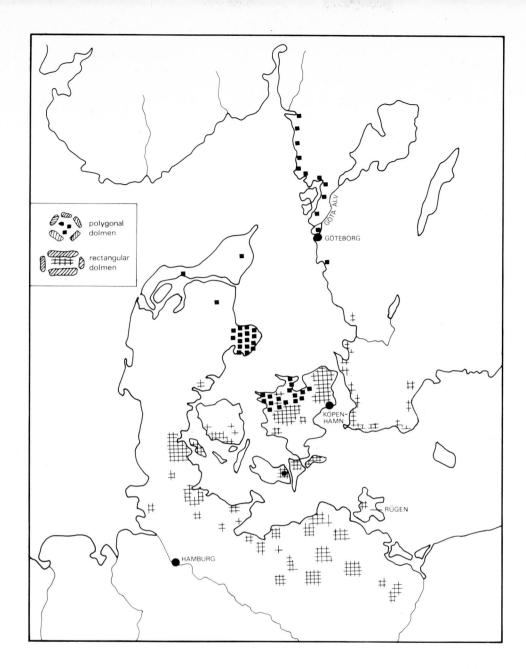

 is embedded above with its legend reading "polygonal dolmen" and "rectangular dolmen".

for the two types of dolmen – that is, the rectangular and the polygonal – had been abandoned and each had been analysed individually, with account taken of the frequency of the different forms of the surrounding barrow, the solution to the problem of origin was in sight (Kaelas 1956, 10–14; Aner 1963).

Aner's analysis of the spread of rectangular and polygonal dolmens in Denmark and Schleswig-Holstein resulted in a survey map of the centres of the respective dolmen types (17, ill. 7). If Aner's map is supplemented with details from the south and west of

5 Areas where rectangular and polygonal dolmens predominate. (E. Aner 1963, with additions.)

Sweden (the counties of Scania, Halland, Bohuslän) and northern Germany (Mecklenburg) the picture is, if possible even more enlightening (ill. 2): Jutland (Djursland peninsula) and adjacent areas in north-western Zealand appear quite clearly as the central areas of the polygonal dolmens. With a few exceptions, on-ly polygonal dolmens are found on the west coast of

145

6 Polygonal dolmen at Haga in Stala, isle of Orust, Bohuslän. Note the 'heart'-shaped entrance. Similar entrances are found in polygonal dolmens in Portugal. (Photo Göteborgs arkeologiska museum (GAM).)

Sweden (Bohuslän and modern Halland) opposite to Jutland. It appears quite clearly from the map that these polygonal dolmens of western European origin reach the coastal area of the Kattegatt through Limfjorden (see also Aner 1963, 13, ill. 5.) (The earliest appearance of the polygonal dolmens is still considered to date from phase C of the Early Neolithic). In other parts of Zealand the rectangular dolmens predominate, just as in Scania. Further eastwards, in Mecklenburg, there are only rectangular dolmens. However, the map showing the central areas of the respective dolmen types should not be read as suggesting that within the central areas in Denmark only one type in fact appears. It shows only where the respective dolmen type is in the majority. As a further comment on the map it can be said that of the more than 300 identifiable polygonal

dolmens in Denmark and Schleswig-Holstein, 40 per cent occur on Djursland and as many on north-western Zealand (Aner 1963, 13).

Passage graves Many of the architectural and technical details recently found through studies of the construction of passage graves in different geographical areas, which were previously thought to be unique to or prevailing in a particular area, have proved to be more general in occurrence. One example of this state of affairs is represented in the two types of passage graves, the 'Lower Saxony' type (with the passage placed in the middle of one of the long sides of the chamber) and the 'Holstein' type (with asymmetrically placed passage). The latter was considered typical of Holstein and Mecklenburg. But more recent research has shown that contrary to earlier belief both types are equally common in Mecklenburg.

Another and yet more eloquent criterion is evident in the division of the chamber into compartments (ill. 7), once believed to be unique to Västergötland. It is now clear that such a division is not an isolated local phenomenon but a general characteristic feature in the layout of passage graves.

Chamber compartments are of course not uncommon in western Europe. Prior to the extensive investigations in Mecklenburg I therefore regarded it as a western European feature of the passage graves of the Funnel Beaker Culture (Kaelas 1956, 22–3). It is now difficult to maintain this view. The Mecklenburg investigations show in fact that chamber compartments appear there in all types of megalithic tombs with the exception of 'urdolmens'. The division of the megalithic tombs of the Funnel Beaker Culture seems to be related to their function, although with local variations in design. However, it is surprising that compartments of this type are not found in Denmark, Schleswig-Holstein or Lower Saxony. Instead, in these areas are found single, about human-length, partitions which divide the chamber transversely, usually into two rooms. Is this a question of two different traditions and functions?

According to observations in Mecklenburg, chamber compartments can be dated to the early Middle Neolithic. They are primarily in the passage graves and originated in connection with the process of building (Schuldt 1972, 62). In my view this interpretation is substantiated both in Västergötland and in Scania, one reason being that the stones in the walls of the compartments are at the same depth as the chamber walls. According to Strömberg (1971, 258), however, the large number of compartments in passage graves – in Scania up to thirteen, in Västergötland closer to twenty, in Mecklenburg between seven and eight –

7 *Compartments in the excavated chamber of passage grave no.2 at Gnewitz, County Rostock, Mecklenburg, seen fromt the west. (Photo Klaus Nitsche, Schwerin, DDR.)*

together with the fact that different compartments may have different floorings, speaks for the probability that they were not built in originally and not all at the same time. On the contrary, the compartments in dolmens are a later addition (Schuldt 1965, 49; 1969, 109; 1972, 62).

What was the function of the compartments? In the case of Mecklenburg, Schuldt (1966, 50–2; 1966, 76–9; 1972, 74) considers it proved that skeletal remains were interred in the burial chambers only after the bodies had lain for some time in another place. Ac-

cordingly, the burial chambers had the function of ossuaries. He supports his view from observations which the majority of archaeologists have made, namely that skeletons from the primary burial period are never complete. They are always discovered in a

8 Funnel Beaker Culture bottom layer of agglomerated bones and bone fragments, bounded by partition walls into compartments. North-eastern part of the chamber in the passage grave at Rössberga, Valltorp, Västergötland, Sweden. (Photo Antikvariskt-Topografiskt Arkivet (ATA), Stockholm.)

more or less chaotic state, whether in compartments or in undivided burial chambers.

This view corresponds well with my own observations on visits during the excavation of the Rössberga passage grave in Västergötland (1962). The passage-grave chamber contained seventeen compartments. The lowest level of finds consisted almost wholly of a (30-cm thick) layer of bones bounded into compartments by the partition walls (ill. 8). Since the osteological analysis – twenty years after the dig – has not been published yet, it is still not known how many individuals are represented in the skeletal remains (a

148

preliminary evaluation suggests forty). Accordingly it is not known how many individuals the fragments in each compartment represent, or whether the remains of one and the same individual are to be found spread over several compartments. It is known, however, from earlier studies that in Västergötland the remains of several individuals have been found also in small compartments. The old ossuary theory, which is now over one hundred years old, has thus been given new relevance through this flood of new evidence. On the other hand, observations of bodies in a sitting position – mentioned in earlier excavation reports – must be questioned.

It should, however, be added that Strömberg, in an investigation of a passage grave in Scania, Carlshög at Hagestad, discovered skeletal fragments in such a position that she – although with certain reservations – considered this to indicate burial in a sitting position (1971, 289). If the observation is valid this suggests that megalithic tombs of the Funnel Beaker Culture in exceptional cases were used as burial places as such and not merely as ossuaries.

In what way was the body prepared before the bones were laid in the ossuary? The question has been discussed from different viewpoints but is still unanswered. It is possible that the unusual buildings of the Tustrup and Ferslöv type, of which there are at least six to seven in Jutland – all of the same type and age and all from the same period (that is, the Middle Neolithic period Ib, possibly at Herrup as early as period Ia and predating the first passage graves) – and of whose function nothing is known, may have had a role in this connection. However, according to Becker (1973, 79) they should rather be regarded as small sanctuaries or temples without direct connection with mortuary houses or funeral rites.

A large number of buildings which seem to have served as mortuary houses in the second half of the Middle Neolithic are found mainly in north-western and mid-Jutland. These are amongst the most remarkable discoveries which have been made in Funnel Beaker Culture burial ritual since the middle of the 1960s. The excavation of a passage grave at Vroue Hede between Viborg and Holstebro indicated that the sacrificial cult, traces of which are usually found outside the entrance of the passage in the so-called 'sacrificial cairn', had ceased at some time during the Middle Neolithic, period III. But at some distance from the passage entrance under level ground were found a large number of later graves, so called stone-packing graves dating from the Middle Neolithic, periods IV and V (Jörgensen 1977, 186). These human-length graves were in pairs and in rows next to their mortuary houses (ill. 9). This type of grave belongs to the

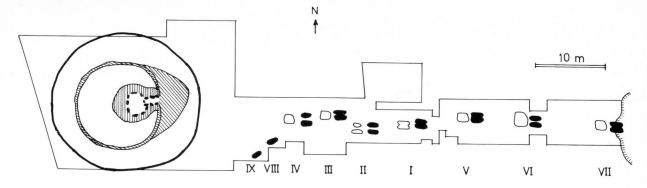

9 Passage grave and stone-packing graves (in black) with mortuary houses at Vroue Hede, Jutland. (Drawing by B. Jakobsson after Jörgensen 1977.)

second half of the Middle Neolithic, possibly originating as far back as the Middle Neolithic, period II (Becker 1967, 28–9). In addition, finds were made in the old sacrificial mound which, to judge from their position, were placed there by the stone-packing grave people. This indicates that the passage graves and their surroundings were still used as a cult and burial area also by a later Funnel Beaker Culture society (Jörgensen 1977, 110, 204–5, 207). These mortuary houses are important for future research because they suggest what traces such constructions leave behind. But in the meantime, the question of how these people treated the dead before the bones were laid in the passage-grave chamber or the dolmen must remain unanswered.

The 'Megalithic' Society

As the previous discussion has made clear, the questions still at the centre of research today, as they were fifteen years ago, are those of the architecture and dating of megalithic tombs, the function of such monuments and the cults connected with them and that of the origin of the tombs. But in addition greater interest is being taken in the question of the society that built them.

The tombs are a manifestation of the activity of a society – 'fossilized behaviour of extinct societies' as Childe expressed it. Under the influence of anthropological models postulated by American and British anthropologists, as well as the predominantly eastern European Marxist models, megalithic tombs are also being studied in their socio-economic aspects.

The construction of megalithic tombs must have been labour-intensive, especially if they are seen in relation to the estimates we have of the population of the societies. A precondition of such work would be a surplus of food supplies for the labour force involved, at least during the building period. How many individuals lived in a community which had the capacity to erect a passage grave? According to Paul Ashbee,

the construction of the Fussell's Lodge long barrow is calculated to have required nearly 5,000 days of labour for the mound alone (Clark 1977, 35). What was the basis of their economy?

Such considerations have made it essential to supplement excavations of tombs with a search for contemporary sites in the vicinity. As yet, few sites which can be assigned with certainty to the building period of a specific tomb are known.

Where are the Dwelling-Sites of the Tomb Builders?

Assuming that each megalithic tomb corresponds to one settlement unit, that is, one community, and that the monument marks the sphere of interest of the community – which is reasonable according to archaeological and ethnographic experience – traces of settlement should be found within the territory in question (cf. Renfrew 1976, 208). This view of the tombs is not new. However, systematic topographical studies and search for dwelling sites in the area around megalithic tombs have not generally been instigated. Where they have been for instance in connection with tomb investigations, good results have been obtained.

In Sweden, in the province of Scania, through systematic search Funnel Beaker Culture settlements have been found which have left culture deposit layers within an area of 1–1.5 km radius from the megalithic tomb, in some cases quite close and sometimes under the tomb as well. Similar results have also been obtained sporadically in other Nordic megalithic tomb areas. As mentioned above, the difficulty has been to connect the dwelling site chronologically to a specific tomb. This is not surprising. The tomb finds are different in composition and often contain a range of more 'valuable' objects than the dwelling-site finds. For a more definite connection it is necessary to have pottery with complicated ornamentation from both the tomb and the dwelling-site in question. To get suitable samples from both sites for radiocarbon dating is also difficult. Up to now extremely few samples of this nature have been found.

In Jutland, however, they have succeeded in finding dwelling-sites beside a group of megalithic tombs at Karups Hede, south of Limfjorden. These sites were populated at the time of construction of the passage graves (Jörgensen 1977, 204). Dwelling-sites are also known near megalithic graves in Mecklenburg, but there too there are difficulties in establishing a chronological connection with the period of building. From Lower Saxony little knowledge exists. Practically no total investigations of dwelling-sites have been carried out there and dwelling-site excavations are also rare (Schirnig 1979, 19). On the other hand, cultural deposits contemporary with the tombs beside the 'chamberless' earthen long barrows are commonly found in Kujavia. Polish scholars generally consider these to stem from earlier dwelling sites above which long barrows have been built. Similar cultural deposits have also been found in connection with long barrows in Jutland, but have been differently interpreted there. It is thought 'that the cultural material was laid down in connection with the use of the structures' (Madsen 1979, 317), that is, as part of cult observances. This may be so, but until the Danish excavation reports are published it will not be possible to form an opinion.

Because of the difficulties commented on, megalithic tomb studies and dwelling-site studies have to some extent run parallel.

The Economy and Structure of Megalithic Tomb Societies
The two main questions are how foodstuffs were produced and how society was structured.

There has been renewed interest in the latter question since recent investigations have discovered earth graves in the areas of the passage graves, e.g. in Scania, Jutland and Lower Saxony. Sometimes the earth grave was very close to the passage grave (Strömberg 1971, 339–40; Tempel 1979, 111–13). Some of these graves are contemporary with the primary period of use of the passage graves (Tempel 1979, 114). Earlier known earth graves date almost exclusively from the non-megalithic groups of the Early Neolithic in southern Scandinavia. The premises for research have thus been changed.

Was it a sign of higher status that the bones were laid in a tomb rather than in an earth grave? Or can the presence of an earth grave beside a tomb possibly indicate an exogenous marriage to a person from a non-megalithic group of the Funnel Beaker Culture? The question must remain unanswered at present.

Archaeological surveys of the economy of megalithic communities and their structure are usually brief and generalized and, as is natural, based on the research of the natural sciences. These have shown considerable agreement between Scandinavia and northern Germany on such matters as cultivated plants and domestic animals. We know from these what the megalithic tomb-building Funnel Beaker Culture groups cultivated and what animals they kept.

Such determinations are, however, qualitative and understandably lack quantitative data. Accordingly they can say nothing about the importance of cultivation and cattle-breeding for the livelihood of these communities compared with what food-gathering, hunting and fishing could yield. Surveys give the general impression that the writer views 'the Neolithic revolution' as quantitatively important for food production.

Those who like myself have had the opportunity of sorting pottery sherds with alleged grain impressions (both in tomb-pottery and dwelling-site material) can hardly have avoided being surprised at the low frequency of sherds with such impressions. It may be claimed that the grains were not necessarily being handled in the same place as the pottery was made. But there also exist impressions which belong to wild edible plants. Fortunately, in certain areas one has the pollen diagram for comparison. But in the majority of cases the evidence of the tombs is the only starting point for judgment on the economy of the megalithic societies.

Since only a few dwelling-sites from the tomb-building period are known one must, in common with Grahame Clark, concentrate on the graves themselves and put the question if and to what extent their distribution pattern can be used for conclusions on the economy of the tomb builders (1977, 34–5). Clark's investigation is based on the hypothesis that 'under subsistence economy most food is obtained within an hour or so's radius of the focus of settlement'. This is an attempt at quantification. The same estimate of distance should also be valid for tomb building but should not be overstated. If anything, the transport of blue stones and sarsens to Stonehenge is proof that people are willing to undertake great exertions for ideological reasons, as Clark points out.

With due respect to the foregoing theory, traces of settlement in the neighbourhood of megalithic tombs suggest that the tombs *are* an indication of where people lived. And people settle down in areas which are favourable to their mode of subsistence.

As one example of this I would like to discuss the well-known inland concentration of passage graves in central northern Västergötland – Falbygden – in

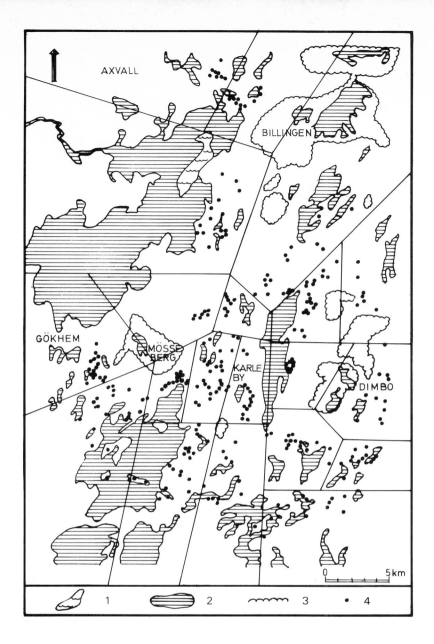

AXVALL

BILLINGEN

GÖKHEM

MÖSSE
BERG

KARLE
BY

DIMBO

0   5km

1   2   3   • 4

Sweden (ill. 10), also treated by Clark in his study of 1977.

The areas is a typical ecological niche. It comprises mainly a very small lime-rich Cambro-Silurian area – an island amid the vast primary rock terrain of which the rest of western Sweden consists. The Cambro-Silurian rock overlies the primary rock and forms an even surface, a plain, covered with moraine clays and surrounded by diabase-covered plateaux. Below the plateaux edges there are extensive marshes. The plain is subject to particular conditions of precipitation and drainage. Some small parts of the

10 Suggested classification of Falbygden's passage-grave area, based on the passage-grave groupings and natural boundaries. (Drawing by B. Jakobsson after Hyenstrand 1979.) 1 lake; 2 marshland; 3 plateaux; 4 passage grave.

area have even been defined ecologically as being of the same nature as the continental steppe. In these steppe-meadows we find a relict from a warmer period, the *Stipa pennata*, the only place it grows in Nordic countries. In this area the majority of Swedish passage graves are found, with 290 known examples, of which

151

about 240 still remain. This means that four-fifths of all the passage graves in Sweden are concentrated in an area of 500 sq.km.

Falbygden today is a prosperous agricultural area. Was it also attractive as farming land for a megalithic tomb-society, when more favourable climatic circumstances existed than those of today? Clark, who mainly seems to rely on soil fertility, moraine clays above Cambro-Silurian lime bedrock, considers that the surplus of food symbolized by the tombs 'was derived substantially at least from farming'. To the extent that this interpretation relates to cereals cultivation it is supported neither by the comparatively few grain impressions on pottery sherds nor by palaeo-botanical studies. The pollen analysis of lake deposits in this area shows that, on the contrary, cereals cultivation during the Middle Neolithic was insignificant (Fries 1958, 31, 59). Magnus Fries, who started from the archaeological postulate according to which passage graves indicate cultivation, was surprised at the weak representation of cerealia in the pollen diagrams. According to his studies the area at this time was covered by deciduous forests, although with some open spaces, possibly man-made (ibid. 36).

When one discusses cereals cultivation during an age when agricultural implements were rudimentary one should remember that primitive cultivation demanded greater manpower than other means of sustenance in relation to yield. Prehistoric fields were small. Just how small they were during the Neolithic period we do not know. It is highly probable that cereals from the small clearings in Scandinavia during the Neolithic and also Bronze Ages were a luxury food. Basic nourishment must have come from other sources. For instance, Fries calls attention to the importance of acorns as human food.

The Silurian area's type of landscape provided better conditions for grazing than the surrounding western Swedish gneiss rock. But it would be too bold to conclude that the passage-grave people's sustenance was based on or dominated by cattle-raising.

On closer inspection of the position of the passage graves in the landscape described above, one finds that they appear in scattered groups, often beside the outskirts of the Silurian plain and adjacent to swamps. The diabase-clad plateaux and the vast marshlands form natural boundaries around the passage-grave area. Attempts have been made to divide the total of passage graves into some twenty groups comprising ten to fifteen graves, each in its own landscape setting (ill. 10), by assuming that an immediate area of 2–2½ km radius from each passage grave group was the supply area for food production (Hyenstrand 1979, 130).

In these settings there are plenty of small watercourses and they were once larger and more numerous. The watercourses, with their fish and waterbirds, together with the rich assets of forest wildlife in the vicinity, gave a good yield in relation to labour input. It is highly probable that such possibilities of sustenance were exploited. If this interpretation is correct, cattle-raising was only a complement to food-gathering, whereas sheep-wool and goat-hair were likely to have been more important. The importance of cereals cultivation was quite marginal. In such an ecological niche the conditions for the sustenance of a sedentary community would have existed all year round in each landscape setting.

Clark (1977, 40–2) points out the environmental circumstances of the west coast of Sweden, Bohuslän, as an example of how the nature of food production is crucial to the localization of megalithic tombs. All dolmens and 85 per cent of the passage graves are found within 3 km of the sea, some only a few metres from the waterline as it then was. Land that was arable by the techniques at that time consisted of washed-down moraine, a particularly meagre soil at the foot of the bare rocks. The pattern of distribution of the tombs cannot therefore depend on cultivation. The coastal meadows certainly were suitable for grazing, but the question is whether cattle-raising was an important means of sustenance in terms of quantity. The known major food supplies on the coast consisted of fish, shellfish, seals and sea birds, etc. The position of the megalithic-tomb communities can hardly have been decided by factors other than just these resources. As further proof of his theory Clark also analyses traces of coastal settlement before and after the Funnel Beaker Culture megalithic-tomb societies and their economy, which were similarly based on fishing and the sources of sustenance available on the coast.

Fishing and the abundance of shellfish in the Limfjord area in Jutland including the coast up to Djursland (where the majority of Jutland's 200 passage graves lie) would also have been decisive for the localization of the settlements and thus the tombs. The concentration of megalithic tombs to the north and south-east of Rügen is not explicable in any other light. In fact, this concentration was greater than what appears from the fifty-four surviving monuments. During the first half of the nineteenth century a good 250 stone-chamber tombs were registered on the island (with few exceptions all were so-called big dolmens with a rectangular chamber and passage on the gable end). This density of monuments clearly emphasizes the nature of food production on the protected bays on the east and southeast coast of the island.

On the other hand, if one studies the natural back-

ground to the megalithic tombs in the Mecklenburg hinterland one is struck by the abundance of watercourses. In this area there existed a rich ecological niche with freshwater fishing, game-hunting and edible herbs, with cattle-raising as a complement.

Mecklenburg has been divided into six different Neolithic settlement areas on the basis of the megalithic tombs, each with its characteristic tomb design (Schuldt 1972, 102 and distribution maps 3–9). Closer analysis of the landscape in these six dwelling areas together with grave finds may perhaps answer the question to what extent the different groups of tombs reflect groups with different economies.

Clark, by focussing on sources of sustenance as the basis for his study of the megalithic tombs distribution patterns, has opened up a fruitful avenue for continued productive research. The reason for the spread of the megalithic tombs along the Atlantic coast is according to his theory, 'the pursuit of fish'. It is an attractive hypothesis and as worth proving as any. The occurrence inland of megalithic tombs requires a different type of food production but not – as has been maintained – cereals cultivation.

The Community

What kind of community is symbolized by the megalithic tomb? One view is that the megalithic

11 Centre portion of 'row-formation' of passage-graves (dotted circles) at Karleby, Västergötland. Remains of the passage-grave 'row-formation', to the north and south of the church, extend along the road. There are large areas of marshland to the right of the farms and below the hill.

tomb is a grave and cult centre for an upper class among the Funnel Beaker Culture peasants (Strömberg 1968, 227). This notion is grounded mainly on the monumental nature of the tombs, since otherwise the finds show no difference in status between tombs and earth graves.

Another interpretation suggests that the megalithic tombs are indicative of a segmentary and thus egalitarian society (Renfrew 1976, 204–11).

Finds of copper objects in some twenty passage graves in Lower Saxony (mainly west of the Weser) show differences in economic resources, both during the Early Neolithic, phase C, and the beginning of the Middle Neolithic (Schlicht 1979, 169–78). Similar differences also occur in the area of the Funnel Beaker Culture earth graves (Tempel 1979, 114). In this respect, therefore, there is no difference between the tombs and the earth graves. At present the theory of segmentary societies seems superior as a working hypothesis.

153

According to Renfrew, the megalithic tombs of north-western Europe are to be interpreted as territorial markers. Examples cited by him (Renfrew 1976, ills 4, 6) show that each territory has one megalithic tomb as a marker of 'territorial behaviour'. Although the thesis seems reasonable it also awakens new questions. Can a group of ten to fifteen megalithic tombs in one and the same territory as those found in Västergötland bear the same significance? Do several contemporary monuments mean a stronger expression of territorial marking? And if so, is this true for all contemporary territorial groups?

A reasonable view is that each group of passage graves in Västergötland is a settlement unit with its own territory (Hyenstrand 1979, 74). In some groups the tombs are positioned in rows, such as in Karleby (10–12 passage graves) (ills 10–11), in others they lie more or less scattered in small clusters of just a few graves only 25–50m apart, thus symbolizing a village-like or more scattered unit of settlement. It is not likely that all passage graves of one and the same unit were built during the same building period. It is not possible to decide which and how many are contemporary without further investigations. Neither from the appearance of the tombs nor from topographical studies can one conclude as to the order of sequence of the tombs. Finds from old studies are mostly of little use for determining the precise chronology of the building of the monuments. It is, however, probable that the passage graves in row formation were built successively – a few graves in each generation and depending on the size of the population. But this is only a hypothesis, which will need to be tested in future investigations.

Just as it is difficult to be precise about the chronological sequence of the tombs in each unit, it is also dif-ficult to decide how many settlement units in this segmentary society were contemporary. Are all twenty settlement units of the same age? Which are the most ancient? In what direction did change take place? How long did the different units survive?

To answer these questions we should remember that the dating of finds shows that the building phase of the passage graves was brief and ended before the middle of the Middle Neolithic in southern Scandinavia and in Mecklenburg (in some parts even before period II, Kjaerum 1966/67, 332; Schuldt 1972, 62). The same is probably true of the Funnel Beaker Culture western group in Lower Saxony and Drenthe-Groningen in Holland. This view is partly supported by radiocarbon data. But to reach certainty on these questions comprehensive field studies will be required, especially of the social and economic aspects. This research is still in its initial stage. Research on the monuments stands in the forefront, as it did fifteen years ago.

In this survey I have stressed the importance of comprehensive studies of megalithic-tomb societies. Research into the tombs appears more and more as a means, albeit a necessary one, to the end of gaining new knowledge. This means that the search for settlement sites should be intensified; so should cooperation with the disciplines of the natural sciences. Different models from the field of anthropology should be tried out. The formulation of problems we have to work with will be increasingly dependent not only on archaeological concepts but also on the general aims and methods of the social sciences.

Translated by Bryan Errington

Bibliography

ANER, E. 1963 'Die Stellung der Dolmen Schleswig-Holsteins in der nordischen Megalithkultur', *Offa* XX, 9–38.

BECKER, C.J. 1947 'Mosefundne Lerkar fra yngre Stenalder', *Aarbøger for nordisk Oldkyndighed og Historie*.

1967 'Gadefulde jyske stenaldergrave', *Nationalmuseets Arbejdsmark*, 19–30.

1973 'Problems of the Megalithic "Mortuary Houses" in Denmark, in Daniel, G. and Kjaerum, P. (eds), *Megalithic Graves and Ritual*, Copenhagen, 75–9.

CLARK, J.G.D. 1977 'The Economic Context of Dolmens and Passage Graves in Sweden', in Markotic, V. (ed.), *Ancient Europe and the Mediterranean*, Warminister, 35–49.

FRIES, M. 1958 'Vegetationsutveckling och odlingshistoria i Varnhemstrakten, Acta Phytogeographica' *Suecica* XXIX, Uppsala.

HYENSTRAND, Å. 1979 *Ancient Monuments and Prehistoric Society*, Stockholm.

JAZDZEWSKI, K. 1973 'The Relations between Kujavian Barrows in Poland and Megalithic Tombs in northern Germany, Denmark and western European Countries', in Daniel, G. and Kjaerum, P. (eds), *Megalithic Graves and Ritual*, Copenhagen, 63–74.

KAELAS, L. 1956 'Dolmen und Ganggräber in Schweden', *Offa* XV, 5–24.

1966/67 'The Megalithic Tombs in South Scandinavia —Migration or Cultural Influence?' *Palaeohistoria* XII, 287–321.

KJAERUM, P. 1966/67 'The Chronology of the Passage-Graves in Jutland', *Palaeohistoria* XII, 323–33.

MADSEN, T. 1979 'Earthen Long Barrows and Timber Structures: Aspects of the Early Neolithic Mortuary Practice in Denmark', *Proc. Preh. Soc.* XLV, 301–20.

PIGGOTT, S. 1956 'Windmill Hill – East or West', *Proc. Preh. Soc.* XXI, 96–101.

1966/67 'Unchambered Long Barrows in neolithic Britain', *Palaeohistoria* XII, 381–93.

RADDATZ, K. 1979 'Zur Funktion der Grosssteingräber', in Schirnig H. (ed.), *Grosssteingräber in Niedersachsen*, Hildesheim, 127–41.

RENFREW C. 1976 'Megaliths, Territories and Populations', in De Laet, S.J. (ed.), *Acculturation and Continuity in Atlantic Europe*, Brugge, 198–220.

SCHIRNIG, H. 1979 'Einführung', in Schirnig, H. (ed.), *Grosssteingräber in Niedersachsen*, Hildesheim, 1–26.

SCHLICHT, E. 1979 'Handels- und Kulturbeziehungen auf Grund von Importfunden aus niedersächsischen Grosssteingräbern', in Schirnig, H. (ed.), *Grosssteingräber in Niedersachsen*, Hildesheim, 169–78.

SCHULDT, E. 1972 *Die Mecklenburgischen Megalithgräber*, Berlin.

STRÖBERG, M. 1968 'Der Dolmen Trollasten', *Acta Archaeologica Lundensia*, VIII, no. 7, Lund.

1970 'Die Megalithgräber von Hagestad', *Acta Archaeologica Lundensia*, VIII, no. 9, Lund.

TEMPEL, W.-D. 1979 'Flachgräber der Trichterbecherkultur', in Schirnig, H. (ed.), *Grosssteingräber in Niedersachsen*, Hildesheim, 111–16.

15   Megalithic Graves in Belgium — A *Status Quaestionis*

Sigfried J. De Laet

ONLY A FEW megalithic tombs exist in Belgium, as distinct from its neighbouring countries, France, the Netherlands and Germany. Just five are known, three of which still exist, the remaining two having been destroyed at the end of the nineteenth century. Though so few in number, they are of interest because of their geographical location which may make it possible to determine the links existing between different cultures in the third millennium BC.

These five tombs are concentrated in a small triangular area, with sides of about 50, 45 and 30 km, lying in the provinces of Namur and Luxemburg and covering part of the Condroz and the Famenne (ill. 2). Very probably they all belong to the Seine-Oise-Marne (SOM) culture; I shall return to this later. First we should study the graves and their contents.

The two best-preserved tombs (still visible) are situated at Wéris, in the north of the province of Luxemburg (Corbiau 1978, 286 ff.). The smaller of these

1 Plan of the two megalithic graves at Wéris (after de Loë 1928). 1 the sunken allée couverte; 2 the gallery-grave built above ground.

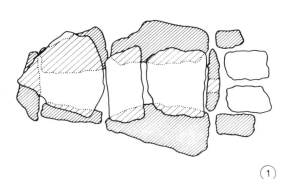

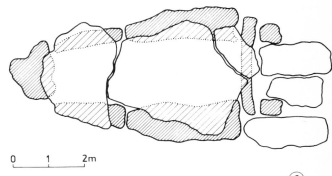

0   1   2m

① ②

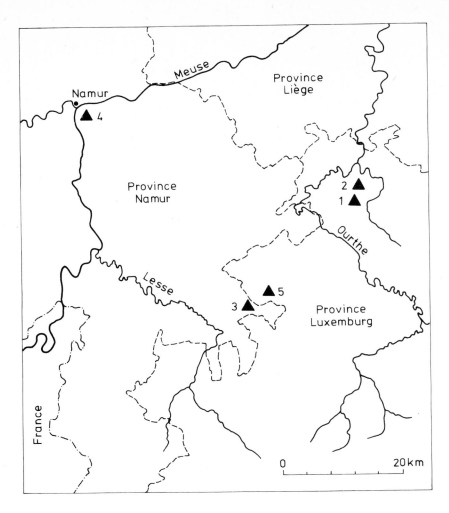

2 Location of the Belgian megalithic graves: 1 sunken gallery-grave (allée couverte) at Wéris; 2 gallery-grave, built above ground, at Wéris; 3 gallery-grave (?) at Jemelle, partly destroyed; 4 destroyed megalithic grave at Velaine (Jambes), type unknown; 5 destroyed megalithic grave (long cist ?) at Jemeppe-Hargimont.

is a gallery-grave, an *allée couverte* of the Paris Basin type, sunk below ground level up to the capstones (ill. 1). The walls of the funerary chamber (length 4.6 m, width 1.2 m: internal dimensions) are made of two pairs of opposing orthostats, and of one slab closing off the chamber at the rear end; the roof is composed of three massive horizontal slabs. Leading to this chamber is an antechamber, only two orthostats of which are left. As a result of the rather questionable restoration of 1906 (Rahir 1928, 71 ff.), this antechamber is now paved with two slabs which are probably fragments of a

broken capstone. Chamber and antechamber are separated by a transverse slab, pierced by a round hole. The interstices between the orthostats were filled in with dry-stone masonry. This tomb was discovered in 1888 and 'excavated' the same year by A. Charneux using the rather clumsy methods customary at that time. If the very cursory report published on this occasion (Charneux 1888a) can be trusted, the grave-chamber yielded traces of a 'hearth' (ritual fire?), human bones, animal bones, artifacts made of flint (scrapers, arrowheads, polished axes) and of sandstone (hammer-stones), sherds of very coarse, thick-walled and plain pottery (probably SOM pottery) and a few sherds of (bell-beaker?) pottery decorated with a herring-bone pattern.

All these finds seem since to have disappeared. When in 1906 the monument was bought by the State and restored, new excavations were carried out but these yielded no results (Rahir 1928, 71–2). The larger megalithic tomb at Wéris is much the same in plan; but it is a gallery-grave built above ground and was originally covered with an earth mound. Here too the chamber (length 5.50 m, width 1.75 m: internal dimensions) is made of two pairs of opposing orthostats, and of one slab closing off the chamber at the rear end. The roof is composed of two capstones, one now broken. Again, funerary chamber and antechamber are separated by a transverse slab pierced by a door-shaped hole. Of the antechamber, only two rather narrow orthostats are left. When the restoration took place in 1906, three slabs lying on the ground in and next to the antechamber were interpreted as paving-stones, but are probably the remains of a broken capstone originally covering this antechamber. *Allées couvertes* of the Paris Basin type almost certainly belong to the SOM, but gallery-graves built above ground and covered by a barrow are less frequent in this culture (Bailloud 1964, 156). Both megalithic tombs at Wéris are made of pudding-stone, coming from a site approximately 3 km distant. The second megalith, which has long been known and publicized, had of course been robbed some time ago. According to local tradition, it had contained several skeletons. When, in 1888, the *allée couverte* was discovered and excavated, Charneux took the opportunity to dig the gallery-grave as well, but he found only traces of a 'hearth' (ritual fire?), some bones and a few flint and sandstone artifacts, and sherds of coarse pottery, all scattered in and around the tomb (Charneux 1888b). When the monument was acquired by the State in 1906 and restored, new excavations were carried out by the Musées royaux d'Art et d'Histoire (Brussels), but they yielded only a single sherd of coarse pottery from the chamber and very few remains scattered around the grave (Rahir 1928, 71).

The two megalithic tombs at Wéris seem to have formed part of a big religious complex, a sacred area (ill. 3). Indeed, on a straight strip about 5 km long and orientated NNE-SSW are to be found successively the site of the menhir of Tour (municipality of Heyd), which was destroyed at the end of the nineteenth century (Danthine 1947a); the gallery-grave at Wéris; a second menhir, 3.6 m high, which had been toppled and buried in a field, but rediscovered in 1947 and reinstated (Danthine 1947b); the *allée couverte* of Wéris; and finally, the three menhirs of Bouhaimont at Oppagne (municipality of Wéris). The last named, the largest of which is 3.6 m high, had also been toppled and subsequently buried, but they were reinstated in 1906 (Rahir 1928, 73–4). All five menhirs were made of the same material as the megalithic graves, namely pudding-stone from the site previously referred to. Another element has possibly to be added to

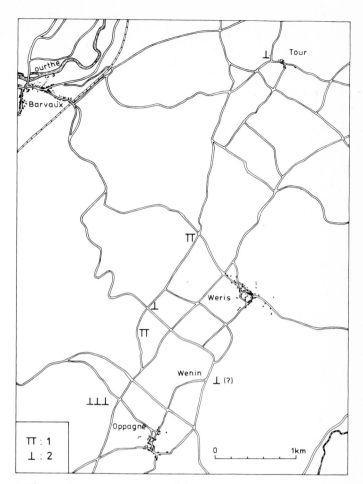

3 The sacred area at Wéris: 1 megalithic grave; 2 menhir.

this group: the so-called 'Pas Bayard' at Wenin (municipality of Wéris), a large pudding-stone about which several local legends have grown up, but it is not possible to tell whether it is a fragment of a broken menhir or the remains of a megalithic grave.

The third megalithic tomb was discovered as recently as September 1976 near the farm of Lamsoul at Jemelle (province of Namur) (Chardome 1979). It was excavated in 1976 and 1977 by a group of amateurs. This tomb, which had been robbed and largely destroyed, appears to have been built above ground and was originally covered by a barrow, some traces of which were discovered. Of the tomb itself only part of the funerary chamber remains: seven orthostats, two of which had fallen down, and one roof-slab. No traces of a possible antechamber were found and therefore it is rather difficult to determine the exact type of this monument, although it is likely to have been some kind of gallery-grave. The excavators found some human bones, sherds of coarse, probably SOM pottery, but also a few Gallo-Roman sherds.

As far as the two graves destroyed at the end of the nineteenth century are concerned, practically nothing is known of the one at Velaine (municipality of Jambes, province of Namur), apart from the fact that it was called 'Pierre du Diable'; there are no clues as to its type (Knapen-Lescrenier 1970, 146 ff.). A little more is known about the megalithic tomb at the 'Bois des Lusce' at Jemeppe-Hargimont (province of Luxemburg) (Corbiau 1978, 119–20; see also Mariën 1952a, 152–4). This tomb – which, according to some traditions, contained several skeletons – was 15 m long and 1.25 m wide (internal dimensions). Very probably it was a dug-out tomb, although this is not mentioned explicitly in the publications. The chamber was bounded by a vertical slab at each end, while its side walls consisted of dry-stone masonry. No roof-slabs are mentioned and it is possible that the tomb originally had a wooden ceiling. There is no mention either of an antechamber or of a pierced slab between chamber and antechamber. From this description, one gets the impression that this tomb is much closer to the West German *einteilige Galeriegräber* than to the *allées couvertes* of the Paris Basin. We will come back to this point later.

For the sake of completeness, I should mention the discovery in 1970 at Gomery (municipality of Bleid, province of Luxemburg) of a jumble of buried blocks of stone, which some amateurs interpreted – wrongly in my opinion – as remains of a megalithic grave (Corbiau 1978, 60–1). In fact, on investigation this structureless heap of stones yielded neither bone remains nor any grave contents whatsoever and I think that they were dumped there fairly recently. An earth-sample taken from *under* the stones was subjected to a palynological analysis by J. Heim of the University of Louvain and showed a typical sub-Atlantic composition with 40 per cent *Carpinus*. Furthermore, charcoal from a hearth discovered at a depth of 70 cm in the immediate neighbourhood of the stone heap gave a radiocarbon date of AD 1390 ± 110 (Lv–496) (Gilot 1971, 50).

In the general context of the European megalithic graves, the Belgian group is rather isolated, geographically speaking. It is situated at least 100 km from the nearest megalithic tombs, namely those of the Ardennes department in France (as can be seen in Kaelas 1967, map on page 307). Notwithstanding the loss of the grave goods almost in their entirety, however, it is generally admitted that the Belgian megalithic graves belong to the SOM culture (Mariën 1952a; De Laet

1958; De Laet-Glasbergen 1959; Bonenfant 1969; De Laet 1974; 1976; 1979): there is the *allée couverte*, of a type characteristic of this culture, and there are the gallery-graves of Wéris and Jemelle, which are paralleled in the SOM, besides the references to 'coarse pottery', which practically always indicate SOM ceramics in the reports concerning Neolithic sites in the regions we are considering. Furthermore, there is the presence in the neighbourhood of very numerous caves, which in the basin of the Meuse and its tributaries have been used as collective graves by the SOM people (after having been, long before, the dwelling-places of Middle and Later Palaeolithic hunters). In Belgium, there are at least eighty caves and rock-shelters which have been used as ossuaries (ill. 4). Most of these belong to the SOM culture, as shown for example by the grave goods. Collective inhumation in caves, however, was continued in this particular region during the whole of the Bronze Age and even during the Hallstatt period. I have discussed this subject more thoroughly elsewhere (for the most recent data, see De Laet 1979, 270 ff.), so there is no need to say more about it here, except to stress the fact that the Belgian megalithic tombs, although isolated as such, are clearly situated in the northernmost part of the SOM area. Naturally, the latter point is a further argument to link these tombs to the SOM culture.

A few decades ago, it was still generally conceded that the SOM was only poorly represented in Belgium (see for instance Mariën 1950, 1952b). Now we know, however, that not only the whole northern half of France, but also Belgium and even part of the southern provinces of the Netherlands lay within the area of SOM culture and that in Belgium the SOM was even the main Neolithic culture of the third millennium BC, surviving there, at least in some regions, during an important part of the Bronze Age (*status quaestionis*: De Laet 1979, 265 ff.). We need only glance at the distribution map for Belgium, however (ill. 4), to see that the SOM occupation there was much denser in the Meuse basin, from the French border to Dutch Limburg, than it was in the Scheldt basin. It has been stressed for some time that there exist striking similarities between the Westphalian and Hessian *Galeriegrab-Kultur* and the SOM, mainly as far as the structure of some megalithic tombs is concerned (recent bibliography in De Laet 1976, to which should be added Louwe Kooijmans 1976; Schrickel 1976; Fischer 1979 and Schwellnus 1979). Dutch Limburg can probably be identified as the main contact zone between the two cultures. It was in this region that P.J.R. Modderman (1964) discovered and excavated the important tomb at Stein, a non-megalithic version of the *allées couvertes*: its structure can best be compared

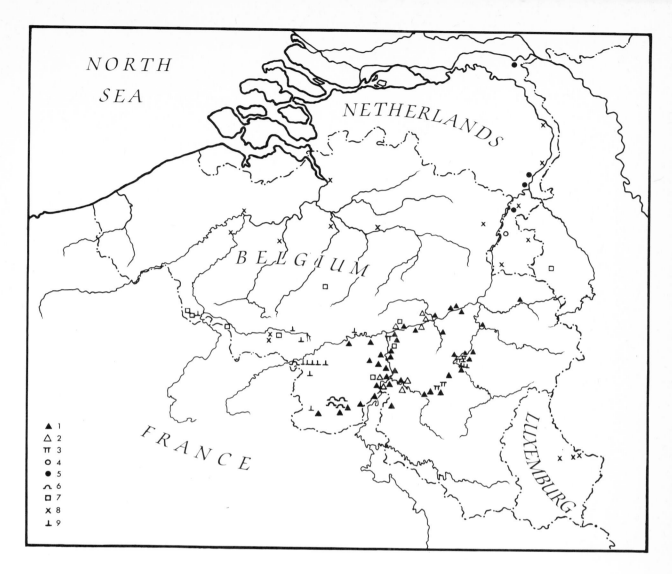

NORTH SEA

NETHERLANDS

BELGIUM

FRANCE

LUXEMBURG

▲	1
△	2
ᴨ	3
○	4
●	5
⌒	6
□	7
✕	8
⊥	9

to that of a number of non-megalithic SOM tombs in France; part of the grave goods point to relations with the *Galeriegrab-Kultur*, while other elements present features analogous to those of the SOM (Modderman 1964; De Laet 1979, 284 ff). Since this discovery, other finds have come to light in Dutch Limburg which present the same mixed character: this 'Limburgs midden-neolithicum' (Middle Neolithic of Limburg) has been studied mainly by Modderman (1964) and L.P. Louwe Kooijmans (1976). All these elements suggest the existence of contacts between the SOM and the *Galeriegrab-Kultur*; one can probably add to that the already mentioned megalithic cist of Jemeppe-Hargimont, which up till now has never been discussed in this particular context. As far as its type can be identified from the older publications which do not include plans or photographs, it seems to be very much

4 *Distribution map of the SOM culture in Belgium and in the southern part of the Netherlands*
1 *sepulchral cave; 2 group of sepulchral caves; 3 megalithic grave; 4 the non-megalithic grave at Stein; 5 site of the 'Middle Neolithic of Limburg'; 6 Bronze Age barrow with SOM pottery; 7 SOM settlement; 8 SOM stray find; 9 menhir.*

akin to some dug-out megalithic non-segmented West German tombs (the *einteilige Galeriegräber*). In his recent book on the Hessian Wartberg group W. Schwellnus (1979) too has touched upon the problem of the contacts between the German gallery-graves and the French *allées couvertes*; he seems to be unaware of the importance of the SOM culture in the Meuse basin in Belgium and in the southern part of the Netherlands, believing the contacts between the two cultures to have been established by way of the Moselle valley. The remains he uses as a basis for this theory are not well known and much poorer than those from the Meuse valley. Of course, it may be that the Moselle was also used as a contact route between the two cultures, but as far as our actual knowledge goes, it was a much less important one than the Meuse route.

From the information available at present, I can only conclude that the small group of Belgian megalithic graves constitute a far from negligible factor when considering contacts and mutual influences between the SOM and the *Galeriegrab-Kultur*. Some years ago the study of this particular problem led me to propose (De Laet 1976) a new solution for another problem, that of the origins of the *allées couvertes* of the Paris Basin type, a question which Glyn Daniel has broached on several former occasions (Daniel 1941; 1955; 1960; 1967; 1973). Till then it was generally accepted that

the Hessian and Westphalian tombs, presenting the same structure as the French *allées couvertes*, derived from the latter, but I tried to demonstrate that the oldest tombs of this type were not those of the SOM but on the contrary those of West Germany, and that the origins of the SOM *allées couvertes* were to be looked for in Germany, the Meuse valley being the main contact route between the two areas. In Germany the *allées couvertes* with chamber and antechamber separated by a pierced vertical slab can easily be derived from the non-segmented dug-out gallery-graves, the *einteilige Galeriegräber*, of which the grave of Jemeppe-Hargimont probably constitutes one of the westernmost specimens. It was quite a joy for me to see my thesis accepted by my friend Glyn Daniel (Daniel 1978), who completed it by suggesting that the ancestry of both the *Galeriegräber* and the *allées couvertes* is to be found in the long-houses of the Linear Pottery people. It is now my turn to stress my full agreement with his view on the subject.

Bibliography

BAILLOUD, G. 1964/1974 *Le néolithique dans le Bassin Parisien,* 2nd edn, Paris, with 'mise à jour' 1972, 387–429.

BONENFANT, P.-P. 1969 *Civilisations préhistoriques en Wallonie. Des premiers cultivateurs aux premières villes,* Brussels.

CHARDOME, J.-M. 1979 'Le monument mégalithique de Lamsoul à Jemelle', *Conspectus MCMLXXVIII = Archaeologia Belgica* CCXIII, 44–8.

CHARNEUX, A. 1888a 'Un second dolmen à Wéris', *Annales Institut archéologique Luxembourg* XX, 203–5.

1888b 'Les fouilles à l'ancien dolmen de Wéris' *Annales Institut archéologique Luxembourg* XX, 207ff.

CORBIAU, M.-H. 1978 *Répertoire bibliographique des trouvailles archéologiques de la province de Luxembourg,* Brussels.

DANIEL, G.E. 1941 'The dual nature of the megalithic colonisation of prehistoric Europe', *Proc. Preh. Soc.* VII, 1–49.

1955 'The *allées couvertes* of France', *The Archaeological Journal* CXII, 1 – 19.

1960 *The Prehistoric Chamber Tombs of France,* London.

1966 'The Megalith-Builders of the SOM', *Neolithic Studies in Atlantic Europe = Palaeohistoria* XII, 199–208.

1973 'Spain and the Problem of European Megalithic Origins', *Estudios dedicados al Professor Dr. Luis Pericot* Barcelona, 209–14.

1978 Review of S.J. DE LAET (ed.), *Acculturation and Continuity in Atlantic Europe, mainly during the Neolithic period and the Bronze Age* (Bruges 1976), in *Helinium* XVIII, 268–9.

DANTHINE, H. 1947a 'Le champ mégalithique de Wéris (Luxembourg)', *Archéologie* 1947, 2 (= *L'Antiquité Classique* XVI, 2), 358.

1947b 'Wéris (Luxembourg). Découverte d'un menhir', *Archéologie* 1947, 2 (= *L'Antiquité Classique* XVI, 2), 358.

DE LAET, S.J. 1958 *The Low Countries,* London and New York.

1974 *Prehistorische Kulturen in het Zuiden der Lage Landen,* Wetteren.

1976 'L'explication des changements culturels: modèles théoriques et applications concrètes. Le cas du S.O.M.' in DE LAET, S.J. (ed.) *Acculturation and continuity in Atlantic Europe, mainly during the Neolithic period and the Bronze Age. Papers presented at the IV.Atlantic Colloquium, Ghent 1975* (= *Dissertationes archaeologicae Gandenses* XVI), Bruges, 67–76.

1979 *Prehistorische Kulturen in het Zuiden der Lage Landen.* 2nd edn, Wetteren.

DE LAET, S.J. AND GLASBERGEN, W. 1959 *De Voorgeschiedenis der Lage Landen,* Groningen.

DE LOË, A. 1928 *Belgique ancienne. Catalogue descriptif et raisonné.I.Les âges de la pierre,* Brussels.

FISCHER, U. 1979 'Europäische Verbindungen der niedersächsischen Groszsteingräber', in *Groszsteingräber in Niedersachsen,* Hildesheim, 27–42.

GILOT, E. 1971 Louvain 'Natural Radiocarbon Measurments X', *Radiocarbon* XIII, no.1, 45–51.

KAELAS, L. 1967 'The Megalithic Tombs in South Scandinavia. Migration or cultural influence?' *Neolithic Studies in Atlantic Europe = Palaeohistoria* XII, 287–321.

KNAPEN-LESCRENIER, A.-M. 1970 *Répertoire bibliographique des trouvailles archéologiques de la province de Namur*, Brussels.

LOUWE KOOIJMANS, L.P. 1976 'Local developments in a borderland. A survey of the neolithic at the Lower Rhine', *Oudheidkundige Mededelingen van het Rijksmuseum van Oudheden te Leiden*, 57, 227–97.

MARIËN, M.E. 1950 'Poteries de la civilisation de Seine-Oise-Marne en Belgique', *Bulletin des Musées royaux d'Art et d'Histoire* XXII, 79–85.

1952a *Oud-België, van de eerste landbouwers tot de komst van Caesar*, Antwerp.

1952b 'La civilisation de Seine-Oise-Marne en Belgique', *L'Anthropologie* VI, 87–92.

MODDERMAN, P.J.R. 1964 'The neolithic burial vault at Stein', *Analecta praehistorica Leidensia* I, 3–16.

RAHIR, E. 1928 *Vingt-cinq années de recherches, de restaurations et de reconstitutions*, Brussels.

SCHRICKEL, W. 1976 'Die Galeriegrab-Kultur Westdeutschlands. Entstehung, Gliederung und Beziehung zu benachbarten Kulturen' in Schwabedissen, H. (hrsg. von-) *Die Anfänge des Neolikums von Orient bis Nordeuropa, Teil V b, Westliches Mittel-Europa*, 188–233.

SCHWELLNUS, W. 1979 *Wartberg-Gruppe und hessische Megalithik*, Wiesbaden.

16 Chambered Tombs and Non-Megalithic Barrows in Britain

Lionel Masters

To the graves, then, of our earliest ancestors, must we mainly turn for a knowledge of their history and of their modes of life; and a careful examination and comparison of their contents will enable us to arrive at certain data on which, not only to found theories, but to build up undying and faultless historical structures.

Llewellynn Jewitt,
Grave Mounds and their Contents (1870)

THREE DECADES have passed since the publication of Glyn Daniel's seminal work on *The Prehistoric Chamber Tombs of England and Wales* (1950). Many changes have occurred since the publication of that work. It would indeed be surprising if they had not, for an active discipline should thrive on changes in perspective and approach. Two of the more important changes have been the application of radiocarbon dating, and the acceptance by many scholars of a more insular interpretation for the development of prehistoric cultures in Britain. The former has given us a greatly extended time-scale for the Neolithic period in Britain as elsewhere, and the latter has challenged us into considering new approaches in explanation of the origins

and functions of chambered tombs and NM (non-megalithic) barrows.

Major works of synthesis have appeared since the publication of *The Prehistoric Chamber Tombs of England and Wales*. Of outstanding importance is Henshall's *The Chambered Tombs of Scotland* (1963, 1972), a work to which I have already paid tribute (Masters 1974). The wealth of detail provided in these two volumes has greatly facilitated not only the study of the Scottish monuments, but also from Henshall's assessment and speculation, the consideration of chambered tombs in general. Sadly, there is still no *corpus* of chambered tombs for England and Wales, a fact which must be a disappointment to Glyn Daniel, for he has championed and encouraged the publication of *corpora* for other areas (Daniel 1976, 187–9). *Megalithic Enquiries in the West of Britain* (Powell *et al.* 1969) does, however, provide useful lists of the tombs in North Wales, the Severn-Cotswold area and the Clyde area, in addition to the respective authors' detailed considerations of the monuments. The NM series of long barrows was considered by Ashbee in *The Earthen Long Barrow in Britain* (1970), and the recent publication of a *corpus* of Neolithic round barrows and ring-ditches has drawn attention to this less well

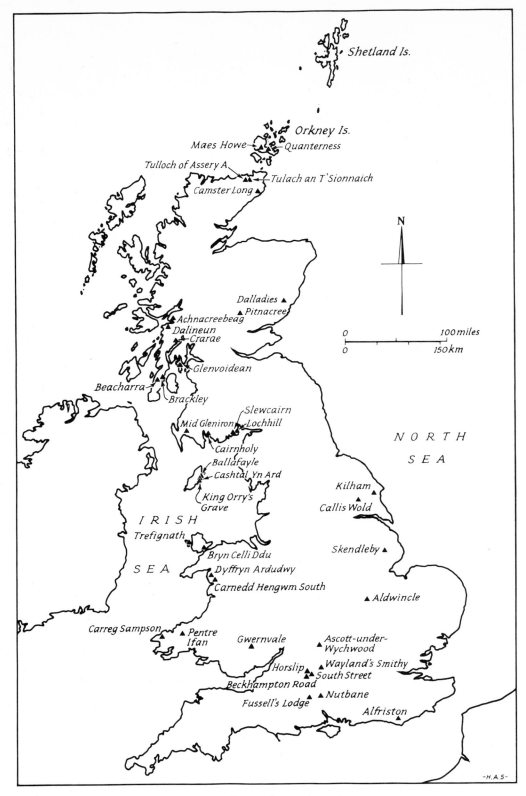

Shetland Is.

Orkney Is.

Maes Howe →← Quanterness

Tulloch of Assery A ▲▲
▲← Tulach an T'Sionnaich
Camster Long ▲

N

Dalladies ▲
▲ Pitnacree

Achnacreebeag ▲
Dalineun ▲← Crarae

0   100 miles
0   150 km

Glenvoidean

Beacharra ▲
Brackley

Slewcairn
Mid Gleniron ▲← Lochhill

NORTH
SEA

Cairnholy
Ballafayle
← Cashtal Yn Ard

King Orry's
Grave

Kilham
▲
Callis Wold ▲

IRISH

Trefignath

Bryn Celli Ddu
Dyffryn Ardudwy ▲
▲ Carnedd Hengwm South

SEA

Skendleby ▲

▲ Aldwincle

Carreg Sampson ▲
▲ Pentre
Ifan

Gwernvale
▲

Ascott-under-
Wychwood ▲

Horslip ▲▲
Beckhampton Road ▲▲
▲ Wayland's Smithy
South Street

▲ Nutbane
Fussell's Lodge

Alfriston
▲

-H.A.S-

1 Map of principal sites mentioned.

documented series of funerary monuments (Kinnes 1979). These works, together with the many excavation reports of chambered tombs and NM barrows, provide the information on which to base an assessment of the origin, function and role of the monuments themselves.

As comprehensive summaries have recently been published of the state of knowledge concerning the Neolithic period in Britain (Smith 1974, 100–36; Ashbee 1978), it is not necessary here to go into detail on the general background. Suffice it to say that the chambered tombs and NM barrows occupy a place in time contemporary with the causewayed enclosures of southern England, and that some monuments must be contemporary with the developing series of stone circles and henge monuments in the latter half of the third millennium BC. In other aspects of material culture, pottery, flint and stone objects of Neolithic date are encountered in both chambered tombs and NM barrows. The significance of such deposits for the understanding of the function of the monuments is discussed later.

One point does, however, demand more detailed consideration. It is generally accepted that the earliest Neolithic in Britain was initiated by people from the continent of Europe. What particular area or areas provided the immediate impetus for settlement in Britain is still a matter for debate. For the initial pioneering phase, Case (1969, 3–27) has cogently argued that the settlers may have brought little of their material culture with them to Britain and Ireland because of the sea journeys involved. He also suggests that the building of large monuments, demanding in terms of communal effort, would not have formed part of the initial colonizing process. This would not rule out the possibility that simple structures were built, some of which may later have been incorporated into monumental mounds. Nor does it rule out the possibility of contact at later stages between established communities in Britain and those of western and northern Europe.

If the arguments put forward by Case are accepted, it makes it all the more difficult to seek a European source for the earliest Neolithic settlers in Britain. In a recent study, Whittle has looked to 'the Linear Pottery culture tradition of the Rhineland and its environs and of northern France . . . as the most likely source of population to have filled Britain from the earlier fourth millennium bc onwards' (1977, 238). General similarities in pottery, flint and stone tools can be demonstrated, as can possible antecedents to the causewayed enclosures. Whilst the characteristic long houses of the Linear Pottery culture have been notoriously absent from Britain, they have frequently been

considered as providing the inspiration behind the form of the NM long barrow. Yet the people of the Linear Pottery culture did not themselves engage in the building of monumental mounds. The question of origins for both chambered tombs and NM barrows in Britain may, therefore, not lie with the initial movements of colonization. Kinnes (1975, 18) has, however, drawn attention to some examples of 'enclosed-space interment', in pits lined and roofed with wood, amongst the flat grave cemetery at the Linear Pottery culture site at Elsloo. It is possible that such unspectacular monuments could provide the basis for the development of the NM series in Britain, and even have formed part of the initial colonization process.

Questions concerning the origin and development of chambered tombs are frequently bound up with the model of the past in current vogue. A general consideration of this is given elsewhere in this volume, but it is necessary here to mention some of the approaches which have a direct effect on the British monuments, for the acceptance or rejection of some of them is of crucial importance to the understanding of origins, developments and function.

Approaches to Interpretation

Piggott (1973, 9–15) has drawn attention to the problems associated with the interpretation of chambered tombs. These may be outlined as questions concerning the nature of the distribution pattern and whether it is the result of independent invention, diffusion or migration, or a combination of two or more of these major determinants of culture change. Tomb typology still looms large in current thinking, though a straightforward linear typology from simple to complex or vice versa may no longer fit the available information. Furthermore, there is the realization that under a term such as 'collective burial' there is a wide variety of modes of deposition, and the questionable assumption that 'grave-goods' represent the personal property of the deceased. At a completely mundane level, the flint knife and the broken pot in a Scottish chambered tomb might represent no more than the detritus of a meal taken in the chamber by a passing traveller sheltering from the cold! I do not make this point too seriously, but it might serve to remind us that, if chambered tombs were left open in the Neolithic period, disturbance of the burial deposit could have taken place for reasons other than the insertion of further burials. The question of dating, and particularly the provenance of samples for radiocarbon dating of chambered tombs, is of crucial importance, and Piggott's strictures on these should be in the minds of every chambered tomb

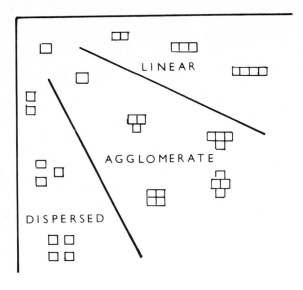

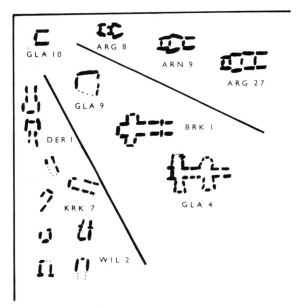

2 (Upper) *Systems of modular combination.*
(Lower) *Modular systems in practice. (After Kinnes.)*

the major control for monument typology. He isolates as the main features the requirements of the ritual, the appearance of the monument at varying stages, the number of chambers, and the nature of any pre-existing structures. Adopting a modular approach the wide variety of plans in British chambered tombs can be seen as the combining and recombining of the existing elements in the architect's repertoire. For the Severn-Cotswold tombs, Fleming suggests that the builders 'may already have been engaged in "systems building"' in thinking of forecourts and trapezoidal cairns as modules to be arranged in the most convenient way. On the function of the tombs themselves, Fleming has considered them as 'attention-focussing devices, part of a signalling system designed to reinforce the existing patterns of leadership' (1973, 190).

The concept of modules has been taken up by Kinnes when he puts forward the view that 'A simple scheme of modular manipulation according to need and intent forms a plausible alternative to linear taxonomy *qua* typology' (1975, 19–20). What is envisaged here (ill. 2) is that a simple box-type chamber can be arranged in three grouping patterns – linear, agglomerate and dispersed. By combining the basic box-type chamber in the groupings suggested, it is possible to reproduce many of the varieties of plans of the chambers of chambered tombs without recourse to external influences. Thus a linear grouping would account for the segmented chambers of the Clyde and court cairns, the agglomerate grouping for the transepted Severn-Cotswold tombs and the transepted court cairns, and the dispersed grouping for the laterally chambered tombs in the Severn-Cotswold, Bargrennan and Clyde cairns.

Acceptance of these ideas 'does much to undermine the diffusionist approach to the study of the origins of British types of megalithic tomb' (Fleming 1972, 66), a point echoed by Kinnes (1975, 20). But it might be considered that whilst these ideas have considerable validity, they are as yet still as incapable of proof as the linear typologies which they seek to replace.

A possible relationship between long barrow length in Britain and the length of long houses in the Linear Pottery and Rössen cultures of Europe has been discussed by Reed (1974, 33–57). It is suggested that a doubling of the length and width of long house dimensions is involved in the consideration of long barrow measurements. There is some evidence that a strict adherence to 'length requirements was the rule among long barrow builders' (Reed 1974, 56), and this is used to promulgate the view that particular lengths might be related to discrete groups. On this basis, movement of the group and settlement strategy may be inferred. This is an interesting series of ideas

excavator. Finally, there are the questions of function and ritual 'which perhaps by their nature will always remain insoluble' (Piggott 1973, 13). With these important points in mind, we can now turn to consider some of the new approaches to the interpretation of British chambered tombs and NM barrows.

Fleming (1972, 1973) has looked at the question of the design of chambered tombs, and has seen design as which could, perhaps, be considered in more detail if and when a full series of radiocarbon dates has been obtained from NM long barrows.

Attempts to define territory using the distribution patterns of chambered tombs and long barrows have been made by Ashbee and Renfrew. For southern England, Ashbee (1970, 104–5) has pointed out that in some areas groups of long barrows are associated with one or more causewayed enclosures. In a more recent account he has developed this concept further (Ashbee 1978) and has pointed to the close association between henge monuments and chambered tombs.

The defining of territories on a more limited basis has been attempted by Renfrew for the islands of Arran and Rousay (1973, 132–42; 1979, 13–20, 216–17). The results for Rousay have suggested that each of the thirteen tombs on the island might represent a population of about twenty people, assuming they were all built and used at the same time. Although the radiocarbon dates for the Knowes of Yarso, Rowiegar and Ramsay support the view that they were all in use during the latter half of the third millennium bc, there are no radiocarbon dates for the putative early tombs like Bigland Round, Knowe of Craie or Cobbie Row's Burden. It may also be inappropriate to make estimates of group size for Rousay on the basis of skeletal remains preserved in the Mainland tomb of Quanterness. At this site parts of 157 individuals were recovered from the partially excavated main chamber and one of the six side chambers. The majority of the Rousay cairns have been excavated, admittedly excavated and published (or not published) to widely different standards, but the skeletal evidence ranges from a skull at the Knowe of Craie, two adults at Blackhammer, to the twenty-five individuals at Midhowe and twenty-nine at the Knowe of Yarso. It might, therefore, be necessary to consider that some of the Rousay monuments are not 'equal access' tombs after the manner of Quanterness, with consequent results for any estimate of population.

Although Renfrew has concluded that 'Quanterness housed the dead of a living group, whose numbers at any time may have been some twenty in number' (1979, 172), and also that because there was no differentiation in the age or sex of the people buried in the tomb, that burial was accorded to every member of the group, this does not appear to be the case for other areas of Britain. A study of the burials from NM long barrows led Atkinson to conclude, on the basis of thirty-five excavated sites, that the population represented would range from 1,500 to 3,000 individuals for the whole of the Neolithic period (1968, 86). Kinnes (1975, 25–6) has also considered this question in relation to NM barrows, arriving at a figure of eighty

people at any one time throughout the whole of the long barrow territory. Even allowing for a population explosion, the figure is unlikely to exceed 250. It is concluded that the burial privilege was reserved for a more socially dominant group. Any apparent conflict between the concept of a more hierarchical society in the south of Britain and Renfrew's 'small-scale, autonomous, segmentary societies' lacking 'indications of high rank or prominent status' (1979, 217) for those buried at Quanterness, can be resolved by the simple expedient that different social orders would prevail at different times and in widely separate areas. It could also be resolved by accepting the last of the new approaches mentioned here.

That some groups of chambered tombs and NM barrows should be considered not as burial places for human remains, but as shrines, has been suggested by Case (1973, 193–5). Following the excavation of the pits at Goodland, Co. Antrim, which are considered to have been filled with settlement debris, Case has pointed to the occurrence of similar deposits in some of the Irish court cairns and NM barrows of England. Assuming that settlement debris was associated in the mind of Neolithic man with soil fertility, it is argued that the 'closed foundation deposits' in the court cairn chambers may have been an attempt by magic rites to provide for the needs of the living against the effects of predatory Neolithic farming and consequent soil-deterioration. This hypothesis has been adopted by Ashbee, who would appear to see the majority of chambered tombs and NM barrows, not as mausolea, but as *fana* where dedicatory deposits were made 'as a response to developing soil deterioration' (Ashbee 1978, 85). This is a stimulating hypothesis, and one which deserves careful consideration in the light of the increasing knowledge of the contemporary environment. But I doubt if it provides a *raison d'être* for all chambered tombs, and I hope it will not be misunderstood if I continue to refer to tombs, chambers and burials, rather than to *fana*, repositories and dedicatory deposits.

This account of new approaches to the problems posed by chambered tombs in Britain has involved considerations of tomb typology and challenges to the assumption of linear typological development and to whether chambered tombs are really tombs at all. Such a maelstrom of conflicting hypotheses makes it difficult to see any clear pattern developing amongst the disparate groups of chambered tombs and NM barrows. Nevertheless, in a period of at least one and a half millennia during which these monuments were built and used, it is hardly surprising that ideas concerning their function may well have changed through time, and in response to local needs and circumstances.

It now remains to outline the current state of re-search and to examine some of the more important results from the large number of excavations which have taken place on both chambered tombs and NM barrows. Obviously such a survey must be selective, but I have tried to indicate those lines of research which seem most profitable for future speculation.

NM Barrows and Cairns

Included in this section are those monuments variously described as 'earthen' or 'unchambered' barrows and cairns which have either proved after excavation to have features similar to those encountered under NM barrows, or can be suspected from fieldwork to belong to this series. Their distribution in Britain is well known, from southern and eastern England to eastern Scotland. From the all too few radiocarbon dates available, they were being built and used throughout the latter half of the fourth millennium and almost all of the third millennium bc (Whittle 1977, 248–9).

A general semblance of unity among the series is provided by the regular occurrence of a long mound, generally trapezoidal in plan, although rectangular and oval plans are also found, the latter recently demon-strated at Alfriston, East Sussex (Drewett 1975). Lengths range from about 18 m to over 120 m, but generally are less than 70 m. The possibility has been put forward 'that differential lengths of Long Barrow were quite deliberate and established according to pre-cise principles' (Reed 1974, 34). Following excava-tion, the mounds have been shown to cover a wide variety of timber and stone structures. It can also be pointed out that round barrows or cairns can cover structures similar to those found under long mounds (Kinnes 1979).

Following Piggott (1967, 381–93) and Manby (1970, 1–27), three main types of structural feature have been discovered under the mounds. First, there are mortuary structures, generally containing cre-mated or inhumed bone, pottery, flint, charcoal and, on occasions, dark soil. Second, there are timber enclo-sures which might be small, as at Nutbane (Morgan 1959, 32–3) or large, as at Fussell's Lodge (Ashbee 1966, 6–7) and Kilham (Manby 1976, 119–23). Final-ly, there are forebuildings or porches set in line with the mortuary structure, and represented by post holes at Fussell's Lodge (Ashbee 1966, 7), Wayland's Smithy (BRK 1) (Atkinson 1965, 130) and in stone at Lochhill (KRK 14) (Masters 1973, 99).

Not all of these features need occur under any one mound. Indeed some barrows have proved to have none of them, as at Horslip, where only a series of in-tersecting pits was recorded (Ashbee *et al.* 1979,

207–28). At the nearby barrows of Beckhampton Road and South Street, there were no indications of mortuary structures or burials, but there was evidence from both for the division of the barrows into a number of bays defined by timber fences (Ashbee *et al.* 1979, 228–75). A similar feature has also been found under the Severn-Cotswold long barrow at Ascott-under-Wychwood (OXF 6) (Selkirk 1971, 7–10).

This is not the place to pursue a detailed comparison of all the features found under long barrows, but a few general comments can be made.

The position of mortuary structures is generally at right angles to the proximal end of the barrow, but ex-ceptions to this can be seen at Dalladies (KNC 8) (Pig-gott 1974) and Skendleby (Phillips 1936), where the mortuary structures are located transversely to the long sides of the barrows. The basic form of the mor-tuary structure comprises a linear area, generally defin-ed by low banks or stone walls. Pits, which may or may not have held posts, sometimes serve to subdivide the mortuary structure. The presence of posts at some sites has led Ashbee to claim that the basic form of these structures is that of a pitched-roof mortuary house. Objections to such an all-embracing recon-struction have been made (Simpson 1968, 142–4; Ashbee and Simpson 1969, 43–5), and with the objec-tors the present writer would agree. Piggott's careful analysis of the successive mortuary structures at Dalladies offered no conclusive evidence for a pitched roof. Mortuary structures are generally quite narrow, sometimes less than 2 m in internal width, a factor which could be used to argue against a pitched roof. There is also some evidence to suggest that the posts may pre-date the mortuary structure. At Pitnacree, the first phase was marked by two large posts, but the stone wall of the second phase mortuary structure clearly overlies the cavity of the western phase one post (Coles and Simpson 1965, 39–41). It is considered that the posts of the first phase mortuary structure at Dalladies had rotted away before the second phase structure, with its boulder walls, was built. Kinnes has proposed that a simpler solution to the pitched roof could be provided by a flat roof resting on the flanking banks or walls of the mortuary structure (1975, 19). Nevertheless, Ashbee continues to maintain his posi-tion regarding pitched-roof chambers (1978, 70), and this certainly seems to be a convincing reconstruction for Wayland's Smithy I (Atkinson 1965).

The contents of mortuary structures have been shown to be very variable. At Dalladies only a frag-ment of a child's skull, a cup-marked stone and a plano-convex flint knife were found. It is doubtful in this instance if the structure was used for mortuary purposes, unless the removal of skeletal remains prior to the building of the barrow is invoked. At the other end of the scale is the burial of the disarticulated remains of between fifty-three and fifty-seven individuals in the area covered by the flint cairn at Fussell's Lodge. In Yorkshire, *in situ* cremation deposits have been found at a number of sites including Garton Slack C34, Helperthorpe, Market Weighton, Rudston, Westow and Willerby Wold (Manby 1970, 10). Inhumation burials do occur, as at Kilham (Manby 1976, 113–14) and, on a stone pavement flanked at either end by massive post pits, at the Callis Wold 275 round barrow (Coombs 1976, 130–1).

The timber enclosures found under some mounds as, for example, at Fussell's Lodge and Kilham, have sometimes been assumed to be free-standing enclosures pre-dating the construction of the mound. The proximal end is sometimes marked by more massive timbers, suggesting the presence of a timber façade, analogous with the stone façades of some chambered tomb groups. At Lochhill, a free-standing timber façade has been shown to pre-date the construction of a trapezoidal long cairn and stone façade (Masters 1973, 96–9). In some cases it can be suggested that the free-standing timber enclosure was later used to revet the barrow.

Arrangements of post holes, variously interpreted as porches or forebuildings, have been found at Wayland's Smithy I and Fussell's Lodge. A similar arrangement has also been found in the forecourt of the Severn-Cotswold tomb at Gwernvale (BRE 7) (Britnell 1979, 132–4). These may be compared with the stone-built porch at Lochhill, and it is interesting to speculate that the covered passage at Pitnacree, incompletely excavated because of tree cover, may have been a similar feature. These porches are normally located in line with the mortuary structure and in front of the façade, but the occurrence of 'avenues' of post holes at Kilham and Kemp Howe (Manby 1976, 148; Brewster 1969, 13) may, as Manby suggests, 'be the ultimate development of an entrance approach'.

The final act at these NM barrows can be seen as the construction of a covering mound, the material being derived from flanking quarry ditches in many cases, but also by turf or stones. How long after the construction and use of mortuary structures is not known with any precision, but it has generally been assumed that the enmounding took place after an appreciable lapse of time. Ashbee has even suggested that the long barrows did not assume their final form 'until more than a millennium after the laying down of the foundation deposit' (1978, 97). That the interval was not so long may be suspected from some sites, but the lack of radiocarbon dates from each of the sequences of construction makes it very difficult to offer any convincing estimate of time-lapse between one stage and the next. A number of stages are clearly involved before the construction of the mound, as can be clearly seen at Nutbane (Morgan 1959), Aldwincle (Jackson 1976) and Kilham (Manby 1976), but less complex monuments also exist, such as the oval barrow at Alfriston covering only two pits, one of which contained a crouched inhumation burial (Drewett 1975, 119–52).

The presence of round barrows in the Neolithic has been known for some time (Piggott 1954, 111–12), but the extent of their presence has recently been demonstrated by Kinnes (1979). From the eighty-eight acceptable Neolithic sites, Kinnes has been able to show that the earlier sites cover features such as crematoria and linear mortuary structures, similar to those found under NM long mounds. Among the later developments, however, is a tendency towards a single-grave tradition with distinctive grave-goods, as at Liff's Low. The important point is made that this development took place well before any beaker presence.

Before concluding this section on the NM monuments, an account can be given of two cairns which clearly belong with the NM series. These sites are situated some 6 km apart in the Stewartry District of Dumfries and Galloway Region.

Excavation at Lochhill (ill. 3) produced evidence for a first phase mortuary structure, consisting of a rectangular trench edged by a low boulder wall, and containing three pits, the end ones of which had held large split tree-trunks, whilst the central pit had held two posts. The mortuary structure contained a burnt plank floor, some small deposits of cremated bone, charcoal, small boulders and dark soil. Associated with the mortuary structure was a timber façade, with four granite orthostats in front forming a porch. The second phase comprised a trapezoidal long cairn, which covered the mortuary structure and timber façade. The cairn was provided with a stone façade, which closely copies the plan of the preceding timber one and was linked to the earlier porch by an additional slab and a panel of dry-walling. Unfortunately, it is not known what interval of time elapsed between the first phase mortuary structure and the building of the cairn. As there were no voids in the cairn above the post pits, the presumption must be that the split timbers had rotted away before the cairn was built. Final activity at the site was marked by the blocking of the forecourt and long cairn walls (Masters 1973, 96–100).

Excavations at Slewcairn (KRK 12) are still in progress, so the account given here must be tentative pending completion of the work (Masters 1973 to 1979). Broadly the same sequence as revealed at Lochhill has been repeated at Slewcairn (ills 3,4). A first phase rectangular mortuary structure contained

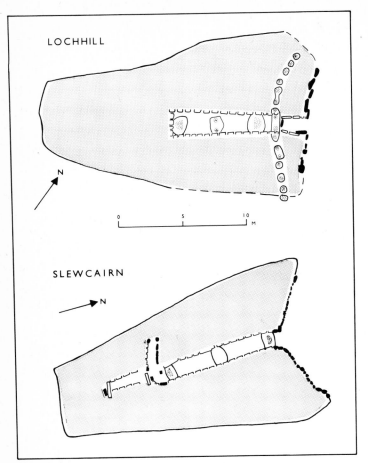

LOCHHILL

SLEWCAIRN

3 Lochhill and Slewcairn: plans of main structural features.

three pits, the outermost of which had held split tree-trunks. The filling of the centre pit proved to be ambiguous, but it may have held two posts in the first phase of its use. The mortuary structure had a filling similar to that at Lochhill, but cremated bone, mostly in the form of minute fragments, was found throughout the length of the structure. Cremated bone was also found in the pits, and it is suggested that the posts had rotted away before the mortuary structure was infilled. No indications of a timber façade have as yet been found, but at the southern end of the mortuary structure there is a setting of vertical stones which might be considered as the equivalent of the porch at Lochhill. When the long cairn was built, these stones were incorporated into a small 'chamber' approached by a passage from the west side of the long cairn. There is, however, one other feature which must be considered to belong to the primary phase. In line with the

mortuary structure, but separated from it by the 'porch' was a paved area bounded by a kerb on its east and west sides, a recumbent block to the north, and a recumbent block and vertical stone over 1 m in height to the south. Scattered over the paving were some sixty sherds of undecorated Neolithic pottery. The major building stage comprised the construction of a trapezoidal long cairn with a concave façade at its north end. Activity within the forecourt area is attested by the finds of over three hundred small sherds of undecorated Neolithic pottery, together with flint scrapers, leaf-shaped arrowheads and knives. Finally, as at Lochhill, the forecourt was blocked and the cairn wall concealed by deliberately placed extra-revetment material.

Taken with the evidence from Dooey's Cairn, Co. Antrim (Evans 1938; Collins 1976) and Ballafayle (Henshall 1978, 172), Lochhill and Slewcairn can be seen as the western outliers of the NM barrow series of eastern and southern Britain.

The Chambered Tombs

It is a daunting task to contemplate the considerable amount of work and speculation which has been undertaken on British chambered tombs within the last decade or so. The perennial problems of chronology, typology and relationships still figure largely in many of the considerations, and changing views are detectable as a reflection of the changing model of the past from one which relied on continental parallels for the monuments to one which sees insular development playing the prominent role. Powell summed up the situation envisaged some three to four decades ago when he wrote 'At that time it was a much discussed working hypothesis that the more elaborate tombs of the British Isles stood at the head of an introduced building tradition for which there existed very general comparisons in "Atlantic Europe"' (1973, 33). Today the general mood is to reverse such a proposition, and to see within the various tomb groups a sequence which begins with simple structures and develops towards more elaborate monuments. Such a process can be illustrated by the sequence proposed for the Maes Howe group. In Piggott's (1954, 245) scheme, followed by Henshall (1963, 131; 1972, 238; 1974, 155), Maes Howe itself is seen as the prototype. Two lines of development are envisaged leading to a slackening of the general plan of the prototype on the one hand, and to a multiplicity of side chambers on the other. Henshall sees a possible origin for the group in the Irish cruciform passage graves (1972, 283; 1974, 155). Renfrew envisages a different situation in which relatively simple tombs are the earliest monuments,

168

*4 Slewcairn: façade and mortuary structure from north.
(Photo C. Provan.)*

followed by a local evolutionary pattern towards stalled cairns in one direction, and his Quanterness-Quoyness group in the other. Maes Howe is seen as the end of the sequence within the Quanterness-Quoyness group. Despite the radiocarbon dates used to support this sequence, the beginning of it rests on the fact that Renfrew 'implicitly accepts that the Orkney tombs of the Orkney-Cromarty class (such as Bigland Round, Sandyhills Smithy and the Knowe of Craie) are part of a tomb building tradition brought to Orkney by the first Neolithic colonists' (1979, 210), a belief for which there is as yet no absolute proof, but seems reasonable in the light of present-day thought. Thus the sequence has been reversed and, at first sight, the 'foreign' connections dismissed. But Renfrew does leave open the possibility of contact between Orkney and Ireland when he writes 'Some scholars have wished to see a connection between the two groups, and this seems perfectly possible' (1979, 210).

This example could be repeated for virtually all the major tomb groups in Britain, and illustrates very well the dilemmas still surrounding questions of origin and development. Chronological problems of a detailed nature cannot as yet be solved by the available radiocarbon dates. Too many of them are, for quite valid

reasons, related either to pre-monument activity, or to the use of the chambers, rather than to the construction of the monument. All that can safely be said is that chambered tombs in Britain were being built and used from towards the end of the fourth millennium to the end of the third millennium BC.

The problems of local development and imported influences can be illustrated by reference to the Clyde group. In his detailed study of these monuments in south-west Scotland, Scott (1969, 175–222) postulated that the earliest were simple closed-box chambers (protomegaliths) set in minimal cairns. This was followed by elaboration at one end to produce an entrance with a pair of portal stones, and later still a second pair of stones could be added to form a two-compartment chamber divided by a septal slab. The next major stage sees the introduction, possibly from the Severn-Cotswold region, of trapezoidal cairns with flat façades. Later developments include more concave façades, an increase in the length of the chamber and its division by septal stones, and finally, influences

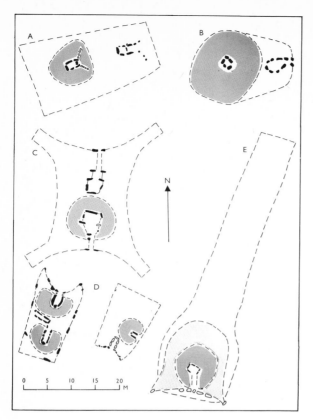

5 Excavated multi-period chambered tombs in Britain
(after Corcoran):
A Dyffryn Ardudwy
B Achnacreebeag
C Tulloch of Assery A
D Mid Gleniron I and II
E Tulach an-t' Sionnaich

from Irish court cairns, detectable in the 'dual court' cairn at Barmore Wood (ARG 9) and in the jambs and septal slabs at such sites as Achnagoul II (ARG 8). The sequence is supported to some extent by the pottery evidence and by Scott's own excavations at Brackley (ARG 28), Crarae (ARG 11) and Beacharra (ARG 27) (1958, 22–54; 1963, 1–27; 1964, 134–58). The excavation of the Mid Gleniron cairns (WIG 1, 2) could also be used to support the sequence, for it is claimed that the long cairns at these sites were added to pre-existing chambers set in minimal cairns (Corcoran 1969a, 29–90).

Leaving aside for the moment the subject of multi-period tombs, Scott has used the evidence of the Clyde sequence to reinterpret the rather unusual plan of Cairnholy I (KRK 2) (1969, 193–5; excavation: Piggott and Powell 1951, 103–23). According to Scott, the first phase could comprise the closed inner compart-

ment with its tall end-stones, to be followed by the addition of the first one, and then another pair of tall stones to form an outer compartment. The final phase would see the building of the long cairn and slightly concave façade. But it would also be possible to see Cairnholy I as a megalithic version of the mortuary structure and porch at Lochhill, with the tall stones of the closed chamber recalling the wooden posts at either end of the Lochhill mortuary structure, and the outer compartment of the Cairnholy I chamber fulfilling a role similar to the porch at Lochhill. As it is considered that the trapezoidal cairn at Lochhill formed part of the original design plan, the same might apply to Cairnholy I. I do not wish to press this point too strongly, for further excavation would be necessary to solve these differences in conjecture. I do, however, use it as an illustration of the differences in view between those who see multi-period sites developing in distinct stages, not necessarily related directly to each other, and those who see multi-period as merely the planned stages in a unitary design, analogous with the situation envisaged for NM sites like Nutbane and Aldwincle (Kinnes 1975, 19).

Some of the more recent hypotheses on the origin and development of tomb groups have, however, been based on the premise that multi-period tombs reached their final form as the result of one or more distinct, and not necessarily related, additional building phases to an original monument. The evidence was conveniently summarized by Corcoran (1972, 31–63) and by Henshall (1974, 137–64), so only a brief statement is necessary here with the addition of a few more recent examples.

Excavations by Corcoran (ill. 5) at Tulach an-t' Sionnaich (CAT 58) and Tulloch of Assery A (CAT 69), together with the evidence from the two cairns at Mid Gleniron (WIG 1, 2), led him to suggest that the monuments had reached their final form as the result of a number of distinct building phases (1967, 1–34; 1969a, 29–90). It should be noted that the evidence for Tulloch of Assery A being a multi-period site is not considered in the original excavation report, but in Corcoran's later consideration of multi-period tombs in general (1972, 34). Taken with the evidence from Dyffryn Ardudwy (MER 3) (Powell 1973, 1–49), what seems to be involved is the encapsulation by means of a long cairn of earlier simple chambers set in minimal cairns. Evidence for addition to an original cairn is provided by the site of Achnacreebeag (ARG 37), where a round cairn with a closed chamber was subsequently enlarged to accommodate a small passage grave (Ritchie 1973, 31–55). At Dalineun (ARG 3), however, Ritchie was able to show that a large cist, visible in the cairn to the south-west of a small Clyde type chamber, was a secondary insertion into the cairn (1974, 48–62).

To this collection of sites, together with the clear evidence for two periods at Wayland's Smithy (Atkinson 1965, 126–33), we can now add information from Camster Long (CAT 12) (ill. 6). At the time of his death, Corcoran had excavated most of the north-eastern half of the cairn, in which are situated the two known passages and chambers. The present writer has now assumed responsibility for the rest of the excavation (Masters 1978, 453–4, 459). Corcoran's work has shown that the simple polygonal passage grave was originally enclosed within a circular cairn, bounded by a well-built dry-stone wall a little over 1 m in height (ill. 7). The round cairn wall meets the passage at a point where the latter takes a slight bend to the right. This change in passage alignment is further emphasiz-ed by a pair of orthostats set into the dry-walling of the passage indicating, perhaps, the original entrance to the tomb. As access was still required to the chamber, the building of the long cairn involved a lengthening of the passage by some 6 m. The second chamber at Camster Long belongs to the classic Camster type as defined by Henshall (1963, 69–70). There are hints from Anderson's excavation that this chamber was also enclosed within a round cairn (Anderson 1870, 484), but further investigation will have to take place before this point can be resolved.

Brief notes of work at Trefignath (ANG 1) have in-dicated that this is a most interesting multi-period site

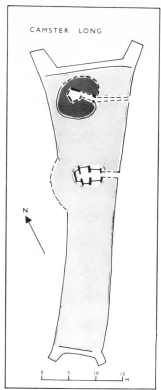

6 Plan of Camster Long.

7 Camster: round cairn enclosing simple passage-grave, from west; wall of long cairn in foreground. (Photo Crown Copyright Reserved.)

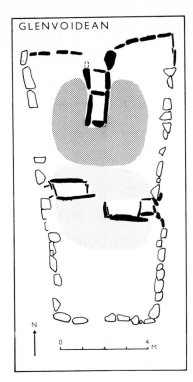

GLENVOIDEAN

N

0   4

M

8 Plan of Glenvoidean (after Marshall and Taylor).

(Smith 1978, 445; 1979, 340). Formerly classified by Lynch as a long grave (1969, 296), it can now be seen that the western group of stones are the remains of a simple passage grave contained within a circular cairn. The next stage was marked by the construction of a portal dolmen to the east, and set in a wedge-shaped cairn, which also incorporated the cairn of the passage-grave. Provision was made, however, for continued access to the passage-grave chamber. Blocking of the forecourt area of the portal dolmen was subsequently removed and a second portal dolmen was constructed in the forecourt of the first. The second portal dolmen was contained within an extension of the wedge-shaped cairn. Lynch's percipient comment that 'the possibility that Trefignath is a composite monument, with chambers juxtaposed over a period of time' (1969, 114) has proved to be correct.

Finally, the evidence for multi-period construction at Glenvoidean (ill. 8) (BUT 1) may be considered (Marshall and Taylor 1979, 1–39). The excavators suggest that the primary monument here was the northern closed chamber, set in its own round cairn. A radiocarbon date of 2910 ± 115 bc (I–5974) was obtained from burnt material under the west slab of this

chamber. Still within the primary phase, a pair of tall portal stones may have been added to the north end of the chamber to form a porch. A second phase is represented by the two lateral chambers, enclosed within a separate oval cairn which abuts the earlier one. It is suggested that the lateral chambers may have started as simple closed structures, to which were added pairs of stones to form porches, and then with the addition of end-stones, outer compartments. The third phase comprised the incorporation of these earlier structures by a trapezoidal long cairn, and within this phase a second pair of stones, one represented now only by a hole, may have been added to the axial chamber to form an outer compartment opening from the centre of the façade. Such a sequence, if accepted, would support Scott's sequence of development for the Clyde cairns (Scott 1969, 175–222). But the excavators emphasize that 'it is very difficult to determine the chronological sequence for the various stages', and they themselves stress that no great period of time need have elapsed between the first and second stages (Marshall and Taylor 1979, 14).

In the absence of a radiocarbon sequence for any of the composite tombs mentioned, considerations of whether the various features form part of a single design plan, or whether they are separate and distinct entities conceptually unrelated to the additions which follow, is something which has to be decided on the basis of the excavation evidence. At the moment, there seems to be no easy way of solving this dilemma, and personally held views will sway the evidence one way or another. In my own view, the evidence from Camster Long is strongly indicative of a situation in which the simple passage grave was built without there being any intention of enclosing it within a long mound. I suspect that the same situation may have prevailed at Mid Gleniron I, but I am not so sure about Glenvoidean. The excavators rightly stress the tentative nature of their interpretation and, apart from the pitching of the cairn stones, I can see little evidence for three distinct phases at this site. The Scottish legal verdict of 'not proven' may be appropriate in this case.

I have considered in some detail the subject of multi-period sites, for they have become a dominant theme for some writers on chambered tombs. Henshall has, perhaps, made most of the opportunities provided by considering that the final appearance of the monuments was the result of different building phases (Henshall 1972, 198–264). On the basis of fieldwork, sometimes supported by evidence from earlier excavations, it can be suggested that sites such as Oban nam Fiadh (UST 25), Rudh' an Dunain (SKY 7), Ormiegill (CAT 42) and Vementry (ZET 45) may be multi-phase in development. In a recent study of the Isle of

172

Man tombs, Henshall has put forward evidence for different building phases at King Orry's Grave and Cashtal yn Ard (1978, 171–6), and Lynch has considered that the cairn at Pentre Ifan might be of two-period construction, the enlargement of the cairn occurring when the façade was added to the portal dolmen (1972, 70–7). A similar situation may have prevailed at Carnedd Hengwm South (MER 6) (Lynch 1976, 69).

Henshall has recently stated that she regards 'all tombs as multi-period constructions, believing that most eccentric plans are due to difficulties of adapting or incorporating earlier structures in later additions', and also that 'there is plenty of evidence, once it is looked for, that this is a valid line of enquiry' (1974, 143). Not everyone would agree that all tombs are even potentially multi-period, but the line of enquiry is certainly valid, bearing in mind the difficulties of interpretation at unexcavated and often ruined sites.

If any general conclusions are to be reached concerning the earliest chambered tombs in Britain, it appears that present opinion would suggest that the earliest examples are simple structures. Into this category can be placed the simple box-like chambers set in minimal cairns. Portal dolmens might also be considered to be early in date on the basis of the pottery found in the forecourt pit of the western chamber at Dyffryn Ardudwy. Although the origins of the portal dolmen are by no means clear, it can be postulated that it could be derived from the simple box-like chambers, with which they share a similar concept of enclosed space burial. Irish evidence might appear to be in conflict with an early date for portal dolmens, if the accepted derivation of this type of monument from the lateral chambers of court cairns is accepted (de Valera and Ó Nulláin 1972, 162–8). This view has now been challenged by Flanagan, who would prefer to see court cairns and portal dolmens 'treated as a continuum instead of two distinct types' (1977, 26).

By using the evidence from Scottish multi-period sites, and the early Neolithic pottery from Carreg Sampson, Lynch (1975, 25–35) has suggested that passage graves with small polygonal chambers and short passages might be considered as early in date. The group, if indeed it can be called a group, has a widespread distribution from southern Brittany to the north of Scotland, and would include such sites as Broadsands, Devon Ty Newydd (ANG 3) and Camster Long (CAT 12).

Subsequent developments in many of the tomb groups seems to proceed towards elaboration of the chambers, and takes such diverse forms as segmented chambers in the Clyde group, tripartite and stalled chambers in the Orkney-Cromarty group, and transepted chambers in the Severn-Cotswold group. The problem of the origin of the long cairn, common to all three groups, is still not resolved, but it is still possible to look to the trapezoidal long barrows of the NM series as a possible progenitor.

The more elaborate passage graves, such as Barclodiad y Gawres (ANG 4) (Powell and Daniel, 1956) and Bryn Celli Ddu (ANG 7) (Hemp 1930, 179–214) can then be seen as later Neolithic monuments related to the Irish cruciform tombs of the Boyne Valley. At the latter site, a late date is indicated for it has been demonstrated that the tomb post-dates a henge monument (O'Kelly 1969, 17–48). The radiocarbon dates from the ditch at Maes Howe would also indicate a late date for this monument.

That we are still unable to offer a more precise picture of the development of the tomb groups is a measure of our ignorance of the chronology and human motivation behind the development of the tomb series. Nevertheless, further fieldwork analysis and excavation, together with sequences of radiocarbon dates, may resolve some of these problems and enable us to see more clearly the history of the various chambered tomb groups.

Origins

Any attempt to seek origins for the NM and chambered tombs of Britain is bound to be bedevilled with difficulties and we can only point to various possibilities.

In the present climate of thought, waves of colonists from Europe introducing various types of chamber plan are less acceptable now than they were three or four decades ago. Acceptance for Britain of a model which emphasizes insular and localized developments during the Neolithic period, following an initial colonization from Europe, still leaves the problem of accounting for the observed similarities in monument plan and function over wide areas of western and northern Europe. Recourse to the transmission of ideas, unaccompanied by archaeologically significant movements of people, or the acceptance of a view that people faced with similar problems will react in broadly similar ways are two constructive lines of approach. Alternatively, consideration can be given to MacKie's version of modified diffusionism, and accept that the passage graves of western Europe, the rite of collective burial, and knowledge of practical astronomy and geometry were disseminated by a professional priesthood. Basing his hypothesis on Darlington's *The Evolution of Man and Society* (1968), MacKie envisages that his professional priesthood may have been formed in Iberia 'due to the genetic and cultural mixing of two or more different ethnic groups of talented people', or even that the priesthood was brought to Iberia 'perhaps from the proto-urban societies of the Near East' (1977, 191). Whatever one's views of MacKie's hypothesis, there is the awesome spectre of Childe's megalithic missionaries returning once more, in different guise, to western Europe.

Whichever hypothesis, or series of hypotheses, is taken to account for the distribution of the chambered tombs and NM barrows, we are still likely to conclude, as Daniel did, by saying that 'in the absence of written evidence we may go on arguing for ever about the historical role of the megalith builders' (1958, 125). It seems reasonable, however, still to think of two broad traditions – that of the NM barrows of northern Europe, and of the chambered tombs of western Europe, which was the position envisaged by Daniel (1967, 313–17).

For the British NM series, many scholars have looked to the North European Plain as a source of origin (Piggott 1955, 96–101; 1961, 557–74; 1967, 381–93; Ashbee 1970, 87–99; Jazdzewski 1973, 63–74), but chronological difficulties, as well as significant differences in material culture, precluded a derivation of the British series from one specific European source. Recent excavations in Denmark have added greatly to our information, and these have been summarized by Madsen (1979, 301–20). Three basic groups are distinguished. The first comprises the gabled and ridge-roof mortuary houses of Konens Høj type, for which there are now between fourteen and sixteen examples. The Troelstrup type consists of rectangular mortuary structures built entirely of wood, or a combination of wood and stone. The third group is characterized by earth graves. Long covering mounds have also been recognized, generally rectangular in plan, but with some trapezoidal examples. The similarities of the Danish examples with the British series can be summarized as a common interest in an east-west orientation of the mound, timber façades and palisade enclosures, transverse rows of poles sectioning the barrows, and mortuary structures. Differences there certainly are, such as the position and number of the mortuary structures and in the burial rite, but the plans of some of the sites, Bygholm Nørromark for example, might not look out of place in the southern British Neolithic. Radiocarbon dates at present available would place some of the monuments in the first half of the third millennium bc, contemporary with the British series. Madsen concludes that the similarities seen in the long barrows of northern Europe are 'the result of structurally similar solutions to religious, ritual and sociopolitical problems' (1979, 319).

The passage graves of western Europe present similar problems of interpretation to those posed by the NM series. Iberia and Brittany can be considered as potential areas of origin on the basis of TL dates for Portuguese examples (Whittle and Arnaud 1975, 5–24) and early fourth millennium bc radiocarbon dates for some Breton passage graves. The two areas need not be connected, however, and both could have had separate origins and developments. It may be possible, as Whittle has suggested (1977, 221), to introduce into Britain those simple passage graves with short passages, although the dating evidence for this is slight, as Lynch has demonstrated (1975, 25–35).

Within Britain it is still possible to offer, with varying degrees of conviction, a whole set of different ideas to account for the various tomb groups. To take but one example, it could still be maintained that the transepted terminal chamber plan in the Severn-Cotswold group was derived from progenitors in the southern Morbihan and the mouth of the River Loire (Daniel 1939, 143–65; 1950, 158). The difficulties over a 'foreign' origin for the trapezoidal cairn could be resolved by accepting influences from the British NM series (Piggott 1962, 59–64). These hypotheses were accepted by Corcoran, who developed the foreign influences theme even further by suggesting that the Severn-Cotswold lateral chambers could be derived from the passage graves of the Hérault, and that more locally, blind entrances were derived from the frontal appearance of portal dolmens. Thus for Corcoran, the Severn-Cotswold group was the result of 'an amalgam of external influences' (1969b, 102). But the present climate of thought would see the Severn-Cotswold group and the NM series as 'expressions of the same set of ideas' with parallel developments and 'adaptation of one kind of idea to suit local needs' (Whittle 1977, 218).

Similar situations could be postulated for almost all the major tomb groups in Britain. Chronological difficulties, differing views on the nature of Neolithic society, and judgments as to whether independent invention, diffusion or migration, should be held to account for the appearance of the monuments in space and time, will inevitably lead to the many views seeking to account for their origin, role and function.

In writing this essay I recall with pleasure the hours spent as an undergraduate discussing with Glyn Daniel the chambered tombs of western Europe. That we have not yet constructed Llewellynn Jewitt's 'undying and faultless historical structures' will come as no surprise to him!

Bibliography

ANDERSON, J. 1870 'On the Horned Cairns of Caithness: their Structural Arrangements, Contents of Chambers &c', *Proc.Soc.Antiq.Scot.* VII, 480–512.

ASHBEE, P. 1966 'The Fussell's Lodge Long Barrow Excavations 1957', *Archaeologia* C, 1–80.

1970 *The Earthern Long Barrow in Britain*, London.

1978 *The Ancient British*, Norwich.

ASHBEE, P. AND SIMPSON, D. D. A. 1969 'Timber Mortuary Houses and Earthen Long Barrows Again', *Antiquity* XLIII, 43–5.

ASHBEE, P., SMITH, I. F. AND EVANS, J. G. 1979 'Excavation of Three Long Barrows near Avebury, Wiltshire', *Proc. Preh. Soc.* XLV, 207–300.

ATKINSON, R. J. C. 1965 'Wayland's Smithy', *Antiquity* XXXIX, 126–33.

1968 'Old Mortality: Some Aspects of Burial and Population in Neolithic England', in Coles, J. M. and Simpson, D. D. A. (eds) *Studies in Ancient Europe*, Leicester, 83–93.

BREWSTER, T. C. M. 1969 'Kemp Howe', in *Archaeological Excavations*, 1968, 13.

BRITNELL, W. 1979 'The Gwernvale Long Cairn, Powys', *Antiquity* LIII, 132–4.

CASE, H. 1969 'Settlement-patterns in the North Irish Neolithic', *Ulster J. Archaeol.*, 32, 3–27.

1973 'A Ritual Site in North-East Ireland', in Daniel, G. and Kjaerum, P. (eds) *Megalithic Graves and Ritual*, Copenhagen, 173–96.

COLES, J. M. AND SIMPSON, D. D. A. 1965 'The Excavation of a Neolithic Round Barrow at Pitnacree, Perthshire, Scotland', *Proc. Preh. Soc.* XXXI, 34–57.

COLLINS, A. E. P. 1976 'Dooey's Cairn, Ballymacaldcrack, County Antrim', *Ulster J. Archaeol.* 39, 1–7.

COOMBS, D. 1976 'Callis Wold Round Barrow, Humberside', *Antiquity* L, 130–1.

CORCORAN, J. X. W. P. 1967 'Excavation of Three Chambered Cairns at Loch Calder, Caithness', *Proc. Soc. Antiq. Scot.* XCVIII, 1–75.

1969a 'Excavation of Two Chambered Cairns at Mid Gleniron Farm, Glenluce, Wigtownshire', *Trans. Dumfriesshire Galloway Natur. Hist. Antiq. Soc.* XLVI, 29–90.

1969b 'The Cotswold-Severn Group', in Powell, T. G. E. (ed.) *Megalithic Enquiries in the West of Britain*, Liverpool, 13–104.

1972 'Multi-Period Construction and the Origins of the Chambered Long Cairn in Western Britain and Ireland', in Lynch, F. and Burgess, C. (eds) *Prehistoric Man in Wales and the West*, Bath, 31–63.

DANIEL, G. E. 1939 'The Transepted Gallery Graves of Western France', *Proc. Preh. Soc.* V, 143–65.

1950 *The Prehistoric Chamber Tombs of England and Wales*, Cambridge.

1958 *The Megalithic Builders of Western Europe*, London.

1967 'Northmen and Southmen', *Antiquity* XLI, 313–17.

1976 'Megaliths Galore', *Antiquity* L, 187–9.

DE VALERA, R. AND Ó NUALLÁIN, S. 1972 *Survey of the Megalithic Tombs of Ireland*, III, Dublin.

DREWETT, P. 1975 'The Excavation of an Oval Burial Mound of the Third Millennium bc at Aflriston, East Sussex, 1974', *Proc. Preh Soc.* XLI, 119–52.

EVANS, E. E. 1938 'Doey's Cairn, Dunloy, County Antrim', *Ulster J. Archaeol.* I, 59–78.

FLANAGAN, L. N. W. 1977 'Court Graves and Portal Graves', *Ir. Archaeol. Res. Forum* IV (Part 1), 23–9.

FLEMING, A. 1972 'Vision and Design: Approaches to Ceremonial Monument Typology', *Man* VII, 57–73.

1973 'Tombs for the Living', *Man* VIII, 177–93.

HEMP, W. J. 1930 'The Chambered Cairn of Bryn Celli Ddu', *Archaeologia* LXXX, 179–214.

HENSHALL, A. S. 1963 *The Chambered Tombs of Scotland*, vol. 1, Edinburgh.

1972 *The Chambered Tombs of Scotland*, vol. 2, Edinburgh.

1974 'Scottish Chambered Tombs and Long Mounds', in Renfrew, C. (ed.) *British Prehistory: A New Outline*, London, 137–64.

1978 'Manx Megaliths Again; An Attempt at Structural Analysis', in Davey, P. (ed.) *Man and Environment in the Isle of Man*, Brit. Archaeol. Rep. 54 (i), Oxford, 171–6.

JACKSON, D. A. 1976 'The Excavation of Neolithic and Bronze Age Sites at Aldwincle, Northants, 1967–71', *Northamptonshire Archaeol.* XI, 12–70.

JAZDZEWSKI, K. 1973 'The Relationship between Kujavian Barrows in Poland and Megalithic Tombs in Northern Germany, Denmark and Western European Countries', in Daniel G. and Kjaerum, P. (eds) *Megalithic Graves and Ritual*, Copenhagen, 63–74.

KINNES, I. 1975 'Monumental Function in British Neolithic Burial Practices', *World Archaeol.* VII, 16–29.

1979 'Round Barrows and Ring-ditches in the British Neolithic', *Brit. Mus. Occasional Paper*, 7.

LYNCH, F. 1969 'The Megalithic Tombs of North Wales', in Powell, T. G. E. (ed.) *Megalithic Enquiries in the West of Britain*, Liverpool, 107–48.

1972 'Portal Dolmens in the Nevern Valley, Pembrokeshire', in Lynch, F. and Burgess, C. (eds) *Prehistoric Man in Wales and the West*, Bath, 67–84.

1975 'Excavations at Carreg Sampson Megalithic Tomb, Mathry, Pembrokeshire', *Archaeol. Cambrensis* CXXIV, 15–35.

1976 'Towards a Chronology of Megalithic Tombs in Wales', in Boon, G. C. and Lewis, J. M. (eds) *Welsh Antiquity, Essays Presented to H. N. Savory*, Cardiff, 63–79.

MacKie, E. 1977 *The Megalith Builders*, London.

Madsen, T. 1979 'Earthen Long Barrows and Timber Structures: Aspects of the Early Neolithic Mortuary Practice in Denmark', *Proc. Preh. Soc.* XLV, 301–20.

Manby, T. G. 1970 'Long Barrows of Northern England; Structural and Dating Evidence', *Scot. Archaeol. Forum* II, 1–27.

1976 'Excavation of the Kilham Long Barrow, East Riding of Yorkshire', *Proc. Preh. Soc.* XLII, 111–59.

Marshall, D. N. and Taylor, I. D. 1979 'The Excavation of the Chambered Cairn at Glenvoidean, Isle of Bute', *Proc. Soc. Antiq. Scot.* CVIII, 1–39.

Masters, L. J. 1973 'The Lochhill Long Cairn', *Antiquity* XLVII, 96–100.

1973–9 'Slewcairn' in *Discovery and Excavation in Scotland.*

1974 'The Chambered Tombs of Scotland', *Antiquity* XLVIII, 34–9.

1978 'Camster Long Chambered Cairn', in Department of the Environment Summary Reports, *Proc. Preh. Soc.* XLIV, 453–4, 459.

Morgan, F. de M. The Excavation of a Long Barrow at Nutbane, Hants.', *Proc. Preh. Soc.* XXV, 15–51.

O'Kelly, C. 1969 'Bryn Celli Ddu, Anglesey: A Reinterpretation', *Archaeol. Cambrensis* CXVIII, 17–48.

Phillips, C. W. 1936 'The Excavation of the Giant's Hills Long Barrow, Skendleby, Lincs.', *Archaeologia* LXXXV, 37–106.

Piggott, S. 1954 *The Neolithic Cultures of the British Isles*, Cambridge.

1955 'Windmill Hill – East or West?' *Proc. Preh. Soc.* XXI, 96–101.

1961 'The British Neolithic Cultures in their Continental Setting', in *L'Europe à la fin de l'âge de la pierre*, Prague, 557–74.

1962 *The West Kennet Long Barrow: Excavations 1955–56*, London.

1967 '"Unchambered" Long Barrows in Neolithic Britain', *Palaeohistoria* XII, 381–93.

1973 'Problems in the Interpretation of Chambered Tombs', in Daniel, G. and Kjaerum, P. (eds) *Megalithic Graves and Ritual*, Copenhagen, 9–15.

1974 'Excavation of the Dalladies Long Barrow,

Fettercairn, Kincardineshire', *Proc. Soc. Antiq. Scot.* CIV, 23–47.

Piggott, S. and Powell, T. G. E. 1951 'The Excavation of Three Neolithic Chambered Tombs in Galloway, 1949', *Proc. Soc. Antiq. Scot.* LXXXIII, 103–61.

Powell, T. G. E. 1969 (ed.) *Megalithic Enquiries in the West of Britain*, Liverpool.

1973 'Excavation of the Megalithic Chambered Cairn at Dyffryn Ardudwy, Merioneth, Wales', *Archaeologia* CIV, 1–49.

Powell, T. G. E. and Daniel, G. E. 1956 *Barclodiad y Gawres*, Liverpool.

Reed, R. C. 1974 'Earthen Long Barrows; A New Perspective', *Archaeol. J.* CXXXI, 33–57.

Renfrew, A. C. 1973 *Before Civilization*, London.

1979 *Investigations in Orkney*, Reports of the Research Committee of the Society of Antiquaries of London, no. 38, London.

Ritchie, J. N. G. 1973 'Excavation of the Chambered Cairn at Achnacreebeag', *Proc. Soc. Antiq. Scot.* CII, 31–55.

1974 'Excavation of a Chambered Cairn at Dalineun, Lorn, Argyll', *Proc. Soc. Antiq. Scot.* CIV, 48–62.

Scott, J. G. 1958 'The Chambered Cairn at Brackley, Kintyre', *Proc. Soc. Antiq. Scot.* LXXXIX, 22–54.

1963 'The Excavation of a Chambered Cairn at Crarae, Loch Fyneside, Mid Argyll', *Proc. Soc. Antiq. Scot.* XCIV, 1–27.

1964 'The Chambered Cairn at Beacharra, Kintyre, Argyll, Scotland', *Proc. Preh. Soc.* XXX, 134–58.

1969 'The *Clyde* Cairns of Scotland', in Powell, T. G. E. (ed.) *Megalithic Enquiries in the West of Britain*, Liverpool, 175–222.

Selkirk, A. 1971 'Ascott-under-Wychwood', *Curr. Archaeol.* XXIV, 7–10.

Simpson, D. D. A. 1968 'Timber Mortuary Houses and Earthen Long Barrows', *Antiquity* XLII, 142–4.

Smith, C. 1978 'Trefignath Burial Chambers, Holyhead, Anglesey', in Department of the Environment Summary Reports, *Proc. Preh. Soc.* XLIV, 445.

1979 'Trefignath Burial Chambers, Holyhead, Anglesey', in Department of the Environment Summary Reports, *Proc. Preh. Soc.* XLV, 340.

Smith, I. F. 1974 'The Neolithic' in Renfrew, C. (ed.) *British Prehistory: A New Outline*, London, 100–36.

Whittle, A. W. R. 1977 *The Earlier Neolithic of Southern England and its Continental Background*, Brit. Archaeol. Rep. Suppl. Ser. 35, Oxford.

Whittle, E. H. and Arnaud, J. M. 1975 'Thermoluminescent Dating of Neolithic and Chalcolithic Pottery from Sites in Central Portugal', *Archaeometry* XVII, 5–24.

17   The Megalithic Tombs of Ireland

Michael J. O'Kelly

I DOUBT if Glyn Daniel remembers our first meeting. It was when he and Terence Powell were on a visit to Seán P. Ó Ríordáin in Cork. I had just begun to study archaeology but knew absolutely nothing of the subject at the time and I was very impressed by the fact that two Cambridge students should deign to visit Cork! I have no very clear memory now either of that visit except that they would not look at anything that was not a megalithic tomb. Time mellowed them both and when they were back in Ireland after the war, they were very ready to look at many things that were not megalithic! I was involved with them again at the excavation of Barclodiad y Gawres and they both many times visited my Newgrange excavations which began in 1962; various pieces about it have appeared in *Antiquity* over the years since. I have benefited so much from my continuous contact and association with Professor Daniel that it gives me the greatest pleasure to contribute this piece on the megalithic tombs of Ireland to a *Festschrift* that he so well deserves.

Since the 1930s, Irish megalithic tombs have attracted much attention and several archaeologists have devoted themselves to their particular study. Early in the field were Professor Daniel himself as well as his fellow student the late Professor Terence Powell. In the north of Ireland Professor Estyn Evans, Oliver Davies and the late Dr John Corcoran contributed mightily to the study as also did the late Professor Seán P. Ó Ríordáin in the south. In more recent times a new generation has taken over the field and contributions have been made by Pat Collins, the late Dudley Waterman and Lawrence Flanagan in Belfast. In Dublin, the leading scholar of the new generation has been the late Professor Ruaidhrí de Valera who devoted his whole archaeological working life from his student days to his untimely death in 1978 to an intensive study of the tombs, and while he was Archaeology Officer at the Ordnance Survey, initiated the official survey of the megalithic tombs of Ireland. Because of all this, de Valera's influence on the course the research has taken has been very great and his lines of thought have been accepted by his co-workers and students. They in turn have made their own considerable contributions and amongst them are the works of Dr Seán Ó Nualláin, who in 1957 succeeded to the post in the Ordnance Survey when de Valera became professor in University College, Dublin. Dr Michael Herity of the same College, also much influenced by de Valera, has dealt with aspects of the portal- and wedge-tombs and has published a major study of the passage-tombs. The art of the passage-tombs has been studied comprehensively by Dr Elizabeth Twohig of University College, Cork, and the Boyne Valley art in particular by Claire O'Kelly. Professor George Eogan, UCD, has also contributed to this aspect in connection with his excavations at Knowth, Co. Meath.

In what I have written here, I have made constant reference to and use of the published work of all these writers and I thank them, one and all not only for their writings, but for information freely given over a long number of years. It is inevitable that different interpretations can be put upon the same archaeological evidence and as will be seen below, my views differ from those of my friends and colleagues in various ways. I trust that they will find my views as interesting as I have found theirs, even when I have drawn as long a bow of speculation as they have done.

The survey of the megalithic tombs of Ireland has been in progress for twenty years and the fieldwork is now well nigh completed. The work has been done by the late Professor Ruaidhrí de Valera of University College, Dublin and by Dr Seán Ó Nualláin, Archaeology Officer to the Ordnance Survey. So far, three volumes have been published and others are in preparation. Since the recent and lamented death of Professor de Valera, the work is being continued by his collaborator, Dr Ó Nualláin, who hopes to bring it all to a successful published conclusion during the next seven or eight years. Volume I (1961) dealt with the tombs of Co. Clare, Volume II (1964) with those of Co. Mayo and Volume III (1972) with those of the counties of Galway, Roscommon, Leitrim, Longford, Westmeath, Cavan, Laoighis, Offaly and Kildare. No proven tombs have been discovered in the three latter counties. The volumes are published by the Stationery Office, Dublin. They have been produced to a very high standard and it is to be hoped that despite present-day costs, it will be possible to maintain this standard throughout.

The survey has given many interesting results. It has shown that there are at least 1,200 megalithic tombs in the whole of Ireland and that this cannot have been the original total. A study of the literature published in the past and of other sources of information has shown that much destruction of sites has taken place and that this destruction has gone on even in recent times. Some sites seen by the surveyors and given a preliminary recording had disappeared when they went back to do a full survey. In the absence of a blanket preservation by the state and because of the land improvement schemes that are in progress throughout the country, sites which have now been fully recorded, will alas also disappear.

The majority of the 1,200 known sites have been classified into four main types but there is a residue which, for a variety of reasons, remains unclassified. Unfortunately, too, there are megalithic structures, which, though they have been examined, have been excluded from publication because in the opinion of the surveyors they were not recognizable by them as tombs. Such sites could have been included in appendices under some heading such as 'doubtful sites' so that other workers holding differing views would be made aware of their existence and so could make their own judgments.

In Volume III, the first which covers an area that includes passage-tombs, a curious policy has been followed. Because this type occurs in cemetery groups, they are to be treated

> separately from other types which do not have a nucleated distribution pattern. The cemeteries will be dealt with as units but examples of Passage-tombs occurring outside the main cemeteries are surveyed during the county surveys. It is proposed to publish plans and descriptions of these scattered sites from time to time in *ad hoc* papers and eventually to include all Irish Passage-tomb cemeteries and isolated sites in one or more volumes of the survey entirely devoted to this class. In the meantime, lists of Passage-tombs, where they occur, will be published in the relevant county volumes (de Valera and Ó Nualláin, 1972, xiii).

Because Dr Michael Herity of the Department of Archaeology, University College, Dublin, is interested in the finds from each class of tomb, the finds will not be published in the survey volumes – they will be published separately by Dr Herity. This means that the survey volumes will not present the complete information which one would expect them to contain. These, however, are minor criticisms and are greatly outweighed by the very valuable body of information now on record.

The four types of megalithic tombs in Ireland are now called court-tombs (329 examples), portal-tombs (160), wedge-tombs (400) and passage-tombs (150), a change in nomenclature made since Volumes I and II were published (de Valera and Ó Nualláin 1972, xiii). In them the names were court-cairns, portal-dolmens, wedge-shaped gallery-graves, and passage-graves, names for the types which had long been current in the literature. The fourfold classification has received widespread acceptance, though there is an appreciable residue of structures which remains outside it. For instance, there is in the south-west of Ireland (Cork/Kerry) a group of fifty-two structures known in the past as 'boulder dolmens' but now called 'boulder burials' by Ó Nualláin (1978). These might have been called 'boulder-tombs' since they are overground structures, the reason given for the change from passage-grave to passage-tomb etc. (de Valera 1979, 102). Only one of them has been excavated – that at Bohonagh, Co. Cork (Fahy 1961). This did contain a cremated burial (no grave goods or dating evidence), but is one out of fifty-two sufficient to enable them all to be called burial structures without even the addition of a question mark? They consist of a large boulder capstone resting on three or more small boulders and some of them stand adjacent to or within stone circles.

The distribution patterns revealed by the megalithic survey are of much interest. The court-tombs (ill. 1) have a very marked northern distribution, all except five of the 329 lying north of a line drawn across the country from Dundalk on the east to Galway on the west. Of the five south of this line, two are in Co. Clare, and one each in the counties of Waterford, Kilkenny and Tipperary (ills. 5 and 6). There is a strong concentration of the tombs in the west particularly in the coastal regions of Mayo, Sligo and Donegal and a lesser one on the east coast in Louth and Down around Carlingford Lough. Apart from these two areas of density there is a general scatter of the tombs throughout the northern third of Ireland. The portal-tomb distribution is also very northern lying within the court-tomb area, though there is a small group in Co. Clare in the west and a spread of them from Dublin to Waterford in the south-east where some very impressive examples are to be seen. There are at least two in Co. Cork (ill. 2).

The wedge-tombs are the largest and most widespread group though they are most strongly represented in the western half of the country from south-west Cork to Donegal. The densest concentrations are in south-west Cork/Kerry, Tipperary and Clare, the latter county having over a hundred tombs (ill. 3).

The passage-tombs also have a northern distribution (ill. 4), but the most impressive of them lie in a cross-country band from the Dublin/Drogheda east coast to Sligo in the north-west and this band includes the four great cemeteries of the Boyne and Loughcrew in Co.

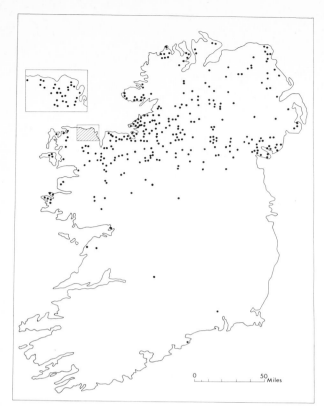

1 *Distribution of court-tombs.*

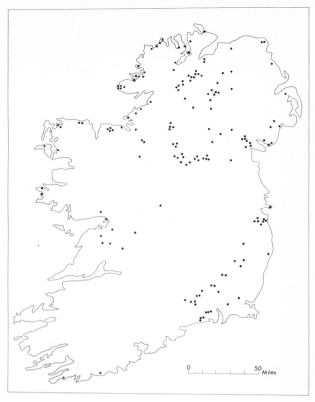

2 *Distribution of portal-tombs.*

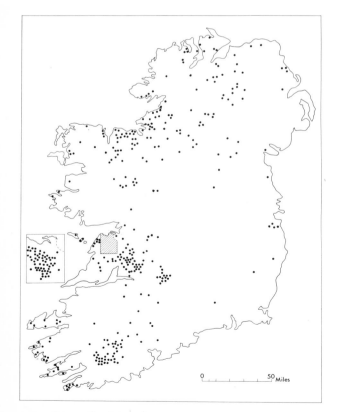

3 *Distribution of wedge-tombs.*

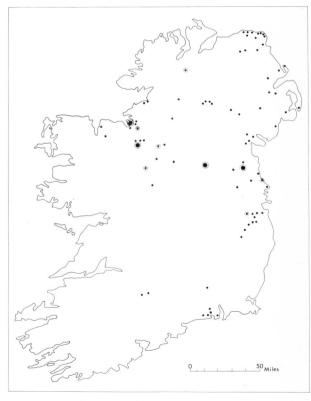

4 *Distribution of passage-tombs.*

1–4 Courtesy Irish Megalithic Survey.

5 Conjectural reconstruction drawing of court-tomb at Shanballyedmond, Co. Tipperary. (From JCHAS *LXIII (1958).)*

6 Plan of court-tomb at Shanballyedmond, Co. Tipperary. (From JCHAS *LXIII (1958).)*

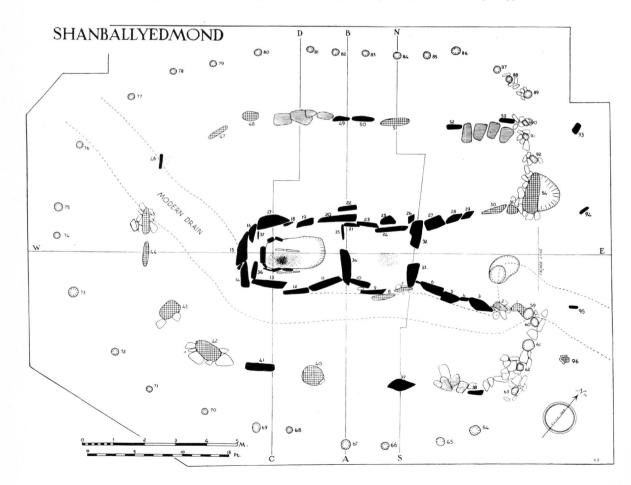

Meath and Carrowkeel and Carrowmore in Co. Sligo. There are small, more scattered groups in the Dublin/Wicklow mountains, in Donegal, in north Antrim and in Co. Waterford. A single slab bearing typical passage-tomb ornament, now in the Cork Public Museum (O'Kelly 1949; Powell 1966, 115), is the only surviving evidence of a site on Clear Island off the coast of south-west Cork. The site was destroyed over one hundred years ago. There is a single passage-tomb in east Co. Limerick.

The passage-tombs differ from the rest of the Irish megaliths in their cemetery groupings and in their hilltop sitings as well as in grave furniture. They have been found to contain personal ornaments such as beads, pendants, bone and antler pins, the enigmatic 'marbles' and round-bottomed pottery called Carrowkeel ware after the Sligo cemetery of that name, but no objects of everyday use in flint or stone. Arrowheads, javelin heads, axes and pottery of types known from domestic sites have been found in the court- and portal-tombs and some of the same objects in the wedges.

The numbers of tombs of all types that have been partially or fully excavated is very small – 37 court-tombs, 19 wedges, about 40 passage-tombs and 20 portal-tombs – a rather small statistical sample of the 1,200 total. The sample is poor in the case of the court-tombs and particularly so in the case of the wedges. The passage-tomb sample may seem large, but one must remember that it is not a random one – over half of it is made up of the two very close-knit groups at Newgrange and Knowth in the Boyne Valley, four sites recently excavated in the Carrowmore cemetery and fourteen of the rest are the old excavations at Carrowkeel of Macalister (*et al.*) in 1912. It does not include the very old 'excavations' of the middle of the last century at Dowth, Loughcrew and Carrowmore.

In the most recently published general statements on the megalithic tombs of Ireland, little that is new has been said (de Valera 1979; Ó Nualláin 1979; Herity and Eogan 1977; Herity 1974). It is assumed that the Neolithic way of life was introduced into Ireland by an incursion/invasion of new people who 'would have found virtually if not totally virgin country' (de Valera 1979, 1). In other words, a denial of a Mesolithic presence in Ireland. It is assumed that the court-tombs, the passage-tombs and the wedge-tombs represent 'three major colonizations by different groups of tomb builders' (de Valera 1979, 102) – people who came from the west of France and Brittany and who landed on the Irish coast at different points from which they extended their colonies into the country. The portal-tombs alone of the four types evolved in Ireland (central Ulster) from the court-tombs. Thus the court-

tomb builders landed in the west around Killala Bay in Co. Mayo and spread eastward across Ulster and eventually into Scotland and the Isle of Man. The passage-tomb builders arrived on the east coast and set up the Boyne Valley cemetery from where the general movement was westward resulting in the founding of the cemeteries at Loughcrew, Carrowkeel and Carrowmore in that order (Herity and Eogan 1977, 57). The wedge-tomb builders came from Brittany, landed in Kerry in the south-west and spread northward to Donegal and in time occupied the greater part of the western half of Ireland.

In the matter of date there is in the accounts cited an ambivalence towards radiocarbon and while dates obtained by this means seem to be accepted where they fit, there is a constant emphasis on the unreliability of the method. The court-tombs are said to be the earliest of the four types, the passage-tombs beginning a little later, but continuing to be built for the same period of time as the court-tombs. The floruit of the portal-tombs is contemporary with the later part of the court-tomb building activity, while the wedge-tombs are the latest and belong to the end of the Neolithic and to the Beaker/Early Bronze Age period. So much for what has recently been said.

There is now emerging quite acceptable evidence that there was a strong early Mesolithic in Ireland. Two recently excavated sites, Mount Sandel, Co. Derry (Woodman 1978, 220) and Lough Boora, Co. Offaly (Ryan 1978) have been shown to be seasonal settlement sites with radiocarbon dates ranging from 6500 to 7000 bc. At Mount Sandel a number of circular huts with hearths, rubbish pits and flint-knapping floors have been uncovered. Animal, bird and fish bones as well as hazelnut shells give some indication of diet, and very numerous microliths of several kinds display a high-level flint technology. Polished stone axes were also in use. All the same things except the hut sites have been found at Lough Boora. The polished axes have occasioned some surprise as it has been so firmly held in the past that such tools were not in Ireland before the Neolithic period proper had begun. It seems likely that these first colonizing immigrants to Ireland came from northern Britain (Woodman 1978), and while they may have come dryshod across landbridges, these connections were cut by the rising sea by 6500 bc and thereafter the people must have had boats. Even though our knowledge of them is still very meagre, they were obviously an able people for whom the developing Irish Sea became a highway, not a barrier, and by 4000 bc they were travelling the length and breadth of it and had maintained their contacts in Britain and probably established others farther afield in north and north-west France. I imagine some of them trading animal skins and furs, smoked salmon and other fish and dried venison as well as raw flint out of Ireland and coming back with calves and lambs, kids and young pigs and probably a new wife or two as well as friends *invited* into Ireland. In due time after other visits abroad, they came back with round-bottomed shouldered bowl pots and sacks full of seed wheat and barley. Thus the Neolithic way of life was introduced by a slow and complicated process resulting from overseas contacts – there was no invasion and no arrival of a great colony of foreigners. But see Case's discussion of the matter (1969).

By 3000 bc, pastoralism and agriculture were well established and an increasing population had developed a settled way of life and a firm social structure. The food supply was assured and abundant, and thought could be given to matters other than just the daily round. Foreign contacts had continued of course, and thus by the later part of the fourth millennium, megalithic tomb-building and its associated cult of the dead was coming into fashion in Ireland, the passage-tomb builders beginning their experiments with the cult in the Carrowmore cemetery in Co. Sligo as the radiocarbon dates that we now have suggest. Site no. 7 there has a date of 3290 ± 80 bc (LU–1441). This has been shown to be a very simple tomb structure with just a hint of a passage, the whole set within a circular kerb of boulders within which there never had been a covering cairn (Burenhult 1980). Site 27 in the cemetery had a simple cruciform structure without a passage proper and just the basal layer of a cairn within the circular boulder kerb. Its radiocarbon date is 3090 ± 80 bc (LU–1698).

As was to be expected these two sites show a local elaboration within a cemetery now reduced to thirty-one monuments from an original one hundred or more. Did the Carrowmore cemetery begin to come into existence out of the same stream of influences that affected Denmark and south Sweden and which way was the stream flowing – Scandinavia to Ireland or the reverse? Clear evidence has come from the excavations at Newgrange (O'Kelly *et al.* 1978) and Knowth (Eogan 1969, 13) that simple passage-tomb types can be and are earlier than the great tombs on the Boyne, and so if there is an evolutionary sequence at all, it must be from the simple to the complex. Thus the three great mounds in the Boyne cemetery mark the zenith of the passage-tomb sect of the cult in Ireland, not the beginning as has so often been said (de Valera 1965, 24; Herity and Eogan 1977, 57). The radiocarbon dates for the building of Newgrange centre on 2500 bc, five hundred radiocarbon years later than at least two of the Carrowmore sites. Meanwhile, be-

tween Carrowmore in the west and the Boyne Valley in the east other passage-tomb builders were carrying out their own experiments at Carrowkeel, Loughcrew and elsewhere. New excavations and more radiocarbon dates will in time place them in the sequence of events.

But what of the other megalithic tomb types in Ireland? We have now been stuck for a long time with the arguments about whether the court-tomb builders entered Ireland in the east at Carlingford Lough or in the west at Killala Bay, this because of the concentrations of the tombs in these two areas. In the last written statement he made before he died, de Valera firmly favoured the western entry and a devolution eastward, but he was constrained to say that

> Excavation has produced evidence of a Neolithic date for the court-tombs . . . The dating evidence . . . does not as yet warrant a judgment between the theory of east-west evolution or that of west-east devolution. The finds from court-tombs present coherent evidence for a Neolithic dating and this is confirmed by radiocarbon determinations. It is clear that examples of both the simpler and more complex types were built in Neolithic times (de Valera 1979, 108).

De Valera has argued that the seven transepted court-tombs which he and Ó Nualláin have found in the north-west of Ireland are very early in the series and that they indicate an origin for the court-tombs in the west of France (1965, 29), but seven sites, some of them very doubtful, can hardly be taken as good evidence of an invasion mounted from the Loire estuary – and where did they pick up the courts? They are not known in the putative homeland of the invaders. The cruciform plans of these sites are more likely due to an idea borrowed from the Sligo passage-tomb builders. But what if no flotillas of boats came up the Irish Sea to Carlingford or sailed up the west coast of Ireland to Mayo from the mouth of the Loire? Is it not more likely that we are dealing here with long settled groups of Irish farmers who had now got themselves caught up in another sect of the megalithic cult of the dead and who were doing their own thing in different parts of Ireland at the same time? Taken as a whole the court-tombs must be an Irish invention sparked off perhaps by influences coming from Scotland and northern Britain amongst other places (Waddell 1978, 122).

It has also been firmly said that the court-tombs are the earliest of the four types and that they were built by the first Neolithic invaders (de Valera 1960, 85), but the radiocarbon dates do not support this view. The earliest dates now available are from the court-tomb at

Ballymacdermot, Co. Armagh, but there are great discrepancies between the four dates obtained from charcoal from chamber 3 of the gallery. These range from 770 ± 75 and 1010 ± 75 *both ad* to 2345 ± 90 and 2880 ± 95 *both bc* (UB-705, 697, 695 and 694) and, therefore, one can have little confidence in them. The dates from the Ballyglass court-tomb site (Ó Nualláin 1972) are for the pre-existing house. They average at 2600 ± 45 bc (S1–1450–54) and so all one can say of this site is that the tomb is later. It may be indeed that earlier dates will be obtained for the court-tombs, but as yet there is no evidence that they belong to the very beginning of the Neolithic period.

Likewise we have been stuck for a long time with theories about the wedge-tombs which are unsupported by the evidence, but which have been repeated so often that their protagonists and others have come to believe them as true and they are no longer prepared to question them or look at any other options. Here the statistics must be emphasized: 400 tombs, 19 excavations, 7 no pottery finds, beaker pottery from 6, tanged-and-barbed arrowheads from 3, fragments of stone moulds for bronze objects very doubtfully associated with 2 (Ó Nualláin 1979, 15), yet on this basis we are told that

> Though several [wedge-tombs] especially in Cork and Kerry, were very poor in finds and produced no primary pottery, *the frequent occurrence of Beaker pottery* [italics mine] and the barbed-and-tanged arrowheads which are typical of the beaker-using people securely assigns the type to the Early Bronze Age. A coarse bucket-shaped pottery is likewise very frequent. A few metal finds are also present (de Valera 1979, 128).

The coarse bucket-shaped pottery is the Neolithic ware that is well known from the court-tombs and from Neolithic domestic sites such as those at Lough-Gur in Co. Limerick (Ó Ríordáin 1954). The six most recently excavated wedge-tombs in the south of Ireland, four in Kerry in the very area where the builders from Brittany are said to have come ashore (Herity 1970, 10; Herity and Eogan 1977, 122) one in Co. Cork (O'Kelly 1958) and one in Tipperary (O'Kelly 1960), contained no beaker pottery, no tanged-and-barbed arrowheads and no evidence that the builders had a knowledge of metal. Herity (1970, 11) said 'No grave furniture has been found . . . though four tombs have been excavated. It may be that no pottery was ever deposited in the tombs, or that it has disintegrated in conditions unfavourable for its preservation . . . a cremated burial from one tomb is the only definite trace of ancient interment . . . ' The four tombs he is talking about are those excavated by

himself in the Ballinskelligs/Waterville area of Co. Kerry and in spite of the lack of evidence from them, he repeats the arguments so often put by de Valera and Ó Nualláin for 'a close association of the Beaker-makers and the wedge-builders' (Herity 1970, 10).

The group of potsherds from burial 1 in the wedge-tomb at Baurnadomeeny, Co. Tipperary, seems to have most affinity with the Neolithic shouldered bowl ceramics while the coarse ware sherds from under the cairn are also of late Neolithic type (O'Kelly 1960, 112). Beaker sherds have been found in the wedge-tomb at Lough Gur (Ó Ríordáin and Ó hIceadha 1955) as one element in a late Neolithic complex of sherds, but beaker material has been found in almost every type of early monument in that area so it is not surprising that it should have been intruded into the tomb. The other wedge-tombs that have contained the ware are in the northern half of Ireland in areas where, like Lough Gur, beaker ware is generally found on domestic sites, and it is probably intrusive in the wedges where it was found. No evidence has come up since 1960 when in writing about Baurnadomeeny (ills. 7 and 8) I said: 'We feel therefore that for the present, caution is necessary and suggest that the beaker-wedge equation should not be allowed to harden in our minds until more evidence in support of it is forthcoming from the monuments of Munster' (O'Kelly 1960, 113). If, as now seems likely, there were no Beaker people as such – that beaker pottery was part of the paraphernalia of a cult practice the ideas for which began to be disseminated in late Neolithic times (Burgess and Shennan 1976, Burgess 1978, 213) – wedge-tombs must represent another sect of the megalithic cult of the dead which Irish farmers evolved in the northern part of Ireland, the cult and tomb type later spreading into the deep south of the country. There is no good reason to derive the tombs from the *allées couvertes* of Brittany (Waddell 1974, 36). The detailed forms which the tombs took are no evidence of an invasion of Beaker or other people into this country.

As a support for the Beaker/Bronze Age dating for the wedge-tombs, the distribution pattern of the latter is linked with the distribution of copper ores and a close relationship between the two is seen particularly in the south-west in the Cork/Kerry area, and in the counties of Tipperary, Wicklow and Mayo (Herity 1970, 13: de Valera 1979, 123; Ó Nualláin 1979, 15) and this despite the absence of any hard evidence that Beaker people had anything to do with the wedge-tombs in these areas (Harbison 1973, 125, 129) or that the wedge-tomb builders, whoever they were, had anything to do with copper-mining (Harbison 1978, 103–4). The densest concentration of wedge-tombs,

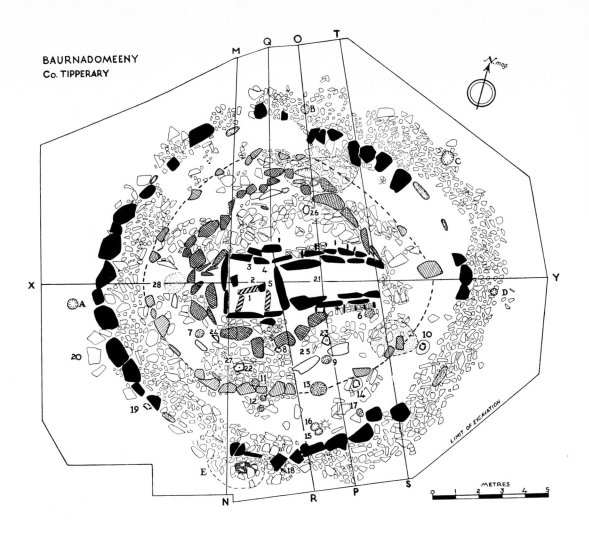

BAURNADOMEENY
Co. TIPPERARY

*7 Plan of wedge-tomb at Baurnadomeeny, Co. Tipperary.
(From* JCHAS *LXV (1960).)*

about seventy, is on the upper limestone plateau of north-west Co. Clare, a region that has no known metalliferous deposits. The reason given for this particular concentration is that the plateau provided grazing for cattle throughout the winter (de Valera 1979, 123; Ó Nualláin 1979, 15). Because most wedge-tombs are situated on hill-slopes and uplands, this is taken by the same writers to mean that the builders were mainly pastoralists, not cultivators, and, living near their tombs, they were on soils which would not have been forested so there would have been round-the-year grazing for their stocks. While all of this is possible and may even be true, there is no hard evidence for any of it. Settlements in upland areas that might even be thought of as belonging to the wedge-

tomb builders are not known (Herity 1970, 13). In some areas in Kerry not far from a few wedge-tombs, field systems enclosed by stone-built fences have become apparent as the blanket peat has been cut away for use locally as domestic fuel, but as yet there is no evidence to connect these fields with the tomb builders, though in time it may be shown that this is the case. Similar field systems recently found under the peat in Co. Mayo by Herity and Caulfield (1977, 50) are said to have belonged to the court-tomb builders of that area.

The most recently offered evidence in support of the wedge-tomb/Early Bronze Age equation is a comparison of the distributions of the wedges and Early Bronze Age cist graves and it is said that because the two distributions are complementary and mutually exclusive, the two types of burial must be contemporary, the wedge-tomb builders invading from the west, the cist-grave people invading from the east (de Valera

1979, 126, Harbison 1977, 20). Ó Nualláin (1979,15) repeats this assertion and says 'The picture is one of two communities living side by side but each preserving its own distinct traditions'. As there is no real evidence to show that the four hundred wedge-tombs were built in the Early Bronze Age, this distribution map comparison is a dubious exercise to say the best of it. Nor indeed is it certain that all the cists on the map made by Waddell (1970, 103) are of the Bronze Age, since several have had no grave-goods associated with the burials and have not been dated by any other means. It may be that some of them are late Neolithic, because the fashion for single-grave burial was already in vogue well before the end of the floruit of the megalithic tomb-building era.

In some respects it is strange that the current theory in regard to the portal-tombs should regard them so positively as an Irish invention with a firm birth-place in central Ulster. The theory of an origin there is based on similarities in structural detail between the portal-tombs and the court-tombs and undoubtedly some similarities do exist, though they are not more compelling than the structural similarities which one can find in all four main classes of tomb if one looks for *similarities* rather than *differences*. From central Ulster

there was an outward spread to east and west and thence down the coasts to Waterford on the one hand and to Clare and Cork on the other, with an extension to Wales and Cornwall from the Waterford limb (de Valera 1979, 112; Ó Nualláin 1979, 9). If one were imbued with an invasionist belief it would be easy to argue on the same evidence for a movement of people from Cornwall via Wales to Waterford and ultimately to central Ulster. The Dyffryn Ardudwy portal-tomb in Wales is an important staging point on the route whichever way the people were marching, for it produced characteristic shouldered bowl pottery of a kind as early as any in these islands (Powell 1963). I do not believe in a mass movement of people in either direction. The portal-tomb is another expression of the house-for-the-dead cult and as portal-tomb builders were living side-by-side with the people of the three other megalithic sects, there was much communication between them all and hence the similarities in their cult buildings.

8 Wedge-tomb at Baurnadomeeny, Co. Tipperary after excavation and conservation. (From JCHAS LXV *(1960); photo M.J. O'Kelly.)*

9 Portal-tomb at Kilmogue, Co. Kilkenny. (Photo M.J. O'Kelly.) (Visible height of right-hand upright: 3m.)

Thirteen of the twenty excavated portal-tombs have produced grave-goods that are comparable with those from the court-tombs: Neolithic period shouldered-bowl and flat-based coarse ware, leaf- and lozenge-shaped arrow- and javelin-heads and hollow scrapers, and all one can argue from this is the contemporaneity of the two classes of monument throughout the floruit periods of both. There is no real evidence for the derivation of one from the other.

Mound or cairn shape for the portal-tombs has occasioned much discussion and no conclusion has been reached. There is good evidence for a primary round mound – Dyffryn Ardudwy is an instance of an excavated site. There it could be shown that the long mound was an addition. This is no surprise because excavation has shown that some of the other tomb types were multi-period structures as for instance Site K, a satellite passage-tomb at Newgrange (O'Kelly *et al.* 1978) and the court-tomb at Annaghmare, Co. Armagh (Waterman 1965, 21, 37). No portal-tomb is known where an appreciable amount of mound survives and in my view this is because there never was a high mound. It is inconceivable that having erected the usually enormous capstone poised high over the entrance portals and sloping downward to the rear, its builders would have done anything to detract from their great feat (ill. 9). The piling up of a high mound would have done this. Just enough stone packing was put around the orthostats to keep them firm. Where some evidence of a long mound is present, this is no more than a token fulfilment of the local cult rule.

186

Orientation was important to the builders of many Neolithic monuments – easterly for court-tombs and some portal-tombs, south-west/north-east for most wedge-tombs, while in passage-tombs no very strong rule can as yet be determined. The dramatic effect of the orientation of Newgrange to the rising sun at the winter solstice has to be seen to be believed.

The carvings on the structural slabs of the passage-tombs have for long excited interest and comment and have been seen as decoration and art, as anthropomorphs and representations of the Earth Mother or Mother Goddess, as symbols of religion or magic, as indications of male and female sex, and more recently as a written language which, if we could only read it, would give us all the answers. Maybe indeed it contains elements of all these things and surely it had a significance for those who created the patterns and did the carvings as well as for those who just saw them in passing. But to what extent are all the interpretations and explanations of it merely the figments of the imaginations of modern-day scholars conditioned consciously or subliminally by the psychological climate in which they have lived? In my years of work at Newgrange I have heard from the general visitor as well as from experts in many fields, explanations and interpretations conceivable and inconceivable, sane and lunatic, all expressed with such conviction that it was often difficult to avoid being influenced and thereby being led into making a false record of what was actually carved on the stone. But the record is now made for Newgrange and will soon be published and all are welcome to make what they like of it. The work has been done by Claire O'Kelly who has also made a detailed study of the Boyne Valley carvings in general (1973; 1978) and I agree with her when she comments as follows:

> Within the relatively restricted framework of geometrical motifs it is clear that there was ample scope for Irish passage-grave builders to express individuality by characteristic groupings of motifs to which names such as Newgrange style, Loughcrew style etc., can be applied. Generally speaking, there is a definite similarity between all the decorated stones of a particular tomb. How much of the various styles are idiosyncratic, how much the product of particular or even personal, beliefs or cults . . . is one of the intriguing problems yet to be solved. Wide as the divergence between the different styles appears to be, it is minimal, however, compared with that between Irish passage-grave art and the Iberian and Breton examples with which it has been so often linked. Heretofore, the tendency has largely been to concentrate attention on alleged

anthropomorphic and representational elements in the Irish material . . . This has led to a linking of Irish carvings with a variety of media far removed spatially as well as chronologically. Irish passage-grave art has been said to be derived from the stone idols, amulets, stone plaques and small anthropomorphic figures found in Iberian tombs, for example, as well as from the designs engraved and painted on the walls of the tombs themselves.

Gavrinis in Brittany, has repeatedly been brought forward as an example, if not an exemplar, of Irish art, often without due regard to the fact that this tomb is an exotic in the context of both Breton and Irish art. Petit Mont (Arzon) has also been cited as an Irish parallel mainly on the strength of its zigzag and radial lines, but non-Irish motifs such as feet, axes and shields (*écussons*) are also present. Other putative sources are designs on pottery from Iberia and Scandinavia, but unless all or any of these proposed models can at the very least be shown to antedate the Irish examples, there is little point in the comparisons . . . Now that Newgrange has been shown to belong to the mid-third millennium BC, many of the above comparisons can be ruled out. Moreover, the overtly representational nature of much of the Breton and Iberian carvings indicates a fundamental difference which is not negatived by the fact that a small range of motifs such as arcs, U's, circles, radials, zigzags, etc., is held in common (O'Kelly, C. 1973, 28–9).

As Fleming (1969, 259) would have it: 'The mother-goddess [from Iberia & Brittany] has detained us for too long; let us disengage ourselves from her embrace.'

10 Kerbstone 52 at Newgrange — detail. (Reproduced by permission of the Commissioners of Public Works in Ireland.)

11 Back of kerbstone 13 at Newgrange. (Reproduced by permission of the Commissioners of Public Works in Ireland.)

*12 Newgrange now. (Reproduced by permission of the
Commissioners of Public Works in Ireland.)*

Conclusions

The introduction of the Neolithic way of life into
Ireland was a complicated process which was initiated
by late Mesolithic Irishmen who were constantly travelling abroad and returning. Pastoralism probably
came first and cereal cultivation a little later. Food production was well established here by 4000 bc.

Continuing to travel abroad, the Irish farmers
became caught up in the megalithic cult of the dead
and by 3000 bc were introducing at home the ideas of
the various sects, and so, while international threads
can be seen in the tomb types, the tombs are native versions built on these ideas.

All four types of Irish tombs were being built during more or less the same period of time. There was
much communication between the sects and many
borrowings took place. Each tomb built was an individual effort so that even within the sects there were
many experiments and elaborations. Many tombs are
multi-period structures, additions having been made as
circumstances demanded.

By 2000 bc, so much man-time/effort had been
spent on tomb building that there was an economic
collapse (Whittle 1978, Burgess 1978, 207). One has
only to think of the strain put upon the economy of
the Boyne Valley by the profligacy shown in the
building of the three great passage-tombs – Newgrange, Dowth and Knowth.

There is little evidence to support the oft repeated
Beaker/Early Bronze Age/wedge-tomb equation. Researches still in progress on the late Neolithic/Beaker
period pottery complex around the edge of the

188

Newgrange passage-tomb are showing that *all* the pottery types including the best beaker ware were locally made. The high-tin bronze axe from this horizon shows that metallurgy was well established in Ireland long before 2000 bc and long before Beaker pottery came upon the scene (O'Kelly and Shell 1978).

Irish archaeologists have so concerned themselves with searches abroad for the origins of Irish megalithic tombs that they have not had time to 'glory in the great achievement of Irish megalithic architecture in the 4th and 3rd millennia bc irrespective of where the first seeds came from. Newgrange is one of the great wonders of the prehistoric world of ancient Europe and far surpasses any comparable achievement in Spain or Brittany' (Daniel, *in lit.*, 21 December 1979). I wholeheartedly agree (ill. 12).

Bibliography

BAR   *British Archaeological Reports*
JCHAS   *Jour. Cork Hist. and Arch. Soc.*
JRSAI   *Jour. Roy. Soc. Antiquaries Ireland*
PPS   *Proceedings Prehist. Soc.*
PRIA   *Proceedings Roy. Irish Academy*
UJA   *Ulster Jour. Archaeology*

BURENHULT, G. 1980 'The Archaeological Excavation at Carrowmore, Co. Sligo. Ireland', in Malmer, M. P. (ed.), *Theses and Papers in North-European Archaeology 9*, Inst. of Archaeology, Univ. of Stockholm.

BURGESS, C. 1978 'The Background of Early Metal-working in Ireland and Britain', in Ryan, M. (ed.), *The Origins of Metallurgy in Atlantic Europe*, Proceedings of the Fifth Atlantic Colloquium, Dublin, 30 March to 4 April 1978, 207–14.

BURGESS, C. AND SHENNAN, S. 1976 'The Beaker Phenomenon: Some Suggestions' in Burgess, C. and Miket, (eds), *Settlement and Economy in the Third and Second Millennia* BC, *BAR* British Series 33, Oxford, 309–31.

CASE, H. J. 1969 'Settlement Patterns in the North Irish Neolithic', *UJA* XXXII, 3–27.

DE VALERA, R. 1960 'The Court Cairns of Ireland', *PRIA* 60, C, 9–140.

1965 'Transeptal Court Cairns', *JRSAI* XCV, 5–37.

1979, in S. P. Ó Ríordáin, *Antiquities of the Irish Countryside* 5th edn, London, 1–28.

DE VALERA, R. AND O NUALLAIN, S. 1972 *Megalithic Survey of Ireland* III, Dublin.

EOGAN, G. 1968 'Excavations at Knowth', *PRIA* 66, C, 299–400.

1969 'Excavations at Knowth, Co. Meath, 1968', *Antiquity* XLIII, 8–14.

1974 'Report on the Excavations at Knowth', *PRIA* 74, C, 11–112.

FAHY, E. M. 1961 'A Stone Circle, Hut and Dolmen at Bohonagh, Co. Cork', *JCHAS* LXVI, 93–104.

FLEMING, A. 1969 'The myth of the mother-goddess' *World Archaeology* I, 247–61.

HARBISON, P. 1973 'The Earlier Bronze Age in Ireland – Late 3rd Millennium – *c.* 1200 BC', *JRSAI* CIII, 93–152.

1977 'The Bronze Age' in Cone, P. (ed.), *The Treasures of Early Irish Art 1500* BC *to 1500* AD, New York, 18–24.

1978 'Who were Ireland's First Metallurgists?' in Ryan, M. (ed.), *The Origins of Metallurgy in Atlantic Europe*, Proceedings of the Fifth Atlantic Colloquium, Dublin, 30 March to 4 April 1978, 97–105.

HERITY, M. 1970 'The Prehistoric Peoples of Kerry: A Programme of Investigation', *Jour. Kerry Archaeological & Hist. Soc.* no. 3, 4–14.

1974 *Irish Passage Graves*, Dublin.

HERITY, M. AND EOGAN, G. 1977 *Ireland in Prehistory*, London.

MACALISTER, R.A.S., Armstrong, E.C.R. and Praeger, R. L1. 1912 'Bronze Age Cairns on Carrowkeel Mountain, Co. Sligo', *PRIA* 29, C, 311–47.

O'KELLY, C. 1973 'Passage-grave art in the Boyne Valley', *PPS* XXXIX, 354–82.

1978 *Illustrated Guide to Newgrange and the other Boyne Monuments*, Cork.

O'KELLY, M. J. 1949 'An Example of Passage-Grave Art from Co. Cork' *JCHAS* LIV, 8–10.

1958 'A Wedge-shaped Gallery-grave at Island, Co. Cork', *JRSAI* LXXXVII, 1–23.

1960 'A Wedge-shaped Gallery-grave at Baurna-domeeny, Co. Tipperary', *JCHAS* LXV, 85–115.

O'KELLY, M. J., LYNCH, F. M. AND O'KELLY, C. 1978 'Three Passage-graves at Newgrange', *PRIA* 78, C, 249–352.

O'KELLY, M. J. AND SHELL, C. A. 1978 'Stone ob-

MICHAEL J. O'KELLY

jects and a Bronze Axe from Newgrange, Co. Meath', in Ryan, M. (ed.), *The Origins of Metallurgy in Atlantic Europe*, Proceedings of the Fifth Atlantic Colloquium, Dublin, 30 March to 4 April 1978, 127–44

Ó NUALLÁIN, S. 1972 'A Neolithic House at Ballyglass near Ballycastle, Co. Mayo', *JRSAI* CII, 49–57.

1978 'Boulder Burials', *PRIA* 78, C, 75–114.

1979 'The Megalithic Tombs of Ireland, *Expedition XXI, 6–15.*

Ó RÍORDÁIN, S.P. 1954 'Lough Gur Excavations: Neolithic and Bronze Age Houses on Knockadoon' *PRIA* 56, C, 297–459.

Ó RÍORDÁIN, S. P. AND Ó HICEADHA, G. 1955 'Lough Gur Excavations: The Megalithic Tomb', *JRSAI* LXXXV, 34–50.

POWELL, T. G. E. 1963 'The Chambered Cairn at Dyffryn Ardudwy', *Antiquity* XXXVII, 19–24.

1966 *Prehistoric Art*, London.

RYAN, M. 1978 'Lough Boora Excavations', *An Taisce* (Ireland's Conservation Journal), II, no. 1 Jan/Feb., 13–14.

WADDELL, J. 1970 'Irish Bronze Age Cists', *JRSAI* C, 91–139.

1974 'On Some Aspects of the Late Neolithic and Early Bronze Age in Ireland', in Scott, B. G. and Walsh, D. E. (eds.), *Irish Archaeological Research Forum*, Belfast, 32–8.

1978 'The Invasion Hypothesis in Irish Archaeology' *Antiquity* LII, 121–8.

WATERMAN, R. D. 1965 'The Court Cairn at Annaghmare, Co. Armagh', *UJA* XXVIII, 3–46.

WHITTLE, A. W. R. 1978 'Resources and population in the British Neolithic', *Antiquity* LII, 34–42.

WOODMAN, P. C. 1978 *The Mesolithic in Ireland: Hunter Gatherers in an Insular Environment*, *BAR* British Series 58, Oxford, 1–360.

190

PART III : ARCHAEOLOGY AND THE PUBLIC

18 Introduction: The Public Face of the Past

Barry Cunliffe

WHEN SOME years ago Jacquetta Hawkes wrote that each generation gets the archaeology it deserves, she was issuing a salutary warning rather than simply making a passing observation. Archaeology is a public discipline – it always has been – but therein lies the problem. Whether we like it or not (and let us admit it there are many who do not) archaeology as a creative pursuit, rather like the theatre, is dependent upon its public. Brilliant plays can be written, yet until they are performed their existence is only partial – so I believe it is with archaeological research. (I can already hear the indrawn breaths between clenched teeth and the gasps of horror – but let us continue.) Unlike many forms of research which deal with increasingly obscure abstraction the archaeologist is attempting to explain the human condition and to provide a sufficient perspective to enable present generations to understand the dynamics, directions and deflections which have shaped our past and are thus determining the future. It is a wide brief and a responsible one and at its heart lies the need to communicate our perceived understanding of the past with present generations, and through their response the better to understand it. The sentiment is brilliantly echoed in T. S. Eliot's lines from East Coker, 'Time present and time past are both perhaps present in time future, and time future contained in time past'.

Those of us who were fortunate enough to study archaeology at St John's College under Glyn Daniel's gentle, concerned, supervision learnt this truth. We learnt to appreciate the strivings of our predecessors in their attempts to understand the past, we learnt that there were no glib short cuts to be taken through the vastly increasing volumes of raw data which had to be mastered, we were made to think across a broad canvas (one of the first undergraduate essays I had to write, on chariots, was entitled 'From Anyang to Anglesey') and above all we were taught that scholarship was not measured by the length of our footnotes, by the liberal use of jargon or by the complexity of our prose style, but by the simple clarity with which we could express our ideas. At a time when it was so easy to become frustrated by blinkered approaches to flint chips and irritated by pretentious theorizing, Glyn taught us that the pursuit of archaeology, properly conceived, could be a way of life of enormous fun. His throwaway line, 'Why does one lecture but to interest oneself?', has a far

deeper humility and awareness of the academic process than might at first be apparent!

This brief digression has served two purposes – it has allowed the writer to pay a deeply felt homage to his teacher and it has gone some way to explain why Glyn's friends have felt it proper to include in this volume a collection of papers reflecting his concern for the public face of the discipline.

Archaeology has always had a public. Until the middle of the nineteenth century that public was admittedly a privileged aristocratic one but already, in the early decades of the century, C. J. Thomsen at Copenhagen was encouraging rural workers to visit the archaeological collections at the National Museum. In Britain it was the Great Exhibition of 1851 that marked the turning point. In the heady days of high Victorian philanthropy which followed – a time when it was thought politically and morally advisable to begin to educate the workers – a knowledge of the past and of communal roots was avidly encouraged. After all, the concept of gradual modification, presented against a background of Darwinian evolutionary theory, was a useful redress to the dangerous ideas, prevalent in some areas, that revolution was the only acceptable form of social change. The Libraries, Museums and Gymnasiums Act of 1845 had empowered local authorities to establish public museums. By the time of the Exhibition there were about sixty in the country. The number rose rapidly and is now about a thousand.

To link the establishment of the local public museum in Britain directly to a deep-seated political fear of social upheaval is of course a gross oversimplification. Nonetheless it is abundantly clear in the writings of many Victorians that a knowledge of the past was fully recognized to provide a potentially stabilizing influence on the public. In the first half of the nineteenth century the population had not only doubled but had changed from being a rural to an urban-based society. As Toynbee pointed out in his famous Oxford lecture published in 1884, large-scale production and the resulting free competition led to the alienation and degradation of a large body of the rural producers. It followed that these people, now cooped up in our cities, cut off from their traditional rural roots, needed to be provided with a sense of perspective and to be shown their place in social evolution. The museum was the appropriate means of achieving this.

After the initial formative fervour of the Victorian era, our archaeological museums, fortunately perhaps, seem to have changed very little to match developing social attitudes. Their values and perspectives are much as they were a hundred years ago – the same emphasis on simple evolutionary theory and the same concern for the importance of the spectacular object. This dynamic conservatism is nowhere better illustrated than in the British Museum. Perhaps it is what the visitor demands but more likely, one suspects, it is because the traditional museum with its static, slice-through-time, approach is becoming so irrelevant that its shortcomings pass unnoticed and uncriticized.

The last twenty years has seen a spectacular increase in the number of special exhibitions presented, mainly, in London. Without enquiring too deeply into the political motives of the countries of origin, the simple fact is that these offerings have proved to be enormously successful – think back to the publicity surrounding the Chinese Exhibition, Tutankhamun, Pompeii, Bulgarian Treasures and the Vikings. Each one has presented spectacular material but set within the context of a people and a landscape, thus offering a cohesive view of a society. If that society was little known so much the better: even the familiar old Vikings have been repacked – trimmed, scrubbed and sanitized for human consumption. A cynic might see all this as pandering to modern demands for transient excitement, rather like the modern cinema – the Vikings, an epic adventure; Tutankhamun, a detective intrigue in an exotic setting; Pompeii 79, a disaster movie? While this may in part be true, the success of these exhibitions is, I believe, a far more healthy response – the demand of an increasingly sophisticated public who have become sufficiently archaeologically aware to want to approach a topic in much greater depth. One has only to read the exhibition captions or the accompanying guide catalogues to appreciate the solid academic content on offer. Yet still the nagging doubt remains: is it perhaps the gold and the gore that really attracts after all? It certainly encourages the colour magazines and the bandwagon publishers to provide publicity largely free of charge. Perhaps our museums might take up the challenge and back equally well-presented exhibitions centred around less that glitters and more that inspires enquiring thought.

An even more recent development in public archaeology is the creation of real-life simulations of the past. They range from the Museum of London's son-et-lumière, with a blast of hot air added, which introduces interminable queues of school children to the Great Fire of London, to full-size replicas of the Roman fort at the Lunt, an Iron Age farm at Butser or to the delights of storming Alesia at the Archeodrome near Beaune in the Côte d'Or. All good family fun and all adding a little to the strength of the discipline by catching a corner of the public imagination.

Of the alternative methods of presenting the results of our researches to the public, through publishing and television, others have written below (Eric Peters and Paul Jordan). Glyn Daniel has used both media to good effect to keep archaeology in the mind of a wide audience, while through the columns of *Antiquity* he has ensured that a more restricted following remain well informed on matters of current interest.

In recent years archaeological publishing has changed out of all recognition. Perhaps most dramatic has been the rise of specialist book clubs which have sprung up in several West European countries and in America to serve a faithful clientele avidly reading (or at least buying!) works on ancient history, local history and archaeology. The definition of this market has encouraged publishers more readily to commission volumes in these fields, secure in the knowledge that bulk sales to book clubs can usually be negotiated. This has had two effects: it has meant that a wide range of books, many of them excellent scholarly works, have been published when even a few years ago they would have been rejected; but it has also opened the flood gates to a lot that is second rate, written by those with little direct contact with archaeological research, as well as a constant stream of lunatic rubbish, usually twilight-of-the-gods nonsense, put together by the deranged or the unscrupulous. If we must accept the right of this fantasy fringe to exist (archaeology's equivalent to space films?), the least we can hope is that our more reputable publishers will forgo the quick returns of this genre in the interests of the integrity of their lists.

If Britain is by and large well served by its archaeological publishers, not so the rest of the world. The United States and many Western European countries do indeed generate their own popular archaeological literature, but a cursory examination of current lists and foreign bookshops gives the strong impression of a much lower annual output of titles (though in America the sales of an individual book can be very large). It could be argued that this shows the backward-looking propensities of the British, revelling in the past because they are scared of the future. Yet this is surely not so. It is much more likely to be because archaeology in Britain is part of the public awareness. We have, after all, a long tradition of communicating our work to a wide audience going back to 1842 when the *Illustrated London News* produced its first archaeological item. Newspaper coverage, and sometimes sponsorship, has

193

continued on an increasing scale since Sir Mortimer Wheeler involved the *Daily Mail* in his excavations at Caerleon in 1926. While more recently, as Paul Jordan describes below, Glyn Daniel and Sir Mortimer were responsible for presenting archaeology in an entertaining guise to the first generation of TV-centred families in the post-war era. It is hardly surprising that, with such a tradition of dedicated communication, an informed knowledge of the past should have entered the British consciousness.

All this is to the good of the discipline, not least because to survive any university-based or state-supported pursuit must constantly demonstrate its social and academic desirability, and whether we like it or not private sponsorship usually requires some guarantee of both. There can be little doubt that the work of those concerned to publicize and popularize archaeology during the last thirty years or so has been a deciding factor in helping archaeology, through public acclaim, to gain its position of pre-eminent respectability in the academic world (witness the number and strength of university archaeological departments) and has encouraged national and local government alike to build a substantial archaeological presence into the administrative structure of the country. A glance at school curricula demonstrates the increasing place of archaeology in teaching at all levels, and is a further reminder that public awareness of the past is still on the increase.

This brief eulogy is not intended to be self-congratulatory but a prelude to a warning. Our subject has benefited enormously from the efforts of people like Glyn Daniel. That benefit has helped to increase our number and magnify our resources and this in turn has led to a dramatic advance in the quality and scope of our research – but herein lies the problem. There is a danger that the discipline of archaeology will soon lose contact with the real world. Its vitality may well be dissipated between the rarefied atmosphere of theoretical model-building, the stifling boredom of computerized data manipulation, and the mindless rescuing of ill-considered trifles.

The dilemma was forcefully brought home to me a few years ago when I was in Tunis negotiating with the government in advance of the arrival of the British archaeological mission. Carthage, the third largest city of the classical world, was rapidly being engulfed by bungaloid growth and the problem was what to do and with what resources. In the evenings, after tramping the sites with UNESCO and Tunisian colleagues, I read David Clarke's magnificently stimulating *Models in Archaeology*. The two worlds of archaeology seemed very wide apart and largely unrelated. And, when on a subsequent visit, an American archaeologist

appeared on the scene concerned only with computerizing every scrap of data about the city, the situation became even more surreal. What we were all in danger of missing in emphasizing our different fringe interests was, in this example, the central reality of that great city and its place in the social development of European culture. It was much to the credit of the project director, Henry Hurst, and his fellow directors of the other national missions that polemics were bypassed, current trends cut down to size and, in consequence, so much was achieved.

The example is relevant here because the funds were made available by the British Government only after the relevant minister had been persuaded of the social and economic value of the work to Tunisia. The Tunisians for their part quite properly insisted that the sites be eventually laid out and explained for the benefit of visitors. Thus the story began with, and will end with, the simple need to communicate. In between archaeology has gained an enormous amount and, if the final levels of popular presentation are properly followed up, future archaeologists will profit from the establishment of an interested and informed public.

At a time when university finance is in an uncertain position and both local and national government are intent on cutting employees, the need for archaeologists to be able to justify their discipline and to present their work to a broader public in clear and interesting terms is all the greater. In its academic sphere, archaeology seems secure: for anyone to attempt to argue against its educational desirability would be perverse in the extreme. In other fields, however, and in particular in ensuring an acceptable level of funding for fieldwork, one suspects that a greater willingness to sell our wares in the market place is now called for. While some diehards may be perfectly content to see the demise of the more ungentlemanly pursuits which those of us who dare to leave the study engage in, the simple fact remains that any discipline that bases itself on the reworking of a static data base, however brilliant its theoretical thinking, is doomed to choke in its own irrelevance. There will only be an acceptable level of progress if the chain, model-building, research-design, fieldwork, assessment, model-building, is unbroken. At the moment we are in danger of losing our facility to forge the vital but costly link of fieldwork – unless, that is, our base of public support is widened.

Glyn well realized all this when, on returning to Cambridge after the war, he decided to devote a part of his time to the difficult and demanding art of *haute vulgarisation* – we are still reaping the benefits but in doing so our responsibilities to the future are immeasurably increased.

194

19 Archaeology and Publishing

Eric Peters

'ONE'S PEN just picks itself up and writes,' said Sir Mortimer Wheeler, possibly with uncharacteristic modesty; probably in perfect awareness that not every archaeologist, however brilliant, is an equally brilliant writer. The two abilities, at their best, are so rarely combined that the publisher often treads, if not a tightrope, a very narrow path between the well-written book or article that imparts little of importance, and the sadly pedestrian account of a subject that deserves something better and livelier. The latter will still interest the academic; it will not appeal to the intelligent but archaeologically only slightly-informed reader. And the former, especially if produced by a non-specialist writer, runs the risk of reaping a whirlwind of academic criticism. 'Bullshit archaeology' is Glyn Daniel's dismissive phrase for the meretricious, over-popularized or under-researched kind of book that lacks substance or significance. His references to sensational Press articles are even more colourful.

Glyn himself is on very safe ground, as an author/academic cast in the authentic Wheeler mould: respected archaeologist, incisive, often witty, writer. An expert, in fact, at *haute vulgarisation* – an expression that, implying as it does, fastidious, well-informed popularization, he regards as in no sense derogatory.

All the same, Glyn Daniel and Mortimer Wheeler, to both of whom is due so much of the credit for the vastly increased public interest in archaeology (and hence in books on the subject) in the last thirty years, must take a little responsibility for the inevitable too-popular or too-hurried (sometimes because topical) spin-offs, simply because spin-offs from the successful *are* inevitable. Their brilliant television series – Wheeler and Daniel were surely the Gielgud and Richardson of archaeology – is discussed elsewhere in this *Festschrift*; it did an immense amount to arouse public interest in the archaeologist's ceaseless task of, to use Jacquetta Hawkes's phrase, 're-awakening the memory of the world'. It helped, if not to create, certainly to nourish, a new market in book publishing.

In the mid-1950s, the biannual special Export edition of *The Bookseller*, which then, as in fact was the practice until 1977, combined archaeology with history in its introductory editorial pages, announced a mere eight to ten archaeological books per issue. The Spring 1980 issue carried two pages (forty-five titles):

'Floreat' (as a – not The – bookseller was heard to remark) 'Archaeologia!'.

Archaeologists had, of course, been publishing for an élite and limited public since the early nineteenth century; far earlier if the great antiquaries such as William Camden, John Aubrey, Edward Lhwyd, William Stukeley and others of that calibre are included, as they should be. Stuart Piggott, introducing his attractive book of essays, *Ruins in a Landscape* (1976), recalls that he had expressed the view some forty years earlier (*Antiquity* 1937) that 'the accurate and precise science which some of us would consider modern archaeology to be, began merely as an episode in the history of taste.'

As far as modern archaeology is concerned, Petrie's *Ten Years' Digging* (1892) may well have been one of the first books to reach a much wider readership. Referring to his work at Naqada, Margaret Murray wrote (*Antiquity* 1961): 'Petrie's previous work had roused so much interest that anyone with any pretensions to culture had some knowledge of the finds.'

The 1920s produced even more general interest in archaeology, with the publication of Howard Carter and Arthur Mace's first accounts of the Tutankhamun tomb discoveries. And for the discipline as a whole, Gordon Childe's *Dawn of European Civilisation* was a landmark. 'It was, and is, in its 1957 edition, a classic of archaeology,' wrote Glyn Daniel in his *Origins and Growth of Archaeology* (1967). Appropriately, its publication is the first entry for 1925 in the useful chronological table of main events in his *A Hundred and Fifty Years of Archaeology* (1975). It is interesting to see, rather lower in the notes on an archaeologically eventful year, 'Wheeler – *Prehistoric and Roman Wales*'. The reader with a taste for significant coincidence will be disappointed to know that this was not *quite* Sir Mortimer's first book; the kudos for that (if a Greek word is permissible in this context) belongs to the previous year, 1924.

A Hundred and Fifty Years. . . is itself a fascinating general survey, incorporating a valuable bibliography which includes many less-than-obvious secondary sources; it would be even more helpful to the amateur or the student had the promised asterisks, indicating books specially recommended for further reading, actually appeared.

1 *Walter Neurath (founder of Thames and Hudson),*
T. G. E. Powell and Glyn Daniel at a party to
celebrate the publication in 1964 of New Grange
by Sean P. Ó Ríordáin and Glyn Daniel.

Nineteen-fifty – the year in which this 'essential'
book (as more than one tutor and ex-student dubbed
it) first appeared in its earlier form – marked the
beginning of three decades from which the task of
choosing other classics of archaeological publishing has
become almost impossibly invidious, on simple
grounds of quantity, generally improving standards,
more precise specialization, and diversity – necessary
diversity – of approach. Challenge an academic, or
a well-qualified archaeological correspondent, to name
a book that he, or she, regards as outstanding, and the
former may well cite a particularly brilliant work in a
specialized field; of more general works, a frequent
choice is Colin Renfrew's *Before Civilisation* (1973)
(now, happily, in Pelican – Penguin Books have an
excellent archaeological publishing record, stretching
back over almost forty-five years, with Glyn Daniel as
archaeological adviser for fifteen of those years

(1965–79)). Rather more technical, *Science in Archaeology* (edited by Brothwell and Higgs) quickly
established itself as a standard work when published
first in 1963, though, as with all works of reference,
advances in knowledge have rendered parts of it out of
date, despite a second edition (1969). Where books on
individual sites are concerned, Leslie Alcock's *By South
Cadbury is that Camelot . . .* has won much praise, one
respected archaeological journalist describing the
author's Introduction as a superb exposition of what
archaeology has done, is doing, and can do.

The beginnings, nearly thirty years ago, of what a
popular newspaper was to describe, infelicitously, as
'the archaeological explosion', occurred partly because
the interest generated by television, and by a few
accessible (in the non-physical sense) books, produced
more would-be students, more university courses, and
hence the demand for more and yet more books.
Archaeology, once, like publishing, described as 'an
occupation for gentlemen', found itself living in two
worlds: academic, and commercial.

Nineteen-fifty also saw the appearance of the first
books from a small and very new publishing house:
Thames and Hudson, then housed in attic, but scarcely

196

2 Simon Young, Glyn Daniel and Eric Peters at a Thames and Hudson publishing party.

Attic, quarters in Holborn. Walter Neurath, its founder (ill. 1), though primarily concerned with the publication of high-quality art and topographical books, had the flair and, equally important, the courage, to back his conviction, based partly on previous European experience, that anthropological and archaeological books that were not strictly academic could succeed in Britain and America, and elsewhere in the world.

The first step was a series, 'The Past in the Present'. Its General Editor was Jacquetta Hawkes, who, as a trained and respected archaeologist and a superb writer, could well be described as having a foot in both camps – literary and academic. She had recently produced a phenomenally successful book, *A Land* (Cresset Press 1951). *A Land* was not strictly an archaeological book; it drew heavily on geology and on recorded history. So did the Thames and Hudson series, which included such titles as *Boats and Boatmen* (T.C. Lethbridge, 1952) and *Soil and Civilization* (Edward Hyams, 1952). It appealed to the kind of reader who had acclaimed *A Land*, and the fact that it was a series seemed to work in its favour. The active interest of the bookseller and the public was confirmed.

This encouraged Thames and Hudson to embark on a more specialized series, with which some readers of this *Festschrift* will not be unfamiliar: 'Ancient Peoples and Places'. It had propitious beginnings. Simon Young, later a Director of John Murray, then on the editorial staff of Thames and Hudson, was a former pupil of Glyn Daniel at Cambridge; a happy state of affairs that eased the introduction, in 1956, of a totally archaeological series under Glyn's General Editorship. The series was planned so that each book should appeal to the intelligent, educated amateur, and – which many titles seem to have done – to the academic whose specific experience lies elsewhere. The choice of titles has been catholic. Examples representing 'peoples' are *The Phoenicians* (Harden, 1962), *The Vikings* (Arbmann, 1961), *The Celts* (Powell, 1958 and 1980) and *The Sea Peoples* (Sandars, 1978); representing 'places', *Peru* (Bushnell, with which the series opened), *Early Christian Ireland* (de Paor 1958 and 1978), *Mexico* (Coe, 1962 and 1976) and *Babylon*

(Oates, 1979) – to select but a few. It has encompassed, moreover, topics that are neither peoples nor places, yet essentially archaeological, such as *Writing* (Diringer, 1962) and *Food in Antiquity* (Brothwell, 1969). This worldwide coverage has ensured an international sale – an essential ingredient in the continuing success of the series. The requirements of the American market have been met by exporting US editions, while foreign-language editions – some fourteen to date – have been produced by publishers in Europe and overseas.

'A P & P', the name by which it is widely known, though Glyn refers to it teasingly as 'Ancient Peepholes', has been, and is, an absorbing publishing experience for – one hopes – all concerned, working well on several levels, including, happily, the personal one. Just as well, since, with some twenty-five titles still in print in Britain, the hundredth is due to appear this year. Appropriately – naturally, in fact – it is written by the General Editor.

Any series, however, successful, has its disadvantages, as several publishers have discovered. 'Not *another* one of those!' may well greet the Rep, or the publisher's Publicity Department. On the other hand, a good reputation, once built up, is helpful; as, for several reasons, is a known and influential General Editor. 'T & H always seem to get exactly the right author', says the Archaeological Correspondent of the *Sunday Times,* Patricia Connor. 'Disadvantages? I can't think of any – except that once a series is established as authoritative, the occasional less-than-first-class book is going to be noticed. Keeping up that kind of standard must get more, not less, demanding.'

Within this series, and others which have followed it, keeping up the standard not only of authorship but also of production while holding the books' prices at a level which, if not low, is not unrealistic, has been helped in two ways. First, by judicious restyling, combining economy with a more up-to-date appearance. And second, by adoption of photolitho offset printing. This process, which has in recent years been very greatly improved, can now give high-quality reproduction of photographs, both monochrome and colour, on uncoated text paper, so that books can be 'integrated' (i.e. illustrations interposed where reference is made to them in the text). The previous system of printing text and line drawings by letterpress, and the photographs by gravure or photolitho, involved not only the use of two different kinds of paper, an expensive printing process and a more complex binding operation; it also meant that the plates were separated both from the relevant section of the text, and from drawings that supplemented or clarified them. This irritated many readers, who blamed

editorial whim rather than technical necessity, and it even evoked criticism from less knowledgeable reviewers and uninformed members of the book trade.

'A P & P' can surely, as it chalks up its century, claim to be the most extensive archaeological series yet published, though by no means the only one. In 1967 Thames and Hudson themselves launched, under the editorship of Sir Mortimer Wheeler, 'New Aspects of Antiquity', books written by archaeologists about their own recent work. And Glyn Daniel has guided the development of the 'World of Archaeology' series for the same publisher, as well as the 'Faber Archaeological Guides' – travel books with short introductory texts and lists of sites to be visited. Indeed, if the 1950s and early 1960s represented the pioneering era of 'A P & P', the 1970s were when archaeological publishing came into its own. Academic Press, a subsidiary of the big American house Harcourt Brace Jovanovich, put its resources behind a series called 'Studies in Archaeology' (Consulting Editor Stuart Struever), which by 1980 could claim some twenty-five weighty and often expensive titles. Arriving on the scene somewhat later, Cambridge University Press sought to tap the same scholarly market with 'New Studies in Archaeology' and (confusingly) 'New Directions in Archaeology'. Duckworth, a smaller concern, could nevertheless rival its larger brethren with 'Peoples of Roman Britain' (edited by Keith Branigan), 'New Approaches in Archaeology' (edited by Colin Renfrew) and a string of successful archaeology textbooks to its name. Smaller still, 'British Archaeological Reports', founded in 1974 by three part-time archaeologists in Oxford, cleverly saw the need for fast, cheap publication of the latest research, and soon established a long list of paperback titles with a worldwide sale by direct mail.

General publishers, too, cashed in on the growing popularity of archaeology. Magnus Magnusson, practised presenter of the BBC 'Chronicle' programme, brought together a strong team of authors in a series intended for teenagers – 'The Bodley Head Archaeologies'. And between 1975 and 1979 the Dutch-owned multinational, Elsevier, published a twenty-one volume history of mankind, 'The Making of the Past', through its subsidiaries, Elsevier-Phaidon in Oxford and E.P. Dutton in New York.

Barry Cunliffe, whose intelligent approach and easy, fluent style are greatly appreciated by publishers, is General Editor of a series for Routledge and Kegan Paul, 'The Archaeology of Britain', which promises to be impressive. Cunliffe's own *Iron Age Communities in Britain* (1974, 2nd edn 1977) was followed by Richard Bradley's *The Prehistoric Settlement of Britain* (1978), of which Glyn Daniel wrote in the *Guardian*:

198

'Could . . . the second volume in this series keep up the high standard set by Cunliffe? It does. It is a fresh and challenging account of pre-Roman Britain . . . making us think in terms of agriculture, herding, transhumance and nomadism.'

This review underlines Glyn's own long-held and, to our mind important, view that 'The craftmanship and the scientific techniques fall short of the fulfilment of archaeology unless transmuted by the art of historical interpretation and writing' (*A Hundred and Fifty Years of Archaeology*). This is a plea, also made by Jacquetta Hawkes ('The Proper Study of Mankind': *Antiquity* 1968), not merely for *haute vulgarisation* but for recognition of the fact that 'Archaeology exists for the service of history'.

The straightforward benefits to history *via* archaeology of scientific techniques such as radiocarbon dating, and the value of 'social archaeology', were brilliantly documented by Colin Renfrew (*Before Civilisation*) and in an interesting full-page article (*Guardian*, October 1973) which was, in fact, an abridged version of his inaugural lecture as Professor at the University of Southampton. (Colin Renfrew will be Disney Professor of Archaeology at Cambridge, as successor to Glyn Daniel.)

Such an article, surprisingly something of a rarity in the *Guardian*, underlines the fact that books are not the only publications to present archaeology to the public at every level from academic, through popular, to worryingly sensational. For reasons of time and space (sometimes far less of the latter than would fill a book is needed to report an important discovery or re-interpretation) periodicals are essential, as are museum publications and those of HMSO; the proceedings of learned societies and their journals (notably the *Proceedings of the Prehistoric Society* and the *Antiquaries Journal*) are of particular interest to the professional archaeologist.

Pride of place, inevitably, and in no way because its Editor's name is much in our minds at the moment, must go to *Antiquity*. Its articles are authoritative and largely topical, its book reviews are exceptionally useful to everyone – academic, student, librarian or knowledgeable amateur – who wishes or needs to buy books, but must discriminate between those that merely sound worthwhile and those that actually are. Since more than adequate space is given, and the most reliable reviewers chosen, they are genuinely informative. Plenty of room is found for both – or all – sides, of controversial issues, such as the 'New Archaeology', and a generous welcome is accorded new archaeological publications, both British and foreign.

The journal's present Editor, ably helped by a staff of 1.5 (this includes the Production Editor, Ruth Daniel, which fact explains the relative frequency of Staff Outings) took over the difficult-seeming task of succeeding the great O.G.S. Crawford in 1958, as Richard Atkinson discusses in more detail elsewhere in this *Festschrift*. *Antiquity*, 'the only archaeological publication with a gossip column', provides some splendid reading, even for those who, though interested, are outside the world of archaeology; this partly because the Editor looks, when it seems useful to do so, outside strictly academic circles. A naval officer who served for many years in the Mediterranean provided a highly practical article on 'The Ship of Odysseus' (XLIV 74, 1970); a practising dentist and extra-mural archaeology student contributed an extremely informative article on environmental and dietary factors in dental pathology (XXXVII 148, 1963). Academics are allowed their lighter moments (*vide* Philip Rahtz (XLIX 193, 1975) 'How likely is likely?' with its probability scale and 'glossary'). Glyn's own suggestion for registering *Antiquity*'s contributors as a religious body, with, for ceremonial purposes, an interesting cast (in order to claim parity with bogus Druids in the matter of entry to Stonehenge) makes hilarious reading – with a serious underlying purpose. Wit is a useful campaigning tool. 'Fiery stuff – bold and fiery, like grocer's port' is Glyn's comment on a controversial item in another periodical, and while we doubt the depth of his experience of grocer's port, the reference stays in the mind – as it was intended to.

The periodical in question, *Current Archaeology*, is in fact (I quote John Evans) 'a useful back-up to *Antiquity*'. Also produced by a husband-and-wife team, Andrew and Wendy Selkirk, it was founded in 1967, in some ways as successor to Miss Heighes Woodford's *Archaeological Newsletter*. *C A* is a small, but essentially practical and readable publication, aiming, to quote Andrew Selkirk, 'to bridge the gap between the full-time academic and the enlightened, perhaps partially-trained amateur'. The journal has, in fact, won approval (tempered, naturally, by occasional disagreements on controversial issues) from both camps. It is well illustrated, with photographs and drawings, and has given useful editorial support to independent projects, to which it now devotes one of its six yearly issues.

On a still less academic level, we now have *Popular Archaeology*, a monthly which, though appropriately titled, should not be dismissed for this reason since, with Magnus Magnusson as its first editor, it undoubtedly catches the eye of the general public, and provides a useful introduction to the subject for those who are interested without being deeply informed.

In too wide a dissemination of the whereabouts of archaeological sites, however, and of archaeological know-how, lies a danger to archaeology itself. Periodicals and Press articles devoted to the encouragement of uninformed and indiscriminate 'treasure hunting' would be better left unpublished. The potential harm, in spite of the fact that the amateur possessor of a metal detector occasionally becomes a genuine enthusiast to the point of accepting instruction and supervision, is too great. *Less* publication of this kind, not more, would be a service to archaeology.

At the opposite end of the 'Popular v. Academic' scale is *World Archaeology*, published by Routledge and Kegan Paul three times yearly, virtually in soft-cover book form. Each issue takes one subject as its theme for different contributions from respected archaeologists. It is usefully indexed, and theme titles of past issues are listed. With Warwick Bray of the Institute of Archaeology as Executive Editor, an Editorial Board that includes Barry Cunliffe, Ian Glover, Joan Oates and Derek Roe, and an Advisory Board drawn from the academics of eleven countries, *World Archaeology* is well placed to select and to attract the best authority on each single aspect of every theme dealt with.

A highly promising new publication is the *Archaeological Advertiser*, an illustrated journal issued by a West German firm of publishers and international booksellers. With its articles by recognized names – in several languages, though mainly in English – and its liberal advertising of archaeological books, this is an enterprising venture.

Among non-British periodicals that should be noted are *Archaeologia* (French), beautifully produced and well illustrated; in the US, *Archaeology* and the *American Journal of Archaeology* are sponsored by the Archaeological Institute of America, *American Antiquity* by the Society for American Archaeology, and now (since 1979) *Early Man* by Northwestern Archaeology, Illinois. Worthy of special mention is *Skalk* (Danish) which, though not unduly popularized, has an astonishing (in view of the total Danish population of little more than five million) subscription list of over 57,000.

Mention must also be made of archaeological features in non-specialist publications: the *Illustrated London News* – first in terms of chronology, and probably of quality – showed a highly intelligent interest in the subject which lasted throughout, and to some extent beyond, the full sixty years of Sir Bruce Ingram's editorship. He began, in 1900, as the youngest, and was finally to become the oldest, editor of a major publication in Britain. In the year when he became editor, a short account of Sir Flinders Petrie's work at Abydos was published. At the time of his death, the total of well-documented articles published was considerably

over 2,000. The *ILN* is now a monthly, and, though sound archaeological contributions are still included, scope for these is naturally limited. All the same, a great many readers (and at least one publisher's editor) of archaeological books were first attracted to the subject by the simple accident of their parents, and even their doctors or dentists, being subscribers to that much respected magazine. *Man, Current Anthropology* and *Nature* also carry the occasional archaeological feature, as does the *Scientific American*.

Newspapers tend, not unnaturally, to look, in archaeology as in other academic subjects, for news. Frauds, fakes, 'amazing finds', especially where valuable items are involved, often take precedence over more mundane-seeming but more significant reports. Archaeologists, professional and amateur, complain about the fact that, where news and features are noticeably separated, archaeology is more often than not treated as 'news' – which means that quite apart from the risk of being sensationalized, i.e. reduced to a paragraph in later editions or handled by sub-editors who lack background knowledge, they are often missed by readers who buy newspapers mainly for the features and arts coverage.

The *Observer*, for example, blotted a clean, though not noticeably well-filled, copy-book twenty years ago (but archaeologists' memories are long) by allowing Professor Palmer to rush into print with his conjectures about possible mis-dating of Minoan Linear B script, headlined with what Glyn described as 'vulgar, catch-fivepenny words' – a puzzling phrase, until one reflects that the *Observer*, at that time (July 1960), did cost five (old) pence. It has an improved, if sparse, record since, though archaeology is still usually treated as 'news', and there is no regular archaeological correspondent.

Both *The Times* and the *Daily Telegraph* (particularly in its excellent colour magazine) have shown active – and often financially useful – interest in archaeology. *The Times* has a long history of archaeological 'scoops' – the paper received constant reports from Schliemann during the Mycenae excavations, and actually secured, via Lord Carnarvon's friendship with John Jacob Astor, exclusive coverage of the Tutankhamun tomb discovery. 'Not so much the Curse of Tutankhamun; more the Curse of Beaverbrook' was the likely cause of subsequent fatalities, according to one of Lord Carnarvon's great-nephews, a certain Mr Auberon Waugh. *The Times* itself survived the curse, and has given good service to archaeology. Some seven years ago, it was decided that archaeological features should no longer take editorial pot-luck; reports from its own correspondent, Norman Hammond, and from contributors should be used as and when preparation time and space allowed, but should be authoritatively edited, and either published complete or held over; a practice that still (Autumn 1980) holds good.

The *Sunday Times* has its own correspondent, Patricia Connor, Cambridge-trained under Grahame Clark; her reports could be called complementary to *The Times'* articles. The *Sunday Times Colour Magazine* has produced effective archaeological features, and has a good record of what might be termed 'three-dimensional publishing', with Fishbourne as a prime example, and Jarrow a more recent one. Says Kenneth Pearson, Assistant Editor in charge of special projects, which have included major exhibitions:

Fishbourne was obviously something of enormous potential interest to the general public; it needed its own on-site museum, and we saw an opportunity of helping, using the kind of visual approach that has a lot in common with journalism. Times Newspapers agreed to provide £20,000-worth of sponsorship. We collected a team of cartographers, architects, designers, headed by Robin Wade – his first independent undertaking.

And indeed as Barry Cunliffe wrote: 'Newspaper techniques and design procedures made communicating a rather complicated archaeological site to the public much easier.' 'We must be mad, throwing away money like this', complained Lord Thomson in the early stages of the enterprise. He thought differently when, six months after the site and museum were opened, 25,000 people had already visited it. Naturally, large-scale coverage in the Colour Magazine helped.

The 1960s saw the growth not only of colour magazines, but of large-format, lavishly illustrated books, sometimes unkindly labelled – not always solely on the grounds of size – 'coffee-table'. In fact, there is no doubt that a subject which, especially for the non-academic, benefits from clear and pleasing visual presentation, merits the occasional large-format book, more particularly if it has a good text. Should such a book come to rest on a coffee table (there are worse places – the 'remainders' section of a bookshop, for example) it may attract attention that is more than cursory; the visual equivalent of 'word of mouth' should not be underestimated.

Thames and Hudson, in 1958, produced *A Picture History of Archaeology*, which was a largely pictorial version of C.W. Ceram's *Gods, Graves and Scholars*, a successful, though perhaps over-popularized book; three years later, *The Dawn of Civilization*: 'The first world survey of human cultures in early times', covering the development of society from 500,000 BC to AD 1600. It contained plates in colour and black and white, maps and reconstructions, plus two parallel texts: extended captions for the casual browser, and over a dozen chapters of scholarly, though never abstruse, text by leading archaeologists. Measuring 35.5 x 27.9 cm, and correspondingly thick, no doubt it fell into the coffee-table category. Many further large-format books followed: *inter alia, Roman Africa* (text by Mortimer Wheeler, photographs by Roger Wood); *Ancient Crete* (texts by Professors Alexiou and Platon, photographs by Leonard von Matt); *Ancient Mexico in Colour* (text by Ignacio Bernal, photographs by Irmgard Groth). The prices now seem ludicrously low, and even in the mid-1960s were reasonable. This fact, and indeed the fact that a large proportion of the big-scale illustrated books being produced came from Thames and Hudson, was the result of Walter Neurath's belief in international publishing. Plates for all editions, English-language and foreign, were usually printed in one country; foreign texts could then be overprinted as and when necessary. Other publishers were, of course, producing beautiful books at that time (midway between the post-war austerity that lingered into the early 1950s, and the poor economic climate of the late 1970s), but Thames and Hudson had the advantage of a strong network of worldwide archaeological contacts, many of them acquired through their own authors.

Economics account partially for the present reduction by all publishers in the number of really lavish books produced (though a big exhibition like 'Tutankhamun' or 'The Vikings' will generate a spate of books, some, if not all, of intrinsic value). The cost of paper, printing and distribution has soared, and in addition, except where new discoveries are made, there is difficulty in obtaining photographs that actually make fresh statements about sites or objects without evoking cries of 'So many obvious gaps' from readers familiar with previous books. Patricia Connor has several times deplored the iconography of recent productions: 'Not more than 10% new photographs in some books; once a standard has been set, too many publishers seem content to do virtually no independent picture research. Or they leave it to the archaeologist, who may not have much experience of photography that's meant to be much more than a factual record.' One sees both sides of that question; economics remain a prime factor in so highly specialized a publishing field.

In such a field, the role of the publisher's editor, if not an uneasy one, can produce some uneasy moments. Obviously, some general background knowledge must be acquired, if only to avoid bombarding authors with elementary queries, and to simplify proof corrections. This necessity, for the present writer, has been

201

one of the more rewarding aspects of the job. Another bonus is the simple fact that archaeologists, though they may be – are, in fact – demanding (when it comes to timing and accuracy; hardly ever in commercial terms) are remarkably pleasant people.

They also, for at least one obvious reason, operate on a different time-scale from those of us who must conform to printing schedules, and who are given to wondering, when dealing with a series such as 'A P & P' whether it will be this year, next year, sometime or never that an obvious gap can be filled.

One consoles oneself with the thought that editors have suffered similarly for at least three centuries. His re-editing of Camden's *Britannia* itself gave Edmund Gibson a few headaches along with the triumphs. To Tanner, 1693-4:

> If you were to trot every day along Cat Street, and after a turn or two in the Schools' quadrangle, to adjourn to Tom Swift's, I could excuse you for not sending your papers sooner. But when a man's cloistered up in an old monkish lodge, and the very Phys of his chamber is nothing but antiquitie itself; for such a one to make delays is a little intolerable. If you knew how I am persecuted, you would not keep them a moment longer; old John Aubrey is dayly upon me . . . (Bodleian MS quoted by Piggott in the Reckitt lecture for 1951, reprinted in *Ruins in a Landscape*).

Now, as then, the pace of the academic life – not to mention its demands, which sometimes include administrative as well as tutorial duties – is not conducive to rapid production of manuscripts. The long-distance record time between signing of contract and delivery of manuscript (still not accomplished) is currently, in the case of 'A P & P', a full twenty years, easily beating the previous one – a mere eighteen years, with the book now safely in print.

Delay is inevitable and understandable when actual fieldwork or excavation on the subject in hand is still in progress; books on archaeology are now all too easily overtaken by events, or by changes in interpretation. As Derek Roe wrote (*Prehistory* 1968): 'No new book on prehistory is now ever likely to be wholly up to date, even at the moment of publication, thanks to the magnificent acceleration of research and discovery,' adding resignedly 'But all any author can do about that is to await with interest, and perhaps trepidation, the new facts which are bound to emerge while his book is in the press.'

When new facts do emerge, the publisher faces the problem of whether, and if so when, to bring out a revised edition. The author will naturally urge him to do this in double-quick time (lest he be considered uninformed). Canny authors firmly date their prefaces – a wise precaution, since a completely revised edition, produced, perhaps, before the previous printing is exhausted, is not feasible, though a certain number of relatively minor changes can be incorporated in a new impression of the original.

Not all textual changes are deliberate. Hell knows no fury like that of the author (and, by implication, the editor) who is chided by reviewers for errors that crept into a text *after* final correction of proofs. That this happens increasingly often may be due to speeded-up printing processes, to more and more complex archaeological terminology, or simply to Murphy's Law, which affects some professions more than others.

At such times, the editor wonders, briefly, whether he might not have slept more peacefully at night (if, perhaps, more frequently during the day) had he undertaken the handling of – say – the novels of Miss Barbara Cartland, whose readers and reviewers are unlikely to cavil at historical or chronological oddities, or indeed, at lesser errors.

These misgivings do not last. A few minutes in a good bookshop, a glowing review in a respected periodical, and, above all, a couple of hours with an articulate, often witty and almost invariably charming archaeological author are enough to restore sanity and even reduce the sensation of total personal uselessness. Helping these books on their way, in however unimportant a capacity, is a good way of spending one's working life. I have spent twenty-five years of *my* working life in intermittent but invariably stimulating semi-subordination to the wide-ranging enthusiasms of Glyn Daniel. The greatest pleasure of all is yet to come – the editing of his long-threatened book on 'The Lunatic Fringe'.

20   Dons and Detection

Jessica Mann

ST CHRISTOPHER's College, Oxford; Fisher College, Cambridge; Shrewsbury College, Oxford; even (since overtaken by reality) St Anthony's: what is the connection between these plausible but non-existent establishments? Those who know the oldest centres of English learning only through literature might be forgiven for believing that 'in the older and more beautiful of the two ancient universities . . . Fisher College lies between Trinity and St. John's, and stretches from Trinity Street down to the Cam,' or that one who drives into Oxford over Magdalen Bridge, down Long Wall Street and St Cross Road, will find Shrewsbury College where Balliol's cricket ground should be. Many tourists search for these colleges unknown to guidebooks.

It is from works of fiction set in these colleges, that outsiders take their ideas of what goes on within their mysterious walls – foremost, of course, murder; but almost without exception such books include descriptions of High Table and Combination Room traditions widely accepted as accurate. What nostalgia and affection has gone into the accounts of the dons' menus, their ceremonies, traditions and cellars! Typical of these celebrations of the civilized life is the opening paragraph of *The Mummy Case* (1933) by Dermot Morrah:

> The hum of after-dinner talk subsided for a moment as the Provost and Fellows of Beaumont College, Oxford, suspended their several conversations to take an informed and critical interest in the opening of another bottle of port. Denys Sargent, the Junior Fellow, on whom the celebration of this rite devolved, manipulated his corkscrew, napkins and decanters with the air of a cardinal. . . .

Typical too is the self-congratulation of those who partake in such rituals. One Master, regretting the absence of visitors from High Table, says, 'Nevertheless, however small, we remain, I hope, as any collection of Fisher dons should be, distinguished and scholarly.' Perhaps this is how the members of Senior Common Rooms do behave; for while the individual colleges and most of their members are products of their authors' invention, it is the familiar university environment that is the most memorable feature of what reviewers tend to call 'Donnish Detection'.

Readers have always loved to be reminded by English detective novels of the places in which the story is set. Cyril Connolly, homesick in Europe, would console himself 'walking with Inspector French round the Mumbles, gazing down winter estuaries, making innumerable railway journeys, exploring Rochester with Thorndyke, going with Mr Fletcher to country towns, till I could find my way in any of them to the Doctor's pleasant Georgian house, the rectory, the spinster's cottage, the eccentric lawyer's office . . . ' In Connolly's opinion, such books were the last repository of the countryside, their local colour beautiful as well as useful. Somerset Maugham was another who always read home-based detective novels on his travels.

Other enthusiasts have written, as well as read, detective novels, partly, at least, in order to re-create beloved landscapes. Fisher College's sixteenth-century courtyards and 'Wren' bridge appeared together in 1945; its founder was in India, on leave in 'The Hills' when he wrote about a precisely detailed college and the life its members led, in a Cambridge swept 'by raw sharp winds which blew from off the dank fens, and the grey-cold North Sea'. The present writer, who for three years devoted to Dilwyn Rees's *The Cambridge Murders*, and other crime stories, time which should have been spent on Glyn Daniel's Chambered Tombs, was relieved to find that even dons sometimes neglected archaeology for detection; for *Welcome Death* (1954) was written not as a distraction from the interpretation of air photographs in India, but when its author, no longer pseudonymous, was back in Cambridge as a university lecturer, and the book is set in his native Wales. His one Cambridge novel is unusual, in that, unlike 'the other place', Cambridge has rarely been the scene of fictional murders, and two of the best detective stories set there, by Margery Allingham and P.D. James, are more to do with town than gown. T.H. White's *Darkness at Pemberley* (1932), a 'locked room' puzzle story set in a Cambridge college, was his one really unsuccessful novel. Margaret Yorke, whose own books include several with an Oxford don as detective, postulated that Cambridge, being 'strong on science', deals with criminological facts, while Oxford, whose atmosphere induces introspection, inspires crime in fantasy (*Murder Ink*, 1977).

Conan Doyle, the initiator of so much in detective fiction, gave Sherlock Holmes only one university problem to solve, in *The Adventure of The Three Students* (1895). Holmes was distracted from his own scholarly pursuit (research into Early British Charters, which Watson hinted had some striking results) by a summons to St Luke's College. Whether it was in Oxford or Cambridge has been the subject of ponderous but inconclusive discussion. Holmes was begged to identify which of three undergraduates had tampered with the examination papers for a valuable scholarship. Holmes finds the bedroom arrangements of the college tutor charmingly old-fashioned, accepts that a cheat wanting to see which passage of Thucydides would be set for translation needed to copy the whole thing out, and agrees that the appropriate punishment for the culprit is to become a police officer – admittedly, in Rhodesia. It is not one of his major achievements.

Once dons themselves are the detectives, and even more when dons are also the authors, university crimes are the prelude to considerably more soul searching and theory.

An Oxford Tragedy, by J.C. Masterman, appeared in 1933. Masterman was a don at Christ Church at the time. Years later, as Provost of Worcester College, he wrote another novel, but his style had been especially suited to The Golden Age of Detective Fiction, as commentators call the period between the two World Wars, and *The Case of the Four Friends* (1956) was less successful. *An Oxford Tragedy* reinforces the message that a don's real life is conducted within his college's walls. A recent crime novel by Amanda Cross (Professor Carolyn Heilbrun) gives an acid, outsider's view of this, and of the behaviour of men in university society. Her amateur detective is an American Professor of English, whose visit to Oxford provides her with a picture of a place where the women are slaves, left hungry and lonely somewhere in the suburbs, while their husbands guzzle elaborate dinners in hall. She returns to liberated America with relief (*The Question of Max*, 1976). This book was written more than half a century after *An Oxford Tragedy*, and generations after dons were first permitted to marry; no wonder that donnish detection set in these conservative institutions seems to 'date' so little.

In Masterman's St Thomas's College, the cloistered quadrangle is contrasted with the harsh outside; the senior tutor realizes how he is unfitted for dealing with a tougher and less academic world.

For years I had lived the easy life of leisure and learning, hurting no one, content with my well ordered, cultured, intellectual life. How easy it had always been over the port and coffee to discuss with

enlightened and broad-minded calm, the affairs of a troubled but distant world.

Murder within the college sanctuary brings home to him that he, like his colleagues, has been too long protected from realities. Violence, in every case, becomes the passport for the outside world's intrusion. It is perhaps the very incongruity between learning and unreason, between the ivory tower and its surroundings, which made dons interested in crime's possibilities. For the essence of the traditional detective novel is that crime should burst upon a community which is accustomed to peace and order. The role of the detective is that of the *deus ex machina*. He must ensure that life can return to normal once the mystery is solved and the criminal punished. It would be pleasant to believe that normality is as blameless as the detective novels imply.

Dorothy L. Sayers also used her Oxford novel as an expression of nostalgia. Hers was the longing of an academic manquée, a brilliant student forced out into the world of commerce. Her version of Somerville ('Shrewsbury College') was resented by the dons of 1933 when *Gaudy Night* appeared, since she had written as though the customs she remembered from her own undergraduate days (1912–1915) had survived unmodernized, and some of the women dons in her novel were both recognizable and, they thought, ludicrous. Sayers intended that this novel should be a vehicle for some of her deepest convictions, and she felt that its message, about intellectual integrity and academic values, was one she needed to impart. She wished to show that both were essential not only in scholarship, but in the conduct of life. Her criminal was driven by emotion uncontrolled by the brain. There has been much dispute as to whether *Gaudy Night* is one of the best crime novels ever written, or whether it is a disastrous misuse of what should be a light and ultimately un-serious branch of fiction. In fact the majority of readers probably ignored the treatise on ethics in their eagerness to follow the prolonged courtship of Peter Wimsey and Harriet Vane; either way, the detection is the least memorable part of the book.

One could never accuse the most prolific of the donnish detective writers of excessive solemnity. Michael Innes's plots occasionally touch upon important issues; *Hare Sitting Up* (1958) is about the uses of nuclear power, and *Operation Pax* (1950) on the merits of artificially neutralizing the aggression in human nature, but Innes is nothing if not passionless. One never for one single moment has the impression that his characters are more than puppets stepping through the plot, and it is the manner, not the matter, which is enjoyable. His places are especially vivid; nobody could forget the description of underground Oxford in the bowels of Bodley, from *Operation Pax*, or, for that matter, Professor Bultitude/Bowra.

Innes was an undergraduate at Oxford, and for 24 years, was a don there. Like other writers, he set his first detective novel in an Oxford from which he was far distant, on a long sea voyage to Australia in 1934. Its self-explanatory title was *Death at The President's Lodgings*. In it he introduced his series detective, the erudite Inspector Appleby, who has a 'schooled but still free intelligence', quotes lavishly from obscure examples of English literature, is knowledgeable about art, music and modern dance, and is often able to discomfit others with his fund of esoteric information. Where else in fiction would somebody confronted by 'the fourteen bulky volumes of the Argentorati Athenaeus' murmur, 'The Deipnosophists. . . . Schweighauser's edition. . . takes up a lot of room . . . Dindorf's compacter . . . and there he is.'? His first book was immediately acclaimed as putting him in the front rank of detective novelists; his second, *Hamlet Revenge* (1936) was said to put him in a class by himself. At the time of writing, he has published forty-two crime stories and many more volumes of fiction and criticism in his real name of J.I.M. Stewart. His combination of urbane learning and sharp plotting, with an occasional excursion into Stevensonian adventure, has made him widely popular. He has said that his aim in writing crime fiction is solely to entertain, 'to make a little merry', and he regards the genre as the purest escape literature. It is not always easy for a reader to see the difference between the crime fiction and Stewart's 'straight' novels, and some of the later work has been convoluted and self-conscious; but his early novels were witty and ingenious, and are among the best detective novels ever written.

Any closed community is particularly suitable for the traditional detective story, and the inward-looking habit of colleges makes them a perfect setting; those rooms with sported oaks, those locked courts or quadrangles, provide endless ways of fictionally limiting opportunities and multiplying motives. Provincial universities have never seemed so enticing. Michael Innes, whose first academic post had been at the University of Leeds, exposed some of the pretensions of redbrick in *The Weight of the Evidence* (1944) and in *Old Hall, New Hall* (1956), in which a sprawl of army huts and red brick boxes around the Old Hall's Georgian façade immediately identify this former University College as something very different from more ancient and august universities.

On the other hand, J. J. Connington (Professor Alfred Walter Stewart, 1880–1947) was a very prolific

crime writer who never mentioned higher educational establishments in his work, although he was the son of the Dean of Faculties at Glasgow University, and later Professor of Chemistry there himself. He was careful not to talk shop, but this very avoidance of using his own special knowledge may be the reason that his work is now forgotten; in his prime, his novels were regarded as among the best of his day. They represent the purest puzzle type of detective fiction, being expanded mathematical problems, in which the permutations and combinations of victims and murderers are discussed in orderly sequence.

Provincial universities do appear in modern crime novels, sometimes very enjoyably; but more contemporary dons choose to write novels which are funny or farcical, rather than mysteries.

It is not only the colleges of Oxford and Cambridge which enhance donnish detection; Oxford and Cambridge dons are among the most successful amateur detectives. What is more, apart from Edmund Crispin's Gervase Fen, who is a Professor of English based on Crispin's Oxford tutor, W.G. Moore, archaeological dons are the most numerous. Naturally the first to be mentioned must be Glyn Daniel's Professor Sir Richard Cherrington, FRS, FBA, D.Sc, MA, Vice-President of Fisher College, Member of the Athenaeum and the United University Club, and Professor of Prehistory in the University of Cambridge. With hindsight we may recognize a certain proleptic, or even prophetic, self-portrayal in this worldly, learned bon-viveur, unable to make up his mind whether scholarship was just another animal pleasure, like a squirrel's in collecting nuts, or whether in it could be found 'something transcending brute nature, something of the spirit – the eternal, unsatisfied, quest for truth.'

It was not surprising that Cherrington's author made him an archaeologist; but writers whose own specialities have lain in other disciplines have also concluded that the qualities of the archaeologist are useful to the detective. One such appears in John Trench's *Docken Dead* (1953), although archaeology is merely the reason for the hero's presence at the events in the story, not the means by which he interprets them. The archaeologist Stanley Casson makes an amateur archaeologist say (*Murder By Burial*, 1938), 'I often think that a highly expert archaeologist would make a perfect detective. He has the education that the best of professional policemen often lack and the knowledge of *things* as such that the theorist and literary man never has at all.'

A few years later, R.G. Collingwood drew this analogy in less frivolous vein. In his chapter on Historical Evidence, in *The Idea of History* (1946), he discussed a tale of the murder of John Doe, the suspicion of Richard Roe and the detection by Inspector Jenkins of Scotland Yard. He used it to show that, apart from the rules of evidence, 'the analogy between legal and historical methods is of some value for the understanding of history'. Elsewhere he says that 'the hero of a detective novel is thinking exactly like a historian when from indications of the most varied kinds, he constructs an imaginary picture of how a crime was committed and by whom.' Collingwood compared the methods of Sherlock Holmes, which were the collection of everything that might conceivably turn out to be a clue, with those of Hercule Poirot, who insisted that the secret of detection was to use 'the little grey cells' – in other words, Collingwood said, 'you can't collect your evidence before you begin thinking'.

The fact is that scientists, scholars and detectives alike must work by similar methods, either the Baconian gathering of minutiae, or the Cartesian use of logic and reason. As Professor Marjorie Nicolson said (*The Professor and the Detective*, 1929), 'scholars are in the end only the detective of thoughts . . . methods and conclusions are the same.'

Of all scholars, the archaeologist's methods most approximate to the detective's; each must accumulate, classify and interpret a wide range of material clues. Perhaps for this reason Dermot Morrah, Fellow of All Souls, not himself an archaeologist, gave that profession to his detective in *The Mummy Case*, who becomes gripped by the interest of collecting murder clues, which he sees as a problem of pure archaeological technique. The murderer and his victim are both Egyptologists, and one of the causes of their mutual hatred is the ownership of 'the oldest royal mummy in the world'. Having committed his crime, the Oxford Professor of Egyptology realizes that this acquisition of a fresh, unpickled, human corpse, is the opportunity of his lifetime, and he spends the long vacation making it into a mummy. 'There's nothing like the empiric method in archaeology,' he says, having solved many of the perplexities which had puzzled Egyptologists for generations.

Academic obsession frequently drives the criminals in such stories. Katharine Farrar, the wife of an Oxford theologian, invented a monomaniac zoologist, who stole a colleague's baby to be the foster child of his favourite chimpanzee (*The Missing Link*, 1952). A scholar equally lacking in sense of proportion is the subject of C.E. Vulliamy's *Don among the Dead Men* (1952), a novel set in the university of Ockham, which is indistinguishable in all but name from Oxford. The murderer is a chemist who discovers an untraceable poison. He decides that he would be performing a

public service by removing some of society's enemies, identified, of course, by himself. At first his motives are worthy, but as the gap between madness and sanity narrows, he uses his poison more selfishly, and less carefully. In the end Vulliamy repeated a trick which he used in other books; the murderer is convicted and punished for the one death he did not cause. Like most academic story-tellers, Vulliamy used fiction to draw moral and philosophical conclusions.

There are many more dons who are detectives, and detective novelists, than there has been space to consider, though it is necessary at least to list the names of Mgr. Ronald Knox, G.D.H. and Margaret Cole and Nicholas Blake (C.Day Lewis). However there are few academic thriller writers, and few donnish adventurers. Action thrillers excite the emotions without necessarily engaging the brain; their form is episodic and romantic. Detective stories offer their readers the classic intellectual satisfaction of what Edgar Allen Poe called, in this context, ratiocination, by their logical elucidation of mystery. This pleasure can be derived even from works otherwise devoid of literary merit. As Jacques Barzun, one of the leading authorities on the history of crime novels, has said, 'detective fiction belongs to the kind of narrative properly called the tale. . . . it does not pretend to social significance, nor does it probe the depths of the soul . . . the tale appeals to curiosity, wonder and the love of ingenuity' (*Catalogue of Crime*, 1971).

It is not surprising that dons, their whole training and experience in ratiocination, should choose this detective form for their fiction, rather than thrillers, or psychological dissection of deviant motive; in that area, they know what unfavourable comparisons with major literature they might attract. For, unlike many less scholarly novelists, dons are usually enthusiastic readers of the type of fiction they choose to write. Glyn Daniel was following a precedent, when he read a detective story and said to Stuart Piggott, 'I could do a better one than that,' and came back from his leave with its manuscript.

Bibliography

Barzun and Taylor 1971 *A Catalogue of Crime*, New York.

Casson, Stanley 1938 *Murder by Burial*, London (Penguin 1943).

Collingwood, R.G. 1946 *The Idea of History*, Oxford.

Connolly, Cyril 1973 *The Evening Colonnade*, London.

CROSS, AMANDA 1976 *The Question of Max*, London.
DANIEL, GLYN 1954 *Welcome Death*, London.
FARRAR, KATHARINE 1952 *The Missing Link*, London.
IINNES, MICHAEL 1934 *Death at the President's Lodgings*, London.
1936 *Hamlet Revenge*, London.
1944 *The Weight of the Evidence*, London.
1950 *Operation Pax*, London.
1956 *Old Hall, New Hall*, London.
1956 *Hare Sitting Up*, London.
MASTERMAN, J.C. 1933 *An Oxford Tragedy*, London.

1956 *The Case of the Four Friends*, London.
MORRAH, DERMOT 1933 *The Mummy Case*, London.
NICOLSON, MARJORIE 1929 *The Professor and the Detective, Atlantic Monthly*.
REES, DILWYN 1945 *The Cambridge Murders*, London.
SAYERS, DOROTHY L. 1933 *Gaudy Night . . .* , London.
TRENCH, JOHN 1953 *Docken Dead*, London.
VULLIAMY, C.E. 1952 *Don Among the Dead Men*, London.
WINN, DILYS (ed.) 1977 *Murder Ink*, Newton Abbot.

21 Archaeology and Television

Paul Jordan

'WELL, dear boy, that was a complete flop and we shall hear no more about it!' Glyn Daniel reports these words of Sir Mortimer Wheeler's as they parted on the Central Line on their way back from taking part in a trial run of a new television archaeological quiz in October 1952. The quiz was to be called 'Animal, Vegetable, Mineral?' and, with Dr Glyn Daniel and Sir Mortimer Wheeler as its star turns (ill. 3), it began transmission only a few weeks later and ran for six years. The late Paul Johnstone, producer of that series and its rich succession, has related that when he joined BBC television at the beginning of October 1952, he was given three weeks to get this series on the air: Sir Mortimer Wheeler's dim view of the programme's prospects could not take into account the treadmill effect in television production, whereby almost anything once written into the schedules, however unpromising and fraught with difficulties, must needs be transmitted on schedule in the end. As it happened in this case, 'Animal, Vegetable, Mineral?' was an immediate success and went on to father a long line of archaeological programmes and series on television.

'Animal, Vegetable, Mineral?' was itself based upon an American television success of the time called 'What in the World?' in which two or three experts were gathered around a plinth, with a chairman in the background under a map of the world, and invited to identify objects placed upon it which might come from anywhere and any period. AVM, as the British

1 *An early appearance before the camera: Glyn Daniel in 'Target for Tonight', 1941. (Photo Imperial War Museum.)*

series is fondly abbreviated, dispensed with the map of the world and sat its three panellists opposite the chairman with his score-card and invited them to accept the challenge of a particular museum in identifying objects from its collection.

The programme's popularity was enormous and its participants, particularly Sir Mortimer Wheeler and Dr Glyn Daniel, became household names. Glyn

207

2 GED broadcasting on Indian radio, 1945.

*3 GED and Sir Mortimer Wheeler on 'Animal,
Vegetable, Mineral?', c. 1954.*

Daniel was voted 'Television Personality of the Year'
in 1955 (Wheeler preceded him by a year). His chair-
manship of AVM was derived from his previous participation in a radio series called 'The Archaeologist'
which had been transmitted since 1949; and in fact the
23rd of October of that year was not the first time he
had 'faced the cameras', for he appears in a brief scene
in the famous war-time drama-documentary 'Target
for Tonight' (ill. 1), interpreting air photographs at
Medmenham.

When Paul Johnstone died in 1976, his *Times*
obituary commented upon the popularity of AVM: 'It
was an instant and spectacular success. Libraries found
that neglected shelves of archaeological books were

suddenly empty.' Archaeology did indeed become a
very popular interest and not only libraries profited by
it – museums too, thanks to the museum challenge
format devised for the programme, experienced an
upsurge of interest in their collections.

Sadly, only an extract of about ten minutes from one
programme of the six years' run of AVM survives:
by today's standards the pace is a little slow, and the
long-held caption cards that tell the audience at home
what the object in question is reckoned to be make few
concessions to popular acquaintance with the arcana of
the subject. But the civilized good humour of the
chairman and panellists and their joint enthusiasm for
the objects of their study come through very clearly (as
luck has had it, Gordon Childe joins Wheeler and
Daniel in this surviving fragment). It seems certain
that it was the combination of a congenial subject
matter, brought to life by attractive or at least
intriguing artifacts, with the signally enthusiastic
learning on the part of the participants that made
AVM so great and influential a success through some
150 programmes. The programme perfectly fulfilled
that part of the BBC charter which calls for broadcasting both to inform and entertain; and the entertainment quite frequently leaned towards the anecdotal and idiosyncratic with stories from Sir Mortimer
Wheeler about 'being there when it was dug up' or
incidents of accidental damage to the precious museum
items or, on one occasion, the unorthodox use of an
Australian Aboriginal death-stick in an attempt to
strike at millions through the medium of the television
tube!

The continuing popularity of AVM caused Glyn
Daniel and Paul Johnstone to ponder the introduction
of a new series of archaeological programmes that
would deal with single topics and give them a full
television treatment. In Paul Johnstone, as in a number
of other cases, the BBC found itself employing a 'don
manqué' as Glyn Daniel has called him (he went on to
be elected F.S.A): he had a sure instinct for what was
reputable in a scholarly way, however ingenious he
might be in popularizing it. Together, Johnstone and
Daniel established the tone of worthwhile archaeological programmes on television that has lasted till
today and spread beyond the BBC to other companies
at home and abroad. Their rectitude about archaeology
on television works to this day to promote serious
programmes about real archaeology and keep out too
much in the way of the lunatic preoccupations of
fringe archaeology.

The new series they created was called 'Buried
Treasure' and ran from the middle of 1955 until early
1959: so that for nearly four years AVM and 'Buried
Treasure' were transmitted more or less concurrently.

Especially for those of us who were in our fifth and sixth forms at the time, this was really the Golden Age of archaeology on television: archaeology was attracting the public in general, exercising museums and libraries, but with these television programmes it was also engaging the interests of the next generation of diggers and archaeology students, making for itself a much broader academic and professional constituency than it had ever enjoyed before. It is not too much to say that these programmes created the 'classes of '59 and '60 and '61' that have gone on to include some of our leading academic archaeologists and excavators and even television producers; and through them, the interest has continued and grown with succeeding years.

But AVM and 'Buried Treasure' were always intended to be popular programmes, and popular they were. Indeed in the days of single channel television, and afterwards when ITV reception was initially restricted, these programmes were phenomenally popular – as the awards of 'Television Personality of the Year' indicate. The proof was there that the viewing public could welcome serious programmes like these about the past history of our human civili-

4 *A caricature of GED and Wheeler in the 1950s, from Punch magazine.*

5 *GED and Wheeler in Brittany for 'Buried Treasure', 1956. (Photo Barbara Johnstone.)*

6 *Paul Johnstone, Richard Atkinson, GED and Stuart Piggott on location.*

zation. A glance at some of the subject-titles of the 'Buried Treasure' series reveals the riches that were broadcast: Tollund Man, The Piltdown Fraud, The Etruscans, Jericho, Pompeii, Mohenjo-Daro, Maiden Castle, The Mammoth Hunters, Skara Brae (ills 7, 8), Zimbabwe. But the powers-that-were in the BBC, with a Sixties' relish for all things new and current as against the past and the reflective, turned away from archaeology on television for several years – to the certain deprivation of a substantial slice of the television audience that had been encouraged to enjoy these programmes.

Glyn Daniel became a founder director of the board of Anglia Television in 1957, when the independent television franchise for the area of East Anglia was awarded to that company. He has maintained a special interest in archaeological and historical programmes there to this day. During the years when the BBC was ignoring archaeology on television – with the exception of some Further Education programmes overseen by Paul Johnstone – Anglia Television made the beginnings of its own career in programmes about archaeology. In 1962, a six-part series was produced on the ecology and prehistory of East Anglia with R. Rainbird Clarke, called 'Once a Kingdom', and two years later came a programme on the prehistory and history of Colchester. And then in 1966 the whole ITV network broadcast the Anglia Production 'Who Were The British?' produced by Forbes Taylor, in which Dr Brian Hope-Taylor (a television 'natural') examined the background and effects of the Roman

occupation of Britain. 'Who Were The British?' was a significant innovation in terms of archaeology on television (at least on network television) for it was a six-part series devoted to a single theme. Thus there had been a progression from the scholarly panel games of AVM, through the single-programme expositions of archaeological topics in 'Buried Treasure', to major series dealing with meaty subjects that expected a dedicated audience to want to keep on watching. Thereafter, the series idea was to go on recommending itself for archaeological programmes.

1966 also saw the revival of the BBC's interest in archaeology. Paul Johnstone attracted a huge audience on BBC-1 with his story of the Sutton Hoo discovery and the elevation of David Attenborough to the controllership of BBC-2 brought about the right circumstances for a new strand of archaeological programmes to be created. An Archaeology and History Unit was formed, with Paul Johnstone as executive producer. Glyn Daniel presented some of the early programmes of this unit and was programme adviser there until the untimely death of Paul Johnstone in 1976. Gordon Watkins, head of General Features in the BBC when the unit was formed, coined the title 'Chronicle' to reflect the historical as well as archaeological element in the series which is still there. Since June 1966, 'Chronicle' has – like the Windmill – 'never closed', and has regularly turned out programmes ranging from magazine round-ups of British archaeological news to, increasingly, single treatments of excavations and archaeological stories at home and often abroad. 'Chronicle' has enjoyed many notable successes – like the re-examination of Tutankhamun's mummy in 1969, the return of Brunel's 'Great Britain', 'The Tree that Put the Clock Back' (on radiocarbon revisions), the Sir Mortimer Wheeler profile, Pompeii with Barry Cunliffe, the Glozel fraud, the Macedonian Tomb. 'Chronicle' broke new ground in sponsoring the Silbury Hill excavation in the late sixties, even if the hoped-for spectacular climax eluded the diggers and programme-makers at the centre of the mound. And 'Chronicle' has also kept up the honourable tradition of experimental archaeology pioneered by Paul Johnstone and Glyn Daniel in 'Buried Treasure', episodes like the punting and sledging of a bluestone replica up the Avon and across Salisbury Plain to Stonehenge or the dressing up of Dr Daniel in cowhide costume to live the Stone Age life at Skara Brae. 'Chronicle' has given us experimental Sumerian war-chariots and the reconstruction of the Lunt fort at Coventry; in the hundredth 'Chronicle', the programme experimented upon the archaeologists themselves, pressing them to a feast made up of reconstructed prehistoric, Egyptian and Roman courses. Sir Mortimer Wheeler, who had once pronounced upon the consolations of suicide when faced with a 'Buried Treasure' reconstruction of Tollund Man's last meal, was here seen more cheerily biting into a huge slice of melon and eyeing the serving girls. In such sponsorship of the actual practice of archaeology as experiments and even digs, television has not merely drawn on archaeology to make its programmes but contributed directly to the progress of the subject.

'Chronicle' has fathered a number of offspring in the form of specials and series. At first the series were of short programmes, like the thirteen-part 'Tutankhamun's Egypt' that coincided with the exhibition, or the industrial archaeology and firearms series, but since 'BC – The Archaeology of the Bible Lands' (and before that, the anthropological 'Tribal Eye') increasingly autonomous and substantial series have been produced.

Anglia TV has been keeping up its archaeological output with more series, like 'The Lost Centuries' with Brian Hope-Taylor of 1971, and programmes about industrial archaeology, aerial photography and urban archaeology. And other countries have been making archaeological programmes too (as well as buying into British ones in co-production arrangements). 'Chronicle' has over the years drawn on, for example, Scandinavian, French, Italian and Australian material – almost always adapting as well as merely translating these offerings. The Americans, whose 'What in the World?' shared in the birth of the whole genre, were for a long time more concerned to co-produce financially on British productions rather than make much of their own. When Glyn Daniel was Visiting Professor at Harvard in the early seventies, Paul Johnstone took over a number of 'Buried Treasure' and 'Chronicle' programmes to show there and elsewhere and, three years later, the exercise bore fruit in a BBC co-production with one of the American public broadcasting stations to make a programme about Colonial Williamsburg. The public broadcasting system is now making archaeological programmes of its own, very much in the British tradition created by Glyn Daniel and Paul Johnstone. Still, no other country in the world maintains the sort of regular programming of serious archaeology programmes that the British enjoy.

Since the beginning, archaeology programmes have been popular on television. Curiously enough, they are often quite difficult to make. The difficulty depends upon the sort of subject involved, for there are several sorts of television archaeology programme. There are programmes which tell an established story, whether of discovery in the past or of some aspect of an

7 *GED being made up for a part in the 'Buried Treasure' programme about Skara Brae.*

8 *GED in his cowhide costume for the Skara Brae film.*

ancient site or culture; and there are programmes which follow the course of a current discovery or investigation. The obvious difficulty with the latter is that, while the chase may be exciting, the quarry may not be brought down at the end. This is the sort of risk that is particularly involved in following the progress of an excavation; and if, as has happened, the results of the digging do not constitute much in the way of what is popularly judged to be 'finding something' (meaning portable objects of reasonable size and completeness), then the recourse of the programme-makers must be to try and explain the intellectual interest of the work. That is in the honourable tradition established by Glyn Daniel and Paul Johnstone with 'Buried Treasure', but there is no doubt that it can be difficult to bring off when the ideas to be presented are abstract and remote from common knowledge. Difficult but not impossible, as Colin Renfrew's exposition of his Melos dig showed. But that programme benefited from an engaging setting and the finding of some attractive pieces: rainy days in England with only desultory and muddied finds make the job harder. But with all the difficulties, and even in the case of programmes which inevitably do not do justice to the intellectual importance of the discoveries they chart, there is no doubt that any television programme about a dig or any sort of archaeological investigation can always at least convey the atmosphere of the work and the personalities of the people involved: it can give the right feel about its subject and stimulate the audience to further interest. At this level, any good archaeological programme also helps in some way to dispel the misapprehensions and mistaken assumptions of the lunatic fringe.

Programmes which set out to tell an established story have some advantages over the ones that follow the course of discoveries. The end is known and the shape established before production begins. 'Buried Treasure' pioneered this sort of programme and 'Who Were the British?' raised it to the level of a concentrated series. Such story programmes can document the course of historical excavations, like Pompeii or Nimrud, or the careers of famous archaeologists, like Schliemann or Wheeler; or they can plot the vagaries of archaeological frauds and the detective work that unmasks them. At their grandest, in the form of many-part series, they can set out to present the audience with comprehensive views of whole ancient cultures, like 'BC – The Archaeology of the Bible Lands' and 'The Lost Centuries'. Such series are terrifically educative and, as they go on being made and extended in scope, their power to enlighten the public as to the best thinking of the archaeological specialists must prove to be not only a valuable source of entertainment

and information but also a needed antidote to the slap-dash irrationalism of the 'ancient-gods-and-spacemen' school. The very popularity of the latter indicates the desirability of some more missionary work in that direction.

There are some difficulties with these expository programmes too, and indeed with all television programmes that carry a heavy information content, whether it be the relative chronologies of Bronze Age sites in the eastern Mediterranean or the complexities of particle physics: the ordinary viewer cannot stop the unfolding of the programme and pause to think about what is being said as he might with a book; if he misses anything, he has missed it for good, unless he watches a repeat or uses a video-recorder; and he can only look at anything for as long as the producers have wanted or been able to leave it on the screen, while he might examine a photograph in a book for minutes on end. These circumstances call for a different level of content on television from what one would offer in a book, and some television archaeology programmes have erred in the direction of too much information too rapidly and too densely purveyed – a fault shared with a good many science and arts programmes in general. Even when this error is perpetrated, however, the virtues of visual atmosphere, of flavour of personalities and of the general 'feel' of the subject can still come through.

Three forms of presentation have evolved till now for the putting over of subjects like archaeology and history, science and the arts on television. The form developed by 'Buried Treasure', which is still in use because it is so useful, involves the presence of an 'anchor-man' to welcome the audience and conduct them through the subject, talking directly to the viewers through the lens of the camera and interviewing any other participants on the audience's behalf. The first such anchor-man was a professional archaeologist, Glyn Daniel himself, and other archaeologists, like Brian Hope-Taylor with the Anglia series and Barry Cunliffe at Pompeii, have made a success of this style: The best known of such presenters is, of course, the redoubtable Magnus Magnusson – not a professional archaeologist by training but a Saga scholar as well as a journalist. His experience and assurance have benefited a huge number of programmes.

Another presentation style uses no anchor-man but lets one or a number of academic and professional archaeologists talk to an unseen presence sitting beside the camera who focusses the audience's curiosities and concerns. A single figure may still dominate the programme, as Colin Renfrew did on Melos, or an assembly of participants may all contribute, but the programme as a whole stands back a bit from the

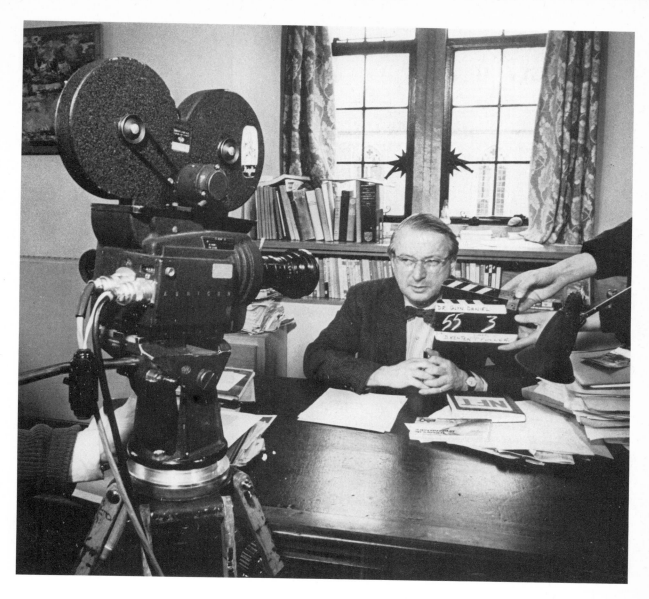

9 Filming GED in his Cambridge rooms for an Anglia Television production, 1971. (Photo Anglia Television.)

subject and its protagonists, and is less of a 'personal view.' The third form uses no contributors at all and is more of a concerted piece of creation on the part of its writer and producer, like the 'Chronicle' film about Champollion and the Decipherment of the Egyptian Hieroglyphics. This sort of thing is more difficult to bring off and there have not been so many programmes like it.

There is no doubt about the popularity of archaeology on television. That archaeology as such is a popular interest has been very largely brought about by the long tradition of television programmes concerned with it: a tradition which reaches back now for getting on for thirty years. Television and archaeology are met in a satisfyingly symbiotic relationship,

feeding upon each other, and generating in the process public information and enlightenment and new recruits for both the academic and the professional pursuit of the study. There will be more archaeology on television, more of the regular strands like 'Chronicle' and more of the substantial series and specials too, and all these programmes will owe a great debt to the pioneering days of AVM and 'Buried Treasure'.

213

22 Amateurs and Archaeologists: Some Early Contributions to British Palaeolithic Studies

Derek Roe

THE ROLE of the amateur in archaeology is increasingly debated in Britain and doubtless elsewhere. Professional archaeologists of the academic kind even set professionally academic examination questions about it for their students and as often as not award a noncommittal 'beta plus' for the answer: of the students, some will become professional archaeologists and some amateurs, while some will take no further part in archaeology at all. These days, the examination results may play a not-insignificant role in determining this. It would be pure speculation if the present writer were to assert that relatively few of those destined to become professional archaeologists answer examination questions on that topic. But the debate is far from being simply an academic one. There is a formidable public appetite for archaeology, nowhere near satisfied by a diet of literature at all levels, television programmes, spectacular exhibitions, visits to sites and monuments, evening classes and local lecture series. Shown how fascinating archaeology is, and how apparently easy – for the failures and difficulties get little publicity – much of the audience wants to get in on the act, muddy boots and all. Some want to render active help in a good cause, some to prove theories or satisfy their own curiosity; for others, it is doubtless the unfailing lure of buried treasure or the chance of themselves making a spectacular find of great antiquity that will redirect the thinking of scholars. In the latter case, only an incorrigible Palaeolithic specialist would overstretch evolutionary theories by tracing such robustly human instincts back to the early Old Stone Age and the primeval urges of man the hunter. In a world where the trophies of the food quest now come packaged in impenetrable polythene and a little too ready to hand, other outlets for the hunting instinct are certainly needed, but it is still a little ironic that Early Man himself has become a quarry pursued with all the cunning of evolving technology. By no means all the discoveries of hominid fossils have been made by professionals; the Swanscombe skull fragments, the only surviving British hominid find of Lower Palaeolithic age, are a case in point.

In any case, there can be no doubt that the massive public desire for participation in archaeology has been the most potent force in creating the present abundance of amateur talent and amateur enthusiasm, which far transcends the simple situation of there being too few professional posts to go round. For this public interest, which has many highly satisfactory aspects, Professor Daniel can claim a fair measure of responsibility. His 1950s 'Animal, Vegetable, Mineral?' television series clearly played an important part in the original capture of the public's imagination, and many still remember the programmes as amongst the best of all television archaeology, even though they were transmitted so long ago that the equipment used is now probably of interest to industrial archaeologists.

How very different is this present situation from that which existed before the explosive expansion of mass communication. Those who debate the roles of amateurs and professionals may not always recall that, to go back only to the beginning of the present century, let alone the last quarter of the nineteenth century, is to enter a world in which professional posts in 'pure' archaeology hardly existed at all. There were a few museum curatorships, but most lacked specialization; archaeology had made no impact on the universities in its own right; there were no prototypes for the regional archaeological units of today. It was scarcely possible, in fact, to make a living as an archaeologist and from this it follows that much of the basic work of archaeological discovery, and even of synthesis and publication, was performed by amateurs. There were, of course, different sorts of amateur, from prominent and wealthy men of considerable scholarship, whose range was international – such as Sir John Evans – to ordinary members of the public with the urge and talent to collect antiquities and study the remote past in their own immediate areas. Amongst the latter, the quality of achievement naturally varies a great deal, and archaeologists of the present day might be forgiven for wondering whether it is worth spending any time at all considering such men and their work. A 'backward-looking curiosity' is all very well, but has not Professor Daniel in several of his books already provided us with an elegant history of archaeology over the past century and a half? What did such people contribute to the development of modern archaeological method or anthropological theory? Should we really spend valuable time on them when sites are being destroyed every day and there is so much to be done and written?

To these questions the present writer would reply, at least in respect of those who worked on the British Palaeolithic, that the early collections and the records left by those who assembled them, so far from being useless, are actually an essential study for anyone who is actively researching in the same field today. 'Gold-mine' is hardly too strong a metaphor, though maybe 'oil-field' is now stronger language – and perhaps more appropriate, because there is also a certain amount of natural gas, not all able to be exploited: some of the local antiquaries got their syntheses right (according to our present criteria), and others got them magnificently wrong. No doubt similar comments could be made about the contribution of early amateurs to the archaeology of the more recent periods in Britain, but one might still draw a certain distinction in that the intensity of local Palaeolithic studies in Britain has declined while the amount of attention devoted to the later periods has increased. Again, there are far more well-preserved sites of all kinds in Britain for the later periods than there are for the Palaeolithic, and amongst them there must be a certain degree of repetition, even if each occurrence has unique features; it is not too difficult to find known sites of the Neolithic onwards that could profitably be excavated or re-excavated to pursue particular lines of research if the funds were in hand. But how many British sites of Palaeolithic age with a similar known potential are now readily available? And, with the exception of caves, which are rare, it is no easy matter to locate promising new ones from surface indications. Whether we like it or not, we must accept that the early amateur workers often made the only direct observations that will ever be made of some of our best Palaeolithic occurrences, especially in the Lower Palaeolithic. As examples we may quote the observations of W.G. Smith (1894, 1916) at Caddington, Stoke Newington, Gaddesden Row and Round Green; J.E. Sainty (1927) and his colleagues at Whitlingham; W. Underwood (1913) and S.H. Warren (1933) at Dovercourt; Warren again at Clacton-on-Sea (1911, 1922 and several well-known later papers); F.C.J. Spurrell (1880, 1884) and R.H. Chandler (1916) at Crayford; or N.F. Layard (1903, 1904) and J.R. Moir (1918, 1931) at various important and interesting sites in the Gipping Valley and the Ipswich area.

Sometimes the aid of professional geologists or palaeontologists was enlisted, or one of the few professional archaeologists might get a look in. R.A. Smith of the British Museum must certainly count as a professional archaeologist: he had experience of many periods and the present writer may be quite wrong in thinking of the Palaeolithic as his chief interest. What little we know of the remarkable Levalloisian factory site at Baker's Hole, Northfleet, depends heavily on his account (1911), and the same might be said of the Acheulian site of Tilehurst near Reading (R.A. Smith 1915). Yet so often, as in these two cases, he was following up the initiative of amateurs who had worked at the sites and brought them to his attention. The same applied to his studies of sites in the valley of the Kentish Stour, notably Sturry and Fordwich (Dewey and Smith 1924, R.A. Smith 1933), where he gives special recognition in his reports to the work of Dr A.G. Ince, a meticulous local amateur. It is distinctly unusual at this period to find reports of wholly 'professional' Palaeolithic fieldwork, like the British Museum sponsored excavations at Swanscombe and Rickmansworth reported by Dewey and Smith (1914, 1915).

Some of the obscure-looking references quoted above are in fact the principal sources for the sites to which they refer, and the sites themselves have long been quarried away. It is true that sometimes deposits remained at sites studied in the nineteenth or early twentieth centuries, for new excavations to be made under 'modern scientific conditions', as we rather arrogantly describe them, though our successors may think otherwise. Hoxne, Swanscombe (Barnfield Pit), the Clacton Channel and High Lodge, Mildenhall, are all outstanding British sites, of considerable importance to the whole European sequence; all were studied during the period we have been considering, and each has been the scene of a major and fruitful programme of excavation in the late 1960s or the 1970s. In other cases, attempts were made to re-excavate old sites and it was found that little or nothing of the former glory remained.

Caddington and Stoke Newington are examples of this, as the present writer can testify at first hand. Yet even where new work has been successfully carried out, the earlier observations have remained crucial and have often been vindicated. Nor should it be thought that the major contributions by amateurs ended with the expansion of professional posts in archaeology: as just a few examples of the many important discoveries made by amateurs of much more recent times might be mentioned the work of P.J. Tester in north Kent, J.B. Calkin in Sussex and Hampshire, J.C. Draper in south Hampshire or L.W. Carpenter in Surrey. And the work of the local amateurs, of course, continues. If it seems that the quantity of information they produce is now less, we should remember that they do not have their predecessors' advantage of watching the slow hand-digging of gravel deposits, and also that many of the important Middle and early Upper Pleistocene gravels are now worked out or built over; modern mechanized gravel extraction is often concerned with

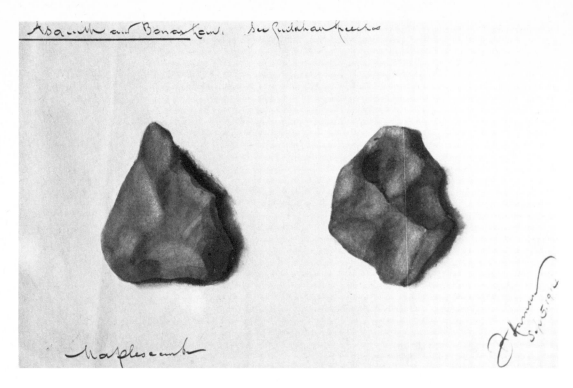

1 *Watercolour drawing by Benjamin Harrison, dated 1914, of two of his finds from Maplescombe, Kent. Original, 28 x 19 cm.*

the lowest and youngest terraces in the river valleys and with deposits below the present water-table.

Space does not permit a proper exploration or evaluation here of the early or more recent work briefly mentioned above, or of an at least equal quantity that has had to be omitted, or even documentation of the examples given with full references, though the writer has listed a good number of these in a forthcoming book (Roe 1981, in press). They make important and often fascinating reading and do not seem to be nearly as widely known in professional circles as they deserve, though few are really difficult to obtain. Those who do not care to make the effort to find them are in effect writing off the study of a major part of the British Palaeolithic. It is true that the terminology of the earlier papers is in places archaic and much of the more general discussion has been superseded, but it is the recorded observations of the archaeological material that are most important. The language is often splendidly clear: indeed, it is to be hoped that many will prefer W.G. Smith's description (1894, 103) of his discovery at Caddington of 'a working

place where every artificial chip of flint is as sharp as a knife, and where every flake rests in the precise place where it originally fell from the hands and stone hammers of the primeval workers in flint' to a more 1980ish version, which might claim 'the hypothesized occurrence of a high-density primary context lithic reduction area rich in debitage'. In fact the quality of Smith's actual description of the Caddington finds in his book *Man the Primeval Savage*, including his work on the conjoining of flakes, has not often been surpassed in the literature of the British Palaeolithic since his day.

Worthington Smith is one of the few local antiquaries to have been the subject of any biographical account other than an obituary: see the two admirable and informative essays about him by J.F. Dyer (1959, 1978). Another is Benjamin Harrison, of eoliths fame, a splendid character and a dedicated and productive worker, whose life and correspondence were recorded by his son, Sir Edward Harrison (1928), in a book that deserves to be far more widely known and has great entertainment value as well as containing much useful information.

To us now, the whole slow course of the great eoliths controversy seems obscure and remote: the passage of some small ship hull down across the horizon of our own experience. Yet at the time an im-

216

mense amount of intellectual energy went into the arguments for and against Benjamin Harrison's specimens: were these chipped stones from the Kentish Tertiary deposits really artifacts, really old, really the work of 'Plateau Man'? Sir Joseph Prestwich was convinced, and his was a powerful voice. Other distinguished figures were ranged on each side: Sir John Evans against, General Pitt-Rivers for, Sir John Lubbock (Lord Avebury) for, Boyd Dawkins against, and so forth. Throughout it all, Benjamin Harrison continued to live in Ightham and to run the village general shop which he had inherited from his father, while the scientific world beat a path to his door. He maintained a lively correspondence with many of the leading experts in archaeology, geology and various of the natural sciences; he roamed and collected all over the land around Ightham for many miles, taking his distinguished visitors to his favourite sites, giving them specimens he had found and sharing his many enthusiasms with them. His fascinating correspondence within and outside the family is profusely quoted in the biography by his son.

There is no doubt that the eolith controversy was a necessary and even a predictable event within the development of British Palaeolithic studies of the late nineteenth and early twentieth centuries, but the inevitable turn of the tide against the proponents of the eoliths, as natural flaking processes became better understood (another great amateur, S.Hazzledine Warren, had an important part in this), regrettably left Harrison marooned in the position of someone who failed to distinguish the work of nature from the work of man and thereby caused a lot of unnecessary bother. Such a judgment is grossly unjust, and a reading of *Harrison of Ightham* should soon put it right. Among other things, we owe to Benjamin Harrison an enormous number of genuine Lower Palaeolithic discoveries on the Kentish greensand and chalk ridges, including some interesting Acheulian and Mousterian sites which, with the exception of the Oldbury group, have never been properly followed up; this contribution of his is quite forgotten. To judge from Harrison as a letter-writer, he could certainly have produced good clear accounts of his finds for publication, but diffidence caused him to leave that task for others and little was ever set down except on the subject of the eoliths, mainly by Prestwich (e.g. 1889, 1892).

It seems now that the eolith controversy is most remembered for the heat of some of the exchanges between the supporters of different points of view. This may have been the case at some of the learned society meetings: heavy artillery does not fire quietly. One feels that the editorial columns of *Antiquity*, had they been available and the present editor in charge, might

2 *Ink and wash drawing by Worthington Smith, undated but inscribed in pencil 'W.G.Smith on one of BH's Eoliths'. Original, 17.5 x 12.5 cm.*

have echoed and re-echoed the noise of the battle and possibly also cast some light on the appropriate wines for the refreshment of the combatants. For his own part, the present writer prefers to remember the moderation, the constructive arguments and indeed the humour shown by Harrison and some of his opponents in the less public moments. To draw together at least two threads in this rather diffuse essay, let us note that amongst those unconvinced by Harrison's eoliths was Worthington Smith. The two wrote to each other quite frequently: a correspondence between firm friends who had agreed to differ gracefully on various favourite topics.

Smith urged Harrison to publish a little volume on the Kentish material like his own *Man the Primeval Savage*, but this seed fell on stony ground (a metaphor of which Harrison would surely have approved). In other letters he deplores Harrison's certainly rather individual handwriting and his practical expertise as a sender of letters: 'I cannot answer your note, for I cannot read it . . . I know that ink has got dearer, but the mud you have substituted for it is not a success.' 'Your letters have been a sore puzzle to me . . . In places where I had read "all humbug" someone suggested that the words were "all harmony" – quite a different meaning.' 'You should use paste for attaching new addresses, your village marmalade is not strong enough.' (Harrison 1928, 151–2). There are, of course, serious discussions by Worthington Smith of specimens sent to him for his opinion by Harrison, but Smith, a brilliant draughtsman, could not resist replying to Harrison's appeals that surely such and such specimens

were human, by decorating the stones themselves with faces – in which a likeness to Harrison himself is not infrequent – and replying that they were human now, or by drawing the outline of an eolith of Harrison's or a stone from his own area around Dunstable, and adding what he regarded as suitable embellishments and an inscription. Some charming examples of these products were for many years in the possession of A.D. Lacaille, and following his death in 1975 passed into the present writer's hands through the kindness of Mrs Lacaille. Lacaille, incidentally, preferred to regard himself as an amateur of the Palaeolithic, notwithstanding his post at the Wellcome Historical Medical Museum, and he has an honoured place in the list of major contributors to the progress of British Palaeolithic archaeology before and after the Second World War. The same collection of documents included a few dozen of Harrison's own sensitive and talented watercolour drawings of his stones, both eoliths and genuine artifacts, and a few works by other hands.

No one would pretend that these delightful documents constitute major sources for scholars of the Palaeolithic, but on the present occasion the writer may perhaps indulge his firm belief that they should be shared with a wider audience by including a small selection, encouraged by the fact that Professor Daniel

3 Drawing by Worthington Smith, dated March 1906, based on a stone from Caddington. Original in ink, 28.5 x 22.5 cm.

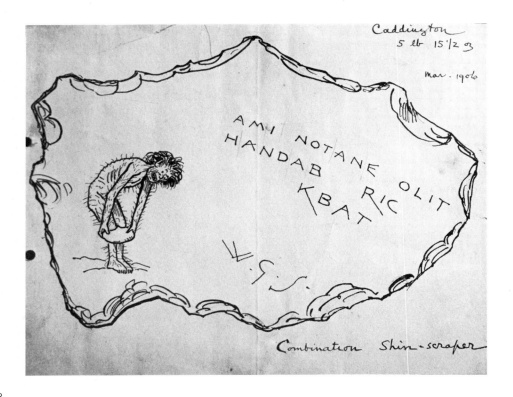

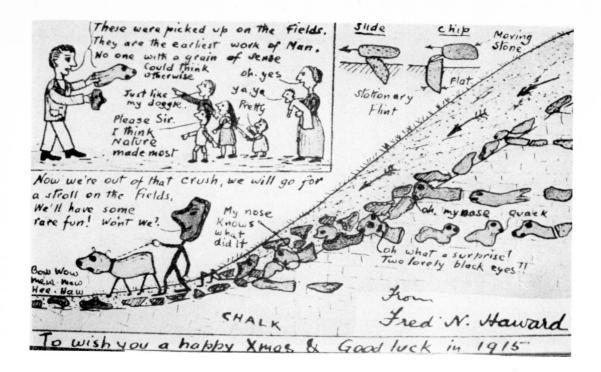

4 *Comment on eoliths by F.N.Haward, 1915. Original on a postcard, ink and colour washes, 14 x 9 cm.*

has himself seen and enjoyed them during a visit to Oxford. The first, a Harrison watercolour (ill. 1), really needs colour reproduction to do it justice. The writer does not know the exact reference that caused Harrison to caption the two implements 'Asquith and Bonar Law. See Guildhall Speeches', but the date is 5 September 1914, and the sentiment is reasonably clear. In the second example (ill. 2), Worthington Smith has 'humanized' an eolith of Harrison's, from its outline. A tracing of another such sketch in the collection, not reproduced here, is captioned 'An Eolithic Deity extirpating Eolithic parasites with Eolithic body-stones'. In the third (ill. 3), Smith has used the outline of a stone found at Caddington, and the human figure demonstrates its use as a 'double shin-scraper'; no great knowledge of any language other than English is required to translate the inscription. The last (ill. 4) is the work of F.N. Haward, dated 1915, and is one of three hand-drawn Christmas cards sent by him (in this case it is not known to whom). Haward was not himself a major figure in the eoliths controversy, but was a serious and successful collector and a participant at various learned society meetings. In his drawing, a little period humour is coupled with a lively appreciation of the processes actually likely to have caused some of the mechanical fractures on the eoliths. In some of his drawings, careful representations of actual published specimens are included.

The amateurs of the late nineteenth and early twentieth centuries who worked on the British Palaeolithic included many who combined sharp minds and a capacity for dedicated hard work with gentleness and a sense of humour, and who were blessed with research opportunities that have now become much rarer. The best of them made contributions of lasting importance in that formative period; in achieving this, they lacked our own advantages of accumulated knowledge and literature, and also our increasingly formidable array of technical aids to the examination and recording of sites and the processing of excavated archaeological material. Who can assert, considering all the circumstances, that they did not do us proud, and who can doubt that there is not a vital role for their successors amongst us today?

Sources of the Illustrations

The originals of ills 1–4 are in the author's possession at the Donald Baden-Powell Quaternary Research Centre, University of Oxford. The photographs were kindly provided by Mr W.H. Waldren.

Bibliography

CHANDLER, R.H. 1916 'The implements and cores of Crayford', *Proc. Prehist. Soc. East Anglia* II, 240–8.

DEWEY, H. AND SMITH, R.A. 1924 'Flints from the Sturry gravels', *Archaeologia* LXXIV, 117–36.

DYER, J.F. 1959 '"Middling for wrecks": extracts from the story of Worthington and Henrietta Smith', *Bedfordshire Archaeologist* II, 1–15.

1978 'Worthington George Smith,' in 'Worthington George Smith and other studies presented to Joyce Godber', *Bedfordshire Historical Record Society* LVII, 141–79.

HARRISON, SIR EDWARD R. 1928 *Harrison of Ightham: a book about Benjamin Harrison, of Ightham, Kent, made up principally of extracts from his notebooks and correspondence*, Oxford.

LAYARD, N.F. 1903 'A recent discovery of Palaeolithic implements in Ipswich', *JRAI* XXXIII, 41–3.

1904 'Further excavations on a Palaeolithic site in Ipswich', *JRAI* XXXIV, 306–10.

MOIR, J.R. 1918 'An Early Mousterian "floor" discovered at Ipswich', *Man* XVIII, no. 60, 98–100.

1931 'Ancient Man in the Gipping-Orwell Valley, Suffolk', *Proc. Prehist. Soc. East Anglia* VI, 182–221.

PRESTWICH, SIR JOSEPH 1889 'On the occurrence of Palaeolithic flint implements in the neighbourhood of Ightham, Kent, their distribution and probable age', *Quart. Journ. Geol. Soc. Lond.* XLVII, no. 2, 290–7.

1892 'On the primitive characters of the flint implements of the chalk plateau of Kent, with reference to the question of their Glacial or pre-Glacial age (with notes by Messrs B. Harrison and De Barri Crawshay)', *JAI* XXI, 246-62.

ROE, D.A. 1981 (in press) *The Lower and Middle Palaeolithic Periods in Britain*, London.

SAINTY, J.E. 1927 'An Acheulian Palaeolithic work-shop site at Whitlingham', *Proc. Prehist. Soc. East Anglia* V, 177–213.

SMITH, R.A. 1911 'A Palaeolithic industry at Northfleet, Kent', *Archaeologia* LXII, 515-32.

1915 'High level finds in the Upper Thames Valley', *Proc. Prehist. Soc. East Anglia* II, 99–107.

1933 'Implements from high level gravel near Canterbury', *Proc. Prehist. Soc. East Anglia* VII, no. 2, 165–70.

SMITH, R.A. AND DEWEY, H. 1914 'The High Terrace of the Thames: report on excavations made on behalf of the British Museum and H.M. Geological Survey in 1913', *Archaeologia* LXV, 187-212.

1915 'Researches at Rickmansworth: report on excavations made in 1914 on behalf of the British Museum', *Archaeologia* LXVI, 195-224.

SMITH, W.G. 1894 *Man the Primeval Savage: his haunts and relics from the hilltops of Bedfordshire to Blackwall*, London.

1916 'Notes on the Palaeolithic floor near Caddington', *Archaeologia* LXVII, 49–74.

SPURRELL, F.C.J. 1880 'On the discovery of the place where Palaeolithic implements were made at Crayford', *Quart. Journ. Geol. Soc. Lond.* XXXVI, 544-8.

1884 'On some Palaeolithic knapping tools and modes of using them', *JAI* XIII, 109–18.

UNDERWOOD, W. 1913 'A discovery of Pleistocene bones and flint implements in a gravel pit at Dovercourt, Essex', *Proc. Prehist. Soc. East Anglia* I, 360–8.

WARREN, S.H. 1911 'Palaeolithic wooden spear from Clacton', *Quart. Journ. Geol. Soc. Lond.* LXVII, cxix.

1922 The Mesvinian industry of Clacton-on-Sea', *Proc. Prehist. Soc. East Anglia* III, 597–602.

1933 'The Palaeolithic industries of the Clacton and Dovercourt districts', *Essex Naturalist* XXIV, 1–29.

23 Archaeological Humour: The Private Joke and the Public Image

Warwick Bray

From the time of Erasmus till about 20 years past, the learning was downright Pedantry. The conversation and habitts of those times were as stiff and starcht as their bands and square beards: and Gravity was then taken for Wisdome.

John Aubrey (1670)

AT A TIME when, once again, Gravity is all too often mistaken for Wisdome, this essay gives an unashamedly personal view of something I believe is important. Within the profession of archaeology we seem to be entering a period like the one described by Aubrey, an era of almost unparalleled gloom and moral earnestness. Few archaeologists will actually admit to enjoying their work, and, more and more, today's professionals are writing to impress each other rather than to inform the general public.

This was not always so. Like it or not (and it is clear that many 'research' archaeologists do not like it at all) we are a branch of the communications industry. Acceptance of public funds for research carries with it the obligation to show the public what it is getting for its money.

The gradual breakdown of communication between professionals and public is reflected by the changing nature of archaeological humour. The theme is an appropriate one for a volume in honour of Glyn Daniel. It was Glyn's interest in the social history of archaeology, coupled with the cartoons pinned up outside his room in College, which first made me realize, as a student, that there are two kinds of archaeology: archaeology as perceived by archaeologists, and archaeology as perceived by the man in the street.

Each of these archaeologies has its own history. The official history, written from within the profession, has been outlined by Glyn himself (1950, 1964, 1967) and by others (Willey and Sabloff 1974). The unofficial history of archaeology as perceived by the outsider at the time, and without benefit of hindsight, has yet to receive the attention it deserves, though the raw materials exist in the form of ephemera of all kinds: newspaper cartoons, television programmes, magazine articles, pulp fiction, advertisements and even pop songs.

These two strands, the academic and the popular, intertwine occasionally in the intellectual journals (though much less so than in the past) but, by and large, the two remain separate, and there is a wide gap – let us call it *the comprehension gap* – between what archaeologists think they are doing (and repeatedly tell each other they are doing) and what most people believe the archaeologist actually does. The existence of this gap, and public misapprehension of what archaeology is all about, is a matter of serious concern.

The 1840s provide a convenient starting point for a survey of archaeological humour. Layard was digging at Nineveh, and many of the 'lost civilizations' were still to be discovered; more importantly, in this pre-Darwinian era, archaeology (as opposed to mere antiquarianism) had not yet emerged as an independent scientific discipline. These years also saw the first publication of *Punch* (1841) and *The Illustrated London News* (1842). Between them, these two journals, middle class and middle brow, mirror the social attitudes and the changing level of scientific knowledge of an influential segment of British society.

The role of the *ILN* in the serious popularization of archaeology can be gauged from Edward Bacon's recent anthology (Bacon 1976) and needs no further emphasis. But *Punch*, too, was doing its bit. Serious anthropological issues, with a good cartoon, appear as early as p.27 of the first volume, and by July of that year (p.129) we have the first of the antiquarian lampoons: 'Bunks's Discoveries in the Thames'. This was followed, shortly afterwards (p.141), by the 'Transactions of the Geological Society of Hookham-cum-Snivey'. Members of local archaeological societies will instantly recognize themselves, and the whole passage is worth reproducing in full. Here we can give only the concluding section, describing Mr Grubemup's excavation below the mile-stone in the Kensington Road 'in the hope of finding some geological facts at the bottom of it'.

After removing the mile-stone:

He found a primary deposit of dark soil, and, on putting his spectacles to his eyes, he distinctly detected a common worm in a state of high salubrity. This clearly proved to him that there must

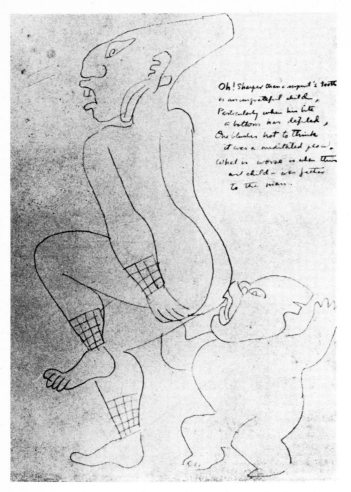

1 Comment by Miguel Covarrubias on the relationship between Olmec and Maya cultures. Radiocarbon dates were just confirming Covarrubias's long-held belief that Olmec was not derived from Maya, but was, in fact, much older.

logist inferred that there were rats on the Kensington-road at a much earlier period than milestones.

For 1841 this is an interesting passage. It demonstrates the strong links between geology and archaeology during these early years (something which sets apart the European tradition from the American), and the writer shows his familiarity with the principles of stratigraphy, type-fossils and cross-dating from one site to another.

More remarkable still, for the detailed, hard-core scientific knowledge it displays, is another of these early pieces, the famous 'Monkeyana' parody of 1861 (Bray 1973). So precise and up to date is the technical detail that 'Monkeyana' can only have been written by a first-rate scientist, and one who could be sure that the general *Punch* reader was well-enough informed to see the joke.

As we write these words, savouring a glass of Aguardiente Cristal in our favourite corner of the Hotel Continental, just round the corner from Bogotá's splendid new Gold Museum, we reflect that the intellectual health of a discipline can be measured by the parodies it generates. To write good parody demands not only a sense of style and an ear for the ridiculous, but also an insider's knowledge and a genuine affection for the subject.

Where are today's parodies? We recall with pleasure the spoof excavation report by Ward and O'Leary (1959), and we remember with glee the arrival, in *samizdat* form, of Lewis D.L. Binclarke's (1970) *New Analytical Archaeological Perspectives* at the 1971 Culture Change conference in Sheffield, where it stole the show, and attracted more interest than any of the official papers. This work, and the history of its publication, were reviewed in the Editorial of *Antiquity* for June 1971. We would have liked to illustrate one of Binclarke's figures here, but every copy in the Institute of Archaeology has disappeared or been stolen, some of them more than once. Instead, as an example of the 'insider cartoon' we illustrate a page from the notebooks of the Mexican artist-archaeologist Miguel Covarrubias (ill. 1).

What is significant about these modern parodies is that they are gibberish to the non-specialist and would never be considered for publication in a mass-circulation magazine today. This was not true a century ago, and it illustrates the way in which the comprehension gap has widened over the years.

Returning to Mr Punch, it is interesting to analyse his treatment of archaeological subjects from 1841 to the present. Not surprisingly, there are no new jokes (all the main themes are present from the start) but certain long-term trends stand out. They indicate not

formerly have been a direct communication between Hookham-cum-Snivey and the town of Kensington, for the worm found beneath the mile-stone exactly resembled one now in the Hookham-cum-Snivey Museum, and which is known as the *vermis communis*, or earth worm . . . Mr Grubemup, encouraged by this highly satisfactory result, proceeded to scratch up with his thumb-nail a portion of the soil, and his geological enterprise was speedily rewarded by a fossil of the most interesting character. Upon close inspection it proved to be a highly crystalized rat's-tail, from which the geo-

222

merely changes in fashion, but also a progressive trivialization of archaeology.

In the earlier years the best of the humour is verbal, and the visual jokes are pretty feeble (ill. 2). The extra space, characteristic of a more leisured age, allows the writer to deal with real scientific issues at a sophisticated level. Archaeology, along with geology, palaeontology

2 (Right) Cartoon from Punch *21 September 1878. The previous year, Canon William Greenwell had published* British Barrows, *describing his excavations in hundreds of barrows in the northern counties.*

'North Country Labourer (who has been engaged to dig). " 'They that eat alane may howk alane!' These archi'logical chaps never so much as asked me if ah'd tak' anything, and while they're havin' their Denners ah've found the 'buryin' " – (Pockets Urn and several flint arrow-heads) – "and they may whustle for't!!" '

3 (Below) Punch's comment (6 October 1954) on the *excavation of the London Mithraeum. Building development was halted to allow the site to be examined.*

REVENGE!

'Start about here and the first man to find a Roman temple gets docked a quid . . .'

'That? That's a place called Piltdown. Uninhabited.'

4–7 (Above *and* opposite) *Cave man cartoons from*
Punch: *28 December 1955, 23 October 1974, 28
September 1977, 6 November 1974.*

and anthropology, was still something which the
well-educated layman was expected to know about.
Symptomatic of this public interest was the popular
success of Layard's account of his excavations, *Nineveh
and its Remains*, which sold eight thousand copies in
one year, enough, as Layard wrote in a letter, to 'place
it side by side with Mrs Rundell's *Cookery*' (Daniel
1964, 154).

With the increasing professionalization of science,
the gap between producer and consumer begins to
open, and the humorist can no longer rely on an
informed audience. The cartoon caption replaces the
full-page column; intellectual issues disappear; the
subject matter of the fun is no longer archaeology, but
something quite different – Archaeologyland. It is
instantly recognizable and, like Disneyland, it is a world
of fantasy: larger than life, eclectic and peopled by
stereotypes – cave men, dinosaurs and missing links,
Druids and Ancient Britons, Vikings in horned
helmets, Pharaohs and mummies, Greek or Roman
soldiers, and the denizens of a mythical Bible Land
which stretches from Babylon to Bethlehem.

By implication, this Archaeologyland is what the
archaeologist investigates – but the jokes themselves *are
no longer about archaeology at all*. There are a few
references to current affairs (the Piltdown hoax, the

Tutankhamun exhibition, and so on) and one of these is
illustrated here (ill. 3). As Professor Grimes has noted
(1968, 236) it refers not only to his discovery of the
London Mithraeum (which attracted an estimated
30,000 visitors), but is also a prophetic comment on
today's uneasy relationship between developers and
archaeologists.

In general, however, most cartoons rely on a single
theme: the incongruity of present-day attitudes when
transferred to an Archaeologyland setting. A classic, and
deservedly successful, example of the genre is the
Astérix series by Goscinny and Uderzo, with a sale of
approximately a million copies of each book. *Punch*'s
equivalent is perhaps Murray Ball's neurotic Stanley,
The Great Palaeolithic Hero, who appeared in 214
consecutive issues during the 1970s. Astérix satirizes
national attitudes, Stanley the manic-depressive element
in modern life – but neither is really about archaeology.

Since cave men are among the most popular inhabitants
of Archaeologyland, a selection of Punch's Palaeolithic
cartoons is presented in ills 4-7. Two of them pre-
suppose a little archaeological knowledge, but most of
the cartoons in this category assume none whatsoever.
In passing, we may note that cave men are equally
popular in literature, and the theme has produced two
fine books of quite different kinds: Roy Lewis's *The
Evolution Man* (Ernest the Ape-man's memoirs of
Pleistocene life at a critical moment of ideological
conflict) and, in complete contrast, William
Golding's *The Inheritors*, which makes a serious and
tragic figure out of Neanderthal Man.

With the decline of archaeology as a subject for humour, the archaeologist tends to disappear as a cartoon protagonist. To get anything like an adequate sample, the scope of enquiry must be broadened to consider the archaeologist in fiction and literature in general – greatly helped by Charles Thomas's (1976) study of the more up-market literature, and M.A. Hoyt's annotated check list with its memorable synopses of the sillier books. Who could resist a heroine like the 'Lovely young archaeological student who also happens to be an Olympic gymnast; an international trouble-shooter; and the resurrection of the Minotaur' (Hoyt n.d., 7)? Are the right people being attracted into archaeology, we wonder?

Although there is some overlapping between the categories, three archaeological stereotypes emerge as clear favourites.

'Once upon a time — well, yesterday, actually . . .'

The Explorer

He comes in various forms, from the cartoonists' standby (an endearing, incompetent figure in pith helmet and baggy shorts, with ill-concealed inclinations towards lechery) to the tough, and sometimes sinister, characters of popular fiction. Frequently the setting is Archaeologyland, and the objective is a lost tribe, lost city or lost treasure: 'They came together in Cairo . . . all propelled by a manic desire for the magnificent treasure of the Pharaohs . . . Harold Barnaby, Egyptologist, half-crazed by his own genius . . .' That quotation (courtesy of Hoyt once again) is taken directly from the publisher's own cover blurb. Contrast ill. 13.

Often the Explorer is directing an excavation (usually, as Thomas noticed, doing so single-handed); sometimes he is simply lucky:

'Listen, honey, I can tell you a thing or two about Peking Man, And I can tell you a thing or two about Heidelberg Man . . .'

> First I have to tell you that I'm not insane
> And that once I was a famous archaeologist name.
> During a recent expedition to a distant land
> I just happened to be passing my hand in the sand
> And then I stopped, looked,
> And then I was hooked.
> I saw a flash then a sparkle from a moonstone . . .
>
> (Cat Stevens 1967)

Admittedly it sounds better with the music, but those who believe a pop song ought not to be taken seriously as a source of misleading information should compare the sales figures of the Stevens disc with those of any archaeological journal.

The strength of the Explorer myth is shown by a letter (quoted in Piggott 1963, 11) from a young man who wanted to go on an excavation, 'You could say I was half trained', he wrote, 'for I am an amateur

'He came rushing up to say he'd just invented something or other and then that rolled over him.'

'Motion carried. The place needs cheering up.'

8 *Archaeologyland: Stonehenge and Druids.* Punch, *19 September 1979.*

9 *Archaeologyland: a Classical joke.* Punch, *2 March 1978.*

10 (Opposite, above) *Archaeologyland: the Egyptian style.* Punch, *15 November 1951.*

11 (Opposite, below) *Archaeologyland: the museum joke in a different setting.* Punch, *18 November 1959.*

rockclimber, and an even shot with a rifle. I have also the full equipment.' He did, however, want to dig in South America.

At the time it seemed funny and slightly sad, but that was before the recently reported shoot-out in Belize, where, we are happy to learn, the archaeologists scored a one-nil victory. In the sober words of the *Latin American Political Report,* XIII (17) for 11 May 1979:

The gunfight came when a team of archaeologists, led by Dr David Pendergast of the Royal Ontario Muse-

'I don't think they're going to fall for it again, sir.'

um, was attacked in its camp by a group of marauders at Indian Church, south of the northern Belizean town of Orange Walk. The archaeologists, accustomed to the threat of being robbed of precious artefacts, fired back. One of the attackers, a United States citizen, Paul Herzog, was hit and captured. When questioned, – Herzog claimed to be an agent sent by the British police headquarters, Scotland Yard.

This is all very good for our macho image, but it gives a curious view of archaeology as normally practised.

The Collector

His characteristic is a single-minded passion. In lurid thrillers he is a sinister stop-at-nothing monomaniac, but, more commonly – in cartoons, at least – he is enthusiastic but gullible, the universal victim described by Ogden Nash:

I met a traveller from an antique show,
His pockets empty, but his eyes aglow.
Upon his back, and now his very own,
He bore two vast and trunkless legs of stone.
Amid the torrent of collector's jargon
I gathered he had found himself a bargain,
A permanent conversation piece post-prandial,
Certified genuine Ozymandial,
And when I asked him how he could be sure
He showed me P.B. Shelley's signature.

(*The Collector*, 1972)

The Antiquarian Scholar

He, or she, is slightly dotty: single-minded, elderly and rather dull, incompetently amorous, possessive about data, jealous of reputation, and concerned with matters of no relevance to the world of real life – in

'Doesn't he want anything else in the other world?'

short, a natural candidate for that much quoted (but, alas, apocryphal) *Directory of Archaeologists Broken Down by Age and Sex*. The type-specimen is the man described by the Revd Charles Churchill Babington (1865) in his inaugural lecture on taking up the Disney Professorship of Archaeology in Cambridge: 'There is some story about a learned antiquary after several years' research coming to the conclusion that two Etruscan words were equivalent to "vixit annos", but which was "vixit" and which "annos" he was as yet uncertain.'

Inaugural lectures, like after-dinner speeches, are privileged occasions, when academics are expected to

'Try and look a little more like an Ancient Briton, Miss Tracy.'

12 Art and archaeology. Punch, *14 July 1954.*

make fun of their profession. More often, however, the fun-pokers come from outside. The antiquarian as a source of comedy has a long ancestry. Stuart Piggott (1976, 133–70) has traced the history of this figure from Richard Graves's *The Spiritual Quixote* (1772) via Sir Walter Scott's *The Antiquary* (1816) to Thomas Love Peacock's *Crotchet Castle* (1831). Charles Thomas continues the survey to the present day, and makes an interesting point: 'In the transformation to a paid, professional, archaeologist, the gentleman-antiquary has necessarily lost caste; what he did for love he now does for money like a dentist or an iron-monger' (Thomas 1976, 311). Not only has the pro-fessionalization of science lost us half our audience, but it has endangered our literary status as well.

This, then, is archaeology as most people see it – and herein lies the danger.

Good caricature, like good propaganda, has its basis in reality. It makes its point not by pure invention, but by distorting and exaggerating something which already exists and which everyone can recognize. The real world of academic science described in Watson's *Double Helix* (1968) is recognizably the same as the fictional world of Angus Wilson's *Anglo-Saxon Atti-tudes* (1956), and the case of the phallic idol in the saintly Eorpwald's tomb is no odder than the true story of the Piltdown hoax.

But, where the real world of science is constantly changing, the cartoonists' stereotypes do not. Once established, they are immutable. *The Explorer*, *The Collector* and *The Antiquary* have been with us, virtually unchanged, for well over a century. The archaeological milieu they inhabit is that of the bygone imperial era so engagingly described by Sir Leonard Woolley in his reminiscences (1962), a time when the great museums behaved like institutional private col-lectors, and even the 'official' archaeologists dug as much for loot as for information. And, there, at about 1939, the clock stopped. For the majority of people, who do not read archaeological journals or watch highbrow television programmes, the technical and intellectual developments of the last forty years have never taken place.

What, then, should we be doing to bridge this comprehension gap? I do not for a moment suggest that the cartoonists and humorists should be made to update their work in the cause of social realism. I do suggest, however, that we are doing archaeology (and, ultimately, ourselves) a disservice by confusing earnestness with seriousness, and Gravity with Wisdome. It is no accident that one of the most stimu-lating, and most quoted, books of archaeological theory in the last decade (and one which got enthusiastic reviews in the trade journals) uses stereotypes in much the same way as the cartoonist uses them. The Real Mesoamerican Archaeologist, The Great Synthesizer and The Skeptical Graduate Student (Flannery 1976) have done more for the cause of archaeology than any number of papers written in gobbledygook – and have done so by making people laugh.

By renouncing the use of wit and humour in our writing, we are wilfully depriving ourselves of the most powerful weapons in the communicator's armoury. Perhaps, in these times of insecurity and job competition, we are simply trying too hard to impress. As long ago as 1954 Ogden Nash (again) summed up the dilemma of the academic cursed with a sense of humour:

People who have a sense of humour have a very good time,
But they never accomplish anything of note, either despicable
or sublime.

I can't believe him, but he gave fair warning. The title of this verse is *Don't Grin, or You'll have to Bear It.*

Bibliography

BACON, E. (ed.) 1976 *The Great Archaeologists*, London.

BINCLARKE, LEWIS D.L. 1970 *New Analytical Archaeological Perspectives: A Logogenetic Inquiry into the Nature of Archaeological Theoretic Theoreticians*, Phu Wiang University Publication No.1.

BRAY, W. M. 1973 'A Page of "Punch"', in Strong, D. E. (ed.), *Archaeological Theory and Practice*, London, 45–60.

COE, M. D. 1968 *America's First Civilization*, New York.

DANIEL, G. E. 1950 *A Hundred Years of Archaeology*, London.

1964 *The Idea of Prehistory*, Harmondsworth.

1967 *The Origins and Growth of Archaeology*, Harmondsworth.

FLANNERY, K. V. (ed.) 1976 *The Early Mesoamerican Village*, New York, San Francisco and London.

GOLDING, W. 1955 *The Inheritors*, London.

GRIMES, W. F. 1968 *The Excavation of Roman and Mediaeval London*, London.

HOYT, M. n.d. *Archaeology in Literature: Semi-Annotated Bibliography*, mimeographed, Wesleyan University.

LEWIS, R. 1963 *The Evolution Man*, Harmondsworth.

NASH, O. 1954 *The Face is Familiar*, London.

1972 *The Old Dog Barks Backward*, New York.

PIGGOTT, S. 1963 'Archaeology and Prehistory', *Proc. Preh. Soc.*, NS XXIX, 1–16.

1976 *Ruins in a Landscape: Essays in Antiquarianism*, Edinburgh.

STEVENS, C. 1967 'Moonstone', in *View from the Top*, Deram DPA 3020, Decca Record Co., London.

THOMAS, C. 1976 'The Archaeologist in Fiction', in Megaw, J.V.S. (ed.) *To illustrate the Monuments: Essays on Archaeology Presented to Stuart Piggott*, London, 309–19.

WARD, C.W. AND O'LEARY 1959 'A preliminary investigation of an early man site in the Delaware Valley', in Fried, M.H. (ed.) *Readings in Anthropology*, New York, 272–9.

WATSON, J. D. 1968 *The Double Helix*, London.

WILLEY, G. R. AND SABLOFF, J. A. 1974 *A History of American Archaeology*, London and San Francisco.

WOOLLEY, L. 1962 *As I seem to Remember*, London.

13 Archaeologists. Punch, *7 December 1938.*

'Many happy returns, Cathcart. I didn't know *what* to get you.'

PART IV : THE EDITOR
OF 'ANTIQUITY'

John D. Evans

IN THE FINAL section of this tribute to Glyn Daniel we strike a more purely personal note. The essays in the three preceding sections all deal with aspects of some major fields in which Glyn has been deeply interested and involved, and to which he has contributed notably in the course of his career. Those which follow attempt to assess and illustrate some of the more purely individual aspects of his life and achievement; his work as an editor and teacher, and the part he has played during so many years in the affairs of his College and of the University of Cambridge as a whole. The list could have been extended, but these are perhaps the most important. Of course, this distinction between

1 Glyn Daniel as an undergraduate, on holiday in Wales.

his various activities is necessarily a rather arbitrary one, for Glyn's personality permeates everything he does and imparts a special flavour to whatever he has a hand in. At the same time, it is reasonable to take the view that those facets of his total activity which are to be considered here are more purely personal, and are some of those in which individual characteristics are likely to be both more obvious and also more important to the end result. For all those who know him it is needless to say that what we present here represents only a selection from his multifarious interests, and one which could be greatly extended if space permitted. Such is their range, and such is Glyn's versatility, that it would obviously be impracticable to attempt more.

What holds together and gives coherence to this diversity of interests and activities is essentially a personality of great warmth and sensitivity, to which, in the most literal sense, nothing which relates to man and his doings is alien, and which finds its greatest satisfaction in the cultivation of human relationships of all kinds. To me, therefore, it comes as no surprise to find Edward Miller saying, towards the end of his contribution to this section, that in the final analysis he remembers Glyn as a person rather than in the context of any particular activity. I imagine that this would be true to a great extent for everyone who has known him. He is indeed the antithesis of the 'faceless man', or of the withdrawn scholar whose personality is completely overshadowed by and submerged in his work. You are always conscious, in any encounter with him, whether face to face or on the printed page, of the person as well as the subject of discussion. He is always in evidence, enlivening the most tedious business, suffusing even the most arid subject matter with the reflected glow of his wit and enthusiasm (or alternatively, from time to time, of his anger or scorn), but above all relishing and bringing out to the full the oddities and absurdities which are present, more or less, in all human affairs. A lovable man, first and foremost; also a man of formidable ability, not just scholarly but also eminently practical, a natural organizer and administrator, and endowed with energy to match.

There can be no doubt that Glyn was conscious from an early stage in his career of the variety of his talents, and that he was anxious to exercise all of them

2 *Glyn Daniel (with Stuart Piggott on his right) in India during the war.*

as far as possible. He had good reason to be so. After his brilliant academic success as an undergraduate and research student in the 1930s (and the beginning of his lifelong involvement with megalithic monuments) the wartime RAF afforded him an early opportunity of testing some of his other abilities. His final rank of Wing Commander testifies to the success with which he did so. Back in Cambridge as a university lecturer after the end of hostilities, teaching and research inevitably claimed a large share of his attention once more, but it is clear that he was determined that they should not become all-absorbing and engulf his other interests entirely.

That this was a conscious decision, deliberately followed up, and not the result of circumstances, is fairly obvious, and for me is confirmed by a conversation which I remember from the early days of my acquaintance with him. I first met Glyn in the summer of 1948. I had decided, after taking Part I of the English Tripos, that archaeology was what I really wanted to study, and that it was now or never if I really intended to do something about it. Glyn was at that time acting as Director of Studies in Archaeology for my college, Pembroke (as also, I think, for several others which did not have a Fellow in the subject), and I was advised by my tutor there to go and see him for advice. My experience of Glyn in the role of teacher was very similar to that recorded by David Wilson in

his contribution to this section, so that there is no need for me to repeat what he has said there, or to try to add to the excellent selection of anecdotes which he has given. However, there is one recollection I have from the later part of my final undergraduate year which bears directly on the present discussion. It was at the end of a supervision – not in his rooms or in a pub, but out of doors (if I remember rightly on one of the St John's College lawns) so that it was probably in the summer term of 1949. Glyn began to talk about the importance of maintaining a proper balance of activities, and went on to say that for his own part he intended always to combine his academic work with a certain amount of administration, and also to be able to give part of his time to other activities, such as, for instance, the popularization of archaeology by means of such things as radio broadcasts (which he was by then doing from time to time), by writing and so on.

He was in fact beginning to put this philosophy into practice in a number of ways. He had already by that time been Steward of St John's for three years, since 1946, an appointment which allowed him to combine administrative activities with two of his other long-standing interests, namely food and wine. Besides this and his broadcasting he was also doing some non-academic writing, and his first detective novel, *The Cambridge Murders*, had been published in 1945. It was not, of course, until a few years later that he became a public figure with the runaway success of the television series 'Animal, Vegetable, Mineral?' and, less spectacular but in some ways more important, the 'Buried Treasure' programmes. But it was already clear that he would become involved with this new and powerful medium which offered quite unprecedented scope for the popularization of a subject with such a strong visual appeal as archaeology, especially when presented by someone who was so clearly a natural 'personality'. In the meantime, however, he was a most stimulating person to be in contact with; certainly this was so for those of us who were his students at that time. Supervisions with him meant so much more than just the discussion for an hour of some archaeological topic. They were essentially unpredictable in all respects – from the place where they might be held, through the kinds of refreshment that might be produced, down to the topics which might be brought up. Although it is true that essays were regularly read and commented on, just as in any run-of-the-mill supervision, the discussions to which they gave rise were generally enlivened by some unusual, not to say often bizarre, slants on the subject contributed by Glyn, often having reference to the personal eccentricities of the archaeologists involved and their relationships with each other. What, more than anything, made them different from other supervisions, though, was what might happen before or after this central ritual of essay-reading – the unscheduled discussions started by, it might be, the subject which had been engaging his thoughts just before we arrived, or, if the session happened to be taking place in his rooms at St John's, by the photographs or publications which he happened to have spread out on every available surface. Looking back on them, I feel, like David Wilson, that these supervisions really were a remarkably valuable educational experience, partly through being so completely informal and unpedantic.

A little later, as a research student, I experienced his help also in the more mundane and practical matter of keeping afloat financially long enough to complete my research and to get established in the profession. He was a never-failing source of good advice in those years as to what the next step should be and where one should apply next for funds. Like many others of his pupils, and others again who were not, I owe a very great deal to his untiring efforts to ensure the material

as well as the mental well-being of all those for whom he was in any way responsible, as well as many for whom he was not.

While Glyn's success on television in the 1950s made him a well-known figure nationally and broadened his field of action enormously, it made remarkably little difference to his personality or to his objectives. These continued to be more or less exactly what they had always been, though of course he now had much greater scope for action. He continued to teach, to write and to lecture, but his other opportunities to further the spread of knowledge about archaeology became much broader and more varied, and he seized them with both hands. As we all know, in 1956 he started the 'Ancient Peoples and Places' series for Thames and Hudson, a series which has now reached its hundredth volume and which is continuing to grow, still under his General Editorship. Two years later, in 1958, after the death of O. G. S. Crawford, he became Editor of *Antiquity*, a position for which he was ideally suited, and with which, over the years, he has become as much identified as the founder himself was in his time. In 1957 he also became a director of the newly established Anglia Television.

All in all the decade of the 1950s was obviously a crucial one for him, since it was the period during which the main lines of much of his subsequent activity were laid down. It was during these years that he became in the full sense a publicist for archaeology, using a variety of media, including television, publishing and archaeological journalism, and reaching different, though overlapping, publics in each instance. Taken together, these activities constitute one of his most substantial achievements, one which has been fully considered and celebrated in the essays which compose the immediately preceding section of this book. It is not necessary, therefore, for me to go into any further detail here about it, except to note the importance, in addition to his inexhaustible energy, of Glyn's unique and always delightful personality in making it possible. It was this which, together with the sharply contrasting but in many ways complementary personal qualities of Mortimer Wheeler, accounted in great part for the quite extraordinary success of the AVM series, and so gave archaeology a flying start as a televisual subject. The bait of a known and much-appreciated personality, first encountered in an amusing panel game, must have lured many a viewer in those days who had hardly heard of archaeology before to become an *aficionado* of the quite serious 'Buried Treasure' programmes. This undoubtedly helped to ensure the success not only of that series, but of those which have followed it down to the present day, on BBC television and elsewhere. A ready public had been created for television archaeology of all kinds, in fact.

Again, the confidence inspired by his personal success in rousing public interest for archaeology on television must have been an encouragement to Walter Neurath in considering the launching of the 'Ancient Peoples and Places' venture, though, of course, there was an obvious need, on the part of students and general readers alike, for such a series of up-to-date syntheses of archaeological information which had remained largely buried in learned journals and massive technical reports. But other personal qualities, including enterprise, tact, charm, and above all endless patience and good humour, were most certainly vital to its success; first of all for securing the services of the numerous specialists from many countries who were needed to undertake what were often daunting tasks of research and synthesis, then for encouraging and coaxing flagging authors to complete their books, and finally for the often quite difficult and complicated process of getting the resulting typescript into shape for publication, which sometimes involved, among other things, the identification and signing up of a suitable translator.

As an archaeological journalist, Glyn's personality has, naturally enough, been no less in evidence and certainly no less a key factor in the success which he has had in this field also. *Antiquity*, a journal created originally by another man of strong, but very different personality, O. G. S. Crawford, who used it, especially the editorials, very much as a vehicle for propagating his own views on every aspect of archaeology, proved to be the perfect medium for Glyn Daniel also. When Crawford died at the end of 1957, *Antiquity* might well have disappeared, so closely was it identified with its founder and editor. It was only saved, as Richard Atkinson tells us below, by Glyn's courageous agreement to take it over, in association with a small panel of Advisory Editors, at less than a month's notice. It has proved to be a fortunate enterprise in all respects and has more than justified the efforts made at that time to keep it in being. Under Glyn's guidance, and with Ruth's help as Production Editor, *Antiquity* has gone from strength to strength. At the same time it has provided, in its editorial section, the ideal forum for Glyn, like 'Ogs' Crawford

before him, to comment freely on matters of topical interest, and to air his views on whatever subjects may be engaging his attention at the time — all this seasoned, of course, with as much anecdote and gossip as he feels like including.

In his contribution on 'Glyn Daniel as Editor' Richard Atkinson has undertaken a fascinating analysis of the enormous range of subjects covered in these editorials over rather more than twenty years, from 1958 up to the end of 1979. It is a most impressive list, but of course in the last analysis it is the way they are written, rather than the intrinsic interest of any particular subject treated, which makes Glyn's *Antiquity* Editorials what they are. It is the inimitable style, and the personality behind the style, which ensures that they are *read*, and that the points made in them really do get across to the wide range of people who either take or consult the journal. The *Antiquity* public is not quite the general public, but it is far from being a merely professional or specialist readership. From its beginnings *Antiquity* was directed at all those who were interested in or concerned for any aspect of archaeology, and Glyn Daniel has, in his editorial policy, ably continued and developed this tradition. As Editor he has therefore an international audience which includes not only experts and serious amateurs, but also many who are neither, yet nevertheless find it both compelling and comprehensible reading.

To write for such a varied readership, to amuse and entertain them, while at the same time discussing and offering opinions on many serious topics and problems, and so perhaps helping to influence to some extent the outcome of many important issues connected with archaeology, has been a task for which Glyn was not only especially well fitted, but it is also one which he has clearly enjoyed enormously. In the editorials of *Antiquity* are to be found both the quintessence of Glyn's personality and also something of his views about every subject, or almost every subject, which has ever interested him. It is for this reason that we have chosen to present him in this section as 'The Editor of *Antiquity*', a congenial *persona* which seems to draw together so many aspects of his life and personality. Long may he continue to appear before us in that guise.

25 Glyn Daniel as Editor

R.J.C. Atkinson

OF *Festschriften*, Glyn Daniel has said in one of his *Antiquity* editorials (174)* that they are 'a cemetery for articles which ought to have been published elsewhere in more accessible form, or not at all'; but his many friends who contribute to this volume have not been deterred by this discouragement, and rightly so.

As an editor, he has played many parts, and two especially for long and equal runs. Since 1956 he has been General Editor of the 'Ancient Peoples and Places' series published by Thames and Hudson, of which one hundred volumes will have appeared by the time that this *Festschrift* can be read, the hundredth to be from the pen of the General Editor himself (though I will not say *finis coronat opus*!). This is one of the most successful and sustained publishing ventures of the twentieth century. I remember making, more than twenty-five years ago, when I had more time for woodwork than I do now, a suite of book-cases with specific and generous provision for volumes of this size; but my allowance has long since been overtaken by this series alone. I salute, with countless other readers, the wise guidance and judgment of the editor of this invaluable series.

My theme here, however, is Glyn Daniel's editorship, since 1958, of *Antiquity*, the only archaeological journal of world-wide scope which is completely independent, because it is not owned by a learned society or a museum or a university, but by Trustees who are *quot homines, tot sententiae*, of whom I have been one (Stuart Piggott is the other) since the beginning and am currently the Chairman.

When O.G.S. Crawford, the founder and first Editor of *Antiquity*, died at the end of November 1957 there were fears that the publication of the journal might cease; but these were allayed by a letter to *The Times* on the last day of the year from the publisher, H. W. Edwards, who announced that it would continue under the editorship of Glyn Daniel, assisted by a panel of five Advisory Editors. The new Editor thus took over at less than a month's notice, to the relief of all the subscribers.

* All the references are to *Antiquity*. To avoid a long and largely repetitious bibliography, by volume and page, I cite the *number* only of each relevant issue. It will be clear from the context whether this refers to an article or to an editorial.

His impact upon *Antiquity* was almost immediate, beginning with the inclusion (126) of the Book Chronicle, which has ever since provided early notice of new publications, whether or not they were to be reviewed later in the same pages. Other changes, recorded below, took a little longer.

In 1960, Mr Edwards announced his intention of ceasing to publish *Antiquity*, and its future was again for a time in doubt. It was assured by the creation of the Antiquity Trust, funded by public subscription (138), the immediate purchase being generously underwritten by I. D. Margary, who became one of the original Trustees (198).

Some day, I hope, the Editor will commit to print the bizarre history of the registration of the Antiquity Trust as an educational charity; but perhaps not yet. When it is written, it will read like a piece of overplayed satirical fiction, with an antagonist quite unbelievably versed in the byways of bureaucratic vacillation and obstruction. In the end reason and equity prevailed, and the Trust achieved charitable status. Otherwise, the subscription to *Antiquity* would have risen, for tax reasons, to a self-destructive level.

Of the content of *Antiquity* under Glyn Daniel's editorship I need say little in detail, because it will be already familiar to almost every reader of this *Festschrift*. Throughout, it has ranged very widely in time and space; from the earliest evidence for Man in East Africa to the present day; and across all the continents, Antarctica excepted.

This wide and truly international coverage reflects the distribution of subscribers and readers. For many years about half of them have been from Britain and the rest overseas, with about 20 per cent of the total from the United States. Two-fifths of subscriptions come from libraries and other institutions, and three-fifths from individuals.

The international character of *Antiquity* has depended, however, upon a great deal of travelling by the Editor to visit sites, museums, exhibitions and fellow scholars, as well as upon a personal intelligence service which is the envy of his friends and colleagues, who are as mystified by its operation as they are gratified by its results.

A simple analysis of the articles published in *Antiquity* during the last twenty-two years shows that 39 per

236

cent of them relate to the British Isles, 32 per cent to Europe and the USSR, 10 per cent to Asia (mainly India and China), 8 per cent to Africa, 6 per cent to the Near East as far as the Arabian Gulf, 3 per cent to the Americas and 2 per cent to the Antipodes. This excludes, of course, many articles which have no specific geographical connotation. A more detailed analysis suggests that the proportion of articles specifically related to the British Isles has risen slowly, though with fluctuations from year to year, at the rate of about two additional articles every five years. This is hardly to be interpreted as chauvinism.

To avoid the indulgence of personal preferences, I refrain almost entirely from commenting upon individual articles; but there are some that must be named (other selectors may make other choices) because they seem to me to be 'scoops' in the jargon of journalism, whether they were commissioned by the Editor in the first place, or eagerly accepted as adventitious offerings. I have in mind particularly the account of the St Ninian Isle treasure (132), with the first colour plate ever to be published in *Antiquity*; Roland Martin's account of the wooden figures from the source of the Seine, with seven plates (156); R. M. Clark's article on the correction of radiocarbon dates (196), which is probably consulted more frequently than any other part of *Antiquity*; David Clarke's 'Archaeology: the loss of innocence' (185) and the rejoinder of Christopher Hawkes (187); and Fred Hoyle's 'Speculations on Stonehenge' (160), which with the later comments (162) and Jacquetta Hawkes's summing-up in 'God in the Machine' (163) constitute some of the primary documents in the controversy, still unresolved, about the possible astronomical significance of Stonehenge and, by extension, about the real or imaginary character of megalithic **astronomy**.

Of the Notes, many of which, unsigned, are from the pen of the Editor, I say no more than that they have increased in length and number, and that they have often given the first news (especially for new radiocarbon dates) of developments only later published elsewhere. This is inevitably a miscellany; but its miscellaneous character should not obscure its value.

As in other journals, the reviews are important, and there can be no doubt that they have had an influence quite disproportionate to the circulation of *Antiquity*. By his choice of reviewers the Editor has encouraged a distinctively open style of comment, sometimes racy, sometimes discursive, but seldom acrimonious and hardly ever dull. This is in very pleasing contrast to the magisterial rebukes and the ponderous nit-picking so often to be found in contemporary journals. The number of books reviewed annually rose from 53 in 1958 to 72 in 1970. Since then it has been slightly lower; but even in the last four years, with only three issues a year, the average has been 59.

Colour printing is normally too expensive for a journal such as *Antiquity*; but since 1959 there have been occasional coloured frontispieces, funded by generous donors, including *Antiquity*'s Custodian Trustees, Barclays Bank Ltd(204). The annual number of black-and-white plates rose steadily from 28 in 1958 to 60 in 1965; but thereafter the increasing cost of printing reduced them, first to 44 or 48, and latterly to between 24 and 32. A notable feature of these has been the regular series of new discoveries from the air, almost all from the camera of Professor St Joseph.

The unique feature of *Antiquity*, however, is its editorials, which have no parallel in any other archaeological periodical. They have been called in print 'a gossip column', and described to me verbally as 'Glyn's private soap-box'. Neither epithet is in the least accurate or just; but each emphasizes the wide-ranging scope and the unfettered personal character of these editorial comments.

I cannot be alone in holding that one of the minor intermittent pleasures of life is to receive (almost always punctually) the latest number of *Antiquity*, and over coffee and toast, with only the briefest glance at the table of contents, to turn to the editorial to see what scandal will now be exposed, what folly will be gently (or not so gently) mocked, what bureaucratic extravagances or exigencies will be rightly reprehended, what footnotes, hitherto unrecorded, will be added to the history of archaeology and of archaeologists, what books I should buy (or at least read) and what exhibitions I should plan to visit. For me each editorial is the literary equivalent of an Indonesian *rijstafel* – many dishes, some bland, some pungent or spicy, a few searing, but in all satisfying and never indigestible.

Allowing for quotations from letters or published sources, the *Antiquity* editorials from 1958 to 1979 amount to well over 250,000 words. To describe, let alone to comment upon, so much writing of an inevitably heterogeneous kind is a labour, even if a labour of love. I attempt it as a token of the pleasure which I have had in reading and re-reading it all.

In the following analysis I have included every topic which has been referred to at least twice in separate editorials. The classification is my own, and would not be that of Glyn Daniel himself or of any one else who might attempt the same task. Subjective though it is, however, it may serve to indicate the mind of the Editor, approximately, through his main preferences as interpreted by a friend and colleague. The figures given are for column-centimetres of the text in its present form, adjusted for the earlier issues (before 1963) when the text was printed right across the page. The matter *not* here classified amounts to about 750 column-centimetres or about 5 per cent of the total length of the editorials. It includes about twenty topics which are mentioned once only, and a rather larger amount of purely ephemeral material, such as notices of forthcoming articles.

History of archaeology – 1682; Necrology – 1543; Fakes and forgeries – 1375; New publications – 1234; Lunacies – 991; Official archaeology abroad – 541; Stonehenge – 490; University archaeology – 409; Radiocarbon dates and dating – 362; Archaeological exhibitions – 354; British Museum – 352; Official archaeology, Britain – 327; Museums abroad – 319; Conferences – 309; The plundered past – 227; Air photography – 197; Other British museums – 190; Philosophy of archaeology – 178; British Schools abroad – 157; Lascaux – 150; Ordnance Survey – 136; Megaliths – 134; Instructions to contributors – 120; Industrial archaeology – 115; Linear B – 104; Excavations – 104; Historical archaeology – 103; History of *Antiquity* – 101; Treasure trove – 96; Archaeology abroad – 87; BBC (Silbury Hill) – 80; Notable finds – 74; Funding of research – 69; RESCUE – 69; Modern antiquarianism – 67; Lecturing techniques – 66; Metal detectors – 55; Thermoluminescence – 39; CBA – 25; Archaeological stamps – 18

To comment upon this long list of topics is perhaps an impertinence, for which I ask indulgence as an amateur historian of *Antiquity*. That Glyn Daniel will forgive me is assured, I hope, by his own great interest in the history of archaeology, of which *Antiquity* is a part. It is not surprising that the author of no less than six books on the origins and growth of archaeology should in his editorials return time and again to this theme. He has stated firmly (193) that for him archaeology is primarily an historical discipline (in contradiction of those 'new archaeologists' who pathetically assert that it is not); and he has always followed in the steps of R. G. Collingwood in believing that a subject of humane or scientific enquiry can be understood only in terms of its own history of conceptual growth and change. In his editorials he has added many new footnotes to the books he has already written.

Antiquity has never published formal obituaries; but no less than 11 per cent of the editorial matter has concerned the lives and achievements (and at times the aberrations and follies) of distinguished contemporaries including, alas, a number of former Trustees and Advisory Editors of *Antiquity*. Such necrologies, written from personal acquaintance and often about friends, are part of the raw stuff of history; and that is why they are there.

Fakes, forgeries and frauds are part, too, of the history of archaeology and a part which all of us can neglect only at our peril. Under this heading pride of place goes to Glozel and its aberrant thermoluminescent dates. No sane archaeologist who has seen the contents of the Glozel Museum will doubt that almost the whole is of modern manufacture. The inference, fortified by these many comments, is that there is some local source of error, still undetected, in this otherwise useful method of dating. One day, perhaps, the Editor will write a book on Glozel, Rouffignac, the Kensington Stone, Piltdown, the Cardiff Giant *et hoc genus omne*.

From frauds it is a short step to self-delusion or lunacy, or what Glyn has called (183) 'our department of folly and nonsense'. Here too he has been urged (201) to write a book entitled *The Wilder Shores of Archaeology*; and stimulated, perhaps, by the claim that an important ley-line passes through his house in Cambridge (208) I hope he will do so. He has rightly warned his readers many times of the rising tide of what is euphemistically called 'alternative archaeology', which in volume of sales already threatens even the more popular works of archaeological scholarship. The time has passed, unfortunately, when such ignorant and uncritical fantasies were published, if at all, in minute editions at the author's own expense.

With a few exceptions, the Editor has not written formal reviews; but nearly 9 per cent of his editorials have noticed new books and journals, often with comment amounting to a review in miniature. Those of us who can still afford to buy some books are correspondingly grateful for his early assessments.

These five leading categories – history, necrology, fraud, publications and lunacies – account for nearly half the content of the editorials. Of the rest, I have space to refer only to those comments which are likely to have had a special influence on public policy. About 14 per cent of the total has concerned the organization and functioning of official archaeology at home and overseas, including the national museums and the British Schools abroad, with praise for achievements but more often due blame for bureaucratic intransigence, folly or *faineantiste* circumlocutions. At shorter length, but perhaps with no less effect, the Editor has adverted several times to the 'plundering of the past' – the trade in valuable antiquities illicitly exported and secretly acquired by museums abroad, with no questions asked (or at least answered). Here his influence, though unknown, is probably substantial.

As a university teacher, he has kept a watchful eye

238

upon the growth and development of academic archaeology in Britain; and I record with gratitude and on behalf of all my university colleagues the conference which he and his college organized in Cambridge in 1975, on the teaching of archaeology in the universities of Britain and Ireland. His initiative, and its success, has borne fruit in a further conference organized by the CBA in May 1980.

Space forbids me to say more of the *Antiquity* editorials. To characterize them epigrammatically, they have not been 'Glyn's private soap-box', but rather 'Glyn's *Private Eye*', though indeed more soberly worded, better informed and without the libel actions.

Antiquity has not only to be edited, but also to be produced in print, so that the Editor and the Production Editor are closely linked in more than one sense. Only those who have had to deal with contributors on the one hand and printers on the other will know how much hard work, frustration and justifiable anger lie between these two extremes of the publication process. Every subscriber and reader of *Antiquity* will join me here in paying tribute to Ruth Daniel for ensuring (even sometimes by candle-light during a powercut) that it has almost invariably reached its subscribers on time; that it has been quite remarkably free from misprints and printers' pies; and that its lay-out and typographical style have not merely kept abreast of current fashion, but have indeed led it, whilst at the same time introducing economies of space which, it is safe to say, have passed largely unregarded. Who noticed, for instance, that from no. 177 the first page of the editorial was longer, or that from no. 201 all the main pages contained three extra lines per column?

Occasionally, in the hope of receiving typescripts which could go to the printer without a great deal of copy-editing, the Production Editor has given instructions to contributors in the editorials (145, 170, 184 (on the quotation of radiocarbon dates); 191 (on the ethics of reviewing), 195). These should be read and re-read by every contributor, invited or hopeful, but with the proviso that an A4 page of typescript contains about 350 words, in double spacing; and in conjunction with the articles on archaeological draughtsmanship by Stuart Piggott (155) and Brian Hope-Taylor (158, 163). If more contributors had been as conscious of solecisms in line-drawing and lettering as they were of those in the written word, there would have been less of a burden on the shoulders of H.A. Shelley, whose sensitive and beautifully lettered interpretations of contributors' 'roughs' have adorned the pages of *Antiquity* since 1965. I suspect that in many cases 'rough' was *le mot juste*. The maps in this *Festschrift* are another example of his craftsmanship.

Glyn Daniel's successor in the twenty-first century, who writes a book called, perhaps, *A Quarter of a Millennium of Archaeology*, will rightly see *Antiquity* as unique, and as an influence upon changing concepts and policies quite out of proportion to its circulation of a few thousands. He (or she) will also recognize that in this formative process the first two Editors (what can we say of the third?) have been paramount, and not least because of their complete independence from any form of external control.

It is too soon, however, to speak of a third Editor of *Antiquity*. The present Editor, writing in the 150th number in 1964, saw himself in 1977 as 'a strange old party then, darting from megalith to megalith in a jet-propelled bath-chair well equipped with portable library and cellar'. Neither the need for the bath-chair, nor the technology to equip and power it, have yet arrived, and Glyn is still in the editorial chair. Later (165) he apostrophized the Editor of *Antiquity* in Orwell's ominous year of 1984. Let us all hope that he was talking to himself, and that he will still then be the Editor.

26 Glyn Daniel as Teacher

David M. Wilson

To WRITE under such a heading one can only be personal, only discuss reality and memory. School and university are too far away to be real and to me memory of the detail of daily life at both is hazy, almost blank. I get a scent of Cambridge as it was thirty years ago when I walk through St John's on a November morning or return to college late on a summer night. Rain and mist, the popping of a gas stove, the smell of brussels sprouts and a few well-constructed funny stories are practically all that remain of undergraduate Wilson or of his teacher, Daniel. Perhaps this chapter should be written when I am seventy; perhaps then I may be able to recover some of the real facts, now I can only recover a few impressions.

Impressions of Glyn. Glyn giving tea to a callow, begowned eighteen-year-old, buying beer for a twenty-year-old sophisticate; Glyn imitating Wheeler (rather well) and Childe (rather badly); Glyn telling stories of Ridgeway, of Macalister, of Chadwick; Glyn at a May ball with Ruth; Glyn in that ancient car (typologically speaking it must have been a Humber); Glyn in a gown or in one of his more ghastly hats, waistcoated, surpliced, or in evening cloak. There are many impressions – but of Glyn the teacher there remain few detailed memories. No vignettes, only an approach to archaeology. Perhaps this is what teaching is all about, effacing oneself and pushing the subject so that the student can remember thirty years later the matter and the approach and not, thank God, the theories . . . do you remember Lindsay Scott?

I went up to Cambridge more or less directly from school – the usual nine months' gap was spent working in a hotel – I did not do National Service (luckily perhaps, for my best friend was killed in Korea). I was surrounded by fellow students sophisticated by army service – Robert Erskine, for example, with whom I shared the odd supervision, had been with the Scots' Guards in Malaya. I was horribly immature and needed all the confidence I could get. Glyn, my Director of Studies and one of my two supervisors, gave me some at least of that. He gave me my first essay, heaven knows what it was about, but I inferred rightly that the first bibliographical references could be found in Childe's *Prehistoric Communities of the British Isles*. As a result I got my first lesson in scholarship, 'All

Gordon's footnote references are approximate; but don't give up, you'll find the source is not too far away'. Sufficiently exaggerated to be fixed in the memory and to be a help years later when trying to bring the PhD perfectionist to the post on his first publication. First lesson learnt and a good one.

Like all undergraduates we suffered from supervisions. We suffered from essays as though they were measles. How Glyn must have been bored by our juvenalia. Page after page of turgid, prosy immaturity. What a horrid way to have had to teach! To hear read aloud undergraduates' definitive discussions of the Huelva hoard in its European context, of the horned cairns of Ireland (do they still exist, one wonders?), or a discussion on the hill-forts of the South Downs, must be excruciating. Later as a teacher I found it hard enough to read written undergraduate effusions without boredom being compounded by hearing essays being read aloud by badly inflected, nervous, stumbling voices. And undergraduate wit! I remember only one essay I wrote in the three years during which I enjoyed Glyn's supervision – I remember it with shame. '''The cistern called Iron Age B has burst and ceased to contain its seething load,'' Wheeler, Discuss'. Discuss it I did with a vengeance and heavy irony – hadn't we learnt all this from Toty de Navarro's lectures? Where Wheeler was 'wrong' he was referred to as Brigadier Wheeler, where he was 'right' he got his professor's title. I shudder now, presumably Glyn shuddered then, but with inexhaustible patience he put me straight, praised my crudities and poured another glass of wine while he heard John Mulvaney hold forth for a further twenty minutes on the same subject.

The pride which Cambridge takes in its system of supervision is not without some foundation. It took the events of 1968 to question much of what the undergraduates of my generation took uncritically as a norm. The extreme waste of time to both student and supervisor of a system which requires the reading aloud of a long essay at regular intervals has still not been sufficiently recognized. Ten to twenty minutes of an hour's supervision can be wasted in this way – and often much more. Why can Cambridge not understand that it is more efficient for a supervisor to read and mark an essay and hold a short discussion with a pupil? This method is used at most other universities with success. It prevents off-the-cuff judgments by the supervisor and provides a more coherent discipline for the student. Free-ranging discussion of a prepared subject is much more worthwhile and whilst I would not deny the value of the discipline of writing essays, I would question their value when read aloud. It does not lend itself to economy in the use of words or to a strict economy of style, both of which are highly desirable commodities in a professional career in academe or elsewhere.

I have never discussed the matter with him, but I suspect that Glyn must have realized that the formal Cambridge supervision system was basically bad; consequently, once we had shown that we could write consecutive prose we were advised instead to write notes and to prepare a subject for discussion. Then the supervisions took off – and with them the process of learning began in earnest.

Glyn's appreciation of the history of the subject struck a chord in me, as it did in many other undergraduates and colleagues. His books, *The Three Ages* and *A Hundred Years of Archaeology*, together with Tom Kendrick's *British Antiquity*, whetted our appetites, while Glyn's encyclopaedic knowledge of the history and folklore of the subject glossed (often in a scandalous but entertaining fashion) the printed page. All Glyn's students have been steeped in the history of archaeology, not through formal teaching (although I believe there was a course in my period at Cambridge), but by process of turning the mind to fundamental sources. Many universities now have a couple of lectures in a course on 'History and Techniques of Archaeology', but nothing is as important as to be soaked in the history of the subject, to be committed to it. Glyn did this for us and equipped archaeologists of my generation to deal with the practicalities of the subject and with the ability to synthesize with confidence. Whether students today get the same wide view is not for me to say: I suspect that in some cases they do not. I remember examining a diploma or an MA in another university some ten years ago and asking the candidate in a *viva* about Childe's attitude to a specific point and how it compared with the ideas of, I think, Buttler, only to be pulled up by the chairman of the board – a distinguished professor who had known both men – who was outraged that I should assume knowledge by a young postgraduate of long out-dated theories. I was equally shocked that the student had not got the critical ability to use such sources.

A dedication to the historical approach then is perhaps a major element in Glyn's success as a teacher. The history of archaeology permeated discussion in

supervisions which were too informal to be called by that term and too unpompous to be designated as seminars. We were encouraged to read long out-dated but influential scholars, warned of crankeries and peculiarities and led lightly through the shifting sands of changing theory.

But there were other matters. Glyn was much exercised by prehistoric art at that time (*A Picture Book of British Art*, you will remember) and was intending to write a major work on the subject. His room was consequently strewn with photographs of painting, sculpture and metalwork and my co-supervisees (mainly John Mulvaney and John Stanford) and I were **tempted to make comparative – even exclamatory –** judgments concerning the different objects about which Glyn enthused. Enthusiasm communicated is another major clue to the quality of Glyn's teaching. He bubbles over at the latest find, surrounding it with judgment, speculation and gossip; drawing from the most immature a response which stretches their minds, tempts them into indiscreet judgments which are kindly corrected and used as a peg on which to hang an access of knowledge. 'Have another glass, and tell me what you think about . . . ' is the phrase which echoes down the years. It is still heard today whenever one meets Glyn and is a measure of the value which he places on the judgment of the least of his students.

Dorothy Garrod was then professor – witty, dry, learned and a terrible lecturer (all those Central European Palaeolithic stations, the names of which she pronounced so lovingly!) – I could not make head nor tail of what she was getting at (even then I was being tugged towards the early medieval period and had no intention of being examined on the Palaeolithic), but I persevered through her lectures and Glyn lightened them for me and I am sure for others. With little system he led us through the art of the Palaeolithic, talked interminably of Lascaux (still a comparatively recent find) and led us thence to the Red Lady of Paviland, Marie Stopes's father, Miles Burkitt (still a force in the faculty) and Peyrony's *Éléments de Préhistoire*. I got the message and, although I never wrote an essay on the subject, I was not put off when later I had to contemplate a, fortunately never taken, examination (in Swedish) on the European Palaeolithic. Only Glyn could have given such confidence.

Glyn has never been what Crawford called 'a slippered archaeologist'. He is always out and about. I took part in what must have been his last excavation (the two seasons at Barclodiad y Gawres) which was exciting and fun: but I don't think even he would label himself an excavator. It is, however, a pleasure to be in the country with him, visiting monuments. He was the teacher *sans pareil* on faculty field-trips. Although my fondest memory of these extraordinary occasions is enshrined in a treasured snapshot of Stonehenge with Stuart Piggott and Grahame Clark pointing in opposite directions, it was Glyn who led us round the Cerne Abbas giant, with appropriate *sotto voce* remarks; Hetty Pegler's Tump, with asides to Elsie Clifford; the pub at Avebury (and of course the monument) with graphic accounts of Keiller and his work; Chedworth and tea with Toty de Navarro at Broadway; Bryn Celli Ddu with love. This was all recalled when he recently led a party of university professors to look at one of the Cambridgeshire dykes and in five minutes got to the heart of the problem. He has taught many of us how to look at monuments, where to be critical, where to accept, where to reject, what questions to ask. His work during the war on aerial photography, and his impressive fieldwork on the British megalithic tombs has given him an eye for field monuments second only to Crawford, a man who is much in his thoughts. Any student who could not learn from this would be dull indeed. Another clue to Glyn as teacher.

Glyn the lecturer I cannot remember. But then I cannot remember any Cambridge lecturer with anything like clarity, save for Toty de Navarro whose style was not a style, whose arguments and material had to be transcribed verbatim as there was no other way of getting the information, who drained us of energy but taught us the Bronze and Iron Ages until we cried for mercy. But of Glyn I have only a vague impression as he shuffles large numbers of 3¼-inch slides in a nonchalant way and comes up with a coherent account of the latest megalithic theories (fortunately for me, pre-computer). Tying his gown-sleeves in knots he holds forth on the relation between folklore and archaeology, on Neolithic pottery, on Spain and Malta, on Hemp. Is that all I remember, and why? The reason is I think simple: I never liked formal teaching and could not do anything but absorb what was said in an incoherent fashion. Glyn is a good lecturer, some might say brilliant, but I can only remember his public performances, never his lecture courses. Strange.

Glyn when he taught me was not the public personality he now is. 'Animal, Vegetable, Mineral?' was taking its first faltering steps in my last undergraduate year – and for the first few programmes Glyn was not even in the chair. But he had then, as he has now, a wide knowledge of the world and of people. Glyn and Ruth gave many people like me the first glimmerings of maturity in our outlook on our non-archaeological life. Like all Welshmen he talks fluently about practically everything. Food and drink, friends, politics, Cambridge; he talks about France, India, America and most of the countries of Europe. He talks cleverly, wittily, forcefully and often to the point. He is a famous story-teller, anecdotes flow from him in an Aubrey-esque fashion. His public persona – television performer, detective-story writer, editor of *Antiquity* – has never occupied him to the exclusion of his pupils. Such activities introduced us to the wider world and encouraged us to popularize and to do detailed research. He also introduced us – young as we were – to the professionals: great names who visited Cambridge only to dine and drink (or so it seemed to us) — Ó Ríordáin, Joffroy, Crawford, Woolley, Leakey, Wheeler, Piggott: these and a hundred more were made to talk to undergraduates over wine in Third Court at St John's or over beer in the Blue Boar. One did not leave Cambridge an innocent to the politics and realities of the profession.

27 Glyn Daniel and Cambridge

Edward Miller

LIKE DAVID WILSON I must begin by disclaiming the pretensions of my title. About a great many of Glyn's Cambridge activities, including a good number that undoubtedly would have appeared most important to him, I am totally uninstructed. Above all, I know nothing of the affairs of the Faculty of Archaeology and Anthropology which Glyn has served for thirty-five years. This, moreover, is merely one gap in my knowledge, although doubtless it is the most serious. On the other hand, Glyn is still, I believe, a Trustee of Cambridge's Arts Theatre and I think that, for a time, he was Steward of the Union: these again are capacities in which I never remember encountering him. I even remember a rumour that somehow associated him with ice-hockey, although I hesitate to claim that this was in a playing capacity. Once more I must plead ignorance both of the sport and of this association. Already, however, intimations of the diversity of Glyn's Cambridge interests begin to build up, so that I need to make clear the very limited angle of my vision: it is virtually confined to the domestic interior of St John's College in the twenty years or so that followed the Second World War. Even within St John's, of course, there were many relevant things that I failed to observe and many more that, in the fifteen years since I left the College, I have forgotten. No less certainly, however, there are others that are firmly printed on the memory.

My first recollections of Glyn go back beyond the war years, although I cannot claim more than a superficial acquaintance with him at that time. After all he had come up, one of a quite astonishingly distinguished series of pupils from Barry County School, a year before I did; so that he had all the seniority conferred by one third of an undergraduate's time-span. I do remember, however, his gifts as a conversationalist and his assurance, the latter amply justified by a distinguished academic record culminating in his election, less than two years after graduating, to a Research Fellowship in 1938. Immediately he had little enough time to enjoy this privilege, for within a year or two he had disappeared into the RAF, and I did not encounter him again until I returned to Cambridge at the beginning of 1946. Glyn had, I think, resumed his Fellowship a little earlier and had celebrated the fact with characteristic panache. As

Jessica Mann has already described above, thinly disguised by the pseudonym Dilwyn Rees (the translation very soon became widely known) he made an impossibly located neighbouring college to St John's, Fisher College, the scene of *The Cambridge Murders* which he published in 1945. This essay in detective fiction appears to me to have enjoyed over the years a not inconsiderable success.

Inevitably, or so it seems in retrospect, Glyn was soon busied about the affairs of the College. Before long he was a member of the College Council and he was, I think, its secretary for a time; but the College's most inspired decision was to invite Glyn in 1946 to become Steward, an office which he held with quite exceptional stamina for nine years. At least in prospect it offered scope, of course, for Glyn's interest in good food and good wine: for, if he took it up in times of austerity and rationing, these had ended before he laid it down. No less did the stewardship offer scope for the exercise of his diplomatic skills. Any Steward of any college inevitably finds himself in the middle: between kitchen staff on the one side and undergraduates and High Table on the other. Undergraduates have always grumbled about their college food and doubtless will continue to do so until the end of time; but dons (or some of them) not infrequently provide a more insupportable cross for a Steward to bear. Glyn himself illustrated the level of asperity with which their dissatisfactions might be expressed when he published certain letters written by that formidable geologist, T.G. Bonney, to one of his predecessors not long before the First World War. In the years immediately following the Second War the dice might seem to have been even more heavily loaded against a Steward; for shortages dictated the serving of such delicacies as whale meat (tasting as I remember rather like india rubber) and the offering of portions that were somewhat less than young appetites demanded. Yet somehow the inevitable critics were appeased, although there still remained what Glyn himself describes as 'the endless staff troubles that every kitchen organization is heir to': but these, too, were got over and from it all Glyn emerged to all appearances both unscathed and in high good humour. That he was able to do so was due in no small measure to his way with people and, what is no less important, his willingness always to offer appreciation where that had been earned. All the same, it took effort and time and trouble to a degree Glyn was always inclined to deprecate; but effort and time and trouble were precisely what he was willing to give towards doing the job well.

There was, however, more than keeping the peace to Glyn's period as Steward: for I think in many ways he also quietly transformed the traditional menus at St John's. Circumstances, of course, favoured this exercise in practical gastronomy. The later years of his stewardship saw an end to rationing and a mitigation of the shortages that since 1939 had severely limited what any kitchen could provide. In the 1950s, therefore, he was in a position to innovate relatively unhampered by the constraints of the past. For someone with Glyn's interests the opportunity was irresistible. His interest in the culinary arts, after all, is practical as well as the interest of a consumer; and he has himself put on record how, with the aid of the then Kitchen Manager at St John's, he invented Les Poires Saliagos in order to provide a sweet suitable for celebrating the wedding of Jane and Colin Renfrew and the latter's election to a Research Fellowship. Another of Glyn's published works, and one that may easily have escaped the notice of those whose concerns are primarily archaeological, is further indication of the breadth and depth of his gastronomic interests: I mean his *Oxford Chicken Pie*, printed quite beautifully for him by Sebastian Carter at the Rampant Lions Press. In this little essay he rescues from oblivion some recipes deriving from Oxford and Cambridge colleges and, at the same time, he punctures a number of culinary myths. Crème Brulée, for example, which so many Cambridge colleges have claimed to be their very own invention, is almost certainly demonstrated to have been a Trinity man's import from Aberdeenshire; and that quintessentially Pembroke dish, Mr Whibley's Soufflé, is traced back to its true origin in the kitchens of the liner *Mauretania*. In Glyn's hands a cookery book is easily transmuted into a historical enquiry or an essay in detection: Dilwyn Rees still lurks in the shadow of Glyn Daniel.

A penchant for gastronomic antiquarianism, however, was merely one of the gifts Glyn brought to life in St John's: another was a hard-headed business capacity. One example among many of the latter was his establishment, soon after becoming Steward, of a college Pig Club. Pig Clubs were institutions that had come Glyn's way while he was in the RAF and the translation of the idea into a collegiate context is merely one instance of how experience in the services influenced life in post-war Cambridge. The application of the idea in St John's was all the more natural because the College had long kept pigs 'in the decent obscurity' as Glyn put it, of the kitchen gardens on Madingley Road. Under existing regulations, however, they had to be fattened for the market, a lamentable deprivation of meat from a Steward's point of view when that commodity was in short supply. Glyn pointed out that, if the College established a Pig Club, only half the meat of the pigs fattened needed to be sold to the Ministry of Food; so a Pig Club was founded and thereafter at intervals over the next few years pork 'by courtesy of the Pig Club' appeared on College menus. Glyn, naturally, was secretary of this institution and found himself acquiring expert knowledge of such recondite matters as deadweight certification and the Government's transit shrinkage allowance.

Inevitably this expertise was not required indefinitely, for the end of meat rationing in 1954 removed the rationale of the Pig Club in its original form. What happened next I believe once again to have been in large measure Glyn's handiwork. To cope with the contingency of its impending redundancy an extraordinary general meeting of the Club was convoked, and it was evident from the very start that some excellent staff work had gone on behind the scenes. The decision of the meeting was a foregone conclusion: that the Club should remain in being for 'social and unspecified purposes as a glorious anomaly'. The meeting concluded with the serving of wine and maupygernons, the latter being a confection of pig meat (to which, I think, Charles II is said to have been particularly partial) which Glyn has rescued from oblivion. What was to have been a final meeting of the Club became the first of many of a new sort which had the merit of preserving one feature of its original dispensation. Membership extends to a number of the assistant staff of the College as well as to a selection from its fellowship; and it is also valid for life, so that the annual summer meeting of the Club, to which ladies are invited, has become a reunion of a special sort. Quite apart from those who continue in the College's service it is likely to bring together a former Master, a former (and famous) head gardener, a former clerk of works now living in Yorkshire and many others.

An anomaly the Pig Club may be, but the idea of preserving it after its practical utility had gone has produced one of those curious institutions contributing positively to the cohesion and continuity of a collegiate community. As I have said, although he had collaborators, I attribute to Glyn a considerable responsibility for the Club's new form – the more particularly because it mirrors so closely his own relationship with those members of the College's assistant staff with whom his activities brought him into contact. This has always been one of his great assets as a

College officer. I do not for a moment claim that either Glyn or anyone else consciously foresaw that the new-style Pig Club would become in fact something more than a mere anomaly; but a good institution is none the worse for having been created in a fit of absence of mind or without precise regard for what the distant consequences of its creation may ultimately be.

Of the things that Glyn initiated or helped to initiate a number have proved enduring. The Pig Club still regularly meets; maupygernons are still served from time to time at its meetings; and at least until fairly recently Les Poires Saliagos was a sweet frequently ordered for Club dinners in College. Not all of his activities, of course, had so permanent an outcome and one that proved more fleeting comes particularly to mind. Glyn had, I think, a principal responsibility for recruiting and organizing the six anonymous Fellows of St John's who, for a number of years, set the Christmas competition in *The Spectator*. I seem to recollect that they sometimes described themselves as the Countess of Shrewsbury's Connection, but the precise implications of that title (if indeed it had any) now escape me. What may have been characteristic, on the other hand, of an enterprise in which Glyn played a leading role was that payment was made, or so at least he persuaded his collaborators, in advance and in the form of quite excellent claret. It was thus possible to attend to the preparation of the competition inspired by consuming the claret at an annual dessert in Glyn's rooms. It is hard to think of circumstances better calculated to stimulate ingenuity and imagination. True, in retrospect, one feels that some tidying of the copy may have been required next morning; but if that had to be done I can only suppose that it was effected surreptitiously and quietly. No doubt it was at this point that Glyn the editor took over from Glyn the genial host.

It was also no doubt quite characteristic that, in this minor enterprise, Glyn should have provided a point of contact between Cambridge and a wider world. No doubt he is fortunate in that his field of study, to say nothing of his manner of cultivating it, conspire to widen his horizons. The full implications of the fact that he is a Knight (1st Class) of the Dannebrog may not be immediately evident to everyone; but no one can misconstrue the significance of one of his publications – *The Hungry Archaeologist in France*. Evidently, perfectly legitimate academic purposes have taken him more frequently to desirable places than happens to most of us. In the meantime, moreover, Cambridge was the centre from which he branched out into a diversity of activities. The television series, 'Animal, Vegetable, Mineral?' made him a national figure; and the volumes of the 'Ancient Peoples and Places' series,

appearing with such rapidity from the mid-1950s onwards, fed a growing general interest in archaeology for the creation of which he had a large responsibility. At the same time these enterprises are by no means irrelevant to the theme of Glyn in Cambridge. I have no doubt they helped in attracting able students of archaeology to Cambridge, and not least to St John's; but they also drew there a stream of scholars in this field, both young and older, whom Glyn would entertain with his characteristic hospitality. It was a further consequence that his colleagues in St John's had exceptional opportunities to meet so many of those who were or would be our leading archaeologists.

In those years what most of us found particularly enviable was Glyn's capacity to do so many things without seeming effort and at the same time. What I have had to say has largely concerned matters that were peripheral to his main preoccupations as a College and University teacher, an active member of his Faculty and a productive scholar; quite apart from that, they by no means exhaust the many things that engaged him. Their diversity and volume might well have been less supportable without Ruth: for she not only shared so many of his interests, but contributed expertise and skill to his mounting burden of editorial work. In so very many ways they struck me as a team, even if to the best of my knowledge Glyn never shared any of Ruth's gifts as a cricketer. One cannot have everything.

In the final resort, however, I remember Glyn as a person rather than in the context of any particular activity or occasion. I think of him, in College matters and no doubt in others, as being on the liberal side of most fences, although never to the extent of jettisoning what was good in old ways or valuable in received tradition. In some ways, in recent times of unusually rapid and frequent changes, this is an uncomfortable stance; for on occasion reasonable change can be made to appear less reasonable by apparent allies who wish to turn it into something more root and branch or merely to justify it on the grounds of irrefutable logic instead of good common sense. No doubt, therefore, Glyn has had his disappointments; but I think he also enjoys for its own sake the process of trying to bring about a desirable end and, in the last resort, he possesses the gift of seeing the ridiculous side of situations. One can also be sure that, in retrospect, the tale about them as told by him will lose none of its savour in the telling.

My clearest memories of all, however, are visual rather than verbal: of Glyn making his way through the courts of St John's from the porters' lodge or kitchens or kitchen office or the Merry Boys (that conveniently located flat just across St John's Street) to his rooms in third court. His appearance in itself was apt to be memorable. His shirt was likely to be of a striking colour, and to be topped with a bow tie that also had a certain gaiety. His jackets, too, were frequently more colourful than those that were commonly worn by others. And all this might be crowned by a remarkable floppy hat. Was there, I wonder, more than one of them or was it the same headgear that persisted eternally over the years? I simply do not know. Be that as it may be, he appeared to move almost at a trot, but his progress was interrupted at frequent intervals by pauses to exchange a confidence, to offer a wry observation, or to convey the latest intelligence on matters of moment. Although he gave the appearance of hastening from one point to another, his progress in fact was probably slow: for he appeared to have something to communicate to almost everyone he met – whether undergraduates or fellows or members

of the College assistant staff. It was equally characteristic of him that, on these peregrinations, he always appeared to be laden with impedimenta: books, packages, letters, papers. He gave the impression that they were somehow clasped precariously, and that at any moment they would fly in every direction. Yet in fact, however often he stopped and started again, they never did. Like everything else they were under a highly individual and totally distinctive control.

Given the circumstances I have been compelled to fall back upon memories of Glyn in times that are now relatively remote. I feel some confidence, however, that many of them reflect qualities and characteristics that would be discernible in today's Glyn Daniel; and, above all, I doubt if the character of his progresses through St John's, where he has been a familiar figure for forty-seven years, has changed at all.

1 Glyn and Ruth Daniel on the Backs at Cambridge.

Belinda Barratt and Ruth Daniel

THE TERMINAL date for this list is 31 October 1980. Periodicals are listed under the year for which they were published, and the abbreviations used are those recommended by the Council for British Archaeology. Reviews (as opposed to review articles) and foreign reprints are not included.

1936

Two polished stone axe-heads from Carmarthenshire, *Archaeol. Cambrensis* XCI, 306–9.

Saxon pottery, *The Eagle: a magazine supported by members of St. John's College* [Cambridge] XLIX, 141–5.

1937

The 'dolmens' of southern Britain, *Antiquity* XI, 183–200.

Excavations at Trehill, Glamorgan, June, 1936, *Archaeol. Cambrensis* XCII, 287–93.

The Four Crosses burial chamber, Caernarvonshire, *Archaeol. Cambrensis* XCII, 165–7.

The chambered barrow in Parc le Breos Cwm, S. Wales, *Proc. Prehist. Soc.* III, 71–86.

1938

The megalithic tombs of Northern Europe, *Antiquity* XII, 297–310.

1939

On two long barrows near Rodez in the south of France, *Antiq.J.* XIX, 157–65.

A note on finds of archaeological interest recently made in the College, *The Eagle* LI, 144–7.

The transepted gallery graves of western France, *Proc. Prehist. Soc.* V, 143–65.

1940

The Rodmarton and Avening portholes (with E. M. Clifford), *Proc. Prehist. Soc.* VI, 133–65.

1941

The dual nature of the megalithic colonisation of prehistoric Europe, *Proc. Prehist. Soc.* VII, 1–49.

1943

The three ages: an essay on archaeological method, Cambridge: University Press.

Air photographs and interpretation in war, *J. United Service Inst. India* LXXIII, 307–13.

1944

Anti-Christ and my cat Toby, *Exposure: a monthly produced somewhere within the frontiers of His Imperial Majesty's Indian Empire by a photographic unit of the Royal Air Force,* The Christmas Miscellany 1944, 20–2.

1945

The Cambridge murders (detective novel, published under the pseudonym of 'Dilwyn Rees'), London: Gollancz. (Reissued 1948.)

1946

Air photography in post-war India (with R. Langhorne), *J. United Service Inst. India* LXXVI, 99–102.

Air photography and archaeology, *Listener* XXXV (9 May), 605.

Why archaeology? *Listener* XXXVI (24 Oct.), 553–4.

1947

Graves of our remote ancestors, *Listener* XXXVII (6 Feb.), 232.

Obituary: Dr H. M. Chadwick: erudition and friendship, *The Times* (8 Jan.), 7d.

1948

Archaeology and broadcasting, *Archaeol. News Lett.* I, no. 2, 1–2, 4.

Reading and writing, *Archaeol. News Lett.* I, no. 4, 7–9.

Danish art and prehistory, *Listener* XL (30 Dec.), 1003–4.

How to look at our cultural landscape (the value of air photography), *Listener* XL (19 Aug.), 276–7.

Ideas and beliefs of the Victorians – X: Archaeology links geology to history, *Listener* XXXIX (8 Apr.), 574–7.

Letter: The wood age, *Spectator* (1 Oct.), 431.

1949

A defence of prehistory, *Cambridge J.* III, no. 3, 131–47.

The heritage of early Britain – I: The prehistoric peoples, *Listener* XLII (15 Dec.), 1037–9.

The Lascaux cave paintings, *Listener* XLII (1 Dec.), 946–8.

The distribution and date of the passage-graves of the British Isles (with T. G. E. Powell), *Proc. Prehist. Soc.* XV, 169–87.

1950

A hundred years of archaeology, London: Duckworth. (Hundred Years series.)

The prehistoric chamber tombs of England and Wales, Cambridge: University Press.

Articles in *Chambers's Encyclopaedia* (New Edition), London: George Newnes. Vol. I: Africa, Archaeology: Neolithic, 143–4; vol. II: Barrow, 138–9; vol. III: Carnac, 123; vol. VI: Hal-Tarxien, 704–5; vol. VII: India, Archaeology: Indus Valley Civilization, 448–50; vol. IX: Megalith, 234–5; Navetas, 711; New Grange, 825–6; vol. X: Nuraghi, 130.

The long barrow in Western Europe, in *The early cultures of north-west Europe* (H. M. Chadwick memorial studies), ed. Sir Cyril Fox and Bruce Dickins, Cambridge: University Press, 1–20.

Prehistoric archaeology in the universities of Great Britain, *Archaeol. News Lett.* II, no. 9, 137–9.

Portrait of a head gardener, *The Eagle* LIV, 144–7.

Letter: 'Hundred years of archaeology', *Times Lit. Supp.* (23 June), 389.

1951

A picture book of ancient British art (with Stuart Piggott), Cambridge: University Press.

Letter: 'Prehistoric chamber tombs of England and Wales', *Archaeol. News Lett.* III, no. 9, 143.

Letter: Prehistoric chamber tombs of England and Wales, *Archaeol. News Lett.* IV, no. 1, 3–4.

Reading and writing, *Archaeol. News Lett.* IV, no. 3, 38–9.

The chronological framework of prehistoric barbarian Europe, *Man* LI, 34–7.

The date of the European megalithic tombs. Summary of a communication to the Royal Anthropological Institute, 6 March 1951, *Man* LI, 63.

1952

Chairman, for six and a half years, of the BBC Television panel game 'Animal, Vegetable, Mineral?'

The Cambridge murders (reissued in paperback), Harmondsworth: Penguin Books.

The heritage of early Britain (with M. P. Charlesworth, J. G. D. Clark, J. M. de Navarro, M. D. Knowles, P. H. Blair, Nora K. Chadwick, and E. Miller), London: G. Bell and Sons. To this GED contributed 'The peoples of prehistoric Britain', 11–32.

The Prehistoric Society: a report of the meeting held in Dublin, September 10th to 15th, 1951, *Archaeol. News Lett.* IV, no. 5, 71–6.

Reading and writing, *Archaeol. News Lett.* IV, no. 6, 87–9.

Reading and writing, *Archaeol. News Lett.* IV, no. 8, 120–2.

Les monuments mégalithiques et la forme des tumuli en France et en Angleterre (with Jean Arnal), *Bull. Soc. Préhist. Française* XLIX, 39–53.

1953

Reading and writing: field archaeology as illustrated by Crawford, *Archaeol. News Lett.* IV, no. 12, 189–90.

Archaeology on the air, *BBC Quart.* VIII, no. 2, 89–95.

The Abbé Breuil and Palaeolithic art, *Listener* XLIX (15 Jan.), 93–5.

Field archaeology (review article of O. G. S. Crawford *Archaeology in the field*), *Listener* XLIX (26 Mar.), 521, 523.

Myth or legend? – I: Lyonesse and the lost lands of England, *Listener* XLIX (19 Feb.), 299–300.

1954

Welcome death (detective novel), London: Gollancz.

Archaeology and television, *Antiquity* XXVIII, 201–5.

The background to antiquarianism and archaeology, *Archaeol. News Lett.* V, no. 1, 1–4.

Letter: Sound and vision, *New Statesman and Nation*, XLVIII (4 Sept.), 266.

Five mysteries of life. 1. How old is man? 2. Man's oldest art; 3. How civilisation came to us; 4. The riddle of the standing stones; 5. Who *were* the Ancient Britons? *News Chronicle* (4–8 Oct.).

Who are the Welsh? (Sir John Rhŷs Memorial Lecture), *Proc. Brit. Acad.* XL, 145–67.

Letter: Vix and the vase, *Spectator* (13 Aug.), 195.

1955

Lascaux and Carnac, London: Lutterworth Press.

Myth or legend? (with D. L. Page, R. F. Treharne, Sir L. Woolley, C. T. Seltman, S. P. Ó Ríordáin, J. M. White, E. R. Leach, T. C. Lethbridge, S. Piggott, J. S. P. Bradford and H. J. Rose), London: G. Bell and Sons. To this GED contributed preface, 5–6, and 'Lyonesse and the lost lands of England', 11–19.

Who are the Welsh? (Sir John Rhŷs Memorial Lecture, read at the British Academy, 10 November 1954, reprinted from *Proc. Brit. Acad.* XL), London: British Academy.

The Brå cauldron and the Danish Early Iron Age, *Antiquity* XXIX, 137–40.

Prehistory and protohistory in France, *Antiquity* XXIX, 209–14.

The *allées couvertes* of France, *Archaeol.J.* CXII, 1–19.

Reading and writing, *Archaeol. News Lett.* V, no. 9, 170–3.

Reading and writing, *Archaeol. News Lett.* V, no. 10, 196–8.

Learning about archaeology, *Literary Guide* LXX, no. 8, 6–8.

Letter: National Library of Wales, *The Times* (16 (Nov.), 11 e.

1956

General Editor, Ancient Peoples and Places series, London: Thames and Hudson.

Barclodiad y Gawres: the excavation of a megalithic chamber tomb in Anglesey, 1952–1953 (with T. G. E. Powell), Liverpool: University Press. (Liverpool Monographs in Archaeology and Oriental Studies).

The back-looking curiosity: the Society of Antiquaries, *Listener* LVI (27 Sept.), 462–3.

Letter: Cave paintings at Rouffignac: seeking evidence of authenticity, *The Times* (22 Sept.), 7e.

Obituary: Professor S. R. K. Glanville: administrator and scholar, *The Times* (7 May), 16d.

1957

The 150th anniversary of the Danish National Museum, *Antiquity* XXXI, 169–71.

The megalithic art of France, *Geogr.Mag.* XXX, no. 8, 335–42.

The wandering megaliths of France, *Geogr.Mag.* XXX, no. 7, 273–82.

The cromlechs of Glamorgan, *Morgannwg* I, 3–12.

1958

Editor: *Antiquity* (from XXXII, no. 125, March). To which GED contributes editorial.

The megalith builders of Western Europe, London: Hutchinson.

The Minnesota petroglyph, *Antiquity* XXXII, 264–7.

Les monuments mégalithiques et leurs relations avec le Rhône, *Cahiers Rhodaniens* V, 22–6.

The earliest people of Wales: recent findings by archaeologists, *Listener* LX (30 Oct.), 689–91.

Snapshot war, *Listener* LIX (27 Feb.), 359–60.

The chronology of the French collective tombs, *Proc. Prehist. Soc.* XXIV, 1–23.

1959

My childhood in the Vale, in *History on my doorstep,* ed. Stewart Williams, Cowbridge, Glam.: D. Brown, 13–18.

Some megalithic follies, *Antiquity* XXXIII, 282–4.

The idea of man's antiquity, *Scientific American* 201, no. 5, 167–76.

1960

The prehistoric chamber tombs of France: a geographical, morphological and chronological survey, London: Thames and Hudson.

Maupygernons and mash, *The Eagle* LIX, 65–74.

The test of the spade: two recent archaeological books, *Listener* LXIV (29 Dec.), 1200.

Writing a new prehistory of man, *Listener* LXIV (8 Sept.), 381, 384–5.

Letter: Education for girls, *The Times* (26 Jan.), 11e.

Letter: Sentenced to death (appeal against death sentence on Francis Forsyth; with others), *The Times* (5 Nov.), 7d.

1961

The pen of my aunt, Cambridge: printed for the author by Rampant Lions Press.

The chronology of the French megalithic tombs, in *Bericht über den V. internationalen Kongress für Vor-und Frühgeschichte,* Hamburg, 24–30 August 1958, ed. Gerhard Bersu, Berlin: Verlag Gebr. Mann, 220–3.

1962

The idea of prehistory, London: C. A. Watts & Co. (The New Thinker's Library).

Welcome death (reissued in paperback), Harmondsworth: Penguin Books.

The megalith builders, in *The prehistoric peoples of Scotland,* ed. Stuart Piggott, London: Routledge and Kegan Paul, 39–72.

A great prehistorian (the late Abbé Henri Breuil; with Miles Burkitt and others), *Listener* LXVII (22 Mar.), 502.

1963

The hungry archaeologist in France: a travelling guide to caves, graves and good living in the Dordogne and Brittany, London: Faber and Faber.

The megalith builders of Western Europe, 2nd edn, London: Hutchinson.

The collective tomb-builders of Iberia: indigenes or colonists? in *A Pedro Bosch-Gimpera en el septuagésimo aniversario de su nacimiento,* Mexico: Instituto Nacional de Antropología e Historia, 103–10.

The personality of Wales, in *Culture and environment: essays in honour of Sir Cyril Fox,* ed. I. Ll. Foster and L. Alcock, London: Routledge and Kegan Paul, 7–23.

Problèmes relatifs à la diffusion des mégalithes, in *Les civilisations atlantiques du Néolithique á l'Age du Fer* (Actes du Premier Colloque Atlantique, Brest, 11 Septembre 1961), ed. P.-R. Giot, Rennes: Laboratoire d'Anthropologie Préhistorique, 15–18.

Letter: A council's action (on Cambridge Midsummer Fair camping ban; with others), *The Times* (21 June), 13d.

Letter: Entrance to Oxbridge, *The Times* (1 June), 9e.

Obituary: Mr R. R. Clarke, *The Times* (13 May), 16c.

The long barrows of the Cotswolds (presidential address, 9 March 1963), *Trans. Bristol Gloucestershire Archaeol. Soc.* LXXXII, 5–17.

1964

New Grange and the bend of the Boyne (with S. P. Ó Ríordáin), London: Thames and Hudson. (Ancient Peoples and Places, 40.)

Megaliths and man: European rock monuments are relics of nascent civilisations, *Natural History* LXXIII, no. 4, 46–53.

1965–79

Archaeological adviser to Penguin Books.

1965

Oxford chicken pie, Cambridge: printed for the author by Rampant Lions Press.

Edited (with I. Ll. Foster) *Prehistoric and early Wales*, London: Routledge and Kegan Paul. To this GED contributed introduction, 1–15.

1966

Man discovers his past, London: Duckworth. (Reissued 1968).

Archaeology and the origins of civilization, *Listener* LXXVI (1 Dec.), 803-4.

Archaeology and the origins of civilization – II: Civilization of the twin rivers, *Listener* LXXVI (8 Dec.), 847–9.

Archaeology and the origins of civilization – III: In the shadow of the pyramids, *Listener* LXXVI (15 Dec.), 884–6.

Archaeology and the origins of civilization – IV: China and the Indus Valley, *Listener* LXXVI (22 Dec.), 924–7.

Archaeology and the origins of civilization – V: Pre-Columbian America, *Listener* LXXVI (29 Dec.), 955–7.

The megalith builders of the SOM, *Palaeohistoria* XII (Neolithic studies in Atlantic Europe: proceedings of the second Atlantic Colloquium, Groningen, 6-11

April 1964, presented to A. E. van Giffen for his 80th birthday), 199–208.

Letter: Russian antiquities (exhibition in The Hague; with Stuart Piggott), *The Times* (17 Nov.), 13d.

Letter: University of Wales, *The Times* (15 Feb.), 11e.

1967

General Editor, Archaeological Guides series, London: Faber and Faber.

The origins and growth of archaeology, Harmondsworth: Penguin Books.

The western Mediterranean (with J. D. Evans), Cambridge: University Press. (Cambridge Ancient History, rev. edn, vol. II, chapter XXXVII; fascicle 57).

Northmen and Southmen, *Antiquity* XLI, 313–17.

Archaeology and the origins of civilization – VI: Causes of 'the great jump forward', *Listener* LXXVII (5 Jan.), 12–15.

Anthropological advice (parts of editorial in *Antiquity*, on gypsies, quoted), *The Times* (5 Dec.), 8h.

Letter: A claim from France (on British discoveries postage stamp issue), *The Times* (14 Aug.), 7e.

Letter: Museum decision (on British Museum), *The Times* (13 Dec.), 11d.

Letter: Tomb of Knowth, *The Times* (16 Aug.), 7e.

Edward Lhwyd: antiquary and archaeologist, *Welsh Hist. Rev.* IV, no. 3, 345–59.

1968

The first civilizations: the archaeology of their origins, London: Thames and Hudson.

One hundred years of Old World prehistory, in *One hundred years of anthropology*, ed. John Otis Brew, Cambridge, Mass.: Harvard University Press, 57–93.

The Lepenski Vir excavations, *Listener* LXXIX (11 Jan.), 42–44.

Obituary: Prof. D. Garrod, *The Times* (20 Dec.), 11h.

Obituary: Prof. H. A. Harris, *The Times* (20 Sept.), 12h.

1969

Knotweed and camomile and bindweed (on Tollund Man), *Listener* LXXXII (17 July), 79.

Letter: 'Post Brenhinol' (on Welsh language), *The Times* (9 Apr.), 9d.

1970–76

Entries in *Dictionary of Scientific Biography*, New York: Charles Scribner's Sons. Vol. I: J. Beddoe, 562–3; vol. II: H. E. P. Breuil, 450–1; vol. VIII: L. S. B. Leakey, 104–5; vol. IX: G. O. Montelius, 489–

90; L.-L. G. de Mortillet, 538–9; vol. X: W. M. F. Petrie, 549–50; L.-E.-S. Piette, 606–7; vol. XI: A. H. L. F. Pitt-Rivers, 5–6; vol. XII: H. Schliemann, 179–82; vol. XIV: C. L. Woolley, 504–5; O. Worm, 505; J. J. Worsaae, 506–7.

1970

Archaeology and the history of art (an inaugural lecture delivered in the University of Hull on 21 January 1969), Hull: University of Hull. (Ferens Fine Art Lectures.)

Carbon 14 dates and the chronology of European megaliths, in *Actes du VIIe Congrès International des Sciences Préhistoriques et Protohistoriques*, Prague, 21-27 August 1966, ed. Jan Filip, Prague: Académie Tchécoslovaque des Sciences, 536–9.

Megalithic answers, *Antiquity* XLIV, 260–9.

1971

The first civilizations: the archaeology of their origins (reissued in paperback), Harmondsworth: Penguin Books.

Osbert Guy Stanhope Crawford, in *Dictionary of National Biography 1951-60*, ed. E. T. Williams and Helen M. Palmer, Oxford: University Press, 268–70.

From Worsaae to Childe: the models of prehistory, *Proc. Prehist. Soc.* XXXVII, 140–53.

1972

Megaliths in history, London: Thames and Hudson. (4th Walter Neurath Memorial Lecture.)

The idea of man's antiquity, in *Old World archaeology: foundations of civilization* (Readings from Scientific American), ed. C. C. Lamberg-Karlovsky, San Francisco: W. H. Freeman and Company, 7–11.

The origin of the megalithic tombs of the British Isles, in *Die Anfänge des Neolithikums vom Orient bis Nordeuropa*, ed. Hermann Schwabedissen: VII, *Westliches Mittelmeergebiet und Britische Inseln*, Cologne and Vienna: Böhlau Verlag, 233–47. (Fundamenta: Reihe A, Band 3.)

The origins of Boucher de Perthes' archéogéologie, *Antiquity* XLVI, 317–20.

The second American, *Antiquity* XLVI, 288–92.

The new archaeology (the claims made for a science of archaeology; with Colin Renfrew, Jacquetta Hawkes and others), *Listener* LXXXVII (20 Jan.), 68–70.

Obituary: Dr Louis Leakey, *The Times* (12 Oct.), 18h.

Obituary: Prof. D. Talbot Rice, The Times (17 Mar.), 16g.

1973

Edited (with Poul Kjaerum) *Megalithic graves and ritual: papers presented at the III Atlantic Colloquium*, Moesgård, 1969, Copenhagen: Jutland Archaeological Society. (Jutland Archaeological Society Publications, XI.)

Did Teilhard do it? (on the Piltdown forgery), *Listener* LXXXIX (24 May), 690.

Spain and the problem of European megalithic origins, in *Estudios dedicados al Professor Dr. Luis Pericot*, Barcelona: Universidad de Barcelona Instituto de Arqueología y Prehistoria, 209–14. (Publicaciones Eventuales, 23.)

1974

Edited (with Stuart Piggott and Charles McBurney) *France before the Romans*, London: Thames and Hudson. To this SP and GED contributed preface, 8, and summary and conclusions, 220–3.

Archaeology, in *The new Encyclopaedia Britannica*, 15th edn: *Macropaedia*, vol. I, Chicago: Encyclopaedia Britannica, 1078–82.

Letter: Perpetrator of the Piltdown forgery, *The Times* (18 Apr.), 15g.

1975

A hundred and fifty years of archaeology (a 2nd edn of *A hundred years of archaeology*), London: Duckworth.

Obituary: Prof. T. G. E. Powell, *The Times* (17 July), 16g.

'Schools need archaeologists' (part of inaugural lecture at Cambridge University quoted), *Times Higher Educ. Supp.* (31 Oct.), 4d.

1976

Cambridge and the back-looking curiosity: an inaugural lecture (delivered in the University of Cambridge on 24 October 1975), Cambridge: University Press.

In memoriam, in *In memoriam Pedro Bosch-Gimpera 1891–1974*, ed. Juan Comas, Mexico: Universidad Nacional Autónoma de Mexico, 61–4.

Stone, bronze and iron, in *To illustrate the monuments: essays on archaeology presented to Stuart Piggott on the occasion of his sixty-fifth birthday*, ed. J. V. S. Megaw, London: Thames and Hudson, 35–42.

Megaliths galore, *Antiquity* L, 187–9.

Letter: Moon temple mystery, *The Times* (4 Feb.), 15f.

Obituary: Mrs E. M. Clifford, *The Times* (7 Sept.), 14g.

1977

A hundred and fifty years of archaeology (reissued in paperback), London: Duckworth.

Consultant editor, *The illustrated encyclopedia of archaeology*, New York: Thomas Y. Crowell Company; Toronto: Fitzhenry and Whiteside.

Letter: A setting for Stonehenge (with Dame Sylvia Crowe, Lord Esher and Stuart Piggott), *The Times* (22 Jan.), 13b.

Letter: 'The Silbury treasure', *Times Lit. Supp.* (14 Jan.), 34.

1978
Consultant editor, *The illustrated encyclopedia of archaeology* (British edn.), London: Macmillan.
Obituary: Dr Calvin Wells, *The Times* (5 Aug.), 14g.

1979
The forgotten milestones and blind alleys of the past (Presidential address to the Royal Anthropological Institute, 5 June 1979), *Rain*, no. 33 (August), 3–6.

1980
Megalithic monuments, *Scientific American* 243, no. 1, 64–76.
Obituary: Professor Ole Klindt-Jensen, *The Times* (18 July), 16g.
Obituary: Mr Keith Muckelroy, *The Times* (13 Sept.), 14g.

processes 198, 202; publishers 196–8
Punch 221–2, *223*, 224, *225–6*

Quanterness 78, 165, 169

radiocarbon dating 97, 161, 163; in Africa 50; in China 66–7; of megaliths 72–3, 78, 85, 87–8; 95–7, 108, 115, 121–2, 128, 150, 165, 172, 174, 182; of Mesolithic 181
religious complex 157
Renfrew, A.C. 95, 97–8, 100–1, 108, 133, 135–6, 144, 149, 153–4, 165, 168–9, 196, 198–9, 212
Ring of Brogar 78–9
Roaix *88, 89*
rock-cut tombs 85, 89, 94, 96, 106–10, 115–16, 118–19, 122, 129, 134; distribution in Mediterranean 106, *107;* plans of *108;* typology 106–8
Romans, attribution of megaliths 24
Rössberga 148, *148*
round barrows 167
Rousay 80, 165
Royal Society 20, 22–3

sacrifice 148; animal 135
Saint-Just 91
San hunter-gatherers 42, 49
Sardinia 106–110, 112–13, *114,* 119, 122–3; list of sites 126
Sayers, Dorothy L. 204
Scandinavia 25–7, 141–54
segmentary societies 76–8, 81, 153–4, 165
Seine-Oise-Marne culture 155–60
settlement pattern 74–5, 76, 79
Shanballyemond *180*
Shang dynasty 67–8; role of cities 68
Shardana 121–2
Shen Kua 13
shrines 165
Sicily 106, 108–9, 128
sites, choice of 30
Skalk 200

skeletal remains 78, 87–9, 103, 108, 111, 115, 148, 167
Skorba *128–9,* 130–1, 135, 138–9
Slewcairn 167–8, *169*
Smith, R.A. 215
Smith, Worthington G. 216–19
social change, processes of 98–9
social structure 135, 150
Spain *see* Iberia
spatial patterning 73–7, 99–101
specialization 31–2, 65
Spencer, Baldwin 60–3; classification of tools 63
Spinden, Herbert Joseph 35–41; Archaic hypotheses 36–7; biography 35
statue-menhirs *see* menhirs
Stewart, J.I.M. *see* Innes, Michael
Stonehenge 22–4, 76, 79
stone-packing graves 148–9
Stones of Stenness 78
stratigraphical investigations, in Mesopotamia 29; Valley of Mexico 36
Stukeley, William 19, 22, 24, 195
Sunday Times 201
surveys of megaliths, in France 82, 84; Ireland 177–8

Tabqa 31–3
Ta Hammut 139
T'ang culture 69
'Target for Tonight' *207*
Tarxien 125, 130, *131–2,* 131–3, *134,* 135, 138, 140
Ta Trapna 129
television 207–13; forms of presentation 212; in other countries 211; popularity 213; problems in presentation 212
Tell Gubba 33
temple 129–38, 148; distribution *136;* evolution *129*
Tène, La 25–6
territorial definition 80, 100, 136, 154, 165
textual evidence 28
Thames and Hudson 196–7, 201; series published 197–8
'The Past in the Present' 197

'The Lost Centuries' 211
thermoluminescence dating 95–7, 174
tholoi 96–7
Three Age Concept 12–13, 35
Tien culture 68–9
Times, The 200
tombe a poliandro 113, 115
tombe di giganti 113–16, 119, 122; typology 114–15
totemism 62
trade 123, 182
tranchés 85
Trefignath 171–2
Trench, John 205
Tylor, E.B. 54–5, 59–60
typology, comparative 111

unchambered long barrows 78, 142, *143,* 144, 166–8
Ur 29
urban development 32
urdolmens 141–2, 144, 146
Ussher, James 20

Velaine 158
Vierville 88
Vroue Hede 148, *149*
Vulliamy, C.E. 206

Warka 29, 32
Wayland's Smithy 166–7
wedge-tombs 178, *179,* 181, 183–6, 188

Weris 155, *155–6,* 157–8
'What in the World? 207
Wheeler, Sir Mortimer 194–5, 198, 201, 207, *208–9,* 210
'Who Were The British?' 210
World Archaeology 200
'World of Archaeology' 198
Worm, Ole 22, 24
Wu-kuan-ts'un 67

Yangshao culture 65–6
Young, Simon *197*

Zimbabwe, dating 46, 48, 50; descent from Acropolis *45;* excavations at 44–6, 48.